Humanism
and the
Northern
Renaissance

Humanism and the Northern Renaissance

edited by
Kenneth R. Bartlett
and Margaret McGlynn

Canadian Scholars' Press Inc.   Toronto   2000

Humanism and the Northern Renaissance
edited by Kenneth R. Bartlett and Margaret McGlynn

First published in 2000 by
Canadian Scholars' Press Inc.
180 Bloor Street West, Suite 1202
Toronto, Ontario
M5S 2V6

CSPI acknowledges the financial support of the Government of Canada through the Book Publishing Industry Development Programme for our publishing activities.

Canadian Cataloguing in Publication Data

Humanism and the Northern Renaissance

ISBN1-55130-178-4

1. Humanism – Europe – History – 16th century – Sources. 2. Renaissance – Sources. 3. Europe – Intellectual life – 16th century – Sources. 4. Christianity and religious humanism – Sources. I. Bartlett, Kenneth R., 1948– . II. McGlynn, Margaret, 1968– .

CB369.H85 2000   940.2'3   C00-930968-3

Managing Editor: Ruth Bradley-St-Cyr
Marketing Manager: Susan Cuk
Proofreading:Linda Bissinger
Production: Linda Bissinger, Kate Zieman
Page design and layout: Brad Horning
Cover design: Amy Seagram and Brad Horning

00   01   02   03   04   05   06   6   5   4   3   2   1

Printed and bound in Canada by AGMV Marquis.

Contents

PART SIX: EDUCATION, LEARNING AND THE OCCULT

Editors' Acknowledgements

A book is the work of many hands. I would like to thank those of my colleagues who generously granted permission to include their translations and editions of the primary source material contained in this text.

Also I must recognize the cheerful, professional and dedicated assistance of everyone at Canadian Scholars' Press: Jack Wayne, Publisher, who encouraged the creation of the book; Ruth Bradley-St-Cyr, Managing Editor, who provided so much excellent advice on every aspect of the project; and, finally, Linda Bissinger, the editorial intern, whose careful work in securing permissions and proofreading the manuscript made my life so much easier.

I also want to acknowledge the collective contributions of years of students in my introductory course on Renaissance Europe. It was their response to my selection of readings which, in the end, determined those which I include in the text.

Equally, my former doctoral student, teaching assistant, colleague and collaborator, Margaret McGlynn, contributed more than selections for many of the sections of the book. Her insightful observations and careful research informed every aspect of this project.

Finally, I must recognize the constant help, support and good humour of my wife Gillian, whose skill and dedication as a teacher has always been an inspiration.

Kenneth Bartlett
Toronto

I would like to thank my students at the University of Toronto, York University and Wellesley College whose responses to these and other texts helped shape the reader. I would also like to thank Richard Moll for his help in translating "The Trial of Mary and Joseph" and Caxton's "Prologue," as well as for his usual support.

Margaret McGlynn
Wellesley, Mass.

Publisher's Acknowledgements

Chapter 1
"Diary of the Council of Constance" by Guillaume Filastre. From *The Council of Constance: The Unification of the Church*, translated by Louise Ropes Loomis, pp. 200–217. © 1961 Columbia University Press. Reprinted by permission of the publisher.

Chapter 2
"The End of the Saintly and Reverend Master John Hus" by Peter of Mladonovice. From *John Hus at the Council of Constance*, translated from the Latin and the Czech with notes and introduction by Matthew Spinka, pp. 224–234. © 1965 Columbia University Press, Ltd. Reprinted by permission of the publisher.

Chapter 3
"First Book of the Commentaries (excerpt)" by Aeneas Sylvius Piccolomini, in *De Gestis Concilii Basiliensis Commentarium: Libri II*, edited and translated by Denys May and W.K. Smith, pp. 17, 19, 21, 23, 25, 27, 29. © 1967 Oxford University Press. Reprinted by permission of Oxford University Press.

Chapter 4
"Of Wedded Men and Wives and of their Children also" by John Wyclif. From *Select English Works of John Wyclif*, edited by Thomas Arnold. Oxford: Clarendon Press, 1871. Translated by Margaret McGlynn.

Chapter 5
"The Imitation of Christ (excerpt)" by Thomas à Kempis. From *The Imitation of Christ*, translated by Harold C. Gardiner, pp. 31–41. © 1955 by Doubleday, a division of Random House, Inc. Reprinted by permission of Doubleday, a division of Random House, Inc.

Chapter 13
"Act in Restraint of Appeals, 1533" and "Act of Supremacy, 1534." From *Tudor Constitutional Documents A.D. 1485–1603*, edited by J.R. Tanner, pp. 40–46. Cambridge: CUP, 1951. Reprinted by permission of Cambridge University Press.

Chapter 14
"Consilium de Emendanda Ecclesia, 1537." From *The Catholic Reformation: Savonarola to Ignatius Loyola*, edited by John C. Olin, pp. 186–197. © 1969 Harper & Row, Publishers. Reprinted by permission of John C. Olin.

Chapter 15
"The Institutes" by John Calvin. From *Calvin: Institutes of the Christian Religion (Library of Christian Classics)*, edited by John T. McNeill, 1960. Reprinted by permission of Westminster John Knox Press and SCM Press.

Chapter 16
"Letter on Obedience" by Ignatius Loyola. From *St. Ignatius' Own Story as told to Luis González de Cámara with a sampling of his letters*, translated by William J. Young, S.J. pp. 110–122. 1956 Henry Regnery Company, Chicago.

Chapter 17
"Spiritual Testimonies" by St. Teresa of Avila. From *The Collected Works of St. Teresa of Avila, Vol. 1*, translated by Kieran Kavanaugh, O.C.D. and Otilio Rodriguez, O.C.D. pp. 404–408, 418–425. © 1976 Washington Province of Discalced Carmelites. ICS Publications, 213 Lincoln Road, N.E. Washington, DC 20002, USA.

Chapter 18
"The Trial of Mary and Joseph." From *Ludus Coventriæ; or The Plaie called Corpus Christi.*, edited by K.S. Block. Published for the Early English Text Society (extra series vol. 120) by H. Milford, Oxford University Press, 1922. Translated by Margaret McGlynn.

Chapter 19
"Book One (excerpt)" by Thomas More (Penguin Classics, 1961). From *Utopia*, translated by Paul Turner, pp. 37–54. © 1961 Paul Turner. Reprinted by permission of Penguin Books Ltd.

Chapter 27
"Excerpt" from *The Fugger Newsletters*, edited by Victor von Klarwill, authorized translation by Pauline de Chary, foreword by H. Gordon Seifridge, pp. 140–50. London: John Lane The Bodley Head Ltd, 1924.

Chapter 28
"To John Asteley" by Roger Ascham. From *English Works: Toxophilus, Report of the Affairs and State of Germany*, edited by W.A. Wright, pp. 125–139. © 1904 Cambridge University Press. Reprinted by permission of Cambridge University Press.

Chapter 29
"Motion of the Heart and Blood" by William Harvey. From *The Circulation of the Blood*, pp. 22–30. © 1923 J.M. Dent and Sons.

Chapter 30
"Gargantua and Pantagruel (excerpt)" by François Rabelais. From *The Northern Renaissance*, edited by Lewis W. Spitz, pp. 57–72. © 1972 Prentice-Hall, Inc. Reprinted by permission of Edna Spitz.

Chapter 31
"Don Quixote (excerpt)" by Miguel de Cervantes. From *The Northern Renaissance*, edited by Lewis W. Spitz, pp. 86–109. © 1972 Prentice-Hall, Inc. Reprinted by permission of Edna Spitz.

Chapter 32
"On the Writing of Letters" by Juan Luis Vives. From *De Conscribendis Epistolis*, translated by Charles Fantazzi, pp. 23, 25, 27, 29, 31, 33, 35, 37. © 1989 E. J. Brill. Reprinted by permission of E. J. Brill, Inc.

Chapter 33
"Advice to his Son (Phillip II), 1555" by Charles V. From *Renaissance and Reformation 1300-1648*, 3rd ed., edited by G. R. Elton, pp. 136–138. © 1976 Macmillan. Reprinted by permission of Prentice-Hall, Inc.

Introduction

The essential elements of humanism were established in Italy during the later 14th and 15th centuries. Beginning with Petrarch (1304–74) Italians began to re-evaluate their relationship with the past, both the immediate past of the Middle Ages and the more distant past of classical antiquity. In the midst of dramatic social, economic and political change, Italians began to search for models of thought, behaviour and society which spoke more directly to their own experience. The great expansion of long-distance trade that followed the crusades, the resurgence in secular education that resulted and the creation of a large class of wealthy, learned, sophisticated and politically ambitious laymen in the Italian city states all contributed to a growing belief that the individual, acting singly or through the community, could improve life in this world. Add to this the dynamic social and political world of the republic of Florence, a world in which social mobility, republican politics, secular values and practical learning were privileged, and the fundamental character of the Italian Renaissance emerges.

In searching for guides for life, these wealthy, lay, urban patricians of cities like Florence found a model particularly well suited to their circumstances: the ancient world of Greece and Rome. These civilizations were not unlike their own, and their literature and thought provided ideal models for Italians looking for principles relevant to their own lives. Clearly, the civilization of the feudal, rural, agrarian, scholastic middle ages held little attraction. Scholastic theology offered no support to men whose lives were dedicated to things of this world, whose riches came from lending at interest or trade and whose professions were practical. However, ancient Roman writers, like Cicero (Marcus Tullius Cicero, 106–43 B.C.) seemed very much like themselves, giving useful advice for ethical behaviour. Moreover, Cicero did so in a rhetorical style so powerful that it seemed necessarily true. For urban patrician merchants exercising guild authority or ambitious for selection as magistrates in their city state, the appeal of Cicero and other ancient authors like him was compelling. He was, after all, a man like them: a lawyer who worked his way to the top of Roman republican political life, a married man with children, but still concerned with ethical behaviour, reflected in his stoic philosophical works.

The problem was, however, that Cicero and his fellow Romans of the golden age were pagans, and that their thought consequently made no allowance for the Christian dispensation. The contribution of Petrarch and his continuators was the recognition that ancient pagans could still be good men, ethical, learned and useful for advice on secular matters. This was in no way to diminish Christianity but rather to admit that the ancients had much to teach modern men in a great many areas. Furthermore, the eloquence and beauty of their Latin style reflected the quality and clarity of their thoughts and minds. The classical belief that good letters mirror good thoughts on the part of good men was widely held. Cicero had to be right and good because his style was so effective and majestic.

Consequently, there was an attempt to recover as much of the ancient world as possible. If individual experience and life in this world are to be recognized and valued, anything which contributed to human experience and understanding would be valuable, especially if written by the ancients whose knowledge of human nature was celebrated. Italian humanists of the Renaissance sought surviving ancient works throughout Europe, discovering long lost classical texts. These texts then had to be studied and reviewed to ensure that they accurately reflected the ancient author's actual words. Philology was invented as was textual editing and comparative stylistics; archeology was first employed to uncover the ruins of the ancient world so visible throughout Italy. Numismatics told Italians what their ancient ancestors looked like; and new styles of painting, sculpture and architecture paid tribute to the inspiration of the past. With the new validity of human experience and ancient models, art was made to describe nature accurately: it was to reflect what the eye sees. Correct human anatomy and linear perspective arose, predicated on the belief that man was the measure of all things.

By the late fifteenth century some of these ideas were moving north of the Alps to influence northern Europeans. However, the circumstances in the north were very different from Italy. Feudalism was still the dominant political structure, with the landholding knightly class in the position of greatest influence. The economies of the dynastic monarchies remained largely agrarian, and trade mostly local. Education and learning were almost solely clerical, with the universities and schools extensions of Church authority and directed mostly towards the training of clergy. The wealthy urban patrician class—the vanguard of humanism in Italy—was small.

Still, there were vehicles for the introduction of Italian humanist learning in the north. The end of the Hundred Year's War and the fall of Constantinople in the middle years of the fifteenth century stimulated trade by making more capital available for peaceful economic activity and breaking the Italian monopoly on the eastern luxury trade. Explorers were beginning to work their way down the coast of Africa until eventually Vasco da Gama sailed around the continent, opening a direct route from the Atlantic seaboard to India and the east. The consolidation of dynastic monarchies added a measure of security through the enforcement of law and the establishment of standardized procedure. Northern scholars had also enjoyed opportunities to experience Italian humanism through direct contact at Church Councils, like Constance, residence at the papal court, or study at the great universities of the peninsula, such as Padua or Bologna; and many Italians—merchants, diplomats, papal collectors or ecclesiastics—spent time in the north, spreading interest in the new learning. Finally, with the invasion of Italy by Charles VIII of France in 1494, there began a period of foreign intervention in the peninsula which would lead to the humiliation of Italy and centuries of foreign domination. However, these events equally resulted in large numbers of northeners spending considerable periods in Italy, bringing home with them the fruits of the Italian Renaissance in all of its manifestations.

By the early sixteenth century the conditions were right for the development of an indigenous humanist culture in the north, dependent upon its different social, political, cultural and religious traditions. The dominant social class remained the landowning nobility, and the models of behaviour were heavily dependent upon the ideals of chivalry and court life. Literary patronage, then, reflected this long memory of chivalric literature, which is so brilliantly burlesqued later in Cervantes' *Don Quixote*. Classical learning, already recovered by the Italians and established as the rhetorical and stylistic ideal, was applied to the needs of different groups in society with a desire to know these texts especially in their own vernacular languages or in their own contexts: hence Caxton's printing of his translation of Virgil's *Aeneid*. Popular traditions in literature were sustained, but with a Renaissance character, as in Rabelais; and elements of folk belief and secular prophecy were recorded in books such as the *Malleus Maleficarum*, a manual for hunting witches, or the learned prognostications of Nostradamus. Classical principles in style were, nevertheless, retained by northern scholars as well as by Italians, as illustrated in Vives' treatise on correct letter writing, or Conrad Celtis, the German arch-humanist's, oration delivered to the University of Ingolstadt.

It is, though, in the area of religion and the church that the character of Northern humanism emerges clearly. Because of the clerical control of education and because of distance from the ruins and traditions of antiquity, the classical past in the north had been transmitted by the Church to a much greater degree than in Italy. Consequently, the place of Christianity in the northern renaissance is central. Christianity is a religion of the book and consequently requires at least a learned clergy. Add to this a powerful tradition of lay piety and a significant degree of control over local churches on the part of kings and princes and the imperative of confessional renewal and ecclesiastical reform and the defining role of religion north of the Alps becomes clear. Learned humanists applied the techniques developed by Italians for the study of pagan texts to patristic and Biblical scholarship. The model of ethical behaviour shifted from the justified pagan exemplified by Cicero and Seneca to early doctors of the Church such as Jerome or Augustine, and, ultimately, the example of Christ himself.

Reform of the Church had, of course, deep roots. The late middle ages had bequeathed to northern Europeans the movements led by John Wyclif in England and Jan Hus in Bohemia. Wyclif was to call for a simpler faith modelled on the apostolic church in which a vernacular Bible, clerical poverty and upright behaviour would be celebrated. Hus took these ideas and used them as the basis for a program of religious and social reform, a program which soon encountered serious opposition from the established orders and resulted in his trial and burning at the Council of Constance. By the early sixteenth century, similar and new ideas, often derived from humanist thought, were animating a powerful new imperative towards Church reform and religious enthusiasm. The mystical tradition continued through writings such as Thomas à Kempis' *Imitation of Christ*; and this northern strain of lay piety was finding powerful support among those Christian humanists who united a sincere and personal piety with superb humanist training. This tradition of Northern, Christian Humanism is ideally represented in Thomas More and Erasmus of Rotterdam, two friends who, with others such as John Colet, sought a regeneration of religion, education and moral behaviour based upon a sound knowledge of Scripture and the tools of classical learning.

This element of uniting profound learning with deep, sincere Christian spirituality was a central element of Christian humanism. The ancient dichotomy between Athens and Jerusalem could be solved by recognizing that for a Christian scholar the purpose of education was to elucidate, propagate and contemplate Christian revelation and teaching. Hence, Erasmus came to accept and profess that secular knowledge was imperfect without the Christian dispensation. Although it might gratify the intellect it could not redeem the spirit. Here, then, was the primary difference between Northern, Christian humanism, exemplified by Erasmus, and Italian humanism. In Italy, man was sufficient and secular knowledge was a goal in itself; but for Erasmus, man is insufficient without God and Christian revelation, to which all human knowledge must defer. This was the *Philosophia Christi*, the Philosophy of Christ, which is the application of human knowledge to divine revelation and the application of the teachings of Christ to each individual's life, to be achieved through a return to the basic elements of the New Testament. The greatest text to be explicated becomes the Bible and Erasmus noted that it should be approached "with a mind sharpened by culture and a heart purified by reverence."

Neither More nor Erasmus wanted to effect a division in the Church. Indeed, More died for the principle of a singular confession rather than submit to Henry VIII's reform of the Church. Nevertheless, the Christian humanists unleashed forces which they could no longer control. In 1517 a German monk, Martin Luther, began an assault on the structure and teachings of the Roman Church, including the supremacy of the pope. The Reformation he began resulted in the universal church being split into Lutheran and Roman confessions. The authority of lay magistrates and princes was greatly increased in Luther's Church, and much Church property was secularized, resulting in a social and political as well as a religious revolution. Despite attempts at accommodation, this division in Christianity was to prove permanent, and lead to other elaborations of theology and church government, most notably that of John Calvin in the generation following Luther's revolt. With Calvin, the liturgy became simpler still and even more authority was transferred to secular powers. And, the traditional Christian belief in Free Will was replaced by an acceptance of divine predestination.

The fragmentation of the Christian church and the social, economic and political changes which attended the Reformation resulted in war and dislocation. Once it was obvious that there would never be any reconciliation with the new sects, the Roman Church began to reform and reorganize itself in defence of its traditional mission. Pope Paul III called a great Council of the Church to meet in the city of Trent with the responsibility of reinvigorating Catholic worship and church organization. This council was to sit, with some interruptions, for almost 20 years and result in the Catholic or Counter Reformation. Among the products of this newly energetic Catholicism was the Society of Jesus, or Jesuits, founded by St. Ignatius of Loyola. This new order was given the mandate to preach, teach and convert souls—whether in Protestant Europe or in the new world empires then being established by Europeans. In addition, new mystical movements of Catholic piety began to influence both the Church and society at large, and saints such as Teresa of Avila became models of renewed faith based not so much on understanding and reason as on obedience and divine illumination.

The disjunction between reason and the supernatural developed in other ways as well during the later sixteenth century. The beginnings of modern science coexisted with the still powerful forces of the occult. Charlatans such as those exposed by the *Fugger Newsletters* shared a continent with Nostradamus, a physician whose opaque predictions were widely read and continue to be quoted, and William Harvey, the English physician trained at the University of Padua in Italy who discovered the circulation of the blood.

Finally, science, technology, religion, adventure and the Renaissance compulsion to extend experience and human knowledge all combined to drive the voyages of discovery in which Europeans extended their understanding of the earth. Impelled by economic and military as well as religious concerns, the early explorers, beginning in the mid-fifteenth century, began the charting, economic exploitation and colonization of parts of the earth previously unknown from either Biblical or ancient texts. It was the crusading spirit of Henry the Navigator of Portugal and the Spanish crown following the consolidation of the Iberian peninsula and the expulsion of the Moors that drove the *conquistadors* to found empires in the Americas. The results were not only the obvious fruits of empire, however. They included the forced reconsideration of the place of Europeans in the world and a reassessment of the human condition. Were the native inhabitants of the new world empires people whom Christ forgot, since they were not part of the Christian dispensation? Equally, if the ancients had not known of the existence of entire continents inhabited by other humans and possessed of vast riches, what else might they not have known, where else might they have erred? These questions are implied in those texts like Thomas More's *Utopia* which use the new world as a corrective or at least a comparison with the old. What was reinforced, though, is the Renaissance belief in the power of the human mind and spirit, the ability of men to comprehend the world and affect its development and the place of genius and fame as the engines of history.

Writers like Bernal Díaz and Gonzalo Fernandez de Oviedo were sophisticated observers of the events of their times. The contacts they record between the old world and the new reflect the complexity of the experience for Europeans. Unfortunately, it was often an experience imposed upon the indigenous inhabitants. Their souls were sought for Christianity, especially through the zealous evangelizing of the Jesuits who were determined that native inhabitants of the Spanish Empire would be Catholic, indicating the renewed vigour of the church after Trent and replacing European souls lost to the Reformation. Equally, the riches of the Indies were for European treasuries, taken home to Spain to advance that kingdom's ambitions on the continent.

Great rulers such as Charles V of Habsburg, who ruled the vast dynastic accumulation of territory in the old world and the new, saw their power as gifts from God to settle accounts in Church and state. In Charles' case, though, the effort was not fully rewarded: he could not stop Martin Luther or John Calvin, nor could he halt the advance of the Turks into Europe and the Mediterranean. He recognized at the end of his life the impossibility of ruling effectively the greatest Empire since Charlemagne; he abdicated and spent the last years of his life in monastic seclusion, having divided his territories. His brother, Ferdinand of Habsburg, was given the territories in Germany and in central and eastern Europe; his son, Philip, received Spain, the Low Countries and parts of Italy, as well as the new world.

Humanism and Renaissance ideals continued to develop in the North, aided by the zeal of religion and the wealth of the new world. The desire for fame and glory, so brilliantly satirized by Cervantes, remained, as did the search for individual autonomy and insight into the secrets of man and nature. The selections excerpted in this collection of readings illustrate the richness of that experience and the magnificence of its achievement in so many areas of human endeavour, and an evident conclusion from these documents is that the age of humanism and the Renaissance was the platform on which our own world was constructed.

Kenneth R. Bartlett   Margaret McGlynn
University of Toronto   Wellesley College

Part One

The Fifteenth Century

Cardinal Guillaume Filastre (1348–1428)

Filastre was born in La Suze, France, educated in law at Paris and taught jurisprudence at Rheims. Although an early defender of French ecclesiastical rights and a proponent of the Avignon pope during the Great Schism, he came eventually to recognize the need for unity in the church at the Council of Constance.

Named a cardinal in 1411 and archbishop of Aix in 1413, he joined with other powerful clerics to try to contain the reform movement supported by the Emperor Sigismond and others. With the end of the Great Schism and the election of Martin V as the singular head of the church, Filastre was sent as papal legate to France to work for church unity.

Filastre was an important scholar as well. He translated several works of Plato and wrote an influential treatise on usury. It is his Diary of the Council of Constance (the general council of the church called to end the great schism) which is best known today, as it provides a detailed commentary on those complex proceedings. Filastre died in Rome in 1428.

Chapter One

Diary of the Council of Constance

The General Council of Constance had its origin in the Council of Pisa. The great and terrible Schism had lasted thirty years, from its commencement at Rome after the death of Gregory XI, in the year of our Lord 1378, when, first, Bartholomew, Archbishop of Bari, was elected Pope, because of the tumults and pressure of the Romans and took the name of Urban VI, and, later, the same cardinals abandoned him, declaring they had been frightened into the election, and chose Cardinal Robert of Geneva, who took the name of Clement VII. Under these two men the famous Great Schism began, unlike any other that has preceded it, in the length of its duration—for it is now in its thirty-seventh year—the perplexing nature of its cause and continuance, and the divisions created by it in kingdoms and provinces.

Those who submitted to Clement were all the Gauls from the Alps inclusive as far as the British Ocean, except Flanders, Hainault, Brabant, and Liège, also all the Spains but Portugal, also Scotland, Cyprus, Rhodes, Majorca, the islands subject to Spain, and finally Genoa. Those who obeyed Urban were the other kingdoms and provinces, such as Italy with her islands, all the Germanies, Bohemia, Hungary, Poland, and England. Urban fixed his seat at Rome, Clement at Avignon. In the Roman line up to the present Council there have been four popes: Urban VI, Boniface IX, Innocent VII, and Gregory XII, who still lives and was known as Angela Corario of Venice. In the Avignon line there have been but two, the above mentioned Clement VII, whose name was Robert of Geneva and who was Pope sixteen years lacking a few days, and Benedict XIII, known as Pedro de Luna of Aragon, who still lives.

When the Schism had lasted thirty years, the said Benedict and Gregory promised and made arrangements to abdicate in order to restore unity to the Church, and agreed upon Savona as the place to meet for their abdication. But when the time of meeting drew near, they both, acting, it is supposed, in collusion, discovered so many insuperable obstacles in the way of obtaining safeguards that they never came together at all. Whereupon the cardinals of both obediences took the situation into consideration and withdrew from them. Pedro de Luna, called Benedict, fled from Portovenere to Perpignan in Aragon, in dread of the King of France, who had now retracted his obedience. Angelo, called Gregory, retired to Siena.

Then cardinals from both obediences assembled and acting in concert summoned a council to meet at Pisa. There the said Benedict and Gregory were deposed from the papacy and the Cardinal of Milan, Peter of Candia, a Franciscan, was elected Pope. He was a native of Crete, also known as Candia, whence he took his title, and a distinguished doctor of theology at Paris. He called himself Alexander V. But all the Spains, except Portugal, still obeyed Pedro de Luna, while the Neapolitan kingdom of Sicily, Charles Malatesta and his lands and all the dukes of Bavaria and the Archbishop of Trier, with the lands subject to them, obeyed Angelo, the deposition at Pisa notwithstanding. However, Ladislas, king of Sicily, later repudiated Angelo and joined the obedience of John XXIII, of whom more anon, making several compacts with him.

After the election of Alexander at Pisa, the Council was ordered by him with its own approval to meet again in three years. The place and day of meeting were to be selected and announced by whoever was pope at the time. But Alexander died at Bologna less than a year after his election and the present John XXIII, cardinal of St. Eustachius, legate at Bologna, known as Baldasarre Cossa of Naples, was elected in his stead. It is said that the election was corrupt, and certainly it was so as regards the merits of the man elected. However, at the end of the three years, he carried out the order to resume the Council of Pisa and convoked a general council at Rome, on the first of April, in the year 1412. But because of the remoteness of the place and the perils of travel no one came but members of the Curia, for everywhere around Rome wars were being fought and there was no safe route of approach. Many people said and believed that these obstructions had been created or aggravated by Pope John so that the council might not be held.

At length, Rome was captured by Ladislas, king of Sicily, and the Curia abruptly forced to take flight, not without some deep connivance on the part of Pope John. He and the Curia then established themselves at Florence. Thither the serene prince Sigismund, king of the Romans and Hungary, sent envoys to ask the Pope for authorization to summon a general council and choose the place and the time. The cardinals then, perceiving that the Pope was trying to escape a general council, put such pressure on him that he sent the Cardinals of Florence and Challant to Sigismund at Como in Italy with power to fix the place and time of holding the council with the advice and consent of the King. So they chose Constance and the day of November first in the year 1414, the fifth of Lord John's pontificate. They also agreed with the King on a day in November in the year 1413, when the Pope and the King would meet in the city of Lodi. There in due time they met with all the cardinals in the presence of the King, and the Pope in a general consistory ordained that the General Council of Constance be convened on the said date and convened it by apostolic decree . . ..

After the Pope had thus ordained the calling of the Council, he returned with his Curia to Bologna at the beginning of Lent and in the month of August following, Ladislas, ruler of the kingdom of Sicily, died. He had taken Rome, as I said before, and was occupying it and all the patrimony and lands of the Church, especially those in Tuscany, the March [of Ancona] and Campania. So our lord Pope John XXIII was bent on going back to Rome to recover it and the lands of the Church. But the cardinals were well aware that if they went back they would not return to the Council and the Council would not be held and the union and reformation of the Church would not be accomplished, and they dreaded the dire consequences to the Church that would probably ensue. They therefore opposed him stubbornly and all in concert urged him by word of mouth and in writing to carry on himself in person his spiritual and ecclesiastical duty, namely, the Council, and to delegate his temporal duty to vicars and legates. He yielded to them but with reluctance.

On the first day of October, he set out from Bologna for Constance. On his way through Merano, a city belonging to Frederick, duke of Austria, he made a compact with him. For a financial consideration the Duke promised to guarantee the Pope's security, even in Constance, to keep him safe and free there, conduct him out of Constance whenever he wished and preserve him safe and free against all comers. Later, in Constance, our lord Pope disclosed this compact, as will appear further on. Hence it may be inferred that the lord Pope did not approach the Council with any sincere intent.

On Sunday, October 28, the feast of Simon and Jude, our lord Pope entered Constance in state, the cardinals having already arrived. He was lodged in the bishop's palace. Later, the order was given to hold a procession and Solemn Mass on Saturday, the third of November, for the opening of the Council. And on that day the Pope, the cardinals and all the prelates and clergy of Constance gathered in the palace, robed in their sacred vestments, and the whole procession was drawn up. But just as it was starting and the Pope had come out from his chamber in pontifical array, he was seized with an illness and obliged to retire again and take off his vestments and lie down on his bed. So the entire performance was at an end for that day. On the following Monday, November 5, the Pope was well again and the procession was held followed by a Solemn Mass with sermon in the cathedral of Constance. Master John of Vincelles of the Order of Cluny and proctor for that order, doctor of theology at Paris, preached the sermon in the Pope's presence. Thus the Council was opened.

[*Session1*.] Then on Friday, the 16th of the month, the first session was held. The Council sat in the place appointed for holding meetings, that is, the nave of the cathedral of Constance. The Pope presided and said Mass and preached a sermon, the text of which was "Love truth." He described truth as threefold, eternal, internal, and external: eternal, which is God; internal, within our consciences; and external, in our words and deeds. Then lord Francis, cardinal of Florence, read from the high pulpit the Pope's memorandum providing for the successful conduct and termination of the Council, as follows:

"Bishop John, servant of the servants of God, for a perpetual memorial. With intention to execute the decree enacted at the Council of Pisa by our predecessor of happy memory, Pope Alexander V, regarding the convocation of another general council, we did some time ago convoke the present Council by our letter, the content of which we think should be presented here." Then was read by the papal secretary the bull convoking the Council included in my prologue above .... [After which the Cardinal of Florence resumed his place in the pulpit and continued reading.]

"Hence, in company with our venerable brothers, the cardinals of the Holy Roman Church, and our Curia, we have come at the time set to this city of Constance. And now by God's grace we are here and with counsel from the sacred synod propose to push on to the peace, exaltation, and reformation of the Church and the tranquility of Christian people.

"And seeing that in so difficult a task we can presume not at all on our own strength but must trust in the help of God, so, beginning with Divine Worship, we have, with the approval of this sacred Council, ordained that this very day a special Mass should be said, appointed for the purpose and repeated every Friday as long as the Council lasts .... [Similar Masses to be said in every church in the city once a week and attended by all cardinals, patriarchs, bishops and abbots, priests and penitents, along with a performance of pious works, fastings, prayers, and alms to obtain God's favor and a happy issue of the Council.] In accordance with the laudable custom of the ancient councils our chief concern is with matters of faith. We exhort all with knowledge of sacred letters to reflect deeply and discuss with themselves and others the things which seem to them helpful and opportune .... In particular, let them consider the errors which for some time past, they say, have been springing up in certain regions, those especially that originated with a certain John, called Wyclif ....

[All who come to the Council are asked to share their wisdom with us.] For it is our will and intention that all who gather here for this reason shall be free to speak, consult, and act in perfect liberty on all and every subject they think pertains to the above.

"Wherefore, that you may know the method to be observed in the proceedings of this sacred synod, both in what will be said and decided and in the action taken and manner maintained, it is our judgment that we return to the practices of the ancient Fathers which are best learned from a canon of the Council of Toledo, the tenor of which should we think, be included here.

"'In the place of benediction, when the lords priests take their seats, no one shall talk noisily or indiscreetly or create any disturbance or turmoil, no one shout frivolous nonsense or ridiculous jokes or, what is worse, insist on obstinate disputations. For, as the Apostle says, "If any man think himself to be religious and bridleth not his tongue but deceived his heart, that man's religion is vain ...." Hence whatever is discussed in sessions of members or proposed by a party bringing an accusation shall be expressed in the mildest words, that the minds of hearers be not confused with contentious voices or the vigor of their judgment shaken by tumult.

"'Whoever, therefore, in the meeting of this Council imagines he may violate this rule and contrary to this interdict disturb the Council with loud noise, vituperation, or laughter... shall be ejected in utter disgrace from the session, leave the general assemblage and for three days lie under sentence of excommunication.' And inasmuch as it may happen that some of the seated members are not placed in their rightful seats, we decree, with the approval of the sacred Council, that no prejudice from such seating shall be created against any Church or individual.

"Whereas for the conduct of the Council certain ministers and officials are essential, we, with the Council's approval, depute those named below, namely, our beloved sons ... [six notaries to supervise and harmonize the records and sign decrees; four scribes to help them; a guardian of the Council, Count Bartoldo Orsini; four inspectors of votes to be always assisted by two notaries and two scribes; four lawyers as Council's advocates; two procurators; and four ushers to assign seats to those entitled to sit in the Council. The date of the second session to be Monday, December 7.]"

At the end of this reading the Cardinal in a loud voice put the question: "Are all and everything contained in the above memorandum approved by the sacred synod?" To which question all the prelates present answered with no dissenting voice: "*Placet.* [Agreed]"

Note that even before the first of November the Pope and the cardinals had assembled in the city of Constance as related above, and also many prelates from Italy, and until after the feast of Our Lord's Nativity few from other nations arrived. So in this general Council of Constance, in which measures were to be taken for the peace and perfect union of the Church and then for its reformation, nothing whatever was achieved from the beginning of November, 1414, when the Pope and the college met there, until the end of January, and the subject of union was not touched upon. For some of the members had the disease *Noli me tangere,* and others who were eager for action did not dare to broach that subject because the French and the English, from whom everyone expected most, were still absent. Meanwhile a few preparations were made but nothing for the reform of the Church was effected. Some cardinals, appointed for the purpose, made certain suggestions but they were always hindered from reaching a conclusion.

However at the first assembly in the palace [December 7], the Pope being absent, a memorandum was presented in the name of the Italian nation on the subject of the Council, to the effect that first of all action should be taken in the Council to confirm the Council of Pisa and put its sentences into execution by an increase of penalties and other methods.But when this memorandum had been read aloud, the lord Cardinal of Cambrai at once offered another and opposing memorandum which he had shown beforehand to the Cardinal of St. Mark and some other French prelates and doctors. It argued, in effect, that they should at least wait until they had heard the ambassadors who were coming from Pedro de Luna and Angelo Corario. So the matter was dropped. Meanwhile some action was taken against the Bohemian heretic, named John Hus, and against the errors of the Englishman, John Wyclif.

The tenor of the memorandum of the lord Cardinal of Cambrai was as follows: "Some conclusions, for the proof and defence of which certain prelates and doctors offer themselves to the general Council and beg the Council, now sufficiently assembled, to deliberate on them.

"The sacred Council of Pisa has bound the lord Pope and the lords cardinals to strive in the present Council by every reasonable way and method for the perfect and complete union and peace of the Church and its due reformation in head and members. To this they are bound not only by the said Council of Pisa but also by the laws of nature and of God. To this the prelates of the Church also are bound, both those already gathered in the present Council and those yet to come. Such persons as obstinately insist that the Council of Constance should be dissolved or prorogued for continuation at another council, when the said union and reformation—in case they cannot now be brought about—may at last be accomplished, are promoters of schism and subject to grave suspicion of heresy.

"Within the present Council no doubt should be raised as to the Council of Pisa. We should maintain as our fundamental hypothesis that that Council was lawfully and canonically held and was therefore valid and authoritative. The Council of Pisa and the present Council are one by continuation and ought to be called one Council. With respect to the Council of Pisa, this Council has properly no power to confirm or sanction it but merely, since it derives from it, the power to continue its work. The request to have the Council of Pisa confirmed by the present Council, before action is taken in full congregation on the ways and means to bring about the union and reformation of the Church, should not at present be either granted or discussed.

"These conclusions will promote the unity of the Church and true faith. Contrary conclusions would promote schism and imply support of heresy."

In time the King of the Romans arrived, during the night of the Lord's Nativity. After his arrival the envoys of Angelo and Pedro de Luna came, some of whom were anti-cardinals. There was then a violent dispute as to whether they should be permitted to enter the city wearing their red hats. For the sake of peace they were permitted to do so and in that garb made their entry. Louis, duke of Bavaria, of the obedience of Angelo Corario, also came.

Finally, the envoys from Angelo made an address in public before the King of the Romans and on behalf of their lord declared themselves advocates of the method of abdication. But they had no mandate to show. Next, the envoys of Pedro de Luna received a hearing but they proposed nothing except a meeting of the King of the Romans with the King of Aragon and Pedro de Luna, which they said, the King of the Romans had requested. And they named Nice as the place and next April as the time. No answer as yet was given them. Then Duke Louis of Bavaria had a memorandum read in public before the King of the Romans and many prelates and others, the tenor of which was as follows:

"[Duke Louis of Bavaria and the Bishops of Worms, Speyer, and Verden, all of the obedience of Gregory, offer to cooperate with the Council in the effort to bring about church unity by the method of abdication] ... on condition, however, that the lord whom some call John XXIII not preside over the Council nor take part in it; further, that every special obligation to him assumed by members of the Council be annulled as far as it affects the matters to be transacted in Council, that no hindrance be put on liberty of conference, speech, and discussion at any point and that the votes of all and everyone be free and honest ...."

On the publication of this memorandum, the Cardinal of St. Mark, seeing that a door had been opened in the Lord which as yet no man could or dared enter, while pretense and friction were the order of the day between King and Pope and there was no mention of union, observing also that the English and the Poles had now arrived and were talking a great deal of plans for the peace of the Church and proposing nothing definite, composed a memorandum and gave it to the lord Cardinal of Cambrai, who praised and approved it. It happened to fall into the King's hands, and he welcomed it heartily and had it immediately copied and sent to all the meetings of all the nations. They too received it favorably, and so it was circulated until it came to the notice of the lord Pope. Many were disturbed at that and others overjoyed. The lord Pope knew that the Cardinal of St. Mark had composed the memorandum and was exceedingly annoyed and bitter against the Cardinal. But the latter, hearing of the Pope's anger, went and told him he had done it for the peace of the Church and did not deny it.

The tenor of the memorandum was as follows: "In the general Council of Constance two objects chiefly are to be accomplished and for that purpose the Council was called together, namely, first, the perfect pacification and union of the Church, second, the reformation of the ecclesiastical state.

"For the pacification and true union of the Church and the ending of the Schism various methods were proposed long before the Council of Pisa. The first was to reduce the disobedient by force. The second was to argue the case and decide by law between the contestants. The third was to bring about the abdication of both contestants .... [Both before and since the Council of Pisa the first two methods have been proved impracticable.]

"Hence it is plain that neither of these two methods should be tried again so long as one other remains, easy and practicable, namely, the last, the abdication of all contestants. This is obviously easy and practicable and advantageous for many reasons.

"Let us ask then whether, circumstances being as they are, the method of abdication should now be tried in the hope of achieving a perfect union; second, whether Lord John should be asked to take that method. (As for the other two, we say we do them a grace if we allow them to take it.) Third, whether, circumstances being as they are, our lord may lawfully be compelled to take it.

"In reply to the first question, I maintain the following propositions ... [Circumstances being as they are, the method of abdication should be tried and preferred above all others to bring about the peace and union of the Church. Obviously it is the quickest and easiest way to reach the goal of peace and perfect union. The other ways look desperate because of their difficulty and numerous other drawbacks.]

"Finally, in the situation in which the Supreme Pontiff now palpably stands, the more truly he is the shepherd of the Church, the more eagerly, ardently, and promptly will he propose and embrace the way of abdication for the peace and union of the Church. This conclusion is plainly supported by the words of the Chief Shepherd, who said: 'The good shepherd lays down his life for his sheep.' It is a mark of a good shepherd that he lays down his life for his sheep, whenever needed. If he does not lay it down, he is not a good shepherd. And if he is bound to lay down his life, how much more should he lay down the accidents of life, honor, power, dominion! ... Nor do I understand Christ's teaching of the good shepherd, if, in view of the present condition of the Church, a true shepherd may not be required to renounce his office for the peace of the Church, seeing that Christ may require him to lay down his life ....

"A soldier in an armed troop is bound to face death for the state; so also is a soldier of Christ. The Vicar of Christ is bound even more than an inferior to follow Christ because of his close relationship to Christ and his obligation to furnish an example to his inferiors, whom he is bound to teach by word an example, even as Jesus began first to do and then to teach....

"In view of the condition of the Church ... the Supreme Pontiff and shepherd of the Church may be compelled for the peace and unity of the Church to offer to abdicate, on condition that the others agree to cease their usurpation of office and carry out their abdications honestly and freely. This conclusion follows plainly from the above. For since he is bound to abdicate, he may be compelled to do so, if he refuses; that is, he may be commanded to do so and compelled, if he does not obey, in order to save God's Church from being rent asunder. For when a man is commanded to make restitution and fails to obey the command, his property may be taken from him by armed force, or other means may be used to oblige him to perform his duty. If the Pope does not obey, he may be deposed as bringing scandal on the Church of God, which he is bound to protect and cherish ....

"Nor should we doubt that a general council is competent to judge in such a case. Otherwise the Council of Pisa would not have possessed its power or passed judgment by the same authority and on the same fundamental grounds....

"Many other reasons might be adduced from the laws of God, of nature and of man to prove that a general Council is superior to a Pope in matters which concern the universal state of the Church, such as the present case and numerous others. Nevertheless, although these conclusions are correct, we recognize the propriety of proceeding mildly at the outset.

"In closing, let us humbly and devoutly entreat our most holy lord John, the true Supreme Pontiff and shepherd of the Lord's flock, that His Holiness deign to open the eyes of a true and good shepherd to the condition of his flock .... Unquestionably the Lord's flock stands in danger of lasting destruction, for already it has experienced grave divisions and suffered for many years the schism of the Greeks. In addition, at the present moment, we are threatened with the loss not only of Spain, as large a part of Christendom as Christian Greece, but of many nations in Germany and Italy besides. It is a fearful spectacle—so many heads for the one body of the Church.

"Let him deign—I will not call him bound—to lay down his life, his soul and his members or, less than that, the office of his members and his body ... to end this spectacle by the sure, easy, and honorable way of abdication. Let him offer to do it on condition that the other members of the flock agree truthfully to renounce the rights they claim and pursue the same way to the goal by sincere and honest paths. Undoubtedly, if he does this, peace will return to the Universal Church of God and the hearts of all Christians will rejoice in secure tranquillity. No nobler act has ever been recorded nor will any Roman pontiff ever possess fame, glory, and renown wider or more lasting than his.

"He must be assured that the Church will provide more richly for his future position than he would ask. No fear of poverty should deter him a moment from so great a benefaction, so bright a glory, and so splendid a reward. But if he refuses to heed, let him consider the two wolves in God's flock, in what scandals they have involved themselves for their causes, and what weapons he may take to resist and eventually overcome them."

In response to this memorandum some sycophants—to describe them correctly—wrote memoranda made up of invectives. Not daring to risk any assertions, they composed them in the form of questions …. "[Does not the course proposed by Filastre involve a repudiation of the work of the Council of Pisa and the reduction of the true Pope to the level of schismatics and heretics?]"

In reply to these memoranda the lord Cardinal of Cambrai composed a memorandum, the tenor of which was . .. . "[It is no derogation to Pope John or to the Council of Pisa to ask him at this juncture to take the lead on the road to peace by voluntarily abdicating. In fact the method of abdication was the one chosen at Pisa as most likely to end the Schism. The Universal Church may depose anyone, even the chief minister of the Church, if its state is disturbed by his continuance in office, and even without guilt on his part.]" The Cardinal of St. Mark also drew up answers to those who were attacking his previous conclusions and advocating compulsory deposition …. Still other memoranda were put forward in the name of the nations, to the effect that the chief business on hand was the union of the Church, and these memoranda were made public.

While all this was going on, the question arose as to who should be admitted to vote on measures in the Council. Some wanted only the bishops and greater prelates and abbots admitted. In opposition to their opinion the cardinal of Cambrai prepared a memorandum, the tenor of which was:

"The following considerations are presented to oppose the pride and ignorance of those who maintain that in this holy Council of Constance, through all its sessions, only the greater prelates, bishops, and abbots should vote in the final verdict on the problems before us.

"To begin with, a distinction should be drawn between the subjects to be treated in the Council. They may either be such as relate solely to the Catholic faith, the sacraments and purely spiritual aspects of the Church, with which the holy fathers of old dealt in their general councils. In such a case the canon law has much to say and what I am now writing nothing at all. Or else they may relate to the ending of the present Schism and the establishment of unbroken unity and peace. In which case the following remarks are pertinent.

"First, we should understand that, just as from the time of the primitive Church different methods were employed in the election of the supreme pontiff, as the laws and ancient histories tell us, so there were differences in the method of convening and conducting general councils. For, as one may read in the Acts of the Apostles and the *History* of Eusebius, which joins directly on to the Acts of the Apostles, at times the whole community of Christians was convened for a council, at other times the bishops, priests, and deacons, at times the bishops alone without the abbots, at other times both bishops and abbots, at times the Emperor summoned and assembled the council and was present in person, while the Pope whose case was under discussion was absent. So a variation in method finds support in the law of nature and of God and in the histories aforesaid ....

"Further, we ought to realize that when bishops alone had the final vote in general councils, it was because they had the administration of the people and were themselves holy and learned men, chosen above the rest in the Christian Church. Later, abbots were added for the same reason and because they had administration over persons subject to them. On the same score priors should now be added and heads of every congregation, in place of the useless bishops or abbots who have merely a titular office and lack the qualifications just mentioned and are possibly under suspicion in this present situation. It seems strange that one such archbishop or bishop or abbot, with few or no suffragans and few or none subject to him, should have as large a vote in the Council as the Archbishop of Mainz or the other great prelates and princes of the Empire or as all the separate archbishops and bishops of France and England and other kingdoms, who govern many parochial churches in which there is a greater congregation than in many of the archbishoprics and bishoprics aforesaid.

"On the same grounds as above the doctors of sacred theology and canon and civil law should not be excluded from the vote. For they, particularly the theologians, have been granted authority to preach and teach everywhere in the world, which is no small authority among Christian people and far greater than that of an ignorant bishop or abbot with merely a titular office. In ancient times, the authority of doctors had not been introduced through the institution of universities, though today it is sanctioned by the church's authority. So there is no mention of them in the ancient common laws, but in the Councils of Pisa and Rome their authority was quoted, and they signed their names to the final decrees. Hence it would be not only absurd but a kind of repudiation of the Council of Pisa if the present Council, which is a continuation of that council, should exclude theologians from similar participation.

"Further, by the same or similar reasoning an equal claim may be made out for kings and princes and their ambassadors and for the proctors of absent prelates and chapters. This is proved by the bull of our lord Pope in which he instructs the members of the present Council that if, through some canonical impediment, they are unable to attend the Council in person at this time and place, those who are thus prevented shall send in their stead, without delay, God-fearing men, equipped with learning and practical experience and furnished with warrant sufficient to fill in the Council the posts of those who sent them.

"With regard to the question of putting an end to the present Schism and restoring peace to the Church, it would seem neither just, right, nor rational to attempt to exclude kings, princes, or their ambassadors from a vote or share in the final decision, since they make up a large and honorable part of the Council and the establishment of peace intimately concerns them and the people under them, and without their advice, assistance and favor the decisions of the Council cannot be put into execution."

The Cardinal of St. Mark composed another memorandum on the same topic, as follows ....

"Whoever you are ... I venture to tell you that in the Gauls, the Germanies, England, and Spain there are a thousand priests of parish churches, each one of whom has a larger district to administer than many prelates, and the care of more souls. Justice would admit these men and no one should exclude them. Would you shut out those whose interest is the keenest because of their great administrative responsibilities?

"For my part, I say we should admit every man in orders or ecclesiastical office, because he is interested, and every doctor, because he may be of use, and should shut none of them out. I do not find they were debarred from the ancient councils. On the contrary, look at the Council of Pisa, of which this is supposed to be a part! You will find in it almost a hundred persons of this sort, especially doctors and licentiates, officially admitted and subscribers to the verdict against Pedro de Luna and Angelo. Why you should make another, contrary rule for this Council, that derives its power from Pisa, I fail to see.

Indeed you will find many councils that admitted priests and deacons. Sometimes, when you do not read they were admitted, we know they were but the names of only the principal men were recorded, so that the numbers might not be too cumbersome.

"It may be that their poverty and distance from this place will keep them from coming. But if they come, I know of no reason, nor do you, why they should be shut out. You admit abbots without discrimination. I do not know why you exclude priests of parish churches, who have definite jurisdiction and an established office in the ecclesiastical hierarchy. They have a more extended cure of souls and administration than abbots. Many of them have a thousand— no, two, three, four, ten thousand—souls under their charge, while some abbots have ten monks or twenty or a handful more. Very few have a hundred. The place of these priests must be within the ecclesiastical order and hierarchy. The abbots minister outside the order and the hierarchy.

"Admit then, of necessity and for our own interest, men of this rank within the body whose ordained and indispensable members they are. Admit also the doctors both for their sakes and for yours, that they may direct and teach you what you do not know. Do not shut out the wise, lest you shut out wisdom and God shut you out. Let Him instruct you by their learning and guide you in the way of eternal salvation.

"As for the proctors of archbishops, bishops, and others above-mentioned, who have the right to admittance but whom you would indiscriminately exclude, I say now that they should neither be altogether excluded nor everyone admitted. I say that proctors for persons who have legitimate excuses for absence should be admitted but others not. That is the rule I find applied in elections .... As for ambassadors of kings and princes, clearly they should be given a voice in matters that concern the Universal Church, such as church union and faith. But in questions of faith they ought to abide by the decision of the scholars and doctors. Other matters too affecting ecclesiastical conduct and orders are not their affair ...."

While this problem was still under debate, another arose as to how decisions should be reached and votes counted on measures before the Council, whether by nations voting as a body—there being four of them, namely, Italy, France, Germany, and England—or by heads! Now the law was clear, that votes should be counted by heads, but there were more poverty-stricken prelates from Italy than from well-nigh all the other nations put together. Besides, our lord Pope had created an excessive number of prelates *in camera,* over fifty. There was also a rumor that he had tried to attach many more to himself by means of promises, bribes, and threats. So if votes were counted by heads, nothing would be done except what our lord wanted. Unquestionably the majority inclined towards the way of abdication. Over these questions the Council halted in suspense a long while.

In the interim, action was taken on the errors of Wyclif and a sentence was written out. But that whole matter was postponed by further developments in the proceedings for abdication. Our lord Pope at last said he was entirely willing to give peace to the Church. Meanwhile the nations, that is, France, Germany, and England, and, later, Italy, were assembling by themselves and so deciding *de facto* the question whether procedure should be by nations or by individuals, for they assembled separately. Finally they all inclined to the method of abdication in accordance with the idea of the first memorandum presented on the subject by the Cardinal of St. Mark, which began: "In the general Councils etc."

Peter of Mladonovice (1390s–1451)

Peter was born in the village of Mladonovice in Moravia near the end of the fourteenth century. He received his BA from Prague university in 1409, and was closely associated with Hus there. While at the council of Constance he shared the same lodging as Hus, and was thus an eyewitness to the proceedings he narrates. He kept in close touch with Hus even after the latter's imprisonment in the Dominican monastery. Peter also played a role in keeping Czech supporters aware of political machinations against Hus at the Council. After Hus' martyrdom, Peter returned to Bohemia to complete his account, part of which had been written while he was in Constance. His account of Hus' death was regularly read along with the Gospel lesson on July 6, a day which became a national holiday.

John (Jan) Hus (c.1370–1415)

Prague was a centre for reform-minded thinkers from the 1360s, and early in his career Hus took a leading position among Czech reform leaders. At first he used the typical reform ideas, calling for a reform in morality, true repentance and the pursuit of holiness in sermons addressed almost entirely to the laity. By 1405, however, he was preaching sermons to the clergy calling for clerical reform and arguing that priests who live in concubinage or commit adultery cannot enter heaven and so should be suspended from their office. He also lashed out against the financial exactions of the clergy and began to turn against the papacy itself; this may represent the beginning of Wycliffite views, which were well known in Prague.

As a parish priest Hus was under pressure to resist the Lollard heresy, but as rector of the university he led the fight against clerical abuses and against German domination of Bohemia. In 1409 the Germans were expelled from the university and the reform movement in Prague intensified. The Czech clergy split over their loyalty to the various popes and Hus was a victim of the rift. In 1409 he was charged with Wycliffite heresies.

Hus's real troubles began, however, when he objected to King Wenceslas' involvement in the selling of indulgences. When the pope turned against Hus, the king was no longer willing to protect him. John XXIII ordered Hus to come to Rome for trial, but Hus refused and was excommunicated. Riots broke out in Prague, and Hus appealed to the patriotism of the people against the popes (there were three at the time) and the German clergy that dominated the church in Bohemia. Finally, under a safe-conduct guaranteed by Emperor Sigismund, Hus agreed to attend the Council of Constance to defend his views.

Chapter Two

John Hus at the Council of Constance

CHAPTER V

The End of the Saintly and Reverend Master John Hus

In like manner in that year of the Lord 1415, on July 5, the Friday after St. Procopius,[1] the noble lords Wenceslas of Dubá and John of Chlum were sent by Sigismund, king of the Romans and of Hungary, along with four bishops, to the prison of the Brothers Minor in Constance to hear the final decision of Master John Hus: if he would hold the above-mentioned articles which had been, as has already been said, abstracted from his books, as well as those that had been produced against him during the course of the trial, and the depositions of the witnesses; or if he would, according to the exhortation of the Council, abjure and recant them, as has been said. When he was brought out of the prison, Lord John of Chlum said to him: "Look, Master John! we are laymen and know not how to advice you; therefore see if you feel yourself guilty in anything of that which is charged against you. Do not fear to be instructed therein and to recant. But if, indeed, you do not feel guilty of those things that are charged against you, follow the dictates of your conscience. Under no circumstances do anything against your conscience or lie in the sight of God: but rather be steadfast until death in what you know to be the truth." And he, Master John Hus, weeping, replied with humility: "Lord John, be sure that if I knew that I had written or preached anything erroneous against the law and against the holy mother Church, I would desire humbly to recant it—God is my witnes! I have ever desired to be shown better and more relevant Scripture than those that I have written and taught. And if they were shown me, I am ready most willingly to recant." To those words one of the bishops present replied to Master John: "Do you wish to be wiser than the whole Council?" The Master said to him: "I do not wish to be wiser than the whole Council, but I pray, give me the least one of the Council who would instruct me by better and more relevant Scripture, and I am ready instantly to recant!" To these words the bishops responded: "See, how obstinate he is in his heresy!"

And with these words they ordered him to be taken back to the prison and went away.

Then the next day, which was July 6, or the Saturday after St. Procopius, in the octave of the blessed apostles Peter and Paul, the said Master John Hus was led by the archbishop of Riga[2] to the cathedral of the city of Constance, where the general session of the prelates was held, presided over by the king of the Romans and of Hungary wearing his crown.[3] In the midst of that session and church a bench like a table was elevated and on it a kind of pedestal was placed, on which the vestments and the chasuble for the mass and the sacerdotal garments were arranged for the purpose of unfrocking him, Master Hus. When, therefore, he was brought into the church and approached the said elevated bench, he fell on his knees and prayed for a long time. In the meantime the bishop of Lodi,[4] ascending the pulpit, delivered a sermon concerning heresies, declaring among other things how much harm heresies cause in the Church of God and how they tear it asunder, and how it is the duty of the king to extirpate such heresies, particularly the heresy of simony, from the Church of God.

In the meantime Henry of Piro, procurator of the Council, rising, made a motion requesting that the Council continue the trial of Master John Hus until a definite decision [could be reached].[5] Then one of the bishops, deputed by the Council,[6] stood up in the pulpit and read the proceedings of the trial that had been carried on between Master John and the Prague archbishop and the prelates in the Roman curia and elsewhere; and after other matters, read the articles against Master Hus himself, drawn from his books and from the trial proceedings, a copy of which, containing the comments and qualifications from the hand of Master John Hus himself, and signed by him in the prison, were delivered to us,[7] as will be further clearly described. Some of them I shall put in here, as to set down the words which he actually used at the time.

The first of these articles was this: the holy universal Church is one, which is the totality of the predestinate, etc. To that, when it was read and finished, as well as to others subsequently, Master John replied in a loud voice with the same qualifications that he had appended to them and signed with his own hand, as has been mentioned previously.[8] When, however, he answered, the cardinal of Cambrai[9] told him: "Be silent now; it were better that you reply later to all of them together." Master John replied: "And how should I reply to all of them together when I cannot reflect upon them all together?" When, therefore, he again attempted to reply to other charges that were being brought up against him, the cardinal of Florence [10] rose and told him: "Be silent now. For we have already heard you enough!" And again rising, he said to the guard: "Order him to be silent!" Master Hus, clasping his hands, implored in a loud voice, saying: "I beseech you for God's sake, hear me, so that those standing about would not believe that I have ever held such errors; then afterward do with me as you please!" When, on the contrary, he was forbidden to say anything whatever or to respond to the charges against him, he fell upon his knees, and clasping his hands and lifting his eyes to heaven, he prayed most devoutly, committing his cause to God, the most just Judge. He did this repeatedly.

After the conclusion of the articles drawn from his books, the articles from the proceedings of the trial were read, which the depositions of the witnesses were said to have proved against him and objected to him. And to each individual accusation they adduced as witnesses pastors, canons, doctors, and other prelates without naming them personally, but mentioning them merely by their official titles and places. Among those articles was the one that after the consecration of the host there remains on the altar the material bread or the substance of the bread. Also another, that a priest in mortal sin does not transubstantiate, nor consecrate, nor baptize; and so forth about others. Then when Master John again arose, wishing to respond, the cardinal of Florence, again shouting at him, forbade him. And he (Hus], responding nonetheless, said: "I pray for God's sake, hear my meaning at least on account of those standing here, lest they believe that I have held those errors. I declare that I have never held, nor taught, nor preached that in the sacrament of the altar the material bread remains after the consecration." And subsequently he responded to other [charges] in accordance with what he had signed with his own hand.

Among other things they also accused him of the article that he wished to be and is the fourth person of the Godhead, as they stated. [11] They attempted to prove that article by [citing] a certain doctor. And the Master cried: "Name that doctor who testified that against me!" But the bishop who was reading it said: "There is no need here now that he be named." And the Master, responding, said among other things: "Be it far from me, a miserable wretch, that I should want to name myself the fourth person of the Godhead, for that has never entered my heart; but I unswervingly assert that the Father, the Son, and the Holy Spirit are one God, one essence, and a trinity of persons."

Thereupon the said lectors read that Master John Hus had appealed to God, and condemned such an appeal as an error. To that Master John responded in a loud voice: "O Lord God, see how this Council already condemns Thy acts and law as an error; and Thou, when Thou wast gravely oppressed by Thine enemies, Thou didst commend Thy cause to God, Thy Father, the most just Judge. Thus Thou host given us wretches an example, that in all grave cases we should resort to Thee, the most just Judge, most humbly asking Thy help in rendering a righteous decision." And to that he added: "I continue to declare that there is no safer appeal than to the Lord Jesus Christ, Who will not be suborned by a perverse bribe, nor deceived by a false testimony, but will render to each one what he deserves."

Among other things they stated that Master John Hus, although excommunicated, bore it contumaciously, etc. He responded: "I did not bear it contumaciously, but having appealed, I preached and celebrated the mass. But although I have twice sent procurators to the Roman curia,[12] advancing reasons for not appearing personally, I was never able to obtain a hearing: instead, some of my procurators were incarcerated [13] and others were ill treated. In all these matters I refer you to the acts of the trial in which all these things are more fully contained. Above all, I even came to this Council freely, having the safeconduct of the lord king here present, desiring to show my innocence and to give account of my faith."[14]

When therefore all the articles offered against him were completed and read, a certain old and bald auditor, a prelate of the Italian nation commisioned thereto, read the definitive sentence upon Master John Hus.[15] And he, Master John, responded, replying to certain points in the sentence, although they forbade it. And particularly when he was declared to be obstinate in his error and heresy, he replied in a loud voice: "I have never been obstinate, and am not now. But I have ever desired, and to this day I desire, more relevant instruction from the Scriptures. And today I declare that if even with one word I could destroy and uproot all errors, I would most gladly do so!" And when all his books, either in Latin written by himself or translated into whatever other language, likewise in that sentence condemned as suspect of heresy, were for that reason condemned to be burned—of which some were burned later, particularly the book *De ecclesia* and *Contra Paletz* and *Contra Stanislaum,* as they were called—he, Master John, responded: "Why do you condemn my books, when I have ever desired and demanded better Scriptural proofs against what I said and set forth in them, and even today I so desire? But you have so far neither adduced any more relevant Scripture in opposition, nor have shown one erroneous word in them. Indeed, how can you condemn the books in the vernacular Czech or those translated into another language when you have never even seen them?" While the rest of the sentence was being read, he heard it kneeling and praying, looking up to heaven. When the sentence was concluded, as has already been mentioned concerning particular points, Master John Hus again knelt and in a loud voice prayed for all his enemies and said: "Lord Jesus Christ, I implore Thee, forgive all my enemies for Thy great mercy's sake; and Thou knowest that they have falsely accused me and have produced false witnesses and have concocted false articles against me! Forgive them for Thy boundless mercy's sake!" And when he said this, many, especially the principal clergy, looked indignantly and jeered at him.[16]

Then at the command of the seven bishops[17] who assisted at his unfrocking, he put on the altar vestments as if he were about to celebrate the mass. When he put on the alb, he said: "My Lord Jesus Christ, when He was led from Herod to Pilate, was mocked in a white garment." And when he was already so dressed and was exhorted by those bishops to recant and abjure, he rose, and ascending the table before which he was being dressed, and turning toward the multitude, weeping sorrowfully, he exclaimed: "Behold, these bishops exhort me to recant and abjure. But I fear to do so, lest I be a liar in the sight of the Lord, and also lest I offend my own conscience and the truth of God. For I have never held those articles that are falsely witnessed against me, but rather have written, taught, and preached their opposite; and also lest I offend the multitude to whom I have preached and others who faithfully preach the Word of God." When he said this, the prelates sitting nearby and others of the said Council remarked: "We see now how obdurate he is in his wickedness and obstinate in heresy."

After he descended from the table, the said bishops at once began to unfrock him. First they took the cup from his hands, pronouncing this curse: "O cursed Judas, because you have abandoned the counsel of peace and have counseled with the Jews, we take away from you this cup of redemption." He replied in a loud voice: "I trust in the Lord God Almighty, for whose name I patiently bear this vilification, that He will not take away from me the cup of His redemption; but I firmly hope to drink from it today in His kingdom." And subsequently taking away from him the other vestments—that is, the stole, the chasuble, and others, etc.—they pronounced in each instance an appropriate curse. And he responded that he humbly and gladly embraced the vilifications for the name of our Lord Jesus Christ. When he was divested of all vestments, as already mentioned, the said bishops proceeded to obliterate his tonsure. Thereupon they began an altercation among themselves, for some wished to shave him with a razor while others asserted that it suffices to obliterate the tonsure merely with scissors; he, turning toward the king presiding on the throne, said: "Look, these bishops so far do not know how to agree in this vilification!" And when they cut his tonsure with scissors into four parts—namely, right, left, front, and back—they spoke during it these words: "The Church has already deprived him of all ecclesiastical rights, and has nothing more to do with him. Therefore, we turn him over to the secular court." But prior to that they placed on his head a paper crown for vilification, saying to him among other things: "We commit your soul to the devil!" And he, joining his hands and lifting his eyes to heaven, said: "And I commit it to the most merciful Lord Jesus Christ." Seeing that crown he said: "My Lord Jesus Christ on account of me, a miserable wretch, bore a much heavier and harsher crown of thorns. Being innocent, he was deemed deserving of the most shameful death. Therefore I, a miserable wretch and sinner, will humbly bear this much lighter, even though vilifying crown for His name and truth." The paper crown was round, almost eighteen inches high, and on it were shown three horrible devils about to seize a soul and to tear it among themselves with claws. The inscription on that crown describing his guilt read: "This is a heresiarch." Then the king said to Duke Ludwig, the son of the late Clem of Bavaria,[18] who then stood before him in his robes, holding the golden orb with the cross in his hands: "Go, receive him!" And the said Clem's son then received the Master, giving him into the hands of the executioners to be led to death.[19]

When so crowned he was then led from the said church; they were burning his books at that hour in the church cemetery. When in passing by he saw it, he smiled at this their act. On his way indeed he exhorted those standing around or following him not to believe that he was to die on account of the errors falsely ascribed to him and deposed by the false testimony of his chief enemies. Indeed, almost all the inhabitants of that city, bearing arms, accompanied him to death.

And having come to the place of execution, he, bending his knees and stretching his hands and turning his eyes toward heaven, most devoutly sang psalms, and particularly, "Have mercy on me, God," and "In Thee, Lord, have I trusted,"[20] repeating the verse "In Thy hand, Lord." His own [friends] who stood about then heard him praying joyfully and with a glad countenance. The place of execution was among gardens in a certain meadow as one goes from Constance toward the fortress of Gottlieben,[21] between the gates and the moats of the suburbs of the said city. Some of the lay people standing about said: "We do not know what or how he acted and spoke formerly, but now in truth we see and hear that he prays and speaks with holy words." And others said: "It would certainly be well that he have a confessor that he might be heard." But a certain priest in a green suit with a red silk lining,[22] sitting on a horse, said: "He should not be heard, nor a confessor be given him, for he is a heretic." But Master John, while he was still in prison, had confessed to a certain doctor, a monk,[23] and had been kindly heard and absolved by him, as he himself stated in one of his letters to his [friends] from prison.[24]

When he was praying, the offensive crown already mentioned, painted with three devils, fell from his head. When he perceived it, he smiled. Some of the hired soldiers standing by said: "Put it on him again so that he might be burned along with the devils, his masters, whom he served here on earth." And rising at the order of the executioner from the place where he was praying, he said in a loud and clear voice, so that his [friends] could plainly hear him: "Lord Jesus Christ, I am willing to bear most patiently and humbly this dreadful, ignominious, and cruel death for Thy gospel and for the preaching of Thy Word." Then they decided to take him among the bystanders. He urged and begged them not to believe that he in any way held, preached, or taught the articles with which he had been charged by false witnesses.[25] Then having been divested of his clothing he was tied to a stake with ropes, his hands tied behind his back. And when he was turned facing east, some of the bystanders said: "Let him not be turned toward the east, because he is a heretic; but turn him toward the west." So that was done. When he was bound by the neck with a sooty chain, he looked at it and, smiling, said to the executioners: "The Lord Jesus Christ, my Redeemer and Savior, was bound by a harder and heavier chain. And I, a miserable wretch, am not ashamed to bear being bound for His name by this one." The stake was like a thick post half a foot thick; they sharpened one end of it and fixed it in the ground of that meadow. They placed two bound bundles of wood under the Master's feet. When tied to that stake, he still had his shoes on and one shackle on his feet. Indeed, the said bundles of wood, interspersed with straw, were piled around his body so that they reached up to his chin. For the wood amounted to two wagon- or cartloads.

Before it was kindled, the imperial marshal, Hoppe of Poppenheim,[26] approached him along with the son of the late Clem, as it was said, exhorting him to save his life by abjuring and recanting his former preaching and teaching. But he, looking up to heaven, replied in a loud voice: "God is my witness," he exclaimed, "that those things that are falsely ascribed to me and of which the false witnesses accuse me, I have never taught or preached. But that the principal intention of my preaching and of all my other acts or writings was solely that I might turn men from sin. And in that truth of the Gospel that I wrote, taught, and preached in accordance with the sayings and expositions of the holy doctors, I am willing gladly to die today."[27] And hearing that, the said marshal with the son of Clem immediately clapped their hands and retreated.

When the executioners at once lit [the fire], the Master immediately began to sing in a loud voice, at first "Christ, Thou son of the living God, have mercy upon us," and secondly, "Christ, Thou son of the living God, have mercy upon me," and in the third place, "Thou Who art born of Mary the Virgin." And when he began to sing the third time, the wind blew the flame into his face. And thus praying within himself and moving his lips and the head, he expired in the Lord. While he was silent, he seemed to move before he actually died for about the time one can quickly recite "Our Father" two or at most three times.

When the wood of those bundles and the ropes were consumed, but the remains of the body still stood in those chains, hanging by the neck, the executioners pulled the charred body along with the stake down to the ground and burned them further by adding wood from the third wagon to the fire. And walking around, they broke the bones with clubs so that they would be incinerated more quickly. And finding the head, they broke it to pieces with the clubs and again threw it into the fire. And when they found his heart among the intestines, they sharpened a club like a spit, and, impaling it on its end, they took particular [care] to roast and consume it, piercing it with spears until finally the whole mass was turned into ashes. And at the order of the said Clem and the marshal, the executioners threw the clothing into the fire along with the shoes, saying: "So that the Czechs would not regard it as relics; we will pay you money for it." Which they did. So they loaded all the ashes in a cart and threw it into the river Rhine flowing nearby.[28]

Thus I have therefore described clearly and in detail the sequence of the death and agony of the celebrated Master John Hus, the eminent preacher of the evangelical truth, so that in the course of time his memory might be vividly recollected. My principle has been not to dress up the account in a mass of highly embellished diction lacking the kernel of fact and deed, wherewith to tickle the itching ears desirous to feast thereon; but rather to speak of the marrow of the substance of the trial proceedings mentioned above, of what I have clearly learned from what I myself have seen and heard. He who knows all things is my witness that I lie not. I would rather suffer the blame of having used inept and awkward words so that it may be recognized that I have brought forth testimony to the truth, that the memory of the Master, its most steadfast champion, may thus live in the future!

Endnotes

1. See Hus's letters written on July 5, in Part II, Nos. 34–36.
2. John of Wallenrode, of the Order of the Teutonic Knights.
3. The crown was held by Henry of Bavaria; it was not actually worn by Sigismund, as the famous painting of Václav Brozík mistakenly shows. In the Czech version of the *Passio,* composed later, but perhaps by Peter of Mladonovice (Novotný in *Fontes rerum Bohemicarum,* VIII, 121–49 ascribes it to him), it is added that the archbishop with Hus had to wait in the entrance while the mass was being celebrated within (p. 127).
4. Jacob Balardi Arrigoni, an Italian Dominican, bishop of Lodi, who preached on the text in Rom. 6:6, which in the Vulgate version reads, "That the body of sin be destroyed." The sermon is found in Novotný, *Fontes,* VIII, 489 ff.
5. This was the usual procedure at the Council: one of the two procurators—Henry of Piro and John of Scribanis of Piacenza—presented the requests for formal actions agreed upon by the nations. When the request was granted, the proposal was then read. In this instance, it was Henry of Piro who requested the formal action against Hus.
6. Berthold of Wildungen, the papal auditor. Peter made a mistake in calling him bishop. The representatives of the other three nations were bishops Anthony of Concordia, Stephen Coevret of Dol, Nicholas of Merseburg, Vitalis Valentini of Toulon, and Patrick Foxe of Cork.
7. Hus succeeded in sending a copy of this document to his friends; cf. Part II, No. 15, for its translation.
8. According to the *Passio,* Hus declared: "I doubt not that the holy Church catholic is one which is the congregation of all the elect here on the earth, and of those in purgatory, and also in heaven; they are the secret body of the head Jesus Christ." Novotný, *Fontes,* VIII, 129-30.

9. Pierre d'Ailly, the president of the Commission and Hus's principal opponent among the cardinals.

10. Francesco Zabarella, one of Hus's former judges, and a member of the Council's Commission.

11. According to Novotný, this fantastically absurd charge represents a twisted deduction from philosophical realism, alleging that there could be more than three hypostates in the Trinity—although Hus neither made any such deduction nor claimed to be the fourth hypostasis of the Godhead!

12. In fact, he sent three procurators successively: Mark of Hradec, John of Jesenice, and Nicholas of Stojcín.

13. This was John of Jesenice, who was imprisoned and excommunicated by the machinations of Michael de Causis.

14. The *Passio* adds: "And when he said that, he turned toward the king; and the king blushed a great deal and reddened." Novotný, *op. cit., p. 135.*

15. This was Anthony, bishop of Concordia. The text is given in Novotný, *op. cit.,* 501 ff., and its translation is to be found in Part II, No. *35. Cf.* also Sedlák, *Studie,* I, 349 ff., where two preliminary texts of the sentence are published. The sentence is correctly summarized by Cardinal Fillastre in his *Diary.* See Loomis, *op. cit.,* p. 256.

16. On the same day, July 6, the Council sentenced Jean Petit, who had defended (1408) the right of regicide in an effort to justify the duke of Burgundy for his assassination of the duke of Orleans. But while Hus was burned, Petit, who had died in 1411, was declared not guilty when the case was reopened several times at the insistence of John the Fearless, the duke of Burgundy. Both Jean Gerson and Cardinal d'Ailly strenuously opposed this as unjust. In the session held on May 2, 1416, the bishop of Arras, the envoy of the duke of Burgundy, criticized Gerson "and asked for his condemnation as the purveyor of calumny." Loomis, *op, cit.,* p. 509.

17. They were Bartolomeo de la Copra, the archbishop of Milan; Henry Scarampi bishop of Belluna-Filtre; Albert Guttuaria d'Agliano, bishop of Asti and abbot of St. Bartholomew in Pavia; Bartholino Beccari of Alessandria; William Barrowe of Bangor; John Belli of Lavour in France; and the suffragan Bishop John of Constance.

18. This was Duke Ludwig of Palatine, the son of the one-time king of the Romans, Ruprecht of Palatine, known as Clem (Clement).

19. The *Passio* adds that Sigismund spoke the words in German and one later Ms. inserts at this place a rather unlikely story that Ludwig, accosting Hus, said to him; "'Master John, recant now and save your life.' Thereupon Master John said to him: 'And who are you?' He then replied: 'The young Hercules' [i.e., Herr zu Klem]. Master John Hus said: 'Do not hold it against me, that I supposed that you were the executioner.' Thereupon he, blushing and looking at the king, took

Master John Hus and turned him into the hands of the executioners." Novotný, *op, cit.,* p. 140.

20. Psalms 51:3 and 31:2, 6.

21. It is now on the western outskirts of the city itself in the vicinity of the municipal gas works on the *Alten Graben Strasse*. A large boulder serves as a monument and is inscribed for both John Hus and Jerome of Prague.

22. Ulrich Schorand, a deputy of the bishop and of the Council. The description written by Richental, who claims to have walked along with the guards and thus was an eyewitness, differs in many details from that of Peter. Cf. Loomis, *op. cit.,* p. 133.

23. The *Passio* adds: "… which confessor the Council had sent, as he [Hus] himself confessed and wrote in a letter written by his own hand, which he sent, among others, from the prison." Novotný, *op. cit.,* pp. 142–43.

24. Cf. Part II, No. 21 of this work.

25. The *Passio* adds that he requested to speak to his jailors; and when they drew near, he thanked them for all the good they had done him. Novotný, *op. cit.,* pp. 143–44.

26. Members of this noble Swabian family held the office of marshal for many generations.

27. Richental's account is strangely confused, for he seems to have conflated Jerome's trial with that of Hus. He asserts that both Hus and Jerome "promised to abandon their wicked beliefs and denounced what they had taught." He dates the death of Hus as taking place on July 8, and of Jerome early in September, 1415, instead of May 30, 1416. Altogether, Richental is surprisingly inaccurate in reporting the trial of Hus and Jerome. Loomis, *op, cit.,* pp. 131-35.

28. The *Passio* adds: "… wishing to destroy, as far as they could, his memory among the faithful," Novotný, *op, cit.,* p. 147.

Aeneas Silvius Piccolomini (Pius II) (1405–1464)

Aeneas Silvius was born in 1405 into the noble Sienese family of Piccolomini. He studied law, but he was more interested in classical letters and humanist learning. In 1431 Aeneas attended the Council of Basle, where his abilities as a scholar and diplomat were widely used; and in 1436 his eloquence and his ambition resulted in his becoming the spokesman for the conciliarist faction.

Aeneas was sent by the Council to the Imperial Diet of Frankfort. He so impressed the Emperor Frederick III that he was crowned poet laureate in 1442 and appointed an imperial secretary. He had also decided to enter the Church, taking holy orders in 1446, and soon after he was given the see of Trieste. In 1450 he was translated to the see of his native city, Siena, and in December of 1456 Aeneas Silvius was raised to the sacred college as a cardinal. Then, in the conclave of 1458, a moment Aeneas himself so powerfully describes in his Commentaries, *he emerged as pope, taking the name Pius II.*

Although guilty of the usual papal nepotism, Pius patronized humanists, and he himself continued to write, despite the demands upon his time. In particular, he completed his Commentaries, *which represents one of the great contributions to Renaissance autobiography, and the unique example of the genre by a Renaissance pope.*

The great issue of his papacy was his calling for a new crusade to liberate Constantinople from the Turks who had conquered the city in 1453. Unfortunately, Pius died in 1464 before his plans could be realized.

Chapter Three

First Book of the Commentaries (excerpt)

While this was happening at Mainz no little uncertainty arose among the theologians who had stayed behind at Basle as to whether Eugenius [Pope Eugenius IV] could be called a heretic, seeing that he was showing such rebellious contempt of the instructions of the Church. Meeting together for that reason, they held a long discussion, some maintaining the negative, some the positive view, knowing that this was the old Socratic method of arguing against another's opinion. For Socrates thought that in this way what was closest to the truth could most easily be discovered. In the course of the discussion three views emerged; some maintained that Eugenius was a heretic, some that he was not only a heretic but relapsed, and the third group was unwilling to admit that he was either relapsed or a heretic. Prominent among the theologians both in authority and knowledge was the bishop of Hebron, ambassador of the serene and puissant king of Castile. Prominent too was a certain Scottish abbot. These, like active boxers putting on an exhibition fight, floored some of their opponents; others either accepted their pleas or gave way to them, and by their efforts the weightier view in the end prevailed: that Eugenius be called both a heretic and relapsed. Eight short resolutions were approved among these theologians, which they asserted to be truths; they published a copy of them. This affair began towards the middle of April, through the industry and shrewdness of a certain Nicolas, a Dominican friar from Burgundy, an acute man with a mind far larger than his body, who did not stop dinning it in the ears of members of deputations and congregations until the matter was accepted and brought to a conclusion. I should not hesitate to assert that the matter would have remained unattempted had not this little man's diligence roused the Fathers, although to look at him you would not have considered him capable of so much. But men are not to be judged by their appearance.

Now when the ambassadors had returned from Mainz, and certainty was felt about the acceptance of the decrees, the Fathers resolved to discuss with greater care and at greater length the short resolutions of the masters, and there were summoned at the order of the deputations all masters and doctors of civil and canon law to the chapter-house of the cathedral to discuss in public with the prelates the heresy of Eugenius. This was a matter very troublesome to the archbishop of Milan, who feared that this discussion might involve the deprivation of Eugenius, which he, as he said, had always opposed through fear of a schism. On that account he admonished some, stirred the sluggish, frightened the bold, and used all his energy to cause confusion in the matter, and though of the duke's ambassadors he alone remained at Basle, yet with notable success he acted for the others as well. For if one works with a will nothing seems hard, and three together would not have done more than he accomplished alone. For as far as he was able he inspired the absent members of his party by letters and those present by words to defend Eugenius. They came to the chapter-house and there was a crowded meeting, for all had been enticed by their eagerness to speak or listen. Discussion lasted for six days altogether, both morning and afternoon. In the midst of them all and occupying first place as judge of faith and director and controller of the whole discussion was Cardinal Louis, archbishop of Arles, a prelate notable for many virtues and in particular for courage and steadfastness. Nicolas Amici, who too is a procurator of faith and very well known among the theologians of Paris, asked each man for his opinion. The votes were recorded by the notary Jean Dieulifist, and there was an excellent discussion and wise examination of several topics. If I were willing to make mention of these, I am afraid some would consider that my judgement was at fault when I entered upon so great a task, as this is very far removed from my promise and my aim. Yet I shall suit myself, and shall not consider that by trespassing within the bounds of holy writings I have "peered into the temple of that goddess from whom males are scared away".[1] Now in beginning to make mention of the actual subject I will state at the outset the resolutions of the theologians as being the foundation of the discussion. I shall not, however, use the same words as they did. It will be sufficient to report the sense. The resolutions were of this nature:

1. It is a truth of the catholic faith that the holy general Council holds power over the pope and anyone else.
2. The Roman pontiff of his own authority can neither dissolve nor transfer nor prorogue the general Council when lawfully assembled without its own consent, and that is part of the same truth.

3. Whoever obdurately opposes those truths must be deemed a heretic.
4. Pope Eugenius IV attacked these truths when first from the plenitude of his apostolic power he attempted to dissolve or transfer the Council of Basle.
5. Eugenius at the warning of the holy Council eventually renounced the errors at variance with these truths.
6. Eugenius's second attempt at dissolution or transference is inimical to the aforesaid truths and contains unpardonable error as regards the faith.
7. Eugenius in attempting a second time to dissolve or transfer the Council is relapsing into the errors he renounced.
8. Eugenius, when warned by the Council to renounce his second attempt at dissolution or transference, by persisting in rebellion after his evident contumacy and by upholding the Assembly of Ferrara, shows himself to be obdurate.

Of this nature, I think, were the resolutions, and when these had been read again and again in the chapter-house in the presence of the Fathers, all were asked individually to give their opinion, and almost all voted for the resolutions. The archbishop of Palermo, however, a man eminent among all for learning, argued at length to the contrary. So too did that ornament of the prelates, the bishop of Burgos, and the almoner of the king of Aragon, distinguished not less for eloquence than learning. These, however, did not oppose the earlier resolutions, but only those affecting Eugenius, and with the subtlety of a most astute mind Panormitanus held forth against the later resolutions, and worked energetically to show that Eugenius was not relapsed; and he had a great dispute with three theologians, the bishop of Ardjisch, John of Segovia, and François de Fuxe. He made a threefold division of the articles of the faith, precise as in the Creed, broad as in declarations made by the Church, very broad as in the consequences of the first two, holding that Eugenius had under none of these headings harmed the faith in the first dissolution that he made, because neither in the Creed nor in the canons of the Church was it maintained that the pope could not dissolve councils; nor did it appear to him that this was a consequence of the canons previously made, but rather of the decrees of the Council of Constance. Such an occasion had been, as it were, left out of account, and was reserved for the pope's ordering, since in the decree *Frequens* the place for a future council was chosen by the pope with the Council's approval, and nothing at all was said about this. But if perhaps Eugenius had done wrong in the first dissolution he ought to be considered excused, as he had acted in accordance with the advice of cardinals representing the Roman Church, the authority of which (he said) was so great that its judgement would be preferred to the whole world's, and which was affirmed by a singular gloss; nor was it found that the holy Council had ever proceeded against Eugenius as a heretic, a sign that it did not think that he had turned aside from the faith. He himself attached no weight to what was said about adherence [to the Council] and about renounced errors. He had read the whole text of [Eugenius's] adherence, and the pope had not renounced the dissolution as contrary to the faith, but as an occasion of scandal. Moreover, in the last dissolution there was nothing of this kind, since in a similar way he had ordered the dissolution on the advice of the cardinals, and to facilitate union with the Greeks, and he should not be compelled to give answer in a criminal case through an agent when he could not put in a personal appearance owing to bad health. So, since from the first dissolution he had not fallen into an error of faith, he was persuaded that Eugenius could not now be called relapsed, seeing that he had not harmed the faith either by the first or the second dissolution.

The speech of Panormitanus met with more general praise than approval. It was, however, so far effective that later the word "relapsed" was taken out of the resolutions, and in its place was put "lapsed." Panormitanus did not venture to clear Eugenius completely of heresy, and placed more weight on the first than the second dissolution, nor did he withdraw without a reply. For John of Segovia, who was very distinguished in theology, rose, and replied with reverence and modesty as befitted so great a prelate. He said he agreed with the remarks of Panormitanus about the threefold division of the articles of the faith, and that supported his own case, because if those things were to be held as articles of faith which were consequences of the canons of the Church, it would be obvious that the resolutions under discussion proceeded from the canons of the Church, that is, the Council of Constance; because if there the pope was in subjection to the general Council, who might say that the Pope had any command over the Council which was his superior? Eugenius should have halted, because he could not dissolve against its will a Council that was superior to himself; and this article he certainly violated. If anyone wished it to be expressly stated that in the first dissolution this article was not infringed because the declaration had not yet been made, the holder of this view should realize that the Roman pontiff must know not only the explicit matters of the faith but the implicit ones too. For being the vicar of Christ and head of all, he had to teach and instruct all men. But if he should dodge this completely, he would be convicted under the head that he persisted in his dissolution for a long time after the declaration of the Council, and did not accept a canon of the Church, and therefore if he did not perhaps commit an error in faith in making the dissolution, he most certainly did in his obduracy. That conclusion was very neatly drawn from a saying of Clement often quoted by Panormitanus to the effect that he who lived in rebellion and neglected to do what was right was shown to be a member of the devil rather than of Christ, and was revealed as being an unbeliever rather than a believer. So it was not absurd to call Eugenius an unbeliever as not obedient to the Church. Nor was it true that the pope was not attacked on a matter of faith. For both in the reply beginning "Considering," and in the other, "They hope, when the pope's ambassadors are given up" these words were openly found: "'This article concerns the faith, and we prefer death to a cowardly surrender"; from which remark it was clear enough that the Synod had warned the pope that he was going against the faith. So when afterwards by his adherence Eugenius had renounced the dissolution, he clearly renounced the error of faith contained in it as well; and the scandal moreover, of which mention was made, arose because of the error of faith, since some said the pope was beneath the Council, others denied this, and the very discrepancy of doctrine brought scandal with it. In the pope's act of adherence those assertions were also expressly renounced which had been made in the name of the pope against the authority of the Council. Though in retractions like these the style and order of legal documents were not observed, still what was done in such matters was enough since the Council was acting against the pope; in which case only the truth was to be respected; nor was the Council subject to positive law that it should keep [legal] terms and follow judicial procedure. Further that "singular gloss" which "preferred the Roman Church to the world," he held in utter contempt; it was a good thing it was "singular," since it made such a fatuous statement, and it did not deserve to have anyone following it. He was surprised at Panormitanus and other doctors of our times who, while thinking they praised the authority of glosses, actually lessened it by adding the "singularity." For a "singular gloss" was one that stood alone; but who would not value more a gloss possessing the same meaning in all places, and always consistently expressed, than one making an assertion in only a single place, which could without doubt seem to have been made in error? As far as the truth was concerned he took Jerome, the most learned of doctors, to be in opposition to that gloss, for he had no doubt that as regards authority the world was greater than the city, that is than Rome.

John of Segovia was not able to finish without interruption. For often Panormitanus broke in upon his words, and actively tried to confute now one remark now another. There rose also the bishop of Ardjisch, a man not only of eloquence but full of courage, who sharply demolished the remarks and arguments of Panormitanus, and matters between them went beyond the requirements of moderate discussion, for they did not refrain from abuse. Yet afterwards (though perhaps he was less at fault), the bishop of Ardjisch asked pardon, as usually happens because subordinates should always submit. The bishop of Ardjisch had happened to say that the Roman pontiff was the servant of the Church, which Panormitanus could not tolerate; and that day so far forgot himself and his learning, which is very great, as not to shrink from claiming that the pope was ruler of the Church. John of Segovia replied, "Watch what you are saying, Panormitanus. It is a very honourable title of the Roman pontiff when he calls himself 'servant of the servants of God.' For that is taken from what Christ said to his disciples when they were asking which of them would be the greatest. For you know he replied that 'the princes of the Gentiles exercise lordship over them, but ye shall not be so,' and so on, when he completely forbade lordship, and Peter, who himself was the first vicar of Christ, says: 'Feed the flock of God which is among you, taking the oversight thereof, not by constraint but willingly'; and a little later: 'neither as being lords over [God's] heritage.' But if Christ, the son of God, 'came not to be ministered unto, but to minister,' how will his vicar exercise lordship or be able to be called lord, as you wish, Panormitanus ? For 'the disciple is not above his master, nor the servant above his lord,' 'neither be ye called masters,' saith the Lord, 'for one is your master [even] Christ,' and 'he that is greatest among you shall be your servant.'"

Panormitanus was rather perturbed by this reply, and the meeting broke up.

Endnotes

1. A quotation (from "introspexisse" to "absterrentur") from Macrobius, *Satur*. i. 24, 12. Bona Dea, sometimes caled Fauna, had a temple at Rome on the Aventine.

John Wyclif (c. 1330–1384)

Wyclif was a trained Oxford theologian, who sought to publicize his views outside the university. He objected to pluralism, simony and the accumulation of church property, which were common targets for church reformers. Wyclif, however, moved into dangerous territory by advocating the return of ecclesiastical property to secular hands and an important role for the secular authority in the reform of the church. Wyclif also believed that the Bible should be available in the vernacular for everyone to read; he made a start on the first English bible, completed after his death.

Up to about 1378 he cannot be considered a heretic, because though his opinions did not follow those of the Church, they had not been condemned. In 1377, however, Pope Gregory XI condemned Wyclif's teachings and ordered him to be arrested and examined. He was protected by John of Gaunt, the uncle of the king, and the examination did not take place, but after this point Wyclif was in defiance of the church.

The Peasants' Revolt of 1381 discredited Wyclif, though there is no evidence that he was involved with it, or agreed with its aims. He was placed under house arrest in 1382, when he seems to have suffered a stroke. It was followed by a second one which killed him two years later. Wyclif's followers became known as Lollards, and the movement passed largely into lay hands. The authorities took measures to suppress it, and persecution by Henry IV forced the Lollards to go underground in 1401. Because Wyclif had never been formally excommunicated, he was buried in hallowed ground. His condemnation came at the council of Constance, in 1415. In 1421 Wyclif's body was dug up and burnt and the ashes thrown into a nearby stream.

Chapter Four

Of Wedded Men and Wives
and of their Children also

Our Lord God Almighty speaks in his law of two matrimonies or wedlocks. The first is spiritual matrimony, between Christ and holy Church, that is, Christian souls ordained to bliss. The second matrimony is bodily or spiritual, between man and woman, by just consent, after God's law.

God speaks of the first matrimony by the prophet Hosea to holy Church; and to each person of holy Church God himself says, I shall espouse you or wed you to me, in righteousness, in judgment, in mercy and in faith; and I shall wed you without end. This is the first matrimony and the best, as God and the soul of true men are better than men's bodies. And this best matrimony is broken for a time by the breaking of the said faith, and default of righteous living. And therefore God says often by his prophets, that his people fornicated and committed adultery, for they worshipped false gods; and St. James (iv.4) says that men that love the world are spiritual adulterers. For he writes thus: you adulterers, do you not know that friendship of this world is enmity of God? And thus all men that love worldly worship or goods of the world more than God and his law and true life are spiritual adulterers, if they were Christian before; and this is worse adultery than breaking fleshly matrimony.

God speaks of the second matrimony, that is bodily, in the first book of Holy Scriptures, when he made matrimony between Adam and Eve in Paradise in the state of innocence, before they sinned. And because God himself made this order of matrimony and he did not make these new religious orders, it is better and more to praise than these new orders. And also Jesus Christ would not be born of the virgin Mary, nor conceived, but in true matrimony, as the gospel of Luke, and St. Ambrose, and other saints witness. Also Jesus Christ was present in his own person with his mother in bodily matrimony, to approve it, as the gospel of John teaches, when he turned water into wine. Also the Holy Spirit warns Christian men, how in the last days some heretics shall depart from the faith of God's law, paying heed to spirits of error, and to teaching of devils, telling lies in hypocrisy, forbidding men and women to be married and teaching men to abstain from meat, which God has made to be eaten by faithful men, thanking God and listening to Him. Also, this bodily matrimony is a sacrament and figure of the spiritual wedlock between Christ and holy Church, as St. Paul says. Also, this wedlock is necessary to save mankind by generation until the day of judgment, and to restore and fulfill the number of angels, damned for pride, and the number of saints in heaven, and to save men and women from fornication. And therefore he that forbids or hinders true matrimony is an enemy of God and the saints in heaven and all mankind. And therefore man punished fornication and adultery in the old law by stoning to death, and in the law of grace by damning in hell, unless men are truly sorry for it.

And therefore, since fornication is so perilous, and men and women so frail, God ordained priests in the old law to have wives, and never forbade it in the new law, neither by Christ nor by his apostles, but rather approved it. But now, by hypocrisy of fiends and false men, many bind themselves to priesthood and chastity, and forsake wives by God's law, and ruin maidens and wives and fall foul of all. For there are many priests and religious, carrying-on, who have a pleasure-loving easy life, being young and strong of complexion, faring well in meat and drink, and they will not toil, neither in penance, nor study of God's law, nor teaching, nor labour with their hands; and therefore they fall into lechery in diverse degrees and in sin against nature. For many gentlemen's sons and daughters have been made religious against their will, when they were children without discretion, in order to give the inheritance wholly to one child that is most loved. And when they come to age, either for fear of their friends or for fear of poverty if they should leave, and for hypocrisy and flattering and fair promises of the religious or for fear of taking their body to prison, they dare not show their heart or leave this state, though they know that they are incapable of it. And from this comes lechery and sometimes murdering of many men.

Nevertheless, though matrimony is good and greatly commended by God, yet pure virginity is much better—and wedlock also, as St. Paul says publicly; for Jesus Christ, who lived most perfectly, was always a pure virgin and not married bodily, and so was his mother ever virgin, and John the Evangelist. St. Augustine and Jerome specially witness this well in many books. Nevertheless, virginity is so high and so noble that Christ did not command it generally, but said, who may take, take it. And therefore Paul gave no commandment of virginity, but gave counsel to them that were able to do it. And thus priests who keep pure chastity in body and soul do best; but many take this burden unwisely and scandalize themselves foully before God and his saints, for new bonds made needlessly by sinful men. And this is a great deceit of the devil under colour of perfection and chastity. For he stirs men to high points of perfection, when he knows or supposes them unable, not for their good, but so that they will fall fouler and deeper in more sin, as St. Augustine teaches. And thus the fiend Satan transfigures or turns himself falsely into an angel of light, to deceive men by colour of holiness.

CHAPTER II

See now how this wedlock ought to be kept in both sides. First this wedlock should be made with full consent of both parties, principally to the worship of God, to live cleanly in the order that he made, and bring forth children to fulfill the chosen number of saints in bliss, and not to have fleshly lusts without reason and fear of God, as mules and horses and swine that have no understanding. For the angel Raphael warned Tobit, that the fiend has mastery upon such men as are wedded, to have thus lusts of flesh as beasts without reason and fear of God. Also this contract should not be made between a young man and an old barren widow, past child-bearing, for love of worldly muck, as men full of covetousness do sometimes—for then comes soon wrangling and adultery and enmity and waste of goods, and sorrow and care enough. And it is a great despite to God to colour thus their wicked covetousness, lechery and adultery by the holy order of matrimony. And many men sin much, for they befoul many women, and hinder them from matrimony and undo them in this world and are sometimes the cause of their damnation; for they are made common women, when they have lost their friends and know no craft to live by. Many hot and courageous men will not take a poor gentlewoman as his wife in God's law, and make her a gentlewoman, and save her own soul, but live in the devil's service all their life, or the more part; and befoul many temples of God to the great peril of their soul, and abide to have a rich woman for muck, and then waste their goods in harlotry and foolish pride, in adultery on gay strumpets, and ever live in wrath and chiding, and in bondage of sin to the fiends of hell. Also some mighty men marry their children, where their heart does not consent willingly, but pretends for fear. For commonly they look for riches and worthiness to the world and not after goodness of virtuous life. And so God and his side is put behind, and the devil and the world and the flesh now have mastery here.

A man may know his rightful wife fleshly for three reasons, the first to beget children, to fulfill the number of men and women that will be saved; the second to keep his wife from lechery with other men; the third is to keep himself from lechery with other women. And no party may keep himself chaste from the acts of wedlock without the assent of the other commonly, for the man has power over the wife's body, and the wife has power over the man's body, as St. Paul says. And if the party desires to be chaste, he should endure without his own lust the acts of matrimony for the other party and he will have God's favour, both for allowing his mate and for the will he has to be chaste; for God gives reward for the good will and not only the deed. Also men say, if both parties assent willingly to perfect chastity, both of will and deed, that it is better than to use forth the acts of matrimony; and if they assent both parties at the beginning to live ever chaste, without bodily knowing, that it is the best kept matrimony of all other, as did our Lady and Joseph, when they were married. Look that each party live well before God and the world, and stir each other to charity, righteousness, and meekness and patience, and all goodness. And each man should beware lest he procure any false divorce, for money or friendship or enmity; for Christ bids that no man divide those that God has joined; but only for adultery the one that keeps himself clean may leave the other's bed, and for no other reason, as Christ himself says. And yet then the clean party may live chaste forever while the other lives, or else be reconciled again to the other. Nevertheless the clean one may dwell forth with the other that forfeits, by way of charity. And men suppose that that way is great charity, if there is evidence that the other party will do well afterwards.

CHAPTER III

See now how the wife ought to be subject to the husband and he ought to rule his wife, and how they both ought to rule their children in God's law. First St. Peter bids that wives be subject to their husbands, insomuch that those who do not believe by word of preaching, may be gained without word of preaching, through the holy living of women, when men behold the chaste living of women. And these women should not have crimped hair, or garlands of gold or over precious or curious clothing on the outside, but they should have a clean soul, peaceable and meek and humble, which is rich in the sight of God. And once upon a time holy women, hoping in God, honoured Him in this manner and were subject to their own husbands, as Sara, Abraham's wife, obeyed Abraham, calling him lord; and women doing well are spiritual daughters of Sara. St. Peter says all this. Also St. Paul speaks thus of husbands and wives; I wish that men would pray in each place, lifting up clean hands, that is, clean works, without wrath and strife. Also I wish that women were in suitable dress, with modesty and soberness adorning them or making fair, not in twisted hair nor in gold, nor in margery stones, or pearls, nor in precious cloth, but in that that becomes women, inspiring pity by good works. A woman ought to learn in silence, with all obedience and subjection. But Paul says, I will not allow a woman to teach, that is, openly in church, as Paul says in a letter to Corinth, and I will not allow a woman to have lordship over her husband but to be in silence and stillness. For, as Paul says in many places, the husband is the head of the wife; and Paul gives this reason, that Adam was first formed and Eve afterwards, and Adam was not deceived in faith, but the woman was deceived in faith, in trespassing against God's commandment. Paul says all this in divers places of holy writ. Also Paul bids that bishops and priests teach wives to love their husbands, to be prudent and chaste and sober, and to have care of the house, and to be benign and submissive or subject to their husbands—so that the word of God is not blasphemed. And that old women should be in holy dress, not putting false crime or sin to another, nor suing too much wine and to teach well, so that they teach prudence. Also Paul teaches thus—that women are submissive or subject, to their husbands as to the Lord. For the husband is head of the woman as Christ is head of the church, he is saviour of the body thereof, that is, the great multitude of all worthy to be saved. But as holy church is subject to Christ, so women are subject to their husbands in all things. Husbands, love your wives, just as Christ loved holy church and took himself willingly to suffer and die for holy church, to make it clean and holy; and made it clean by washing with water in the word of life, to give the church glorious to himself, not having blemish nor reveling nor any such filth, but that it should be holy and without spot or blemish. And husbands ought to love their wives as their own bodies, for he that loves his wife loves himself. For no man has ever hated his body, but nourishes and furthers it, as Christ does holy church. For we are members of his body, of his flesh and of his bones. For this thing a man shall forsake, or leave, his father and his mother and shall cleave to his wife and they shall be two in one flesh. This sacrament is great, but I say, says Paul, in Christ and holy church. But forsooth, you husbands, each by himself, love your wife as yourself and wives, fear your husbands. Children, honour your elders, father and mother, in the Lord, for this is the right thing to do. Worship your father and mother—that is the first commandment in behest; that Christ will look after you and you will live long upon earth. And, fathers, don't stir your children to wrath, but nourish them and bring them forth in discipline or learning and chastising of God. St. Paul says all this together. Also Paul commands thus in another letter; women be submissive to your husbands, as it behoves in the Lord. Men, love your wives and be not bitter to them. Children, honour your elders in all things, for this is pleasing to the Lord. Fathers, stir not your children to indignation, lest they of little understanding offend or trespass against God or man.

Here obstinate husbands and cruel fighters with their wives, without reasonable cause, are blamed by God. But many, when they are drunk, come home to their wives and sometimes from their cursed strumpets and throwers of dice, and chide and fight with their wife and household, as if they were Satan's brats and they allow neither rest, peace nor charity among them. But they shall pay dearly for this bitterness, for if they will have mercy from God they must have mercy on other men, though they had deserved beating— amend them in fair manner.

CHAPTER IV

Of this may wedded men and wives know, how they ought to live together and teach their children God's law. For at the beginning a child may easily be taught, and good morals and manners, according to God's law, are easily printed in his heart; and then he may easily hold them forth and increase in goodness. And therefore Paul bids that the father nourish his children in the lore and chastising of God; and God commands in the old law that the fathers should tell God's commandments to their children and the wonders and miracles that he did in the land of Egypt, and in the Red Sea, and in the water of the Jordan and in the promised land. And much more are fathers and mothers bound to teach their children to the belief of the Trinity, and of Jesus Christ, how he is true God without beginning, and was made man through most fervent charity, to save mankind by strong penance, hard torment, and bitter death. And so all come in points of Christian belief, but they are most beholden to teach them God's commandments, and the works of mercy, and points of charity, and to govern their five wits well, and to fear God before all other things, and to love him most of all things, for his endless might, endless wisdom, endless goodness, mercy and charity. And if they trespass against God's deeds, they ought to blame them for it sharply, and chastise them a thousand-fold more than for spite or unkindness done against their own person. And this teaching and chastising will in a few years make good Christian men and women, and namely the good example of holy life of old men and women, for that is the best teaching to their children.

And Christian men, above all many priests, charge godfathers and godmothers to teach the children the Our Father and the Creed; and this is well done; but it is most needful to teach them the commandments of God, and give them good example by their own life. For though they have been christened and know the common points of belief, yet they will not be saved without keeping God's commandments, but will be full hard and deep damned in hell, more than heathen men. And it would have been better for them never to have received Christendom, unless they continue truly in God's commandments, as St. Peter teaches plainly.

But some teach their children stories of battles and false chronicles not needful to their souls. Some teach new songs to stir men to jollity and harlotry. Some set them to needless crafts, for pride and greed; and some allow them in idleness and lying flattery to breed forth strumpets and thieves; and some with great cost set them to law, for gain and worldly honour, and for this spend hugely in many ways. But in all this God's law is left behind, and thereof hardly any man speaks a good word, to magnify God and that, and to save men's souls. Some teach their children to swear and stare and fight, and curse all men about, and have great joy in their hearts from this. But certainly they are Satan's teachers, and procurators to lead them to hell, by their cursed example and teaching and nourishing and maintaining in sin; and they are cruel slayers of their own children, indeed more cruel than if they hacked their children as small as morsels to their pot or mouth. For by this cursed teaching, and ending therein, their children's bodies and souls are damned without end in hell. And though their bodies were thus hacked so small, both body and soul will be in bliss of heaven, if they truly keep God's commandments. And St. Paul says a dreadful thing about such negligent fathers and mothers, that do not teach their children God's laws and do not chastise them when they trespass against God's commandments. He that has not care of his own and especially of his household has denied the faith and he is worse than a man outside Christendom. And such fathers and mothers, who maintain their children knowingly in sin, and teach them wickedness are worse than the cursed fathers that kill their children, and offer them up to sticks, worshipping false idols. For those children in their youth were dead and destroyed and did no more sin; but these children of cursed fathers and mothers, that teach them pride, theft, lechery, anger, covetousness and gluttony and keep them in them, have a long life and increase in sin to the greater damnation of both (parent and child). And thus little wonder though he take vengeance on our people both old and young, for all commonly despise God and have joy and mirth at his anger and reproving. And God must punish this sin for his rightful majesty.

CHAPTER V

But though husbands thus have power over their wives' bodies, nevertheless they ought to use this in measure and reason, and somewhat refrain their foul lusts and not take a superfluity of hot wines and spiced ale and delicate meats to delight them in this occupation, but consider that they are guests and pilgrims in the world and do not have a dwelling place here forever. And therefore they must give themselves to holiness, without which no man shall see God; and they must abstain from fleshly desires that fight against the soul, as Peter and Paul teach by the authority of God himself; and think on this word of Saint Paul; The time is short; the other part is that they that have wives are as if they have none; that is to say, that they use them for and in dread of God, and measure, not to fulfill their lusts, as beasts without understanding; and that they keep in mind the dreadful coming of Christ to the last judgment, how they shall then answer for each deed, each word, and each thought—and each evil sufferance of their children and household, and principally of evil example to their subjects. And no quibbling or procurator shall be there, but their own good life to save them, or cursed life to damn them. And fleshly lusts, and gluttony, drunkenness, and over much liking in fleshly deeds, make men most to forget this dreadful judgment. And therefore the gospel says, that the third servant that had married a wife, said that he could not come to the supper of Christ; and that servant is understood to be he that gives himself to over much liking in fleshly lusts. And therefore Christ bids in the Gospel, that we take heed that our hearts are not charged with gluttony and drunkenness and business of this life, for the day of judgment will come as a snare, or trap, upon all those that sit upon the face of all the earth.

But wives beware that they stir not their husbands to wrath, nor envy against their neighbours, nor to falseness and over much business of the world, to find too costly estate. For the wife was made to be as a helper to the husband, each to help the other in cleanness and holy life, and true before God and man. But if the husband is stirred to vengeance and pride and envy, the wife ought to stir him to penance and patience, meekness and charity, and all good manner of Christian life. And when God's law bids the husband and wife to love each other, they should beware that they do not turn this love all to fleshly love, and not to love of the soul, for they are encouraged to love the soul much more than the body, for God loves that more than the body, and for the soul Christ died. And indeed love of the body is truly hate unless it is in help to save the soul and keep it in holy life.

But yet three great faults fall many times among married men and women. The first fault is, as Saint John with the gilded mouth says, that they make sorrow if their children are naked or poor, but though their children are naked of virtues in their soul, they think nothing of it. And with much labour and cost they get great riches and high status and benefices for their children, often to their greater damnation, but they will not get their children goods of grace and virtuous life, nor allow them to receive such goods, freely offered by God, but hinder it as much as they can; and say, if their child is inclined to meekness and poverty, and flees covetousness and pride, for dread of sin and to please God, that he will never be a man, and they never spend a penny on him, and curse him if he lives well and teaches other men God's law, to save men's souls. For by this deed the child gains many enemies for his elders and they say that he slanders all their noble kin, that were always considered true and honorable men.

The second fault is, that wives give their husband's goods to strong and rich beggars and other churls, to get them sweet morsels and sometimes spend their husband's goods about fornicators and lechers, while their husbands travel in far countries or grievous travels. And to remain holy and excuse this wickedness, wives many times give a little alms openly, and find hypocrites to say mass and make the silly husbands maintain such hypocrites in their falseness, to rob the poor and hinder true men from teaching God's law, and to favour false slanders of their brethren. And if wives favour and maintain such hypocrites and stir their husbands to it, for private lechery between themselves, and for false security that the hypocrites give them, though they dwell still as swine in sin, it is so much the worse.

The third fault is this; if Almighty God, of his righteousness and mercy, takes their children out of this world by fair death, these rich wives weep, grumble and cry against God, as though God should not act against their will; and ask God why he takes their children from them rather than taking a poor man's, since they may better care for their children than poor men. See now the insanity of this grumbling! It is a great mercy of God to take a child out of this world; for if it shall be safe, it is delivered out of woe into bliss, lest malice turned the understanding of children to sin, and that is a great mercy of God, and therefore all men should be glad. If he shall be damned, yet it is a mercy of God to take him soon to death, lest he live longer and do more sin and therefore be in more pain. And since they grumble thus against God's rightful judgment, they tell God that he is unjust, unaware, that he does not know when is the best time for the child and, without mercy and charity he punishes so sorely the child and its elders. But indeed they are cursed Lucifer's children, wayward anti-Christs, and unnatural heretics and blasphemers. Therefore they should be glad and thank God for all his mercies and benefices and rightful judgments. Amen.

Also each party should look to keep the order made by God, and do not break it for any temptation or liking of the flesh. And many reasons help this. First, because God, who is the author of this order, loves it to be kept in cleanness, and present in every place, and for his righteousness must punish him that breaks it. And no defouling of it may escape unpained, for he knows all things, no matter how secret; and nothing, no matter how mighty, may stand against his punishing. Also, think how soon this stinking flesh, that now delights in lechery, shall turn to ashes and powder, and earth and worm's meat;

and for such short liking to lose everlasting bliss and get everlasting pain in hell, in body and soul, were a cursed exchange; and no man knows how soon he will die and in what state. Also good angels, keepers of men and women, present to God a grievous complaint when this holy order is thus broken, and Christian souls, temples of the Holy Ghost, are thus wickedly blackened with filth of sin and made like the fiends of hell. And for this reason, men and women should be well occupied in good works and not idle, for idleness is the devil's snare, to tempt men to sin; and they should live in devout prayers and reasonable abstinence of meat, and namely of hot and strong drinks, and visit their poor neighbours that are bedridden, and clothe them, and lodge them, to get remission of over-much liking of fleshly deeds; and ever cry to God, with great desire and good life, that he grant them grace to keep cleanly his holy order, and do true penance for their old sins, to end in perfect charity, and so ever have their true spouse, Jesus Christ, in bliss of heaven without end. Amen.

Thomas à Kempis (1379/80–1471)

Thomas's surname comes from his birthplace of Kempen in the Rhineland. The younger of two sons of a blacksmith and a schoolteacher, in 1393 he began his studies at Deventer. The school at Deventer was run by the Brethren of the Common Life, and during his time there Thomas was greatly influenced by Florens Radewijns, successor to the founder of the Brethren, Gerhard Groote. In 1399 he left the house at Deventer to join a house of regular canons at Mount St. Agnes (near Zwolle), where his older brother John was prior. After some delay Thomas was professed in 1407 and ordained in 1413 or 1414.

Thomas remained at Mount St. Agnes for the rest of his long life, and was a prolific writer of devotional works, homilies and saints' lives. He also wrote a chronicle of his monastery which provides much of our knowledge of his life. His most famous work, the Imitation of Christ *is one of the most-published and best known works of Christian devotion. It is a prime example of the message and methods of the* Devotio Moderna *inspired by the Brethren of the Common Life.*

Chapter Five

The Imitation of Christ (excerpt)

1. Of the Imitation or Following of Christ and the Despising of All Vanities of the World

He who follows Me, says Christ our Saviour, walks not in darkness, for he will have the light of life. These are the words of our Lord Jesus Christ, and by them we are admonished to follow His teachings and His manner of living, if we would truly be enlightened and delivered from all blindness of heart.

Let all the study of our heart be from now on to have our meditation fixed wholly on the life of Christ, for His holy teachings are of more virtue and strength than the words of all the angels and saints. And he who through grace has the inner eye of his soul opened to the true beholding of the Gospels of Christ will find in them hidden manna.

It is often seen that those who hear the Gospels find little sweetness in them; the reason is that they do not have the spirit of Christ. So, if we desire to have a true understanding of His Gospels, we must study to conform our life as nearly as we can to His.

criticizing theologians

What avail is it to a man to reason about the high, secret mysteries of the Trinity if he lack humility and so displeases the Holy Trinity? Truly, it avails nothing. Deeply inquisitive reasoning does not make a man holy or righteous, but a good life makes him beloved by God. I would rather feel compunction of heart for my sins than merely know the definition of compunction. If you know all the books of the Bible merely by rote and all the sayings of the philosophers by heart, what will it profit you without grace and charity? All that is in the world is vanity except to love God and to serve Him only. This is the most noble and the most excellent wisdom that can be in any creature: by despising the world to draw daily nearer and nearer to the kingdom of heaven.

It is therefore a great vanity to labor inordinately for worldly riches that will shortly perish or to covet honor or any other inordinate pleasures or fleshly delights in this life, for which a man after this life will be sorely and grievously punished. How great a vanity it also is to desire a long life and to care little for a good life; to heed things of the present and not to provide for things that are to come; to love things that will shortly pass away and not to haste to where joy is everlasting. Have this common proverb often in your mind: The eye is not satisfied or pleased with seeing any material thing, nor the ear with hearing. Study, therefore, to withdraw the love of your soul from all things that are visible, and to turn it to things that are invisible. Those who follow their own sensuality hurt their own cause and lose the grace of God.

2.   Against Vain, Secular Learning, and of a Humble Knowledge of Ourselves

Every man by nature desires to know, but of what avail is knowledge without the fear of God? A humble farm laborer who serves God is more acceptable to Him than an inquisitive philosopher who, considering the constellations of heaven, willfully forgets himself. He who knows himself well is mean and abject in his own sight, and takes no delight in the vain praise of men. If I knew all things in this world, but knew without charity, what would it avail me before God, who judges every man according to his deeds? Let us, therefore, cease from the desire of such vain knowledge, for often great distraction and the deceit of the enemy are found in it, and so the soul is much hindered and blocked from the perfect and true love of God.

Those who have great learning desire generally to seem to be accounted wise in the world. But there are many things whose knowledge brings but little profit and little fruit to the soul; he is most unwise who gives heed to any other thing except what will profit him to the health of his soul. Words do not feed the soul, but a good life refreshes the mind, and a clean conscience brings a man to a firm and stable trust in God. The more knowledge you have, the more grievously will you be judged for its misuse, if you do not live according to it. Therefore, do not lift yourself up into pride, because of any skill or knowledge that is given you, but have the more fear and dread in your heart—for it is certain that, hereafter, you must yield a stricter accounting. If you think that you know many things and have great learning, then know for certain that there are many more things you do not know. So with true wisdom you may not think yourself learned, but ought rather to confess your ignorance and folly. Why will you prefer yourself in knowledge before another, since there are many others more excellent and more wise than you and better learned in the Law? If you would learn anything and know it profitably to the health of your soul, learn to be unknown and be glad to be considered despicable and as nothing.

The highest and most profitable learning is this: that a man have a truthful knowledge and a full despising of himself. More, not to presume of himself, but always to judge and think well and blessedly of another, is a sign and token of great wisdom and of great perfection and of singular grace. If you see any person sin or commit any great crime openly before you, do not judge yourself to be better than he, for you know not how long you shall persevere in goodness. We are all frail, but you shall judge no man more frail than yourself.

don't Lord yourself, we all screw up.

3.   Of the Teaching of Truth

Happy and blessed is he whom truth teaches and informs, not by symbols and deceitful voices, but as the truth is. Our opinion, our intelligence, and our understanding often deceive us, for we do not see the truth. Of what use is the knowledge of such things as will neither help us on the day of judgment if we know them, nor hurt us if we do not know them? It is, therefore, great folly to be negligent of such things as are profitable and necessary to us, and to labor for such things as are worthless and to be condemned. Truly, if we so act, we have eyes but see not.

And of what avail is knowledge of the variety and operations of creatures? Truly, nothing. He to whom the everlasting Word, that is, Jesus, speaks, is freed of many vain opinions. From that Word all things proceed and all things openly show and cry that He is God. Without Him, no man understands the truth, or judges rightly. But a person to whom all things are one, and he who draws all things into one and establishes all things in one and desires nothing but one, may quickly be made firm in heart and fully at peace in God.

[O Truth that is God, make us one with You in perfect charity, for all that I read, hear, or see without You is grievous to me; in You is all that I will or can desire! Let all learned ones be quiet in Your presence and let all creatures keep themselves in silence and do You only, Lord, speak to my soul.] The more a man is one with You, and the more he is gathered together in You, the more he understands without labor high secret mysteries, for he has received from above the light of understanding. [A clean, pure and constant heart is not broken or easily overcome by spiritual labors, for he does all things to the honor of God, because he is clearly mortified to himself. Therefore, he desires to be free from following his own will. What hinders you more than your own affections not fully mortified to the will of the spirit? Truly, nothing more.

A good devout man so orders his outward business that it does not draw him to love of it; rather, he compels his business to be obedient to the will of the spirit and to the right judgment of reason. Who wages a stronger battle than he who labors to overcome himself? And it should be our daily desire to overcome ourselves, so that we may be made stronger in spirit and go daily from better to better. Every perfection in this life has some imperfection attached to it, and there is no knowledge in this world that is not mixed with some blindness or ignorance. Therefore, a humble knowledge of ourselves is a surer way to God than is the search for depth of learning.

Well-ordered learning is not to be belittled, for it is good and comes from God, but a clean conscience and a virtuous life are much better and more to be desired. Because some men study to have learning rather than to live well, they err many times, and bring forth little good fruit or none. Oh, if they would be as busy to avoid sin and plant virtues in their souls as they are to dispute questions, there would not be so many evil things seen in the world, or so much evil example given to the people, or so much dissolute living in religion. On the day of judgment we will not be asked what we have read, but what we have done; not how well we have discoursed, but how religiously we have lived.

Tell me, where now are all the great students and famous scholars whom you have known? When alive, they flourished greatly in their learning, but now, others have succeeded to their posts and promotions, and I cannot tell whether their successors give them a thought. In their lifetime they were considered great in the world; now, little is spoken of them. Oh, how swiftly the glory of this world, with all its false, deceitful pleasures, passes away. Would to God their life had accorded well with their learning, for then would they have studied and read well. How many perish daily in this world by vain learning who care little for a good life and for the service of God. And because they desire to be great in the world rather than to be humble, they vanish away in their learning as smoke in the air.

He is truly great who has great charity. And he is great who is little in his own sight and who sets at naught all worldly honor. And he is very wise who accounts all worldly pleasures as vile dung, so that he may win Christ. And he is very well taught who forsakes his own will and follows the will of God.

4.   That Easy Credence Is Not to be Given to Words

It is not good, truly, to believe every word or impression that comes; they ought to be pondered and considered advisedly and leisurely, so that Almighty God may not be offended through our fickleness. But alas, for sorrow, we are so frail that we quickly believe evil of others sooner than good. Nevertheless, perfect men are not so ready to give credence, for they well know that the frailty of man is more prone to evil than to good, and that he is very unstable in words. It is great wisdom, therefore, not to be hasty in our deeds, not to trust much in our own wits, not readily to believe every tale, not to show straightway to others all that we hear or believe.

Always take counsel of a wise man, and desire to be instructed and governed by others rather than to follow your own ingenuity. A good life makes a man wise toward God and instructs him in many things a sinful man will never feel or know. The more humble a man is in himself and the more obedient he is to God, the more wise and peaceful will he be in everything he will have to do.

5.   On the Reading of Holy Scripture

Charity and not eloquence is to be sought in Holy Scripture, and it should be read in the same spirit with which it was first made. We ought also to seek in Holy Scripture spiritual profit rather than elegance of style, and to read simple and devout books as gladly as books of high learning and wisdom. Do not let the authority of the author irk you, whether he be of great learning or little, but let the love of every pure truth stir you to read. Ask not: Who said this; but heed well what is said. Men pass lightly away, but the truth of God endures forever.

Almighty God speaks to us in His Scriptures in various manners, without regard for persons, but our curiosity often hinders us in reading Scripture when we reason and argue things we should humbly and simply pass over. If you will profit by reading Scripture, read humbly, simply, and faithfully, and never desire to gain by your reading the name of learned. Ask gladly and heed humbly the sayings of saints, and do not disdain the parables of the ancient Fathers, for they were not spoken without great cause.

6. Of Inordinate Affections

When a man desires anything inordinately, he is at once unquiet in himself. The proud and covetous man never has rest, but the humble man and the poor in spirit lives in great abundance of rest and peace. A man not mortified to himself is easily tempted and overcome by little and small temptations. And he who is weak in spirit and is yet somewhat carnal and inclined to worldly things can with difficulty withdraw himself from worldly desires; when he does withdraw himself from them, he often has great grief and heaviness of heart and rebels if any man resists him. And if he obtains what he desires, he is disquieted by remorse of conscience, for he has followed his passion which has not helped at all in winning the peace he desired. By resisting passion, and not by following it, the truest peace of heart is won. There is, therefore, no peace in the heart of a carnal man or in the heart of a man who gives himself all to outward things. But in the heart of spiritual men and women who have their delight in God great peace and inward quiet are found.

7. That Vain Hope and Elation of Mind Are to be Fled and Avoided

He is vain who puts his trust in man or in any created thing. Be not ashamed to serve others for the love of Jesus Christ, and to be poor in this world for His sake. Trust not in yourself, but set all your trust in God: do all in your power to please Him and He will well assist your good will. Trust not in your own wisdom or in the wisdom or plans of any living creature, but instead, in the grace of God who helps humble persons and allows those who presume of themselves to fall until they are humbled. Glory not in your riches, or in your worldly friends, because they are mighty; let all your glory be in God only, who gives all things and desires to give Himself above all things.

Exult not in the strength or fairness of your body, for by a little sickness it may soon be disfigured. Rejoice not in your ability or readiness of wit, lest you displease God, of whose free gift comes all that you have. Do not think yourself better than others, lest perhaps you be thereby belittled in the sight of God who knows all that is in man. Be not proud of your good deeds, for the judgments of God are different from the judgments of man, and what pleases man often displeases God. If you have any goodness or virtue, believe firmly that there is much more goodness and virtue in others, so that you may always keep yourself in humility. No harm comes if you hold yourself worse than any other, though it may not in truth be so, but much harm results if you prefer yourself above any other, even if he is ever so great a sinner. Great peace is with the humble man, but in the heart of a proud man are always envy and anger.

8.   That Much Familiarity Is to be Avoided

Open not your heart to every person, but only to him who is wise, discreet, and reverent. Go seldom among strangers; neither flatter the rich nor bear yourself as an equal among the great. Keep company with the humble and the simple in heart, who are devout and of good deportment, and treat with them of things that may edify and strengthen your soul. Be not familiar with any woman, but commend all good women to God. Desire to be familiar only with God and with His angels; have a care to avoid the familiarity of man as much as you can. Charity is to be had toward all; familiarity is not expedient.

Sometimes it happens that an unknown person, whose good reputation commended him much, does not appeal to us when afterwards we meet him. We think sometimes to please others by our presence, but we displease them instead by all the evil manners and evil conditions they see and will consider in us.

9.   Of Humble Subjection and Obedience
and That We Should Gladly Follow the Counsel of Others

[It is a great thing to be obedient, to live under authority and to seek our own liberty in nothing. It is a much surer way to stand in the state of obedience than in the state of authority. Many are under obedience more out of necessity than of charity and they have great pain and easily murmur and complain; they will never have liberty or freedom of spirit until they submit themselves wholly to their superiors. Go here and there where you will, you will never find perfect rest, save in humble obedience, under the governance of your proper superior. Dreaming of a change of place has deceived many a person in religion.]

It is certainly true that many a person in religion is disposed to act after his own will and can agree best with those who follow his own ways, but, if we desire that God be among us, we must sometimes set aside our own will (though it seem good) so that we may have love and peace with others. Who is so wise that he can fully know all things? No one, surely. Therefore, trust not too much in your own judgment, but gladly hear the advice of others. And if, perhaps, the thing you would have done might be good and profitable, and yet you set aside your own will with regard to it and follow another's will, you will thereby find much profit. I have often said that to hear and take counsel is a more sure way than to give it. It is good to hear every man's counsel; not to agree with it, when reason demands agreement, is a sign of a great isolation of mind and of much inward pride.

10. That We Should Avoid Superfluity of Words
and the Company of Worldly-Living Persons

Flee the company of worldly-living persons as much as you can, for the treating of worldly matters greatly hinders the fervor of spirit, even though it be done with a good intention. We are soon deceived by the vanity of the world and in a manner are made a slave to it, unless we take good heed.

I would I had held my peace many times when I spoke and that I had not been so much among worldly company as I have been. But why are we so glad to speak and commune together, since we so seldom depart without some harm to our conscience? This is the cause: By communing together we think to comfort each other and to refresh our hearts when we are troubled by vain imaginations, and we speak most gladly of such things as we most love, or else of things that are most irksome to us. But alas, for sorrow, all we do is vain, for this outward comfort is no little hindrance to the true inward comfort that comes from God.

It is necessary, therefore, that we watch and pray that time does not pass away from us in idleness. If it is lawful and expedient, speak, then, of God and of such things as are edifying to your soul and your neighbor's. Bad habits and neglect of our spiritual profit often make us take little heed how we should speak. Nevertheless, a devout communing on spiritual things sometimes greatly helps the health of the soul, especially when men of one mind and spirit in God meet and speak and commune together.

Part Two

Humanism in Northern Europe

Sir Thomas More (1478–1535)

Thomas More was born in London and educated in the law. He considered taking monastic vows but decided instead to marry and devote himself to the service of the crown, holding among others the offices of speaker of the House of Commons (1523) and Lord Chancellor of England (1529–1532). The issue of Henry VIII's divorce from Catherine of Aragon resulted in More's resignation; and after his refusal to acknowledge the king as head of the English Church (the Act of Supremacy), he was charged with treason. After an unfair trial, he was executed in July 1535.

More is remembered not only as King Henry's most principled opponent but also as the author of Utopia *(1516), one of the great books of the Northern Renaissance. Sharing with his close friends Erasmus and John Colet a strong belief in the need for church reform, he wrote of a previously unknown island where charity, reason, cooperation, and virtue operated. This mythical island of Utopia (No Place) he contrasted to the England he knew. The book is also an evocative expression of the values of northern humanism, a movement More strongly supported both privately and officially.*

In 1518 he learned that the opposition to his friend Erasmus's Greek New Testament included his own university of Oxford and that gangs of students calling themselves Trojans were interfering in their fellow students' attempts to learn Greek. More responded with a letter to Oxford University supporting the new learning, especially Greek studies, a discipline, he notes, also favoured by the King and the Lord Chancellor, Thomas Wolsey.

———————

Chapter Six

Sir Thomas More to the Professors and Masters of the University of Oxford

Abingdon
29 March (1518)

Thomas More to the Reverend Fathers, the commissary (i.e. the Vice-Chancellor), proctors, and others of the guild of masters of the University of Oxford, greeting.

I have been wondering, gentlemen, whether I might be permitted to communicate to scholars of your distinction certain conclusions to which I have recently come. Yet I have hesitated in approaching so brilliant a group, not so much on the ground of my style as on that of seeming to give an exhibition of pride and arrogance. Who am I, the possessor of little prudence and less practice, a scholar of mediocre proportions, to arrogate to myself the right to advise you in anything? And how can I dare to offer advice in the field of letters especially, when any one of you is fitted by his wisdom and erudition to give advice in that field to thousands?

At first sight, Venerable Fathers, I was therefore deterred by your unique wisdom. But, on second thought, I was encouraged; for it occurred to me that only ignorant and arrogant fools would disdain to give a man a hearing, and that the wiser and more learned you were, the less likely you would be to think highly of yourselves or to scorn the advice of others. I was further emboldened by the thought that no one was ever harmed by just judges, such as you are above all, simply on the ground that he offered advice without thinking of the consequences. On the contrary, loyal and affectionate advice, even if imprudent, has always deserved praise and thanks.

Finally, when I consider that, with God's help, I ought to offer you whatever slight learning I have acquired, since it was at your University that my education began, it seems the duty of a loyal friend not to pass over in silence what I deem it serviceable to bring to your attention. Since, then, the only danger in putting my pen to paper seemed to lie in the fact that a few might deem me too audacious; while I know that my silence would be condemned by many as ingratitude, I have preferred that the whole world should condemn my audacity rather than that anyone should have the chance to say that I showed myself ungrateful to your University, the honor of which I feel myself bound to defend to the uttermost. Moreover, no situation has, I believe, arisen in recent years, which, if you desire to maintain the honor of that institution, more urgently requires your serious attention.

The matter is as follows: when I was in London recently, I rather frequently heard that some members of your teaching body, either because they despised Greek or were simply devoted to other disciplines, or most likely because then possessed a perverse sense of humor, had proceeded to form a society named after the Trojans. The senior sage christened himself Priam; others called themselves Hector, Paris, and so forth; the idea, whether as a joke or a piece of anti-Greek academic politics, being to pour ridicule on those devoted to the study of Greek. And I hear that things have come to such a pass that no one can admit in public or private that he enjoys Greek, without being subjected to the jeers of these ludicrous "Trojans," who think Greek is a joke for the simple reason that they don't know what good literature is. To these modern "Trojans" applies the old saw, "Trojans always learn too late."

[The affair aroused much comment, all very critical; and I myself felt somewhat bitter that even a few academics among you had nothing better to do in their spare time than to cast slurs on their colleagues' subjects. But I kept in mind that one could not expect the whole crowd of academics to possess wisdom, temperance, and humility; and so I began to dismiss the matter as a triviality. However, since I have been here in Abingdon in attendance at the court of His Victorious Majesty (Henry VIII), I have found that the silliness is developing into a form of insanity. For one of the "Trojans," a scholar in his own estimation, a wit of the first water in that of his friends, though slightly deranged in that of anyone observing his actions, has chosen during Lent to babble in a sermon against not only Greek but Roman literature, and finally against all polite learning, liberally berating all the liberal arts.]

His whole performance was of a piece. Perhaps such a body of nonsense could not be preached on the basis of any sensible text; in any case, he followed neither the old custom of elucidating a whole passage of Scripture, nor the recent one of expounding some few words of Scripture; instead he elaborated on some stupid British proverbs. So I have no doubt that his frivolous sermon very deeply disturbed those who heard it; since I see that all who have heard fragmentary reports of it are unfavorably impressed.

What man in the audience, in whose breast burned even a spark of Christianity, would not groan at the degradation of the royal office of sacred preaching, which gained the world for Christ—above all at the hands of those whose supreme duty it was to protect it with the authority of their office? Who could possibly have devised a more outrageous insult than for an avowed preacher, during the most solemn season of the Church's year, in the presence of a large Christian congregation, in the sanctuary itself, from the elevation of the pulpit (as it were from the throne of Christ), and in view of the Sacred Body of Christ, to turn a Lenten sermon into Bacchanalian ravings? What a look must have been on the faces of the audience, who had come to hear spiritual wisdom, and saw the laughable pantomime he put on in the pulpit! They had expected to listen in reverence to the Word of Life; when they departed, all they could record they had heard was an attack on humane letters and a defamation of the preaching office by a fatuous preacher.

It would have been no reproach to secular learning if some good man, who had retired from the world to monastic life, suddenly returned and used this speaker's phrases: "much in watchings, much in prayer" or "the path to be trod by those who seek for heaven" or "other matters like humanistic education, trivial if not a positive hindrance to the spiritual life," or "simple country folk, and the unlettered, flying quicker to heaven," etc., etc. All this could have been borne from such a man. His simplicity would have been pardoned by his audience. They would have generously admitted his saintliness, and given serious consideration to his piety, devotion, and righteousness. But when they saw a man with the academic ermine over his shoulders, step on to the platform in the midst of a gathering composed solely of academics, and calmly proceed to rant against all humane learning, one would have had to be stone blind not to notice a signal pride and wickedness, a positive hatred of the higher arts. Many must have wondered indeed how such a man could get the idea that he had to preach either about Latin, of which he did not know much, or about the liberal arts, of which he knew less, or about Greek—in which he could not even grunt that it was "all Greek" to him!

If such an abundance of material had been supplied by the seven deadly sins, an altogether suitable theme for sermons, who would have believed him totally inexperienced therein! Though, as a matter of fact, what is it but sloth, when one is in the habit of denouncing rather than of learning that of which one is ignorant? And what is it but hatred, when one defames those who know what one deprecates but does not comprehend? And what is it but supreme pride, when he wishes no kind of knowledge to be prized save what he has falsely persuaded himself that he knows, and when he even—not from modesty, as might be the case with other people—arrogates more praise to himself for his ignorance than for his knowledge?

[Now as to the question of humanistic education being secular. No one has ever claimed that a man needed Greek and Latin, or indeed any education in order to be saved.]Still, this education which he calls secular does train the soul in virtue. In any event, few will question that humanistic education is the chief, almost the sole reason why men come to Oxford; children can receive a good education at home from their mothers, all except cultivation and book learning. Moreover, even if men come to Oxford to study theology, they do not start with that discipline. They must first study the laws of human nature and conduct, a thing not useless to theologians; without such study they might possibly preach a sermon acceptable to an academic group, without it they would certainly fail to reach the common man.[And from whom could they acquire such skill better than from the poets, orators, and historians?]

Moreover, there are some who through knowledge of things natural (i.e. rational) construct a ladder by which to rise to the contemplation of things supernatural; they build a path to theology through philosophy and the liberal arts, which this man condemns as secular; they adorn the queen of heaven with the spoils of the Egyptians! This fellow declares that only theology should be studied; but if he admits even that, I don't see how he can accomplish his aim without some knowledge of languages, whether Hebrew or Greek or Latin; unless, of course, the elegant gentleman has convinced himself that there is enough theology written in English or that all theology can be squeezed into the limits of those (late scholastic) "questions" which he likes to pose and answer, for which a modicum of Latin would, I admit, suffice.

But really, I cannot admit that theology, that august queen of heaven, can be thus confined. Does she not dwell and abide in Holy Scripture? Does she not pursue her pilgrim way through the cells of the holy Fathers: Augustine and Jerome; Ambrose and Cyprian; Chrysostom, Gregory, Basil, and their like? The study of theology has been solidly based on these now despised expositors of fundamental truth during all the Christian centuries until the invention of these petty and meretricious "questions" which alone are today glibly tossed back and forth. Anyone who boasts that he can understand the works of the Fathers without an uncommon acquaintance with the languages of each and all of them will in his ignorance boast for a long time before the learned trust his judgment.

But if this foolish preacher pretends that he was not condemning humanistic education in general but only an immoderate thirst for it, I can't see that this desire was such a sin that he had to deal with it in a public assembly, as if it were causing society to rush headlong to ruin. I haven't heard that many have gone so far in such studies that they will soon be overstepping the golden mean. [Further, this fellow, just to show how immoderate *he* could be in a sermon, specifically called students of Greek "heretics," teachers of Greek "chief devils," and pupils in Greek "lesser devils" or, more modestly and facetiously as he thought, "little devils"; and the zeal of this holy man drove him to call by the name of devil one whom everybody knows the Devil himself could hardly bear to see occupy a pulpit. He did everything but name that one (D. Erasmus), as everybody realized just as clearly as they realized the folly of the speaker.]

[Joking aside—I have no desire to pose as the sole defender of Greek learning; for I know how obvious it must be to scholars of your eminence that the study of Greek is tried and true. To whom is it *not* obvious that to the Greeks we owe all our precision in the liberal arts generally and in theology particularly; for the Greeks either made the great discoveries themselves or passed them on as part of their heritage. Take philosophy, for example. If you leave out Cicero and Seneca, the Romans wrote their philosophy in Greek or translated it from Greek.]

I need hardly mention that the New Testament is in Greek, or that the best New Testament scholars were Greeks and wrote in Greek. I am but repeating the consensus of scholarship when I say: however much was translated of old from Greek, and however much more has been recently and better translated, not half of Greek learning has yet been made available to the West; and, however good the translations have been, the text of the original still remains a surer and more convincing presentation. For that very reason all the Doctors of the Latin Church—Jerome, Augustine, Bede, and a host of others—assiduously gave themselves to learning Greek; and even though many works had already been translated, they were much more accustomed to reading them in the original than are many of our contemporaries who claim to be erudite; nor did they merely learn it themselves, but counseled those among their successors who wanted to be theologians above all to do the same.

So it is not as if I were just giving your Worships good advice about preserving the study of Greek. I am rather exhorting you to do your duty. You should not allow anyone in your university to be frightened away from the study of Greek, either by public assemblies or private inanities, since Greek is a subject required in every place of learning by the Church Universal. Common sense is surely enough to convince you that not all of your number who give themselves to the study of Greek can be blockheads; in fact, it is in part from these studies that your university had acquired its pedagogical prestige both at home and abroad.

[There seems to be an increasing number of cases where Oxford has benefited from the presence of men nominally studying Greek only, but really taking the whole liberal arts course. It will be a wonder if their enthusiasm for you does not evaporate when they realize that so serious an enterprise is held in such contempt. Just think, too, what they are doing at Cambridge, which you have always outshone; those who are *not* studying Greek are so moved by common interest in their university that they are actually making large individual contributions to the salary of the Greek professor!]

You see what I mean; and much more could be said to the point by men with better minds than mine. All I am doing is warning you of what others are saving and thinking, not telling you what it behooves you to do. You see much better than I that, if wicked factions are not suppressed at birth, a contagious disease will spread, and the better half be slowly absorbed by the worse, and that outsiders will be forced to take a hand in helping the good and wise among you. Any former student of the university takes its welfare as much to heart as you who are its living members. And I am sure that the Reverend Father in Christ who occupies the See of Canterbury (William Warham), who is the Primate of all our Clergy, and who is also the Chancellor of your university will not fail to do his part. Whether for the clergy's sake or yours, he rightly feels interested in preventing the decay of learning; and learning will perish if the university continues to suffer from the contentions of lazy idiots, and the liberal arts are allowed to be made sport of with impunity. And what about the Reverend Father in Christ, the Cardinal of York (Thomas Wolsey), who is both a patron of learning and himself the most learned of the episcopate? Would he endure patiently if aspersions were cast in your university on the liberal arts and the study of languages? Will he not rather aim the shafts of his learning, virtue, and authority at these witless detractors from the arts?

Last but not least: what of our Most Christian Kings? His Sacred Majesty has cultivated all the liberal arts as much as ever a king did; indeed, he possesses greater erudition and judgment than any previous monarch. Will his wisdom and piety suffer him to allow the liberal arts to fail—through the interests of evil and lazy men—in a place where his most illustrious ancestors wished that there be an illustrious seat of letters, a place which is an ancient nursery of learning, whose products have been an ornament not only to England but to the whole Church, a place which possesses so many colleges that have perpetual endowments specially designated for the support of students (in which respect there is no university outside the kingdom that can compare with Oxford), a place in which the aim of all its colleges and the purpose of all its endowments is none other than that a great body of academics, delivered from the necessity of earning their daily bread, might there pursue the liberal arts?

I have no doubt that you yourselves will easily in your wisdom find a way to end this dispute and quiet these stupid factions; that you will see to it not only that all the liberal arts may be free from derision and contempt but that they shall be held in dignity and honor. By such diligence in intellectual pursuits you will reap benefit for yourselves; and it can hardly be said how much you will gain favor with our Illustrious Prince and with the above-mentioned Reverend Fathers in Christ. You will forge an almost miraculous bond between yourselves and myself, who have thought that all this had to be written now in my own hand out of my deep personal affection for you. You know that my services are at the disposal of each and all of you. May God preserve your glorious seat of learning unharmed; and may He grant that it flourish continually in virtue and in all the liberal arts.

Thomas More

Conrad Celtis (1459–1508)

Celtis rose through learning from the peasantry to appointments at the universities of Ingolstadt and Vienna. After studies in Germany, he visited Italy (1487) but returned to the north where the emperor Maximilian granted him a professorship in Vienna. He was also a major neo-Latin poet, crowned poet laureate by the emperor Frederick III. Concerned that German humanist scholars should enjoy mutual support against both the Italians and the medieval scholastics, Celtis established academies or sodalities in Cracow, Budapest and Heidelberg and encouraged particularist German scholarship and style. His own research discovered the plays of the medieval German nun, Hrotswitha, and, in his Oration Delivered Publicly in the University of Ingolstadt *(August 1492) on the occasion of his acceptance of his professorship in that university, he encouraged German students to apply themselves to humanist disciplines.*

———————

Chapter Seven

Oration Delivered Publicly
in the University in Ingolstadt

I would not have considered it something special, most excellent fathers and distinguished youths, that I, a German and your fellow countryman, can speak to you in Latin, if those ancient talents of our Germany still flourished, and if that age had returned in which our ambassadors are said to have spoken Greek rather than Latin. But, since through the adverseness of the ages and the change of the times, not only amongst us but even in Italy, the mother and ancient parent of letters, all the past splendor of literature has perished or been extinguished, and all the noble disciplines have been driven away and ruined by barbaric tumults, I am not at all confident that, given the slowness of my mind and the poverty of my powers, I can speak to you adequately in Latin. This is especially true since I have not lacked industry or good teaching, which many of you have up till now experienced and deplored in yourselves. However, lest I be accused of coming in total silence to this place, so richly adorned by your presence, I would rather offend by stammering than lightly pass over by silence your love for me and for the commonwealth of letters. I shall hope for your indulgence if you consider that a little man born in the midst of barbarity and drunkenness, as they say, cannot speak so sensibly as is required by your most sagacious ears and by this auditorium, assigned to me for oratory and poetry by the most illustrious prince, our [Duke] George [the Rich of Bavaria Landshut], and by you most distinguished gentlemen who are privy to all his counsels.

I have decided, moreover, that I can say nothing to you more worthy and pleasant, or more appropriate for me and fitting for you to hear, than to exhort your minds to virtue and the study of the liberal arts. For through them true glory, immortal fame, and happiness can be attained even in this brief life of ours. None of you should be found so sluggish and lazy that you do not regard it as a beautiful, excellent, and magnificent thing to strive toward these lofty goals which can make one truly happy. I have not thought it necessary to discuss with any particular acumen the favors of fortune and the delights of the body, or those sensual pleasures, worthy of slaves, that extinguish the light of the spirit. For these are all perishable, transitory, and destined to die with their body in a brief moment of time or will soon have other masters. Wherefore no wise man is remembered to have striven for these things. Rather, if we examine their lives, we find that these wise men of ancient times so loved learning and wisdom, with which the human spirit is nourished as with nectar and ambrosia, that in order to attain them they left their fatherland, wives, and beloved children, dispersed the richest patrimonies, endured injustices, insults, and infamy at the hands of the common crowd, and suffered exile with the greatest patience and peace of mind. Moreover, it is related that they willingly accepted labors, suffered cold and heat, and undertook arduous journeys because they wished to perceive and to see with their sense what they had learned, tired out by their deepest reflection and constant reading—so great was their incredible zeal to acquire wisdom and their love for searching into celestial things and nature. For these accomplishments they finally attained divine honors and are destined to have an immortal name. Greatly venerated and reverenced by all posterity, they come to be solemnly named "philosophers."

The Scythian race is so brutish, uncultivated, and horrid, like wild beasts, that they wander about in vast and inaccessible solitudes like herds of cattle, protecting themselves from the inclemency of the atmosphere and the harshness of the climate only with the skins of wild animals and their hides, from which they take their name. Nevertheless, glory and the desire for praise have so inspired them that three times they ruled over vanquished Asia. Nor did they carry away any gold or silver, things which we most desire, but considered it more glorious for it to be said of them that by their bravery they added such great splendor and amplitude to their dominion. We thus have great examples of a barbarous people for the pursuit of virtue and glory. While they were not able by genius and learning or by gentle customs, contrary to their nature, to contend with other mortals, they at least seem to have provided for their glory and immortality by their unbridled barbarity and the impetuosity of their spirits, which they regarded as a virtue. But if I were to turn my address to the histories of other tribes and what they did in peace and war, I would have a very broad field for recounting, and this present day would not be long enough to tell them all. So I purposely pass over what you are easily able to apply to this subject from your reading of illustrious authors.

I shall regard it as enough, and more than enough, men of Germany and illustrious youths, if by my presentation today, such as it is, I shall have added, impressed, and as it were, branded upon your spirits some stimulus to glory and virtue, so that you keep ever before your eyes that immortality which you must seek only from the fountain of philosophy and the study of eloquence. I cannot easily declare with what great labors and vigils you must linger and sweat over these two things—that is to say, over the writings of the ancient philosophers, poets, and orators. For they alone have prescribed for us the way to live well and happily and have set before us Nature, which is both the parent of the human race and the cause of all things (as it were), as an example and mirror of life to be imitated. From them you will learn to praise good deeds and to detest evil deeds, and from them you will learn to console yourselves, to exhort, to impel, and to hold back. You will strive to contemplate the Ruler of all things and Nature itself, which is the summit of human happiness. Although all these things can be done by others, nevertheless, and I still do not understand just how, the power to arouse compassion, to reawaken, and to repress the whole spirit lies in the hand of the orator and the poet. Indeed, those ornaments of words and thoughts, which like stars illumine the oration, are the proper instruments of the orator and poet. You must borrow them and use them as the occasion demands for your own use in your daily conversations. For what, by the immortal gods, does it profit us to know many things, to understand the beautiful and the sublime, if we are prevented from speaking of them with dignity, elegance, and gravity, and if we are not able to transmit our thoughts to posterity, which is the unique ornament of human happiness? So it is, by the faith of men: nothing shows a man to be learned and erudite unless it be the pen and the tongue—the two things which eloquence governs.

But to you, excellent gentlemen and noble youths, I now direct my address, to whom, thanks to ancestral virtue and invincible German strength, the empire of Italy has passed and who frequent this university rather than all the other centers of study in our Germany, make it fruitful, and serve as a great adornment and elegance. I exhort you to turn first to those studies that can render your minds gentle and cultured and call you away from the habits of the common crowd, so that you dedicate yourselves to higher studies. Keep before your eyes true nobility of mind, and consider that you are bringing not refinement but dishonor to our empire if you merely feed horses and dogs and pursue ecclesiastical prebends rather than the study of letters. As you seek splendor for your dignities with virtue, knowledge, and erudition, reflect on how to add honor to your holy morals so that men may esteem you worthy of those honors, so that they pursue you, and not you them, like fowlers a flock of birds. Noble men, emulate the ancient Roman nobility who, after they had taken over the empire of the Greeks, combined all their wisdom and eloquence so that it is a question as to whether they equalled or actually surpassed all the Greek faculty of invention and apparatus of learning. So you, too, having taken over the rule of the Italians and having cast off your vile barbarity, must strive after the Roman arts. Take away that infamy of the Germans among the Greek, Latin, and Hebrew writers, who ascribe to us drunkenness, barbarism, cruelty, and whatever is bestial and foolish. Regard it as a great shame for yourselves not to know the histories of the Greeks and the Latins, and beyond all shamelessness not to know the situation, the stars, rivers, mountains, antiquities, peoples of our region and land—briefly, all that foreigners have shrewdly gathered together concerning us. It seems a great miracle to me how the Greeks and Romans with such precise diligence and exquisite learning surveyed our land—"the greatest part of Europe," to use their own words, but rough and crude, I think, compared with the South; and they expressed our morals, affections, and spirits with words like paintings and the lineaments of bodies. Cast out, noble men, cast out and eliminate those villanies which they relate were bestowed among us as proofs of manly excellence. It is a wonder that this native sickness has endured for nearly fifteen hundred years in some parts of Germany. For even now we still do not compel the chiefs of that robber band to surrender, in a happier climate when we have eliminated bogs, cut down vast forests, and peopled our land with famous cities—so difficult is it to correct what has become a custom, spread about for ages, because it is generally approved. Thus it has happened that neighboring peoples make us smart and persecute our name with such awful eternal envy and calumny, proclaiming that with the Empire we have taken on many vices of the foreign nations. They always distrust and fear our talents. We should feel ashamed, noble gentlemen, that certain contemporary historians [Sabellicus], by publishing an edition of new *Decads,* so glory in having equalled the ancient Roman Empire, that they insult and bitterly jeer the German name, and that they call our most glorious princes barbarians, suppressing their natal names. So great has been the old and inexpiable hatred between us and the ancient hatred of our gods, that because of the hostility on both sides we would never have been restrained from mutual slaughter if provident nature had not separated us by the Alps and by cliffs raised up to the stars. Let us feel ashamed, I pray, that although we have successfully waged many memorable wars in Pannonia [Hungary], Gaul, and Italy, and against the most monstrous tyrant of Asia [the Turk], brandishing his sword wet with Christian blood, there is no one found among you today who records for eternity the deeds performed by German courage. But there will be many foreigners who will in their histories, without regard for the law of history, hiss like vipers against our bravery with a great verbal show and enticement of speech, not to say with fictions and mendacious invention, with which that kind of men are most effusive in singing their own praises and belittling the most glorious deeds which we perform. I do not really know whether it is due to our wisdom or to our thoughtlessness that in recent times we returned the insignia of writers and the accompanying imperial laurel beyond to the Tarpeian Hill [Rome]. It is an unhappy omen for our Empire, since having conceded to others the license for bestowing the laurel wreath, that finally no honor of the Empire remains ours.

O men of Germany, assume those ancient passions by which you were so often a dread and terror to the Romans, and turn your eyes to the wants of Germany and consider her lacerated and divided borders. What a shame to have a yoke of servitude imposed on our nation and to pay tributes and taxes to foreign and barbaric kings. O free and strong people, O noble and brave nation, clearly worthy of the Roman Empire, your renowned seaport [Danzig] is held by the Pole and your ocean gateway is occupied by the Dane! In the east the most vigorous tribes are held as slaves; the Marcomanni [Bohemians], Quadi [Moravians], and Bastarnae [Slovaks] live, as it were, separate from the body of our Germany. I do not even speak of the Transylvania Saxons, who also use our national culture and native language. In the west, however, upper Gaul [France] is so friendly and munificent toward us, thanks to the immortal virtue and incredible wisdom of Philipp of the Rhenish Palatinate, who rules the shore on either side of its renowned river and ever will rule with an auspicious reign, "As long as the pole rotates the stars, as long as the breezes strike the shores." But to the south we are burdened with a kind of distinguished servitude, for new colonies are continually being established, thanks to that ancient and detestable avarice for fostering luxuries by which our land is being emptied of its wonderful natural resources, while we pay from the public treasury to others what we need for ourselves [papal exploitation]. So determined is fortune or fate to pursue and destroy the Germans, the remnants of the Roman Empire. But I fear I have progressed more freely than I desire, so disgusted am I with my Germany when I consider the things in the store of books taken from the Greeks and the Latins and preserved by the power of our Emperors, books which we have till now abandoned like the detested spoils of the enemies, as if locked in a prison, covered with dust, untouched, and not well protected from the rain.

I come back to you, O noble youths, and admonish above all things that you recall to mind before you proceed to the science of law that the knowledge of many things is necessary for you, because that discipline can teach you nothing beyond opinion. For if one is to believe antiquity, the philosophers and poets, the first theologians, called out the people, who were roaming and wandering about, from the haunts and caves of animals to the cities and social abodes, after their crude spirits had been tamed by speech. They taught them religion and the fear of the gods with many and varied arguments and then ruled with laws and ordinances. Who of you will doubt, O most distinguished fathers, that before the study of law it is necessary to pay close attention to true philosophy and especially to those things by which eloquence can be acquired, which you agree are very necessary for the lawyer. Therefore you will also consider those people quite mistaken and responsible for many abuses who, passing by all philosophy (except the low variety), make themselves leaders in law and religion without reflecting on what kind of legislators there were in ancient times—men who spent their day on laws and arms but spent every night on the study of philosophy. Inasmuch as philosophy, like a kind of seminary, teaches fully the knowledge of things human and divine and their jurisdiction, who without drinking of the fountain of philosophy shall judge himself able to manage these two things? I shall not at this point offer as evidence for you the Greeks, Solon, Plato, Alcibiades, Themistocles, or Philip, the father of Alexander the Great. With what great care he commended his son to Aristotle, the greatest philosopher of that age, and with what great joy he eagerly desired a son born to him at a time when philosophers enjoyed such very great prestige! For that master of arms, so experienced in ruling the state, knew that if his own son were initiated into the precepts and ordinances of philosophy, he would be worthy to be entrusted with the administration of the whole universe. Nor shall I remind you of Anacharsi who, when he introduced his laws to Scythia, first wanted to learn philosophy from the Attic philosophers.

I remain silent about the Roman kings, Numa, Cato, the Scipios, the Caesars, and the later ones, the Antonians, the Valerians, the Aurelians, Theodosius, finally also Charlemagne, born of the noble stem of the Franks, by whose learning and by whose concern and zeal for the liberal arts a most glorious empire was procured and preserved, which flourished as long as it maintained philosophy as its partner and assistant. I now pass over Moses the legislator of our ancient religion, most wise in all philosophy, who was a most prudent governor in impelling, curbing, and overcoming the minds of the masses. In writing the sacred laws he began with the creation of the world and with the remembrance of the majesty of Nature and its Maker. He thereby clearly demonstrated that any legislator or student of the legal discipline must first be initiated into the precepts of philosophy as though into sacred rites.

But such great men do not move us, for by the narrow boundary of destiny now among us, by fortune, circumstances, and the dregs of these last times, the Empire grows old; and we, neglecting all philosophy, prostitute our servile spirits to base complaint alone and hire them out for mercenary wages. Hence, when we come from such pursuits to the princes, we suggest to them only those which we have learned. And these are the reasons—I say with great bitterness—why our princes despise learning and always remain unlearned, why they are regarded with derision by others and are ridiculed as "barbarous," because, even in these otherwise prosperous times, they neglect the liberal arts and their proponents. There is nothing more vile and abject at their courts than those who profess with a word or gesture a knowledge of letters—so greatly our barbarity pleases us and the sickness of an intractable mind. Even among our high churchmen and, to use an ancient term, the "sacred flames," to whom the care and protection of letters rightly belongs, they have been so contemptuous of the trifling value of letters and of those devoted to them that they prefer the wild animals of the forests, the long-eared dogs, the snorting and spirited horses, and other pleasures and amusements like Rhea, the wife of Mars [mother of Romulus and Remus], [Emperor] Claudius, and Sardanapalus [effeminate king of Assyria]. We know some bishops, come up from obscure origins, who, when they receive studious men from abroad at their courts, refuse to speak to them to show their knowledge, to such an extent does the silence of Pythagoras please them, lest they seem to be dishonored in their barbarous majesty by the parsimony of the Roman language. Meanwhile they pant with greed like rapacious hawks for money or for the approbations of kings, which they dare exhibit before their doors like common eager whores. So much has Italian luxury and savage cruelty in extorting pernicious silver corrupted us that it would clearly have been more godly and holy had we lived that rude and silvan life of olden times, when we lived within the limits of moderation, rather than bringing in so many instruments of gluttony and luxury, and adopting foreign manners. So it happens that our rulers take those men into their familiar circle who are similarly inclined and exclude those who cherish learning and wisdom. The founders of the Greek and Roman Empire, in contrast, so honored wise men that they bestowed upon them imperial honors and called their secretaries friends. They ordered that those who died should be interred in their own sepulchers, because they believed that power and immortality were preserved for them by those wise men through the benefit and use of letters by which alone immortality is attained. That way they could aid mankind not only while alive but even after they had died. Therefore they live until today and will continue to live as long as Roman and Greek letters exist. I will give no other reason for Italy's flourishing than that they excel us in no other felicity than the love and study of letters. With these they intimidate other nations as though with weapons and lead others to admire them by their talent and industry. But with us there are frequent changes, and among us there is an improper desire for new things, so that a very wise poet says of us:

> *Brothers eager to know new things and mad with hate*
> *Of peace and with genius and quick desire.*

So that our horses do not contract the gout and our weapons rust, we raise a tumult among ourselves by dissension like Sulla and Marius of Caesar and Pompey. I cannot be temperate as long as we are involved in our vices and domestic strifes and neglect our very rich territories, whose titles we brandish as though for our own consolation, while we tie bootstraps and stretch out the deliberations in our councils up to the fifth new moon, as a certain historian has written of us, by nature given to worthless goods and eager for small advantages. Meanwhile in the heart of our Germany we tolerate the reign of a pertinacious religion most sumptuous in its use of a foreign tongue [Hussites in Bohemia]. Although their university [Charles University in Prague] weeps and sighs over the ruin of its ancient felicity, they must nevertheless render thanks to the gods because an Italian is their leader [Augustinus Lucianus of

Vicenza]. Because the university had no cultivators of true philosophy, it left behind a strong proof by its fall that the foundations of religion can be strengthened and preserved by no one better than by a true philosopher, rather than by those who regard the highest wisdom as ignorance and who merely accommodate themselves by habit to ostentation for the common crowd and set forth only a small shadow of learning and virtue. They are very much like little scarecrows that peasants put up in their orchards and fields to frighten away small birds, but if you come closer you see that they have neither movement nor sense.

I now return to you, then, youths of Germany. Act no longer in a childish manner, but learn to know the secrets of literature, for those writers relate that you flee from them and sing to our shame:

> *The Castalian liquids [wines] and the prescient rivers of fate*
> *No barbarian shall ever drink with his polluted mouth.*

It should shame us that such things should be read and applied to you, the possessors of the Roman Empire, and persist down to the present day. Someone might want to argue against me on the basis of the large number of our universities, of which we have fourteen, and might say that because of them barbarity has been eliminated and care has been taken for good morals and honorable arts, and the way has been opened while the crowd flatters and exults us with the titles of masters and doctors! With tears I say it—you will find few who acquire a true knowledge of things and search into the nature and purity of the Roman language or retain it. This is because in our studies of (not to say triflings with) such subjects those who interpret the poets and the writers of the Roman language are repressed and those who uncover the work of nature and the wisdom of its governor with mathematical truthfulness and who think a bit more deeply than the common crowd are regarded as infamous. To such an extent is philosophy trampled underfoot and boiled down by some who have deformed the most beautiful majesty of Nature into incorporeal thoughts and monstrous abstractions and empty chimeras, like poets. For poets with their imagery and apt fables have transposed natural things figuratively so that sacred things should be hidden from the common crowd, for they know that open and naked exposure is inimical to Nature and that Nature must therefore be revealed under respectable coverings and a sacramental veil. For should the common crowd understand certain mysteries as the philosophers do, it might be difficult to restrain their impulses.

Nor shall I now interpret the fables of the Greek and the Latin poets in the manner of the naturalists, who reveal the foundations of all divine inventions under the cloud of poetic fiction to the truly wise. But we accuse such poets of lies and execrate them as imposters and vile men. So much do our baseness and our foul barbarity please us, the gods being hostile, I believe, that we do not, together with the Roman imperium, also assume the splendor of Italian letters and seek to rival them in this most beautiful kind of writing, even though we admire them. We may to be sure find among us those who labor with my vice, usurping for themselves the name "poet" and "orator." But they, ignoring every precept of philosophy and rhetoric, strain every nerve of their genius to produce futile banter and to allure the minds of the adolescents with strange fantasies. They devise smoothness with watery words, spewing forth shamelessly whatever comes into their mouths, making chaste ears drunk with obscene and shameful fables, as if vices should be opened up to us for our understanding, although they always sprout up more densely of their own accord without encouragement, like useless weeds. If someone would give more careful attention to our erudition such as it is, he would come upon an arena without a goal and a voice without blood, although we are quite prepared to fault others for their vocabulary, like schoolboys. But our own stench we do not smell, and I think that the immortal gods have decreed well toward us, for they have conceded to us at least a certain plebeian and vulgar learning. Otherwise by our bleating and vile medley of words we would not permit others who are more learned than we to murmur a sound. Although it pleases us to hear such men, it is not because they nourish our minds with true teaching, while we persecute with hatred those who cry out against and carp at our obsolete manner of teaching, offer new approaches from the true Roman instruction, and compel the aged, trifling grammarians to learn the elements of the Greek language and to cry once again in learning the art of grammar, like infants in the cradle. As if Cato were not at hand as an example, a most serious man and most learned in all erudition and doctrine, who when already an octogenarian began to learn Greek in order to be able to speak Latin correctly. We, boys and old men alike, neglect both languages and, in defense of our slothfulness and inertia, ascribe divine power and miracle to St. James and St. Augustine because they learned so many languages and wrote so many books, which we do not attain in our whole age, rather than crediting their long vigils, the greatest labors, and longest journeys. For by these efforts learning, sanctity, and an eternal name are handed on to all posterity, not by sleep and gluttony, spending on feasting, with dice and Venus, evils with which we are inflamed, thanks to our stupidity; we gormandize our whole life as though we had been born for this alone. But we who wish to appear more cultivated in learning tarry in childish contention about our terms and quiddities on which we grow old and die, as on the rocks of the Sirens. Nor do we want others to know anything except what is stained with our dregs. Therefore we are chosen as leaders and princes of our most beautiful religion. We look longingly with the zeal of avarice and burn with an insatiable thirst for all powers, while we bury away money with ourselves like the corpses of the dead beneath the earth. This is what our vulgar philosophy has taught us with its worthless harvest of empty words, for which we neglect the most restrained and the most fluent writers of our religion. We are able to attain nothing magnificent, high and excellent, while we seek only inferior things, as though certain basic teachings of our religion were not to be found in Plato and Pythagoras, in whom the most beautiful association of the light of nature and of grace may be perceived. But concerning this another time.

For that reason turn, O Germans, turn about to the more gentle studies, which philosophy and eloquence alone can teach you. Consider well that it is not without reason that the Greek and Roman founders of the Empire devoted such great efforts and watchful attentions to those matters and decorated the teachers of those subjects with the highest honors, for they understood that by the power of language and the lessons of wisdom the assemblies of men, cities, religions, the worship of the gods, the most holy morals, and the broadest empires could be preserved and governed. That divine poet [Virgil], the ornament and delight of Roman eloquence, splendidly expressed this truth thus when he sang:

> *And, as in times of revolt, which often afflict a great nation,*
> *When the ignoble throng are roused to a frenzy of passion,*
> *Firebrands and stones are beginning to fly, for fury finds weapons,—*
> *Then, if they chance to behold some man, for his faith and his virtue*
> *Highly revered, they are awed, and attentively listen in silence,*
> *While he controls their minds by his words, and quiets their passion.*
> [Virgil, *Aeneid*, I, X 48–53; Harlan Ballard, trans.]

Great indeed was that nearly divine element in administering their state that they aimed to join wisdom with eloquence; and, in order to master these, they instituted public performances in which by sublime persuasion and remarkable inventive faculties, they exhorted the spirits of the viewers to virtue, piety, modesty, fortitude, and endurance of all things. They deterred the idle youth from vices and inflamed them to glory, so that whatever they owed to the fatherland, friends, strangers, and their dear parents, they learned as from living portraits. Therefore that allegory of the poets is not unseemly, according to which Orpheus is said to have tamed wild animals, moved stones, and led them where he wished; for it shows by metaphor the power of eloquence and the duty of the poet, who is able to move ferocious, monstrous, and intractable spirits to gentleness, a right spirit, and love for the fatherland. These things being so, the states of Greece and now of Italy wisely educated their boys from the very beginning with the hymns of poets. In those hymns they learned to perceive musical tunes and the sweetest modulations of harmony, on which that age is very keen; and they provided for those tender spirits, inclined to inertia and laziness, a stimulant to industry so that they were excited to learning with a cheerful zeal, a lively spirit, and eagerness. The gravity of words and meanings imbibed by tender minds will thus endure to a more advanced age and until death, and will continually sprout forth again through an entire lifetime. Aristotle prescribes this plan when he stipulates that adolescents should be educated in musical hymns. Because it—that is, harmony—stirs up the talents of boys and impels them to the acumen of oratory and the production of song. That discipline is very well adapted for relaxing the spirit and for consoling and uplifting minds; it sounds forth in sacred hymns their praises of the gods and carries them off in divine meditations. For this reason Pythagoras and Plato, the loftiest philosophers, named poetry the first philosophy and theology, which uses hymns for its demonstrations and arouses with melodious speech. But the other discipline—that is, oratory—spreads out with humble, loose, and free speech. Poetry is more concise in rhythm and a bit more free with words, but similar and almost equal in many kinds of embellishment. Neither the one nor the other must be neglected; but from the very beginning, O men of Germany, the minds of the boys must be instructed in and, if I may say so, allured with songs. And when the sublime admiration of things resides in these, the beauty and polish of words, the spirits of the youths easily gain strength from them. In an intellectually stronger age, when the youthful spirit has already been hardened by those beginnings, and thought has been invigorated, they are better instructed and better prepared to lead themselves to the reading of more serious philosophers and orators. From these they can finally rise to their own inventions and to the sublimity of the poetic discipline and its figures, attaining to the praises of illustrious authors in writing histories and poems. They will then procure immortality for themselves and glory and praise for the fatherland. I have spoken.

Desiderius Erasmus of Rotterdam (1466?–1536)

Erasmus was the greatest figure of the Northern, or Christian, Renaissance. He used his encyclopedic scholarship in ancient Greek and Latin literature and patristic texts to define a new ideal of Christian learning. His biblical scholarship was equally profound, producing in 1516 his Novum Instrumentum, *a new translation of the New Testament with the original Greek on facing pages.*

Erasmus's influence during his lifetime and after was immense. His wide circle of friends and acquaintances throughout Europe resulted in a voluminous correspondence. Popular, as well as learned, books made him the best read author of his age. Works such as The Praise of Folly *(1509), the* Adagia *and the* Colloquies *contributed to northern Europe's appreciation of the heritage of the classical world and publicised Erasmus's concerns for religious reform. This central element of Erasmus's work and thought—indeed of northern Christian humanism—was defined as learned piety (*docta pietas*) and the philosophy of Christ (*philosophia Christi*), an attitude towards religion and scholarship which helped shape the culture of the Northern Renaissance and Reformation. Although initially sympathetic to some of Martin Luther's program of reform, Erasmus refused to join with the Lutherans, preferring a single, united Church but reformed to reflect more clearly what he saw as the simple message of Scripture.*

Chapter Eight

Letter to Jodocus Jonus on Vitrier and Colet; June 13, 1521

It may indeed be that Colet deserves the greater praise of the two on this account, namely, that neither the smiles of fortune nor the impulse of a far different natural bent could divert him from the pursuit of a Gospel life. For he was the son of wealthy and distinguished parents; born, too, in London, where his father had twice filled the highest municipal office in his city, called by them the mayoralty. His mother, who still survives, is a most worthy woman. She bore her husband eleven sons and as many daughters; of whom John, as the eldest, would have been heir to the entire estate, according to the English law, even had the others been alive. But at the time when my acquaintance with him began, he was the sole survivor of the band. To these advantages of fortune was added that of a tall and graceful figure.

During his younger days in England he diligently mastered all the philosophy of the schools and gained the title expressive of a knowledge of the seven liberal arts. Of these arts there was not one in which he had not been industriously and successfully trained. For he had both eagerly devoured the works of Cicero and diligently searched into those of Plato and Plotinus, while there was no branch of mathematics that he left untouched.

After this, like a merchant seeking goodly wares, he visited France and then Italy. While there, he devoted himself entirely to the study of the sacred writers. He had previously, however, roamed with great zest through literature of every kind, finding most pleasure in the early writers, Dionysius, Origen, Cyprian, Ambrose, and Jerome. I should add that among the old authors there was none to whom he was more unfavorable than Augustine. At the same time he did not omit to read Scotus and Thomas and others of that stamp, if the occasion ever required it. He was also carefully versed in treatises of civil and canon law. In a word, there was no work containing either the chronicles or enactments of our forefathers which he had not perused. The English nation has poets who have done among their own countrymen what Dante and

Petrarch have done in Italy. And by the study of their writings he perfected his style, preparing himself even at this date for preaching the Gospel.

Soon after his return from Italy he left his father's house, as he preferred to reside at Oxford, and there he publicly and gratuitously expounded all St. Paul's Epistles. It was at Oxford that my acquaintance with him began, some kind providence having brought me at that time to the same spot. He was then about thirty years old, some two or three months younger than myself. Though he had neither obtained nor sought for any degree in divinity, yet there was no doctor there, either of divinity or law, no abbot or other dignitary but came to hear him and brought his textbooks with him as well. The credit of this may have been due to Colet's personal influence, or it may have been due to their own good will in not being ashamed to learn, the old from the young, doctors from one who was no doctor. However, the title of doctor was spontaneously offered him some time later and accepted by him, though rather to oblige the offerers than because he sought it.

From these sacred occupations he was called back to London by the favor of Henry VII and made dean of St. Paul's, so as to preside over the cathedral of that Apostle whose epistles he loved so much. This takes precedence over all the deaneries in England, though there are others with richer incomes. Hereupon our good Colet, feeling his call to be for the work and not for the empty honor, restored the decayed discipline of the cathedral body and—what was a novelty there—commenced preaching at every festival in his cathedral, over and above the special sermons he had to deliver now at Court, now in various other places. In his own cathedral, moreover, he would not take isolated texts from the Gospels or Apostolic Epistles but would start with some connected subject and pursue it right to the end in a course of sermons: for example, St. Matthew's Gospel, the Creed, or the Lord's Prayer. He used to have a crowded congregation, including most of the leading men both of the city and the court.

The dean's table, which in former days had ministered to luxury under the guise of hospitality, he brought within the bonds of moderation. For having done without suppers entirely for some years before, he was thus free from company in the evening. Moreover, as he dined rather late, he had fewer guests on those occasions as well, and all the fewer because the repast, though neat, was frugal, and the sitting at table short, and lastly, the conversation such as to have no charms but for the good and learned. When grace had been said, a servant would read aloud in a clear, distinct voice a chapter from St. Paul's

Epistles or the Proverbs of Solomon. He would then usually repeat some passage selected from the part read and draw a topic of conversation from it, inquiring of any scholars present, or even of intelligent laymen, what this or that expression meant. And he would so season the discourse that, though both serious and religious, it had nothing tedious or affected about it. Again, towards the end of the meal, when the requirements of nature, at any rate, if not of pleasure had been satisfied, he started some other topic; and thus bade farewell to his guests, refreshed in mind as well as in body and better men at leaving than they came, though with no overloaded stomachs. The pleasure he took in conversing with friends was extreme, and he would often prolong the talk till late at night. But still it was all either about literature or about Christ. If there was no agreeable person at hand to chat with—and it was not every sort that suited him—a servant would read aloud some passage from Holy Scripture. Occasionally he took me with him for company on a journey, and then nothing could be more pleasant than he was. But a book was ever his companion on the road, and his talk was always of Christ.

[He could not endure any slovenliness, so much so as not to tolerate even an ungrammatical or illiterate mode of expression. All his household furniture, his service at table, his dress, his books he would have neat; as for splendor, he did not trouble himself. He used to wear only dark-colored robes, though priests and divines in England are usually robed in scarlet. His outer garment was always of woollen cloth, not lined; but if the cold required it, he would protect himself with an inner lining of fur.]

All the revenue that came in from his preferments he left in his steward's hands, to be laid out in household expenses. His private fortune, a very large one, he would himself dispose of for charitable purposes. At his father's death he had inherited a large sum of money; and fearing lest, if he hoarded it up, it might breed some distemper of mind in him, he built with it in St. Paul's Churchyard a new school of splendid structure, dedicated to the Child Jesus. He attached to it also a handsome residence for the two masters to dwell in and assigned them a liberal stipend to teach free of charge, but on condition that the school should only admit a fixed number. The school was divided by him into four partitions. The one first entered contains those whom we may call the catechumens, none being admitted but such as can already both read and write. The second contains those under the surmaster's teaching, and the third those who are instructed by the high master. Each of these partitions is separated from the others by a curtain, drawn to or drawn aside at pleasure.

Over the high master's chair is a beautifully wrought figure of the Child Jesus seated in the attitude of one teaching, and all the young flock as they enter and leave school salute it with a hymn. Over it is the countenance of God the Father, saying: HEAR YE HIM (an inscription added at my suggestion). At the far end is a chapel in which divine service may be held. The whole school has no bays or recesses, so much so that there is neither any dining room nor dormitory. Every boy has his own proper seat on regularly ascending tiers with gangways left between. Each class contains sixteen, and the head boy in each class has a stall somewhat higher than the rest. Boys of all kinds are not admitted promiscuously, but a selection is made according to natural capacity and ability.

A most farsighted man, Colet saw that a nation's chief hope lay in having the rising generation trained in good principles. But though the undertaking cost him a very large sum of money, he allowed no one to share it. Some person had left a legacy of a hundred pounds sterling toward the building. But when Colet perceived that on the strength of this outsiders were claiming some rights or other, he obtained his bishop's sanction to apply the sum toward providing sacred vestments for the cathedral. Over the revenues and the entire management of his school he placed neither priests, nor the bishop, nor the chapter (as they call it), nor noblemen, but some married citizens of established reputation. And when asked the reason, he said that, while there was nothing certain in human affairs, he yet found the least corruption in these.

This was a work that no one failed to approve. But many were surprised at his building a magnificent dwelling within the precincts of the Carthusian monastery, not far from what is called Richmond Palace. He said that he was preparing an abode for his old age, when he should be no longer equal to his work or be enfeebled by sickness and so compelled to retire from society. There he was minded to philosophize with two or three chosen old friends, among whom he was accustomed to reckon myself. But death forestalled him. For having been seized a few years before with the sweating sickness (a disease that is the special scourge of England), he was now for the third time attacked by it; and though he recovered from it to some degree, an internal disorder ensued from what the disease left behind it, of which he died. One physician pronounced him dropsical. Nothing fresh was discovered by the post-mortem examination except that the liver was found to have the extremities of the lobes rough with tuftlike excrescences. He was buried at the south side of the choir in his cathedral, in a modest grave chosen by himself some years before for the purpose, with the inscription placed over it: IOAN. COL. –John Colet

Before I conclude, my friend Jonas, I will mention a few particulars, first of his natural disposition, then of his peculiar opinions, and lastly of the stormy scenes in which his sincere religion was put to the test. It was but a very small portion of this religious spirit that he owed to nature. For he was gifted with a temper singularly high and impatient of affront; he was, as he himself confessed to me, naturally prone to incontinence, luxuriousness, and indulgence in sleep; overmuch disposed to jests and raillery; and he was besides not wholly exempt from the taint of covetousness. But these tendencies he combatted so successfully by philosophy and sacred studies, by watching, fasting, and prayer that he led the whole course of his life free from the pollutions of the world. As far as I could gather from my intimate acquaintance and conversations with him, he kept the flower of chastity even unto death. His fortune he spent on charitable uses. Against his high temper he contended with the help of reason, so as to brook admonition even from a servant. Incontinence, love of sleep, and luxuriousness he vanquished by a uniform abstinence from supper, by constant sobriety, by unwearied exertions in study, and by religious conversation. Yet if an occasion had ever presented itself either of conversing with ladies or being a guest at sumptuous repasts, you might have seen some traces of the old nature in him. And on that account he kept away, as a rule, from laymen's society, and especially from banquets. If forced at times to attend them, he would take me or some similar companion with him in order, by talking Latin, to avoid worldly conversation. Meanwhile he would partake sparingly of one dish only and be satisfied with a single draught or two of ale. He was abstemious in respect of wine, appreciating it if choice, but most temperate in the use of it. Thus keeping a constant watch upon himself, he carefully avoided everything by which he might cause anyone to stumble, not forgetting that the eyes of all were upon him.

I never saw a more highly gifted intellect. But though he felt a peculiar pleasure on this account in kindred intellects, he liked better to bend his mind to such things as fitted it for the immortality of the life to come. If at times he sought relaxation in sprightlier talk, he would still philosophize on every topic. He took a delight in the purity and simplicity of nature that is in children, a nature that Christ bids His disciples imitate, and he was wont to compare them to angels.

To complete, now, the second part of my promised account, his opinions differed widely from those commonly received. But in this matter he showed a remarkable discretion in adapting himself to others, so as to avoid giving offence to any persons or bringing any slur on his good name. For he knew well how unfair men's judgments are, how ready they are to believe evil, and how much easier a thing it is for slanderous tongues to tarnish a man's good name than for kind-spoken ones to repair it. Among friends and scholars, however, he would express his sentiments with the utmost freedom. As to the Scotists, for example, to whom the common run of men ascribe a subtlety peculiarly their own, he said that he considered them dull and stupid and anything but intellectual. For it was the sign of a poor and barren intellect, he would say, to be quibbling about the words and opinions of others, carping first at one thing and then at another, and analysing everything so minutely. Yet for some reason he was even harder on Aquinas than on Scotus. For when I once praised Aquinas to him as a writer not to be despised among the moderns, since he appeared to me to have studied both the scriptures and the early Fathers—such being the impression I had formed from his *Catena aurea*— and had also a certain unction in his writings, he checked himself more than once from replying and did not betray his dislike. But when in another conversation I was reiterating the same opinions more strongly, he looked hard at me, as if watching whether I were saying this in seriousness or in irony. And on perceiving that I was serious in what I said, he broke out like one possessed: "Why do you preach up that writer to me? For without a full share of presumption, he never would have defined everything in that rash and overweening manner; and without something of a worldly spirit, he would not have so tainted the whole doctrine of Christ with his profane philosophy." Struck with his impetuous manner, I began a more careful study of this author's writings, and, to be brief, my estimate of him was undoubtedly diminished.

Though no one approved of Christian devotion more warmly than he, he had yet but very little liking for monasteries—undeserving of the name as many of them now are. The gifts he bestowed upon them were either none or the smallest possible, and he left them no share of his property even at his death. The reason was not that he disliked religious orders but that those who took them did not come up to their profession. It was in fact his own wish to disconnect himself entirely from the world, if he could only have found a fraternity anywhere really bound together for a Gospel life. And he had even commissioned me to seek for such a one when I was about to visit Italy, telling me that among the Italians he had discovered some monks of true wisdom and piety. Moreover, he did not consider what is popularly deemed religion to be really such, being as it often is mere poverty of intellect. He was accustomed also to praise certain Germans, among whom there even yet lingered, as he said, some traces of primitive religion. He was in the habit of declaring that he nowhere found more unblemished characters than among married people, on whom such restraints were laid by natural affection and family and household cares that they were withheld, as by so many barriers, from rushing into all kinds of wickedness. [Though himself living in perfect chastity, yet of all in the list of offenders he was less hard on those—were they priests or even monks—whose only offence was incontinence. It was not that he failed to abhor the vice of unchastity but that he found such persons not nearly so bad, in comparison, as some others who thought no small things of themselves—though overweening, envious, slanderous, backbiters, hypocrites, empty-headed, ignorant, given up heart and soul to money-making and ambition—while their acknowledged infirmity rendered the former more humble and unassuming. Covetousness and pride, he would say, were more detestable in a priest than keeping a hundred concubines.]

I would not have anyone strain these opinions to such a degree as to suppose incontinence in a priest or monk to be a slight offence, but only to infer from them that those of the other kind are still further removed from true religion.

There was no class of persons to whom he was more opposed or for whom he had a greater abhorrence than those bishops who acted the part of wolves instead of shepherds, showing themselves off before the people with their guise of sanctity, their ceremonies, benedictions, and paltry indulgences, while at heart they were slaves to the world, that is, to ostentation and gain. He had a leaning to some opinions derived from Dionysius and the other early divines, though not to such a degree as to make him contravene in any points the decisions of the Church. Still, they made him less hard on such as disapproved of the universal adoration of images in churches, whether painted or of wood, or stone, or bronze, or silver; or again, on those who doubted whether a priest, openly and notoriously wicked, had any efficacy in the administration of the sacraments. Not that he in any way leaned to this error of theirs, but he was indignant against such as, by a life of open and unmixed depravity, gave occasion to surmises of this kind.

The colleges established in England at a great and imposing cost he used to say were a hindrance to profitable studies and merely centers of attraction for the lazy. And in like manner he did not attach much value to the public schools, on the ground that the race for professorships and fees spoilt everything and adulterated the purity of all branches of learning.

While strongly approving of auricular confession, saying that there was nothing from which he derived so much comfort and spiritual advantage, he yet as strongly condemned its too solicitous and frequent repetition. It is the custom in England for priests to celebrate the Holy Eucharist every day. But Colet was content to do so on Sundays and festivals, or at the most on some few days in addition, either because it kept him away from the sacred studies by which he used to prepare for preaching and from the necessary business of the cathedral, or because he found that he sacrificed with devouter feelings if he let an interval elapse. At the same time he was far from disapproving of the principles of those who liked to come every day to the Table of the Lord.

Himself a most learned man, he did not approve of that painful and laborious erudition which is made complete at all points, so to speak, by an acquaintance with all branches of learning and the perusal of every author. It was his constant remark that the natural soundness and simplicity of men's intellects were impaired by it, and they were rendered less healthy-minded and less fitted for Christian innocence and for pure and simple charity. He set a very high value on the Apostolic Epistles; but he had such a reverence for the wonderful majesty of Christ that the writings of the Apostles seemed to grow poor by the side of it. He had with great ability reduced almost all the sayings of Christ to triplets, intending to make a book of them. The rule that priests, even though busily occupied, must say long prayers right through every day, no matter whether at home or on a journey, was a thing that he greatly wondered at. As to the public service of the Church, he was quite of the opinion that that should be performed with proper dignity.

From numbers of the tenets most generally received in the public schools at the present day he widely dissented and would at times discuss them among his private friends. When with others, he would keep his opinions to himself for fear of coming to harm in two ways; that is to say, only making matters worse by his efforts, and sacrificing his own reputation. There was no book so heretical but he read it with attention. For from such, he said, he many a time received more benefit than from the books of those who so define everything as often to flatter their party leaders, and not seldom their own selves as well.

He could not endure that the faculty of speaking correctly should be sought from the trivial rules of grammarians. For he insisted that these were a hindrance to expressing oneself well and that result was obtained only by the study of the best authors. But he paid the penalty for this notion himself. For though eloquent both by nature and training, and though he had at his command a singularly copious flow of words while speaking, yet when writing, he would now and then trip on such points as critics are given to mark. And it was on this account, if I mistake not, that he refrained from writing books, though I wish he had not so refrained, for I should have been glad of the thoughts of such a man, no matter in what language expressed.

And now, that nothing may be thought wanting to the finished religious character of Colet, listen to the storms by which he was harassed. He had never been on good terms with his bishop, who was, to say nothing about his principles, a superstitious and impracticable Scotist, and thinking himself on that account something more than mortal.[2] I may say that, whilst I have known many of this school whom I should not like to call bad men, I have yet never to this day seen one who, in my opinion at least, could be termed a real and sincere Christian. Colet was no great favorite either with many of his own college, being too strict about canonical discipline; and these were every now and then complaining of being treated as monks, though in fact this college was formerly what in ancient deeds it is styled, the Eastern Monastery. However, when the animosity of the old bishop (who was, I should have said, full eighty years of age) was too virulent to be suppressed, he took as his coadjutors two other bishops, as wise and as acrimonious as himself, and began to give Colet trouble. His weapons were just what such persons resort to when plotting anyone's destruction, that is to say, he laid an information against him before the archbishop of Canterbury, specifying certain articles taken from his sermons. One was that he had taught that images ought not to be worshiped. Another, that he had done away with the hospitality commended by St. Paul, seeing that in expounding the passage from the Gospel with its thrice repeated "feed my sheep," while he was in accordance with other expositors on the first two heads (feed by example of life; feed by the word of doctrine), he had disagreed with them on the third, saying that it was not meet that the Apostles, poor as they then were, should be bidden to feed their sheep in the way of any temporal support; and he had substituted some other interpretation in lieu of it. A third article was that having said in the pulpit that there were some who preached written sermons—the stiff and formal way of many in England—he had indirectly reflected on his bishop, who, from his old age, was in the habit of so doing. The archbishop, to whom Colet's high qualities were perfectly well known, undertook the protection of the innocent, and as Colet himself disdained any reply to these and still more frivolous charges, he became a protector instead of a judge. Still the old bishop's animosity was not allayed. He tried to excite the court, with the king at its head, against Colet, having now got hold of another weapon against him. This was that he had openly declared in a sermon "an unjust peace was to be preferred to the justest war,"[3] a war being at that very time in preparation against the French. A leading part in this play was being taken by two Franciscan friars, of whom one, a very firebrand of war, earned a miter while the other used to declaim like a Stentor in his sermons against poets—meaning Colet, who had not the least taste for poetry, though in other respects not unskilled in music. At this juncture the noble young king gave a conspicuous token of his kingly disposition, for he privately encouraged Colet to go on without restraint, and improve by his teaching the corrupt morals of the age, and not to withdraw his light from those dark times. He was not unaware, he said, of the motive that incited those bishops against him, nor unconscious of the benefits he had conferred on the English nation by his life and doctrine. He added, that he would put such a check on their attempts that others should clearly see that whoever assailed Colet would not go unpunished. On this, Colet expressed his gratitude for such kind feeling on the king's part but prayed leave to decline the offer. He would have no one, he said, worse off on his account: sooner than that, he would resign the office which he bore.

Some time afterwards, however, the faction had an occasion given them for hoping that now at last Colet might be crushed. An expedition was being got ready against the French, to start after Easter. On Good Friday, Colet preached a noble sermon before the king and his court on the victory of Christ, exhorting all Christians to war and conquer under the banner of Him their proper King.[3] For they, he said, who through hatred or ambition were fighting, the bad with the bad, and slaughtering one another by turns, were warring under the banner not of Christ but of the Devil. At the same time, he pointed out to them how hard a thing it is to die a Christian death, how few entered on a war unsullied by hatred or love of gain, how incompatible a thing it was that a man should have that brotherly love without which no one would see God and yet bury his sword in his brother's heart. Let them follow, he added, the example of Christ as their Prince, not that of Julius Caesar or an Alexander.[4] Much more to the same effect he gave utterance to on that occasion, so that the king was in some apprehension lest the soldiers whom he was on the point of leading abroad should feel their courage gone through this discourse. On this, all the mischief-makers flocked together like birds setting upon an owl, in the hope that now at last the mind of the king might be exasperated against him. By the king's order Colet was sent for. He came and had luncheon in the Franciscan convent adjoining Greenwich Palace. When the king was apprised of his arrival, he went down into the convent garden, dismissing his attendants as Colet came out to meet him. As soon as they were alone, the courteous young prince bade him be covered and converse with him without ceremony, himself beginning in these terms: "To spare you any groundless alarm, Mr. Dean, we have not sent for you hither to disturb your sacred labors, which have our entire approval, but that we may unburden our conscience of some scruples, and with the help of your counsel may better discharge the duties of our office." (I will not, however, repeat the whole conversation, which lasted nearly an hour.) Meanwhile Bricot, who from a Franciscan friar had now become a bishop, was in high spirits in the palace, supposing Colet to be in danger; whereas the king and he were at one upon all points, save only that the king wished him to say at some other time, with clearer explanation, what he had already said with perfect truth, namely, that for Christians no war was a just one. And this was for the sake of the rough soldiers, who might put a different construction on his words from that which he had intended. Colet, as became his good sense and remarkable moderation of temper, not only set the king's mind at rest but even increased the favor in which he stood before. On returning to the palace, the king had a wine cup brought to him and pledged Colet in it before he would let him depart. Then embracing him most courteously and promising all that could be expected from the most gracious of sovereigns, he let him go. And as the throng of courtiers was now standing round, eager to hear the result of this conference, the king, in the hearing of all, said, "Let every man have his own doctor, and every one follow his liking; but this is the doctor for me." Thus they departed, like the baffled wolves in the adage, Bricot more than all; nor did anyone from that day forward venture to molest Colet.

Endnotes

1. Regarding Erasmus' view of Thomas Aquinas, see Renaudet, *Etudes érasmiennes*, pp. 123–25. Also see Denys Gorce, *op. cit.,* pp. 233 ff.
2. The bishop referred to is Richard Fitzjames (c. 1440–1522), who had become bishop of London in 1506. Allen (IV, 518.365n) indicates his theological orientation was other than that described by Erasmus. He possessed manuscripts of Origen, Jerome, Augustine, Seneca, et al.
3. Erasmus uses practically the same quotation, taken from Cicero, in the letter to Guy Morillon which appears in the Appendix.
4. This forthright sermon was preached before the court on Good Friday 1513. Erasmus' summary is all that remains of it. The only one of Colet's sermons that is extant is his Convocation Sermon of 1511 on the reformation of the Church, the English translation of which is reprinted in Nugent, *op. cit.,* pp. 358–64.
5. A clear and pointed reference by Colet to Pope Julius II, who had died just the month before (February 1513), and to his predecessor, Alexander VI.

William Roper (c.1495-1578)

Roper was Thomas More's son-in-law, having married his daughter, Margaret (d.1544), in 1521. The son of a lawyer, Roper entered More's household in 1518, the same year the young man was admitted to Lincoln's Inn to study law, and continued to live with More even after the marriage. Originally a follower of the Reformation, Roper was brought back to the catholic faith by More and remained loyal for the rest of his life. He served as chief clerk of the court of King's Bench (1524) and as M.P. for Bramber in 1529. After his resignation as Lord Chancellor in 1532, More assigned some of his Chelsea property to Roper.

Unlike his father-in-law, Roper swore the oath attached to the Act of Supremacy but continued to live as a catholic. He refused to flee England for the continent, although he sent aid to those of his family who did. Under Mary he received much honour, being elected M.P. in 1554, 1555 and 1558, and serving as Sheriff of Kent. With the religious settlement of Elizabeth, Roper was harassed as a catholic but remained steadfast in his faith. He died in 1578.

Chapter Nine

The Life of Sir Thomas More (excerpt)

In the fourteenth year of his grace's rein was there a Parliament holden,[1] whereof Sir Thomas More was chosen Speaker. Who, being very loath to take that room upon him, made an oration (not now extant) to the King's highness for his discharge[2] thereof. Whereunto when the King would not consent, he spake unto his grace in the form following:

> Sith I perceive, most redoubted Sovereign, that it standeth not with your high pleasure to reform[3] this election and cause it to be changed, but have by the mouth of the most reverend father in God, the legate, your highness's Chancellor, thereunto given your most royal assent, and have of your benignity determined—far about that I may bear—to enable me, and for this office to repute me meet,[4] rather than you should seem to impute unto your Commons that they had unmeetly chosen, I am therefore, and always shall be, ready obediently to conform myself to the accomplishment of your high commandment—in my most humble wise beseeching your most noble majesty that I may with your grace's favor, before I farther enter thereunto, make mine humble intercession unto your highness for two lowly petitions; the one privately concerning myself, the other the whole assembly of your Common House.
>
> For myself, gracious Sovereign, that if it mishap me[5] in anything hereafter that is on the behalf of your Commons in your high presence to be declared, to mistake my message, and in the lack of good utterance, by my misrehearsal[6] to pervert or impair their prudent instructions, it may then like your most noble majesty, of your abundant grace, with the eye of your accustomed pity, to pardon my simpleness—giving me leave to repair again to the Common House and there to confer with them, and to take their substantial advice what thing and in what wise I shall on their

behalf utter and speak before your noble grace, to the intent their
prudent devices and affairs be not by my simpleness and folly
hindered or impaired. Which thing, if it should so mishap, as it were
well likely to mishap in me, if your gracious benignity relieved not
my oversight, it could not fail to be during my life a perpetual
grudge[7] and heaviness to my heart. The help and remedy whereof,
in manner aforesaid remembered, is, most gracious Sovereign, my
first lowly suit and humble petition unto your most noble grace.

[Mine other humble request, most excellent prince, is this:
forasmuch as there be of your Commons, here by your high
commandment assembled for your Parliament, a great number which
are after the accustomed manner appointed in the Common House
to treat and advise of the common affairs among themselves apart;
and albeit, most dear liege-lord, that according to your prudent
advice, by your honorable writs everywhere declared, there hath
been as due diligence used in sending up to your highness's Court
of Parliament the most discreet persons out of every quarter that
men could esteem meet thereunto—whereby it is not to be doubted
but that there is a very substantial assembly of right wise and
politick persons; yet, most victorious prince, sith among so many
wise men neither is every man wise alike, nor among so many men,
like well-witted, every man like well-spoken. And it often happeneth
that, likewise, as much folly is uttered with painted, polished
speech; so many boisterous and rude in language see deep indeed,
and give right substantial counsel.]

And sith also in matters of great importance, the mind is often
so occupied in the matter that a man rather studieth what to say
than how, by reason whereof the wisest man and the best spoken in
a whole country fortuneth among,[8] while his mind is fervent in the
matter, somewhat to speak in such wise as he would afterward wish
to have been uttered otherwise, and yet no worse will had when he
spake it than he hath when he would so gladly change it; therefore,
most gracious Sovereign, considering that in your high Court of
Parliament is nothing entreated[9] but matter of weight and
importance concerning your realm and your own royal estate, it
could not fail to let[10] and put to silence from the giving of their

advice and counsel many of your discreet commons, to the great hindrance of the common affairs, except that every of your Commons were utterly discharged[11] of all doubt and fear how anything that it should happen them to speak should happen of your highness to be taken.[12] And in this point, though your well known and proved benignity putteth every man in right good hope, yet such is the weight of the matter, such is the reverend[13] dread[14] that the timorous hearts of your natural subjects conceive toward your high majesty, our most redoubted King and undoubted Sovereign, that they cannot in this point find themselves satisfied, except your gracious bounty therein declared put away the scruple of their timorous minds, and animate and encourage them, and put them out of doubt.

It may therefore like your most abundant grace, our most benign and godly King, to give all your Commons here assembled your most gracious license and pardon, freely, without doubt of your dreadful displeasure, every man to discharge his conscience, and boldly in every thing incident among us to declare his advice. And whatsoever happen any man to say that it may like your noble majesty, of your inestimable goodness, to take all in good part, interpreting every man's words, how uncunningly[15] soever they be couched, to proceed yet of good zeal towards the profit of your realm and honor of your royal person, the prosperous estate and preservation whereof, most excellent Sovereign, is the thing which we all, your most humble loving subjects, according to the most bounden duty of our natural allegiance, most highly desire and pray for.

At this Parliament Cardinal Wolsey found himself much grieved with the burgesses thereof, for that nothing was so soon done or spoken therein but that it was immediately blown abroad in every alehouse. It fortuned at that Parliament a very great subsidy[16] to be demanded, which the Cardinal fearing would not pass the Common House, determined for the furtherance thereof to be personally present there. Before whose coming, after long debating there, whether it were better but with a few of his lords (as the most opinion of the house was) or with his whole train royally to receive him there amongst them—"Masters," quoth Sir Thomas More, "forasmuch as my Lord Cardinal lately, ye wot well, laid to our charge the lightness[17] of our tongues for things uttered out of this house, it shall not in my mind be amiss with all his pomp to receive him, with his maces, his pillars, his pole-axes, his crosses, his hat, and Great Seal, too—to the intent, if he find the like fault with us hereafter, we may be the bolder from ourselves to lay the blame on those that his grace bringeth hither with him." Whereunto the house wholly agreeing, he was received accordingly.

Where, after that he had in a solemn oration by many reasons proved how necessary it was the demand there moved to be granted, and further showed that less would not serve to maintain the prince's purpose, he—seeing the company sitting still silent, and thereunto nothing answering and contrary to his expectation showing in themselves towards his requests no towardness of inclination,[18] said unto them:

"Masters, you have many wise and learned men among you, and since I am from the King's own person sent hither unto you for the preservation of yourselves and all the realm, I think it meet you give me some reasonable answer."

Whereat every man holding his peace, then began he to speak to one Master Marney, after Lord Marney: "How say you," quoth he, "Master Marney?" Who making him no answer neither, he severally asked the same question of divers others accompted the wisest of the company.

To whom, when none of them all would give so much as one word, being before agreed, as the custom was, by their speaker to make answer—"Masters," quoth the Cardinal, "unless it be the manner of your house, as of likelihood it is, by the mouth of your speaker, whom you have chosen for trusty and wise, as indeed he is, in such cases to utter your minds, here is without doubt a marvellous obstinate silence."

And thereupon he required answer of Master Speaker. Who first reverently upon his knees excusing the silence of the house, abashed at the presence of so noble a personage, able to amaze[19] the wisest and best learned in a realm, and after by many probable arguments proving that for them to make answer was it neither expedient nor agreeable with the ancient liberty of the house, in conclusion for himself showed that though they had all with their voices trusted him, yet except every one of them could put into his one head all their several wits,[20] he alone in so weighty a matter was unmeet[21] to make his grace answer.

Whereupon the Cardinal, displeased with Sir Thomas More, that had not in this Parliament in all things satisfied his desire, suddenly arose and departed.

And after the Parliament ended, in his gallery at Whitehall in Westminster, uttered unto him his griefs, saying: "Would to God you had been at Rome, Master More, when I made you Speaker!"

"Your grace not offended, so would I too, my lord," quoth he. And to wind such quarrels out of the Cardinal's head, he began to talk of that gallery and said: "I like this gallery of yours, my lord, much better than your gallery at Hampton Court."[Wherewith so wisely brake he off the Cardinal's displeasant talk that the Cardinal at that present (as it seemed) wist[22] not what more to say to him] But for revengement of his displeasure counselled the King to send him ambassador into Spain, commending to his highness his wisdom, learning, and meetness for that voyage; and, the difficulty of the cause considered, none was there, he said, so well able to serve his grace therein.

[Which, when the King had broken to Sir Thomas More, and that he had declared unto his grace how unfit a journey it was for him, the nature of the country and disposition of his complexion[23], so disagreeing together, that he should never be likely to do his grace acceptable service there, knowing right well that if his grace sent him thither, he should send him to his grave. But showing himself nevertheless ready, according to his duty (all were it with the loss of his life), to fulfill his grace's pleasure in that behalf.]

[The King, allowing well[24] his answer, said unto him: "It is not our meaning, Master More, to do you hurt, but to do you good would we be glad. We will therefore for this purpose devise upon some other, and employ your service otherwise." And such entire favor did the King bear him that he made him Chancellor of the Duchy of Lancaster upon the death of Sir Richard Wingfield,[25] who had that office before.]

And for the pleasure he took in his company would his grace suddenly sometimes come home to his house at Chelsea to be merry with him. Whither on a time, unlooked for, he came to dinner to him; and after dinner, in a fair garden of his, walked with him by the space of an hour, holding his arm about his neck.

As soon as his grace was gone, I, rejoicing thereat, told Sir Thomas More how happy he was, whom the King had so familiarly entertained, as I never had seen him to do to any other except Cardinal Wolsey, whom I saw his grace once walk with, arm in arm. "I thank our Lord, son," quoth he, "I find his grace my very good lord indeed; and I believe he doth as singularly favor me as any subject within this realm. Howbeit, son Roper, I may tell thee I have no cause to be proud thereof, for if my head could win him a castle in France (for then was there war between us) it should not fail to go."

[This Sir Thomas More, among all other his virtues, was of such meekness that, if it had fortuned him with any learned men resorting to him from Oxford, Cambridge, or elsewhere, as there did divers,[26] some for desire of his acquaintance, some for the famous report of his wisdom and learning, and some for suits of[27] the universities, to have entered into argument (wherein few were comparable unto him) and so far to have discoursed with them therein that he might perceive they could not, without some inconvenience, hold out much further disputation with him, then lest he should discomfort them—as he that sought not his own glory but rather would seem conquered than to discourage students in their studies, ever showing himself more desirous to learn than to teach—would he by some witty device courteously break off into some other matter and give over.]

Of whom for his wisdom and learning had the King such an opinion that at such time as he attended upon his highness, taking his progress[28] either to Oxford or Cambridge, where he was received with very eloquent orations, his grace would always assign him, as one that was prompt and ready therein, *ex tempore* to make answer thereunto. Whose manner was, whensoever he had occasion either here or beyond the sea to be in any university, not only to be present at the readings and disputations there commonly used, but also learnedly to dispute among them himself. Who being Chancellor of the Duchy was made ambassador twice, joined in commission with Cardinal Wolsey— once to the Emperor Charles into Flanders, the other time to the French King into France.

Not long after this, the Water-bailly of London,[29] sometime his servant, hearing (where he had been at dinner) certain merchants liberally[30] to rail against his old master, waxed so discontented therewith that he hastily came to him and told him what he had heard. "And were I, sir," quoth he, "in such favor and authority with my prince as you are, such men surely should not be suffered so villainously and falsely to misreport and slander me. Wherefore I would wish you to call them before you, and to their shame for their lewd[31] malice to punish them."

Who, smiling upon him, said: "Why, Master Water-bailly, would you have me punish those by whom I receive more benefit than by you all that be my friends? Let them, a God's name, speak as lewdly as they list of me and shoot never so many arrows at me. As long as they do not hit me, what am I the worse? But if they should once hit me, then would it indeed not a little trouble me. Howbeit I trust, by God's help, there shall none of them all once be able to touch me. I have more cause, I assure thee, Master Water-bailly, to pity them than to be angry with them." Such fruitful communication had he oft-times with his familiar friends.

So on a time, walking with me along the Thames-side at Chelsea,[32] in talking of other things he said unto me: "Now would to our Lord, son Roper, upon condition that three things were well established in Christendom, I were put in a sack and here presently cast into the Thames."

"What great things be those, sir," quoth I, "that should move you so to wish?"

"Wouldst thou know what they be, son Roper?" quoth he.

"Yea, marry, with good will, sir, if it please you," quoth I.

"In faith, son, they be these," said he. "The first is that where the most part of Christian princes be at mortal war, they were all at an universal peace. The second, that where the Church of Christ is at this present sore afflicted with many errors and heresies, it were settled in a perfect uniformity of religion. The third, that where the King's matter of his marriage is now come in question, it were to the glory of God and quietness of all parts brought to a good conclusion." Whereby, as I could gather, he judged that otherwise it would be a disturbance to a great part of Christendom.

Thus did it by his doings throughout the whole course of his life appear that all his travail and pains, without respect of earthly commodities[33] either to himself or any of his, were only upon the service of God, the prince, and the realm, wholly bestowed and employed. Whom I heard in his later time to say that he never asked the King for himself the value of one penny.

As Sir Thomas More's custom was daily, if he were at home, besides his private prayers, with his children to say the Seven Psalms, Litany and Suffrages following, so was his guise[34] nightly before he went to bed, with his wife, children, and household, to go to his chapel and there upon his knees ordinarily to say certain psalms and collects[35] with them. And because he was desirous for godly purposes sometime to be solitary, and sequester himself from worldly company, a good distance from his mansion house builded he a place called the New Building, wherein there was a chapel, a library, and a gallery. In which, as his use was upon other days to occupy himself in prayer and study together, so in the Friday there usually continued he from morning to evening, spending his time only in devout prayers and spiritual exercises.]

And to provoke[36] his wife and children to the desire of heavenly things, he would sometimes use these words unto them:

["It is now no mastery[37] for you children to go to heaven, for everybody giveth you good counsel, everybody giveth you good example—you see virtue rewarded and vice punished. So that you are carried up to heaven even by the chins. But if you live the time that no man will give you good counsel, nor no man will give you good example, when you shall see virtue punished and vice rewarded, if you will then stand fast and firmly stick to God, upon pain of my life, though you be but half good, God will allow you for whole good."]

Stand for virtue in bad times and God will provide

If his wife or any of his children had been diseased or troubled, he would say unto them: "We may not look at our pleasure to go to heaven in featherbeds. It is not the way, for our Lord himself went thither with great pain and by many tribulations, which was the path wherein he walked thither. For the servant may not look to be in better case than his master."

[And as he would in this sort persuade them to take their troubles patiently, so would he in like sort teach them to withstand the devil and his temptations valiantly, saying:

"Whosoever will mark the devil and his temptations shall find him therein much like to an ape. For, like as an ape, not well looked unto, will be busy and bold to do shrewd turns and contrariwise, being spied, will suddenly leap backward and adventure no farther, so the devil finding a man idle, slothful, and without resistance ready to receive his temptations, waxeth so hardy that he will not fail still to continue with him until to his purpose he have thoroughly brought him. But, on the other side, if he see a man with diligence persevere to prevent and withstand his temptations, he waxeth so weary that in conclusion he utterly forsaketh him. For as the devil of disposition is a spirit of so high a pride that he cannot abide to be mocked, so is he of nature so envious that he feareth any more to assault him, lest he should thereby not only catch a foul fall himself but also minister to the man more matter of merit."]

advice to his kids to live a virtuous life

Thus delighted he evermore not only in virtuous exercises to be occupied himself, but also to exhort his wife, children, and household to embrace and follow the same.

Endnotes

1. In April 1523.
2. relief from that obligation (to be Speaker).
3. revoke.
4. *repute me meet:* declare me qualified.
5. *if … me:* if it is my bad luck.
6. misrepresentation.
7. uneasiness.
8. now and then.
9. treated.
10. hinder.
11. relieved.
12. interpreted.
13. reverenced.
14. fear.
15. unskilfully.
16. money granted by Parliament to the Crown to meet specific needs.
17. looseness.
18. *towardness of inclination:* readiness to accede (to Wolsey's requests).
19. confound.
20. minds.
21. unqualified.
22. knew.
23. More apparently felt that the Spanish climate might fatally affect his constitution ("complexion").
24. *allowing well:* accepting as satisfactory.
25. Interestingly enough, shortly after he arrived in Spain, Sir Richard (who replaced More on the mission) was taken ill in Toledo and died there in July 1525. More succeeded him as Chancellor of the Duchy in the same year.
26. on sundry occasions.
27. *suits of:* petitions from.
28. formal state journey.
29. An important official, one of four attendants upon the Lord Mayor of London.
30. unrestrainedly.
31. villainous.
32. The site of More's beloved country estate. In his day Chelsea was about ten miles up the Thames River from the City of London. All contemporary authors who allude in any detail to the estate rhapsodize over its idyllic setting and character.
33. benefits or profits.
34. custom.

35. short prayers.
36. stimulate.
37. achievement.

Part Three

The Reformation of the Church

Desiderius Erasmus of Rotterdam (?1466–1536)

The Colloquies

The first edition of the Colloquies *appeared in 1518. It proved so popular that Erasmus enlarged and revised it throughout the rest of his life. It consists of a collection of short stories which illustrate a wide range of human experience, folly and wisdom, written with wit, humanity, insight and gentle satire. In particular, many of the stories satirize one of Erasmus's greatest concerns: the reduction of religion to ritual or superstition without the requisite inner spirit.*

Chapter Ten

A Pilgrimage for Religion's Sake (excerpt)

MENEDEMUS: Did you overlook Thomas, Archbishop of Canterbury?

OGYGIUS: By no means. No pilgrimage is more devout.

MENEDEMUS: I long to hear about it, if that's not too much trouble.

OGYGIUS: Oh, no, I want you to hear. There's a section of England called Kent, facing France and Flanders. Its chief city is Canterbury. In it are two monasteries, almost adjacent, both of them Benedictine houses. That named for St. Augustine is evidently the older; the one now called after St. Thomas[1] appears to have been the Archbishop's seat, where he used to live with a few chosen monks; just as today, too, bishops have residences adjoining the churches but apart from the houses of other canons. (In old time both bishops and canons were usually monks; evidence abounds to prove that.) The church sacred to St. Thomas rises to the sky so majestically that it inspires devotion even in those who see it from afar. Thus by its splendor it now dims the glory of the neighboring one and, so to speak, overshadows the spot that was anciently the most sacred. It has two huge towers, as though greeting visitors a long way off and making the region ring far and wide with the wonderful sound of its bronze bells. At the south entrance of the church are stone statues of three armed men, who with sacrilegious hands murdered the blessed saint. Their surnames are added: Tusci, Fusci, Berri.[2]

MENEDEMUS: Why is so much honor paid to impious men?

OXYGIUS. Obviously they have the same honor as Judas, Pilate, and Caiaphas, that band of wicked soldiers whom you see carefully carved on gilded altars. The surnames are added lest anybody in the future speak well of them. Attention is called to them in order that hereafter no courtier lift a hand against bishops or Church property. For those three conspirators went mad ; after committing their crime, and would not have recovered had they not begged help of the most holy Thomas.

MENEDEMUS: O the everlasting mercy of martyrs!

Oxygius. When you enter, the spacious grandeur of the building is disclosed. This part is open to the public.

Menedemus: Is there nothing to see there?

Ogygius: Nothing but the mass of the structure, and some books—among them the Gospel of Nicodemus—fastened to pillars, and a tomb, I don't know whose.[3]

Menedemus: Then what?

Ogygius: Iron screens prevent you from going any farther, but they permit a view of the space between the end of the building and the choir, as it is called. This is ascended by many steps, under which a certain vault[4] gives access to the north side. A wooden altar sacred to the Holy Virgin is shown there; a very small one, not worth seeing except as a monument of antiquity, a rebuke to the luxury of our times. There the holy man is said to have spoken his last farewell to the Virgin when death was at hand. On the altar is the point of the sword with which the crown of the good bishop's head was cut off, and his brain evidently smashed to make death come more quickly. Out of love for the martyr we reverently kissed the sacred rust of this sword.

Leaving this place, we went into the crypt. It has its own custodians. First is shown the martyr's skull,[5] pierced through. The top of the cranium is bared for kissing, the rest covered with silver. Along with this is displayed a leaden plate with "Thomas of Acre"[6] carved on it. The hair shirt, girdle, and drawers by which the bishop used to subdue his flesh hang in the gloom there—horrible even to look at, and a reproach to our softness and delicacy.

Menedemus: Perhaps to the monks themselves, too.

Ogygius: I can neither affirm nor deny that, nor is it any of my business.

Menedemus: Very true.

Ogygius: From here we return to the choir. On the north side mysteries are laid open. It is wonderful how many bones were brought forth—skulls, jaws, teeth, hands, fingers, whole arms, all of which we adored and kissed.[7] This would have gone on forever if my fellow pilgrim, a disagreeable chap, had not cut short the enthusiasm of the guide.

Menedemus: Who was this?

Ogygius: An Englishman named Gratian Pullus,[8] a learned and pious man but less respectful toward this side of religion than I liked.

Menedemus: Some Wycliffite, I suppose.

OGYGIUS: I don't think so, though he had read his books. Where he got hold of them isn't clear.

MENEDEMUS: Did he offend the guide?

OGYGIUS: An arm was brought forth, with the bloodstained flesh still on it. He shrank from kissing this, looking rather disgusted. The custodian soon put his things away. Next we viewed the altar table and ornaments; then the objects that were kept under the altar—all of them splendid; you'd say Midas and Croesus were beggars if you saw the quantity of gold and silver.

MENEDEMUS: No kisses here?

OGYGIUS: No, but a different sort of desire came to my mind.

MENEDEMUS: What was it?

OGYGIUS: I was sad because I had no such relics at home.

MENEDEMUS: A sacrilegious wish!

OGYGIUS: Admitted, and I begged the saint's forgiveness before I left the church. After this we were conducted to the sacristy. Good Lord, what an array of silk vestments there, what an abundance of gold candelabara! There, too, we saw St. Thomas' stall. It looked like a cane plated with silver. It was not at all heavy, had no ornamentation, and was no more than waist-high.

MENEDEMUS: No cross? [9]

OGYGIUS: None that I saw. We were shown a pallium, silk to be sure, but coarse, without gold or jewels, and there was a facecloth, soiled by sweat from his neck and preserving obvious spots of blood. These memorials of the plain living of olden times we gladly kissed.

MENEDEMUS: They're not shown to everyone?

OGYGIUS: Certainly not, my good friend.

MENEDEMUS: How did you manage to make such an impression of devoutness that no secrets were kept from you?

OGYGIUS: I had some acquaintance with the Reverend Father William Warham,[10] the Archbishop. He gave me a note of recommendation.

MENEDEMUS: I hear from many persons that he is a man of remarkable kindness.

OGYGIUS: More than that: you would call him kindness itself if you knew him. His learning, integrity, and holiness of life are so great that you would find him lacking in no quality befitting a perfect prelate. Next we were led up above, for behind the high altar you ascend as though into a new church. There, in a small chapel,[11] is shown the entire face[12] of the saint, gilded, and ornamented with many jewels. Here a certain unlooked-for accident almost upset all our good luck.

MENEDEMUS: I'm waiting to hear what misfortune you mean.

OGYGIUS: My friend Gratian made a *faux pas* here. After a short prayer, he asked the keeper, "I say, good father, is it true, as I've heard, that in his lifetime Thomas was most generous to the poor?" "Very true," the man repied, and began to rehearse the saint's many acts of kindness to them. Then Gratian: "I don't suppose his disposition changed in this matter, unless perhaps for the better." The custodian agreed. Gratian again: "Since, then, the saint was so liberal towards the needy, although he was still poor himself and lacked money to provide for the necessities of life, don't you think he'd gladly consent, now that he's so rich and needs nothing, if some poor wretched woman with hungry children at home, or daughters in danger of losing their virtue because they have no money for dowries, or a husband sick in bed and penniless—if, after begging the saint's forgiveness, she carried off a bit of all this wealth [13] to rescue her family, as though taking from one who wanted her to have it, either as a gift or a loan?" When the keeper in charge of the gilded head made no reply to this, Gratian, who's impulsive, said, "For my part, I'm convinced the saint would even rejoice that in death, too, he could relieve the wants of the poor by his riches." At this the custodian frowned and pursed his lips, looking at us with Gorgon eyes, and I don't doubt he would have driven us from the church with insults and reproaches had he not been aware that we were recommended by the archbishop. I managed to placate the fellow by smooth talk, affirming that Gratian hadn't spoken seriously, but liked to joke; and at the same time I gave him some coins.

MENEDEMUS: I quite approve of your sense of duty. But seriously, I wonder sometimes what possible excuse there could be for those who spend so much money on building, decorating, and enriching churches that there's simply no limit to it. Granted that the sacred vestments and vessels of the church must have a dignity appropriate to their liturgical use; and I want the building to have grandeur. But what's the use of so many baptistries, candelabra, gold statues? What's the good of the vastly expensive organs, as they call them? (We're not content with a single pair, either.) What's the good of that costly musical neighing when meanwhile our brothers and sisters, Christ's living temples, waste away from hunger and thirst?

OGYGIUS: Every decent, sensible man favors moderation in these matters, of course. But since the fault springs from excessive devotion, it merits applause, especially when one thinks of the opposite vice in those who rob churches of their wealth. These gifts are generally given by kings and potentates, and would be worse spent on gambling and war. And removal of anything from there is, in the first place, regarded as sacrilege; next, those who are regular contributors stop their giving; above all, men are incited to robbery. Hence churchmen are custodians of these things rather than owners of them. In short, I'd rather see a church abounding in sacred furnishings than bare and dirty, as some are, and more like stables than churches.

MENEDEMUS: Yet we read that in former times bishops were praised for selling the sacred vessels and using the money to relieve the poor.

OGYGIUS: They're praised today, too, but only praised! In my judgment, to imitate them is neither allowable nor agreeable.

MENEDEMUS: I'm holding up your story. Let's have the conclusion.

OGYGIUS: Hear it, then; I'll be brief. While this was going on, the chief official came forward.

MENEDEMUS: Who? The abbot of the place?

OGYGIUS: He has a miter and abbatical revenue; he lacks only the name of abbot and is called prior,[14] because the archbishop serves instead of an abbot. For in ancient times whoever was archbishop of this diocese was also a monk.

MENEDEMUS: Well, I wouldn't mind being called camel if I had an abbot's income.

OGYGIUS: He seemed to me a good, sensible man; something of a Scotist[15] theologian, too. He opened for us the chest in which the rest of the holy man's body is said to lie.

MENEDEMUS: You saw the bones?

OGYGIUS: No, that's not allowed, nor would it be possible without the use of ladders. But within the wooden chest is a golden chest; when this is drawn up by ropes, it reveals inestimable treasure.

MENEDEMUS: What do I hear?

OGYGIUS: The cheapest part was gold. Everything shone and dazzled with rare and surpassingly large jewels, some bigger than a goose egg.[16] Some monks stood about reverently. When the cover was removed, we all adored. The prior pointed out each jewel by touching it with a white rod, adding its

French name, its worth, and the name of the donor. The principal ones were gifts from kings.

MENEDEMUS: He must have had a remarkable memory.

OGYGIUS: Your guess is correct, although practice helps too, for he often does this. From here he leads the way back to the crypt. There the Virgin Mother has a residence, but a somewhat dark one, enclosed by a double row of iron rails.

MENEDEMUS: What's she afraid of?

OGYGIUS: Only robbers, I suppose, for I've never seen anything more loaded with riches.

MENEDEMUS: You tell me of dark riches.

OGYGIUS: When the lanterns were brought closer, we saw a more than regal sight.

MENEDEMUS: More wealth than that of St. Mary-by-the-Sea?

OGYGIUS: It looks like much more. She alone knows her secret wealth. It isn't shown to any but people of the highest importance or to special friends. At last we were led back to the sacristy. There a chest with a black leather cover was brought out, placed on the table, and opened. Immediately everyone worshiped on bended knee.

MENEDEMUS: What was inside?

OGYGIUS: Some linen rags, many of them still showing traces of snivel. With these, they say, the holy man wiped the sweat from his face or neck, the dirt from his nose, or whatever other kinds of filth human bodies have. At this point my friend Gratian again displayed imperfect manners. To him, since he was English, and a well-known person of considerable standing, the prior kindly offered one of the rags as a gift, thinking he was giving him a present that would please him very much. But Gratian was hardly grateful for it. He touched the piece with his fingers, not without a sign of disgust, and put it back scornfully, puckering his lips as though whistling. (This is what he ordinarily did if he came across anything he thought despicable.) Shame and alarm together embarrassed me dreadfully. But the prior, no stupid man, pretended not to notice this incident, and after offering us a glass of wine dismissed us kindly, for we were returning to London.

MENEDEMUS: Why did you have to do that when you were already fairly close to your own shore?

OGYGIUS: Yes, I was, but I willingly avoided that shore as much as possible. It's more notorious for frauds and robberies than any Malean rocks[17] are for shipwrecks. I'll tell you what I saw on my last crossing. Many of us were ferried in a rowboat from the Calais shore to a larger vessel. Among the passengers was a poor, ragged French youth. He was charged half a drachma; so large a sum do they wring from each passenger for the very short ride. He pleaded poverty. To amuse themselves they search him, and when they pull off his shoes they find ten or twelve drachmas between the soles. These they take, laughing in his face and jeering at the damned Frenchman.

MENEDEMUS: What did the young fellow do?

OGYGIUS: Mourned his loss. What else could he do?

MENEDEMUS: They had no right to do such things, had they?

OGYGIUS: Exactly the same right they have to rob passengers' luggage and to snatch purses whenever they get a chance.

MENEDEMUS: It's extraordinary that they should dare to commit such a serious crime in the presence of so many witnesses.

OGYGIUS: They're so used to doing it that they think it's quite all right. Many persons watched from the larger boat. In the rowboat were some English merchants, who protested in vain. Those fellows boasted about catching the damned Frenchman as if it were a practical joke.

MENEDEMUS: I'd gladly crucify those pirates as a practical joke!

OGYGIUS: But both shores are full of such men. Guess "what masters might do when knaves dare do such deeds."[18] So from now on I prefer roundabout routes to that short cut. In these respects, just as "the descent to hell is easy"[19] but the return very hard, so entry by this shore is not altogether easy, exit very hard. Some Antwerp sailors were hanging about London; I decided to take my chances with them.

MENEDEMUS: Does that place have such conscientious sailors?

OGYGIUS: As an ape is always an ape, I confess, so a sailor's always a sailor. But if you compare them with professional thieves they're angels.

MENEDEMUS: I'll remember that if ever I, too, get the urge to visit that island. But go back to the road I took you away from.

OGYGIUS: On the way to London, shortly after you leave Canterbury, you find a very deep and narrow road; moreover, it has such steep banks on each side that you can't get out of it. There's no other road you can take, either. On the left side of this road is a little almshouse[20] for some old beggars. As soon as they see a rider coming one of them runs up, sprinkles him with holy water, and presently holds out the upper part of a shoe fastened to a brass rim. In it is a glass that looks like a jewel. People kiss it and make a small contribution.

MENEDEMUS: On that sort of road I'd rather meet a house of old beggars than a gang of able-bodied thieves.

OGYGIUS: Gratian was riding on my left, closer to the almshouse. He was sprinkled with water, but he managed to put up with that. When the shoe was thrust at him, he asked the man what he meant by this. He said it was St. Thomas' shoe. Gratian turned to me and said heatedly, "What, do these brutes want us to kiss all good men's shoes? Why not, in the same fashion, hold out spittle and other excrements to be kissed?" I felt sorry for the old man and cheered him up with a tip, poor fellow.

MENEDEMUS: In my opinion, Gratian's anger was not entirely unreasonable. If soles of shoes were kept as evidence of a temperate life, I wouldn't object, but I consider it shameless to push soles, shoes, and girdles at one to be kissed. If one kissed them of his own accord, from some overwhelming feeling of piety, I'd think it pardonable.

OGYGIUS: I won't pretend it wouldn't be better to leave those things undone, but from what can't be amended at a stroke I'm accustomed to take whatever good there is. Meantime, I was pleasing myself with the reflection that a good man is like a sheep, a bad one like a beast of prey. When an adder's dead, it can't sting, true but its stench and blood are injurious. A sheep, while alive, nourishes by its milk, provides clothing by its wool, enriches by its offspring; dead, it furnishes useful hide; and all of it can be eaten. So rapacious men, addicted to this world, are troublesome to everybody while alive; when dead, they're a nuisance to the living by reason of the tolling of bells, grandiose funerals, and sometimes by the consecration of their successors—because that means new exactions. Good men, truly, are in every respect useful to everyone: as this saint, during his lifetime, encouraged people to holiness by his example, teaching, and exhortations, comforted the forsaken, and raised up the needy. In death his usefulness is almost greater. He built this very wealthy church; he won more power for the clergy throughout England. Lastly, this piece of shoe supports a whole house of poor men.

MENEDEMUS: A noble thought indeed, but since you're of that mind I'm surprised you've never visited St. Patrick's cave,[21] of which marvelous tales are told. To me they're not entirely plausible.

OGYGIUS: On the contrary, no story about it can be so marvelous that it is not surpassed by the fact itself.

MENEDEMUS: And have you been in it, then?

OGYGIUS: I sailed in Stygian waters, to be sure; I went down into the jaws of Avernus; I saw what goes on in hell.

MENEDEMUS: You'll do me a favor if you'll be kind enough to tell me about it.

OGYGIUS: Let this serve as prologue to our conversation; and it's long enough, in my opinion. I'm on my way home to order dinner; I haven't lunched yet.

OGYGIUS: Oh, no, because of a grudge.

MENEDEMUS: Why haven't you? Not because of religious observance?

MENEDEMUS: A grudge against your belly?

OGYGIUS: No, against greedy tavern keepers who, though they won't serve a decent meal, don't hesitate to charge their guests outrageous prices. I get even with them in this way: if I expect a good dinner with an acquaintance, or at an innkeeper's who is a little less niggardly, my stomach won't stand much lunch; but if luck has provided the sort of lunch I like, I get a stomachache at dinnertime.

MENEDEMUS: Aren't you ashamed to seem so stingy and mean?

OGYGIUS: Menedemus, those who take shame into account in such matters, believe me, are bad bookkeepers. I've learned to keep my shame for other purposes.

MENEDEMUS: I long to hear the rest of the tale, so expect me as a guest for dinner. You'll tell it more comfortably there.

OGYGIUS: Well, thanks very much for inviting yourself, since so many who are pressed to come decline. But my thanks will be doubled if you'll dine at home today, for my time will be taken up with greeting my family. Besides, I have a plan more convenient for us both. Have lunch at *your* home tomorrow for me and my wife. Then I'll talk until dinner—until you admit you're satisfied; and if you like, we won't desert you even at dinner. What are you scratching your head for? You get dinner ready; we'll be sure to come.

MENEDEMUS: I'd prefer stories I wouldn't have to pay for. All right: I'll furnish a bit of lunch, only it will be tasteless unless you season it with good stories.

OGYGIUS: But look here! Don't you itch to go on these pilgrimages?

MENEDEMUS: Maybe I'll itch after you've finished talking. As matters stand now, I have enough to do by going on my Roman stations.[22]

OGYGIUS: Roman? You, who've never seen Rome?

MENEDEMUS: I'll tell you. Here's how I wander about at home. I go into the living room and see that my daughter's chastity is safe. Coming out of there into my shop, I watch what my servants, male and female, are doing. Then to the kitchen, to see if any instruction is needed. From here to one place and another, observing what my children and my wife are doing, careful that everything be in order. These are my Roman stations.

OGYGIUS: But St. James will look after these affairs for you.

MENEDEMUS: Sacred Scripture directs me to take care of them myself. I've never read any commandment to hand them over to saints.

Endnotes

1. "That named for St. Augustine": formerly the abbey of SS. Peter and Paul; "the one now called after St. Thomas": the priory of Christ Church.
2. William de Tracy, Reginald Fitzurse, and Richard le Breton or Brito. Erasmus omits the name of the fourth, Hugh de Morville.
3. The tombs of two archbishops, Islip and Whittlesey.
4. Beneath the steps leading to the choir. Ogygius is being led to the scene of the martyrdom in the northwest transept.
5. "More probably the new relic of St. Dunstan which had recently been enclosed in a mitred bust of silver, since there is no other record of any part of St. Thomas's head being kept in the crypt" (C. E. Woodruff and W. Danks, *Memorials of the Cathedral and Priory of Christ in Canterbury,* 1912, p. 275).
6. There was a legend that the saint's mother was a Saracen.
7. The relics, we are told, included part of the table at which the Last Supper was eaten and some of the clay out of which God made Adam (Woodruff and Danks, op. cit., p. 276–277).
8. "Pullus" ("colt") is undoubtedly John Colet, the Dean of St. Paul's. He was a friend and patron of Erasmus. On the identification see *Erasmi Epistolae,* IV, 517. 327n.
9. "No cross on the staff?" An archbishop's staff is surmounted by a cross.
10. He was archbishop from 1504 to 1532. Erasmus, who owed much to his patronage, dedicated his edition of Jerome (1516) to Warham.
11. The Chapel of the Holy Trinity, at the east end of the church. The shrine was in this chapel.

12. "This was the mitred bust of St. Thomas which enclosed what at Canterbury was always called Corona—i.e., St. Thomas's crown—but was known to the world as the *Caput sancti Thome* or St. Thomas's head" (Woodruff and Danks, op. cit., p. 279).
13. The shrine was later destroyed and the treasures plundered by Henry VIII. Note Erasmus' prophetic remark in "The Godly Feast," p. 162.
14. Thomas Goldston, prior from 1495 to 1517.
15. Learned in the philosophy of Duns Scotus, the "subtle doctor." The Scotists were one of the principal schools of philosophers and theologians in the later Middle Ages.
16. One of these, the "Regale of France," said to have been the gift of King Louis VII, was especially famous.
17. On the coast of southeastern Peloponnesus.
18. Virgil, *Eclogues* iii, 16.
19. Virgil, *Aeneid*, vi, 126–129.
20. At Harbledown, about two miles from Canterbury.
21. St. Patrick's Purgatory, a cave in County Donegal, Ulster, which became a place of pilgrimage. According to medieval legend, some pilgrims who went down into the cave witnessed the tortures of hell.
22. Processions to certain churches in Rome on certain days.

Desiderius Erasmus of Rotterdam (?1466–1536)

The Paraclesis

The Paraclesis is Erasmus's preface to his new translation of the New Testament (*Novum Instrumentum*) of 1516. Although only a few pages in length, it contained many of his fundamental beliefs about learning and religion. It argues for a vernacular Bible, for placing Christ's teachings above all else and for the essential harmony between scholarship and revelation, but observes that Christ's teaching is the ultimate wisdom.

Chapter Eleven

The Paraclesis

The illustrious Lactantius Firmianus, good reader, whose eloquence Jerome especially admires, as he begins to defend the Christian religion against the pagans desires especially an eloquence second only to Cicero's be given him, thinking it wrong, I believe, to want an equal eloquence.[1] But I indeed might heartily wish, if anything is to be gained by wishes of this kind, so long as I exhort all men to the most holy and wholesome study of Christian philosophy and summon them as if with the blast of a trumpet, that an eloquence far different than Cicero's be given me: an eloquence certainly much more efficacious, if less ornate than his. Or rather [I might wish for that kind of eloquence], if such power of speech was ever granted anyone, as the tales of the ancient poets not entirely without cause attributed to Mercury, who as if with a magic wand and a divine lyre induces sleep when he wishes and likewise snatches sleep away, plunging whom he wished into hell and again calling them forth from hell; or as the ancient tales assigned to Amphion and Orpheus, one of whom is supposed to have moved hard rocks, the other to have attracted oaks and ashes with a lyre; or as the Gauls ascribed to their Ogmius, leading about whither he wished all men by little chains fastened to their ears from his tongue; or as fabled antiquity attributed to Marsyas; or really, lest we linger too long on fables, as Alcibiades imputed to Socrates and old comedy to Pericles, an eloquence which not only captivates the ear with its fleeting delight but which leaves a lasting sting in the minds of its hearers, which grips, which transforms, which sends away a far different listener than it had received. One reads that the noble musician Timotheus, singing Doric melodies, was wont to rouse Alexander the Great to a desire for war. Nor were they lacking in former times who considered nothing more effective than the entreaties which the Greeks call *epodes*. But if there were any such kind of incantation anywhere, if there were any power of song which truly could inspire, if any Pytho truly swayed the heart, I would desire that it be at hand for me so that I might convince all of the most wholesome truth of all. However, it is more desirable that Christ Himself, whose business we are about, so guide the strings of our lyre that this song might deeply affect and move the minds of all, and, in fact, to accomplish this there is no need for the syllogisms and exclamations of the orators. What we desire is that nothing may stand forth with greater certainty than the truth itself, whose expression is the more powerful, the simpler it is.

And in the first place it is not pleasing to renew at the present time this complaint, not entirely new but, alas, only too just—and perhaps never more just than in these days—that when men are devoting themselves with such ardent spirit to all their studies, this philosophy of Christ alone is derided by some, even Christians, is neglected by many, and is discussed by a few, but in a cold manner (I shall not say insincerely). Moreover, in all other branches of learning which human industry has brought forth, nothing is so hidden and obscure which the keenness of genius has not explored, nothing is so difficult which tremendous exertion has not overcome. Yet how is it that even those of us who profess to be Christian fail to embrace with the proper spirit this philosophy alone? Platonists, Pythagoreans, Academics, Stoics, Cynics, Peripatetics, Epicureans not only have a deep understanding of the doctrines of their respective sects, but they commit them to memory, and they fight fiercely in their behalf, willing even to die rather than abandon the defense of their author. Then why do not we evince far greater spirit for Christ, our Author and Prince? Who does not judge it very shameful for one professing Aristotle's philosophy not to know that man's opinion about the causes of lightning, about prime matter, about the infinite? And neither does this knowledge render a man happy, nor does the lack of it render him unhappy. And do not we, initiated in so many ways, drawn by so many sacraments to Christ, think it shameful and base to know nothing of His doctrines, which offer the most certain happiness to all? But what purpose is served to exaggerate the matter by controversy, since it is what I might call a kind of wicked madness to wish to compare Christ with Zeno or Aristotle and His teaching with, to put it mildly, the paltry precepts of those men? Let them magnify the leaders of their sect as much as they can or wish. Certainly He alone was a teacher who came forth from heaven, He alone could teach certain doctrine, since it is eternal wisdom, He alone, the sole author of human salvation, taught what pertains to salvation, He alone fully vouches for whatsoever He taught, He alone is able to grant whatsoever He has promised. If anything is brought to us from the Chaldeans or Egyptians, we desire more eagerly to examine it because of the fact that it comes from a strange world, and part of its value is to have come from far off;

and oftentimes we are anxiously tormented by the fancies of an insignificant man, not to say an impostor, not only to no avail but with great loss of time (I am not adding a more serious note, for the matter as it stands is most serious). But why does not such a desire also excite Christian minds who are convinced— and it is a fact—that this teaching has come not from Egypt or Syria but from heaven itself? Why do not all of us ponder within ourselves that this must be a new and wonderful kind of philosophy since, in order to transmit it to mortals, He who was God became man, He who was immortal became mortal, He who was in the heart of the Father descended to earth? It must be a great matter, and in no sense a commonplace one, whatever it is, because that wondrous Author came to teach after so many families of distinguished philosophers, after so many remarkable prophets. Why, then, out of pious curiosity do we not investigate, examine, explore each tenet? Especially since this kind of wisdom, so extraordinary that once for all it renders foolish the entire wisdom of this world, may be drawn from its few books as from the most limpid springs with far less labor than Aristotle's doctrine is extracted from so many obscure volumes, from those huge commentaries of the interpreters at odds with one another— and I shall not add with how much greater reward. Indeed, here there is no requirement that you approach equipped with so many troublesome sciences. The journey is simple, and it is ready for anyone. Only bring a pious and open mind, possessed above all with a pure and simple faith. Only be docile, and you have advanced far in this philosophy. It itself supplies inspiration as a teacher which communicates itself to no one more gladly than to minds that are without guile. The teachings of the others, besides the fact that they give hope of a false happiness, drive off the natural talents of many by the very difficulty, it is clear, of their precepts. This doctrine in an equal degree accommodates itself to all, lowers itself to the little ones, adjusts itself to their measure, nourishing them with milk, bearing, fostering, sustaining them, doing everything until we grow in Christ. Again, not only does it serve the lowliest, but it is also an object of wonder to those at the top. And the more you shall have progressed in its riches, the more you shall have withdrawn it from the shadow of the power of any other. It is a small affair to the little ones and more than the highest affair to the great. It casts aside no age, no sex, no fortune or position in life. The sun itself is not as common and accessible to all as is Christ's teaching. It keeps no one at a distance, unless a person, begrudging himself, keeps himself away.

Indeed, I disagree very much with those who are unwilling that Holy Scripture, translated into the vulgar tongue, be read by the uneducated, as if

Christ taught such intricate doctrines that they could scarcely be understood by very few theologians, or as if the strength of the Christian religion consisted in men's ignorance of it. The mysteries of kings, perhaps, are better concealed, but Christ wishes his mysteries published as openly as possible. I would that even the lowliest women read the Gospels and the Pauline Epistles. And I would that they were translated into all languages so that they could be read and understood not only by Scots and Irish but also by Turks and Saracens. Surely the first step is to understand in one way or another. It may be that many will ridicule, but some may be taken captive. Would that, as a result, the farmer sing some portion of them at the plow, the weaver hum some parts of them to the movement of his shuttle, the traveller lighten the weariness of the journey with stories of this kind! Let all the conversations of every Christian be drawn from this source. For in general our daily conversations reveal what we are. Let each one comprehend what he can, let him express what he can. Whoever lags behind, let him not envy him who is ahead; whoever is in the front rank, let him encourage him who follows, not despair of him. Why do we restrict a profession common to all to a few? For it is not fitting, since Baptism is common in an equal degree to all Christians, wherein there is the first profession of Christian philosophy, and since the other sacraments and at length the reward of immortality belong equally to all, that doctrines alone should be reserved for those very few whom today the crowd call theologians or monks, the very persons whom, although they comprise one of the smallest parts of the Christian populace, yet I might wish to be in greater measure what they are styled. For I fear that one may find among the theologians men who are far removed from the title they bear, that is, men who discuss earthly matters, not divine, and that among the monks who profess the poverty of Christ and the contempt of the world you may find something more than worldliness. To me he is truly a theologian who teaches not by skill with intricate syllogisms but by a disposition of mind, by the very expression and the eyes, by the very life that riches should be disdained, that the Christian should not put his trust in the supports of this world but must rely entirely on heaven, that a wrong should not be avenged, that a good should be wished for those wishing, it, that we should deserve well of those deserving ill, that all good men should be loved and cherished equally as members of the same body, that the evil should be tolerated if they cannot be corrected, that those who are stripped of their goods, those who are turned away from possessions, those who mourn are blessed and should not be deplored, and that death should even be desired by the devout, since it is nothing other than a passage to immortality. And if anyone under the inspiration of the spirit of Christ preaches this kind of doctrine, inculcates it, exhorts, incites, and encourages men to it, he indeed is truly a theologian, even if he should be a common laborer or weaver. And if anyone exemplifies this doctrine in his life itself, he is in fact a great doctor. Another, perhaps, even a non-Christian, may discuss more subtly how the angels understand, but to persuade us to lead here an angelic life, free from every stain, this indeed is the duty of the Christian theologian.

But if anyone objects that these notions are somewhat stupid and vulgar, I should respond to him only that Christ particularly taught these rude doctrines, that the Apostles inculcated them, that however vulgar they are, they have brought forth for us so many sincerely Christian and so great a throng of illustrious martyrs. This philosophy, unlettered as it appears to these very objectors, has drawn the highest princes of the world and so many kingdoms and peoples to its laws, an achievement which the power of tyrants and the erudition of philosophers cannot claim. Indeed I do not object to having that latter wisdom, if it seems worthwhile, discussed among the educated. But let the lowly mass of Christians console themselves certainly with this title because, whether the Apostles knew or other Fathers understood these subtleties or not, they surely didn't teach them. If princes in the execution of their duties would manifest what I have referred to as a vulgar doctrine, if priests would inculcate it in sermons, if schoolmasters would instill it in students rather than that erudition which they draw from the fonts of Aristotle and Averroës, Christendom would not be so disturbed on all sides by almost continuous war, everything would not be boiling over with such a mad desire to heap up riches by fair means or foul, every subject, sacred as well as profane, would not be made to resound everywhere with so much noisy disputation, and, finally, we would not differ from those who do not profess the philosophy of Christ merely in name and ceremonial. For upon these three ranks of men principally the task of either renewing or advancing the Christian religion has been placed: on the princes and the magistrates who serve in their place, on the bishops and their delegated priests, and on those who instruct the young eager for all knowledge. If it happen that they, having laid aside their own affairs, should sincerely cooperate in Christ, we would certainly see in not so many years a true and, as Paul says, a genuine race of Christians everywhere emerge, a people who would restore the philosophy of Christ not in ceremonies alone and in syllogistic propositions but in the heart itself and in the whole life. The enemies of the Christian name will far more quickly be drawn to the faith of Christ by these weapons than by threats or arms. In the conquest of every citadel nothing is more powerful than the truth itself. He is not a Platonist who has not read the works of Plato; and is he a theologian, let alone a Christian, who has not read the literature of Christ? Who loves me, Christ says, keeps my word, a distinguishing mark which He himself prescribed. Therefore, if we are truly and sincerely Christian, if we truly believe in Him who has been sent from Heaven to teach us that which the wisdom of the philosophers could not do, if we truly expect from Him what no prince, however powerful, can give, why is anything more important to us than His literature? Why indeed does anything seem learned that is not in harmony with His decrees? Why in the case of this literature that should be revered do we also allow ourselves, and I shall say almost to a greater extent than do the secular interpreters in the case of the imperial laws or the books of the physicians, to speak what ever comes to mind, to distort, to obscure? We drag heavenly doctrines down to the level of our own life as if it were a Lydian rule, and while we seek to avoid by every means appearing to be ignorant and for this reason gather in whatever is of account in secular literature, that which is of special value in Christian philosophy I shall not say we corrupt, but—and no one can deny it—we restrict to a few, although Christ wished nothing to be more public. In this kind of philosophy, located as it is more truly in the disposition of the mind than in syllogisms, life means more than debate, inspiration is preferable to erudition, transformation is a more important matter than intellectual comprehension. Only a very few can be learned, but all can be Christian, all can be devout, and—I shall boldly add—all can be theologians.

Indeed, this philosophy easily penetrates into the minds of all, an action in especial accord with human nature. Moreover, what else is the philosophy of Christ, which He himself calls a rebirth, than the restoration of human nature originally well formed? By the same token, although no one has taught this more perfectly and more effectively than Christ, nevertheless one may find in the books of the pagans very much which does agree with His teaching. There was never so coarse a school of philosophy that taught that money rendered a man happy. Nor has there ever been one so shameless that fixed the chief good in those vulgar honors and pleasures. The Stoics understood that no one was wise unless he was good; they understood that nothing was truly good or noble save real virtue and nothing fearful or evil save baseness alone. According to Plato, Socrates teaches in many different ways that a wrong must not be repaid with a wrong, and also that since the soul is immortal, those should not be lamented who depart this life for a happier one with the assurance of having led an upright life. In addition, he teaches that the soul must be drawn away from the inclinations of the body and led to those which are its real objectives although they are not seen. Aristotle has written in the *Politics* that nothing can be a delight to us, even though it is not in any way despised, except virtue alone. Epicurus also acknowledges that nothing in man's life can bring delight unless the mind is conscious of no evil, from which awareness true pleasure gushes forth as from a spring. What shall we say of this, that many—notably Socrates, Diogenes, and Epictetus—have presented a good portion of His teaching? But since Christ both taught and presented the same doctrine so much more fully, is it not a monstrous thing that Christians either disregard or neglect or even ridicule it? If there are things that belong particularly to Christianity in these ancient writers, let us follow them. But if these alone can truly make a Christian, why do we consider them as almost more obsolete and replaced than the Mosaic books? The first step, however, is to know what He taught; the next is to carry it into effect. Therefore, I believe, anyone should not think himself to be Christian if he disputes about instances, relations, quiddities, and formalities with an obscure and irksome confusion of words, but rather if he holds and exhibits what Christ taught and showed forth. Not that I condemn the industry of those who not without merit employ their native intellectual powers in such subtle discourse, for I do not wish anyone to be offended, but that I think, and rightly so, unless I am mistaken, that that pure and genuine philosophy of Christ is not to be drawn from any source more abundantly than from the evangelical books and from the Apostolic Letters, about which, if anyone, should devoutly philosophize, praying more than arguing, and seeking to be transformed rather than armed for battle, he would without a doubt find that there is nothing pertaining to the happiness of man and the living of his life which is not taught, examined, and unraveled in these works. If we desire to learn, why is another author more pleasing than Christ himself? If we seek a model for life, why does another example take precedence for us over that of Christ himself? If we wish some medicine against the troublesome desires of the soul, why do we think the remedy to be more at hand somewhere else? If we want to arouse a soul that is idle and growing listless by reading, where, I ask, will you find sparks equally alive and efficacious? If the soul seems distracted by the vexations of this life, why are other delights more pleasing? Why have we steadfastly preferred to learn the wisdom of Christ from the writings of men than from Christ himself? And He, since He promised to be with us all days, even unto the consummation of the world, stands forth especially in this literature, in which He lives for us even at this time, breathes and speaks, I should say almost more effectively than when He dwelt among men. The Jews saw and heard less than you see and hear in the books of the Gospels, to the extent that you make use of your eyes and ears, whereby this can be perceived and heard.

And what kind of a situation is this, I ask? We preserve the letters written by a dear friend, we kiss them fondly, we carry them about, we read them again and again, yet there are many thousands of Christians who, although they are learned in other respects, never read, however, the evangelical and apostolic books in an entire lifetime. The Mohammedans hold fast to their doctrines, the Jews also today from the very cradle study the books of Moses. Why do not we in the same way distinguish ourselves in Christ? Those who profess the way of life of Benedict hold, study, absorb a rule written by man, and by one nearly uneducated for the uneducated. Those who are in the Augustinian order are well versed in the rule of their founder. The Franciscans reverence and love the little traditions of their Francis, and to whatever corner of the earth they go, they carry them with them; they do not feel safe unless the little book is on their person. Why do these men attribute more to a rule written by man than does the Christian world to its rule, which Christ delivered to all and which all have equally professed in baptism? Finally, although you may even cite a thousand rules, can anything be holier than this? And I wish that this may come to pass: just as Paul wrote that the law of Moses was not full of glory compared with the glory of the Gospel succeeding it, so may all Christians hold the Gospels and Letters of the Apostles as so holy that in comparison with them these other writings do not seem holy. What others may wish to concede to Albert the Great, to Alexander, to Thomas, to Egidio, to Richard, to Occam, they will certainly be free, as far as I am concerned, to do, for I do not want to diminish the fame of anyone or contend with the studies of men that are now of long standing.[2] However learned these may be, however subtle, however seraphic, if they like, yet they must admit that the former are the most tried and true. Paul wishes that the spirits of those prophesying be judged whether they are of God. Augustine, reading every kind of book with discretion, asks nothing more than a just hearing also for his own works. But in this literature alone [i.e. Holy Scripture] what I do not comprehend, I nevertheless revere. It is no school of theologians who has attested to this Author for us but the Heavenly Father Himself through the testimony of the divine voice, and He has done this on two occasions: first at the Jordan at the time of the Baptism, then on Mount Tabor at the Transfiguration. "This is my beloved Son," He says, "in whom I am well pleased; hear Him."[3] O solid and truly irrefragable authority, as the theologians say! What is this phrase, "Hear Him"? Certainly He is the one and only teacher, let us be the disciples of Him alone. Let each one extol in his studies his own author as much as he will wish, this utterance has been said without exception of Christ alone. A dove first descended on Him, the confirmation of the Father's testimony. Peter next bears His spirit, to whom the highest Pastor three times entrusted the feeding of His sheep, feeding them without a doubt, however, on the food of Christian doctrine.[4] This spirit was born again, as it were, in Paul, whom He himself called a "chosen vessel" and an extraordinary herald of His name.[5] What John had drawn from that sacred font of His heart, he expressed in his own writings. What, I pray, is like this in Scotus (I do not wish that this remark be taken as a pretext for abuse), what is like this in Thomas? Nevertheless, I admire the talents of the one, and I also revere the sanctity of the other. But why do not all of us apply ourselves to philosophy in these authors of such great value? Why do we not carry them about on our persons, have them ever in our hands? Why do we not hunt through these authors, thoroughly examine them, assiduously investigate them? Why devote the greater part of life to Averroës rather than to the Gospels? Why spend nearly all of life on the ordinances of men and on opinions in contradiction with themselves? The latter, in fact, may now be the views of the more eminent theologians, if you please; but certainly the first steps of the great theologian in the days to come will be in these authors [of Holy Scripture].

Let all those of us who have pledged in baptism in the words prescribed by Christ, if we have pledged sincerely, be directly imbued with the teachings of Christ in the midst of the very embraces of parents and the caresses of nurses. For that which the new earthen pot of the soul first imbibes settles most deeply and clings most tenaciously. Let the first lispings utter Christ, let earliest childhood be formed by the Gospels of Him whom I would wish particularly presented in such a way that children also might love Him. For as the severity of some teachers causes children to hate literature before they come to know it, so there are those who make the philosophy of Christ sad and morose, although nothing is more sweet than it. In these studies, then, let them engage themselves until at length in silent growth they mature into strong manhood in Christ. The literature of others is such that many have greatly repented the effort expended upon it, and it happens again and again that those who have fought through all their life up to death to defend the principles of that literature, free themselves from the faction of their author at the very hour of death. But happy is that man whom death takes as he meditates upon this literature [of Christ]. Let us all, therefore, with our whole heart covet this literature, let us embrace it, let us continually occupy ourselves with it, let us fondly kiss it, at length let us die in its embrace, let us be transformed in it, since indeed studies are transmuted into morals. As for him who cannot pursue this course (but who cannot do it, if only he wishes?), let him at least reverence this literature enveloping, as it were, His divine heart. If anyone shows us the footprints of Christ, in what manner, as Christians, do we prostrate ourselves, how we adore them! But why do we not venerate instead the living and breathing likeness of Him in these books? If anyone displays the tunic of Christ, to what corner of the earth shall we not hasten so that we may kiss it? Yet were you to bring forth His entire wardrobe, it would not manifest Christ more clearly and truly than the Gospel writings. We embellish a wooden or stone statue with gems and gold for the love of Christ. Why not, rather, mark with gold and gems and with ornaments of greater value than these, if such there be, these writings which bring Christ to us so much more effectively than any paltry image? The latter represents only the form of the body—if indeed it represents anything of Him—but these writings bring you the living image of His holy mind and the speaking, healing, dying, rising Christ himself, and thus they render Him so fully present that you would see less if you gazed upon Him with your very eyes.

Endnotes

1. Lactantius Firmianus was an early fourth-century Christian writer, the author of a defense of the Christian faith entitled *Institutiones divinae.* He had a reputation for great eloquence.
2. The names are those of medieval theologians: Albert the Great, Alexander of Hales, Thomas Aquinas, Egidio of Rome, Richard of St. Victor, and William of Occam.
3. Mathew 3:17; 17:5.
4. John 21:15 ff.
5. Acts 9:15.

Martin Luther (1483-1546)

Luther was born in Saxony in 1483 and educated by the Brethren of the Common Life. In 1501 he went to university at Erfurt and by 1505 he had become a master of Arts. In 1508 he was sent to the Augustinian house at Wittenberg to teach in the university which had recently been founded there. As he lectured on St. Paul's letters to the Romans in Wittenberg, Luther came to the realization that salvation was possible only through faith. Luther was only starting to work out the implications of this new revelation when he was prompted into the publication of his views in 1517 by his outrage at the sale of indulgences.

Luther's 95 theses were quickly printed and flew through Germany. The enthusiasm his ideas generated in Germany was not shared in Rome, and between 1518 and 1520 Luther worked to avoid an open breach with the church. At the same time he developed and publicized his ideas in a number of pamphlets, including the Appeal to the Christian Nobility of the German Nation *(published in the summer of 1520) which became best sellers.*

In July of 1521 Luther was formally excommunicated by Pope Leo X, and the pope called on the emperor to enforce the bull. Charles V would have been glad to enforce the proclamation, but the political situation in Germany simply did not allow it. Luther was receiving a great deal of support from the German princes, and the emperor could not afford to antagonize them.

Luther wanted to return the church to a purer form of what had been, not to create something entirely new, and so he stood against extreme reform. Luther was always concerned to play down any kind of social revolution or any kind of re-organization of the temporal world. His concern was with the spiritual world, and he had no desire to put forward ideas on the re-organization of the temporal world that would raise difficulties in having his entirely spiritual ideas accepted.

Chapter Twelve

To the Christian Nobility

To His Most Illustrious, Most Mighty, and Imperial Majesty, and to the Christian Nobility of the German Nation, from Doctor Martin Luther.

Grace and power from God, Most Illustrious Majesty, and most gracious and dear lords.

It is not from sheer impertinence or rashness that I, one poor man, have taken it upon myself to address your worships. All the estates of Christendom, particularly in Germany, are now oppressed by distress and affliction, and this has stirred not only me but everybody else to cry out time and time again and to pray for help. It has even compelled me now at this time to cry aloud that God may inspire someone with his Spirit to lend a helping hand to this distressed and wretched nation. Often the councils have made some pretense at reformation, but their attempts have been cleverly frustrated by the guile of certain men, and things have gone from bad to worse. With God's help I intend to expose the wiles and wickedness of these men, so that they are shown up for what they are and may never again be so obstructive and destructive. God has given us a young man of noble birth as head of state,[1] and in him has awakened great hopes of good in many hearts. Presented with such an opportunity we ought to apply ourselves and use this time of grace profitably.

The first and most important thing to do in this matter is to prepare ourselves in all seriousness. We must not start something by trusting in great power or human reason, even if all the power in the world were ours. For God cannot and will not suffer that a good work begin by relying upon one's own power and reason. He dashes such works to the ground, they do no good at all. As it says in Psalm 33 [:16], "No king is saved by his great might and no lord is saved by the greatness of his strength." I fear that this is why the good emperors Frederick I[2] and Frederick III[3] and many other German emperors were in former times shamefully oppressed and trodden underfoot by the popes, although all the world feared the emperors. It may be that they relied on their own might more than on God, and therefore had to fall. What was it in our own times that raised the bloodthirsty Julius II[4] to such heights? Nothing else, I fear, except that France, the Germans, and Venice relied upon themselves. The children of Benjamin slew forty-two thousand Israelites[5] because the latter relied on their own strength, Judges 30 [:21].

That it may not so fare with us and our noble Charles, we must realize that in this matter we are not dealing with men, but with the princes of hell. These princes could fill the world with war and bloodshed, but war and bloodshed do not overcome them. We must tackle this job by renouncing trust in physical force and trusting humbly in God. We must seek God's help through earnest prayer and fix our minds on nothing else than the misery and distress of suffering Christendom without regard, to what evil men deserve. Otherwise, we may start the game with great prospects of success, but when we get into it the evil spirits will stir up such confusion that the whole world will swim in blood, and then nothing will come of it all. Let us act wisely, therefore, and in the fear of God. The more force we use, the greater our disaster if we do not act humbly and in the fear of God. If the popes and Romanists[6] have hitherto been able to set kings against each other by the devil's help, they may well be able to do it again if we were to go ahead without the help of God on our own strength and by our own cunning.

The Romanists have very cleverly built three walls around themselves. Hitherto they have protected themselves by these walls in such a way that no one has been able to reform them. As a result, the whole of Christendom has fallen abominably.

In the first place, when pressed by the temporal power they have made decrees and declared that the temporal power had no jurisdiction over them, but that, on the contrary, the spiritual power is above the temporal. In the second place, when the attempt is made to reprove them with the Scriptures, they raise the objection that only the pope may interpret the Scriptures. In the third place, if threatened with a council, their story is that no one may summon a council but the pope.

In this way they have cunningly stolen our three rods from us, that they may go unpunished. They have ensconced themselves within the safe stronghold of these three walls so that they can practice all the knavery and wickedness which we see today. Even when they have been compelled to hold a council they have weakened its power in advance by putting the princes under oath to let them remain as they were.[7] In addition, they have given the pope full authority over all decisions of a council, so that it is all the same whether there are many councils or no councils. They only deceive us with puppet shows and sham fights. They fear terribly for their skin in a really free council! They have so intimidated kings and princes with this technique that they believe it would be an offense against God not to be obedient to the Romanists in all their knavish and ghoulish deceits.[8]

May God help us, and give us just one of those trumpets with which the walls of Jericho were overthrown [9] to blast down these walls of straw and paper in the same way and set free the Christian rods for the punishment of sin, [and] bring to light the craft and deceit of the devil, to the end that through punishment we may reform ourselves and once more attain God's favor.

Let us begin by attacking the first wall. It is pure invention that pope, bishop, priests, and monks are called the spiritual estate while princes, lords, artisans, and farmers are called the temporal estate. This is indeed a piece of deceit and hypocrisy. Yet no one need be intimidated by it, and for this reason: all Christians are truly of the spiritual estate, and there is no difference among them except that of office. Paul says in I Corinthians 12 [:12–13] that we are all one body, yet every member has its own work by which it serves the others. This is because we all have one baptism, one gospel, one faith, and are all Christians alike; for baptism, gospel, and faith alone make us spiritual and a Christian people.

The pope or bishop anoints, shaves heads,[10] ordains, consecrates, and prescribes garb different from that of the laity, but he can never make a man into a Christian or into a spiritual man by so doing. He might well make a man into a hypocrite or a humbug and blockhead,[11] but never a Christian or a spiritual man. As far as that goes, we are all consecrated priests through baptism, as St. Peter says in I Peter 2 [:9], "You are a royal priesthood and a priestly realm." The Apocalypse says, "Thou hast made us to be priests and kings by thy blood" [Rev. 5:9–10]. The consecration by pope or bishop would never make a priest, and if we had no higher consecration than that which pope or bishop gives, no one could say mass or preach a sermon or give absolution.

Therefore, when a bishop consecrates it is nothing else than that in the place and stead of the whole community, all of whom have like power, he takes a person and charges him to exercise this power on behalf of the others. It is like ten brothers, all king's sons and equal heirs, choosing one of themselves to rule the inheritance in the interests of all. In one sense they are all kings and of equal power, and yet one of them is charged with the responsibility of ruling. To put it still more clearly: suppose a group of earnest Christian laymen were taken prisoner and set down in a desert without an episcopally ordained priest among them. And suppose they were to come to a common mind there and then in the desert and elect one of their number, whether he were married[12] or not, and charge him to baptize, say mass, pronounce absolution, and preach the gospel. Such a man would be as truly a priest as though he had been ordained by all the bishops and popes in the world. That is why in cases of necessity anyone can baptize and give absolution. This would be impossible if we were not all priests. Through canon law[13] the Romanists have almost destroyed and made unknown the wondrous grace and authority of baptism and justification. In times gone by Christians used to choose their bishops and priests in this way from among their own number, and they were confirmed in their office by the other bishops without all the fuss that goes on nowadays. St. Augustine,[14] Ambrose,[15] and Cyprian[16] each became [a bishop in this way].

Since those who exercise secular authority have been baptized with the same baptism, and have the same faith and the same gospel as the rest of us, we must admit that they are priests and bishops and we must regard their office as one which has a proper and useful place in the Christian community. For whoever comes out of the water of baptism can boast that he is already a consecrated priest, bishop, and pope, although of course it is not seemly that just anybody should exercise such office. Because we are all priests of equal standing, no one must push himself forward and take it upon himself, without our consent and election, to do that for which we all have equal authority. For no one dare take upon himself what is common to all without the authority and consent of the community. And should it happen that a person chosen for such office were deposed for abuse of trust, he would then be exactly what he was before. Therefore, a priest in Christendom is nothing else but an officeholder. As long as he holds office he takes precedence; where he is deposed, he is a peasant or a townsman like anybody else. Indeed, a priest is never a priest when he is deposed. But now the Romanists have invented *characteres indelebiles*[17] and say[18] that a deposed priest is nevertheless something different from a mere layman. They hold the illusion that a priest can never be anything other than a priest, or ever become a layman. All this is just contrived talk, and human regulation.

It follows from this argument that there is no true, basic difference between laymen and priests, princes and bishops, between religious and secular, except for the sake of office and work, but not for the sake of status. They are all of the spiritual estate, all are truly priests, bishops, and popes. But they do not all have the same work to do. Just as all priests and monks do not have the same work. This is the teaching of St. Paul in Romans 12 [:4–5] and I Corinthians 12 [:12] and in I Peter 2 [:9], as I have said above, namely, that we are all one body of Christ the Head, and all members one of another. Christ does not have two different bodies, one temporal, the other spiritual. There is but one Head and one body.

Therefore, just as those who are now called "spiritual," that is, priests, bishops, or popes, are neither different from other Christians nor superior to them, except that they are charged with the administration of the word of God and the sacraments, which is their work and office, so it is with the temporal authorities. They bear the sword and rod in their hand to punish the wicked and protect the good. A cobbler, a smith, a peasant—each has the work and office of his trade, and yet they are all alike consecrated priests and bishops. Further, everyone must benefit and serve every other by means of his own work or office so that in this way many kinds of work may be done for the bodily and spiritual welfare of the community, just as all the members of the body serve one another [I Cor. 12:14–26].

Consider for a moment how Christian is the decree which says that the temporal power is not above the "spiritual estate" and has no right to punish it.[19] That is as much as to say that the hand shall not help the eye when it suffers pain. Is it not unnatural, not to mention un-Christian, that one member does not help another and prevent its destruction? In fact, the more honorable the member, the more the others ought to help. I say therefore that since the temporal power is ordained of God to punish the wicked and protect the good, it should be left free to perform its office in the whole body of Christendom without restriction and without respect to persons, whether it affects pope, bishops, priests, monks, nuns, or anyone else. If it were right to say that the temporal power is inferior to all the spiritual estates (preacher, confessor, or any spiritual office), and so prevent the temporal power from doing its proper work, then the tailors, cobblers, stonemasons, carpenters, cooks, innkeepers, farmers, and all the temporal craftsmen should be prevented from providing pope, bishops, priests, and monks with shoes, clothes, house, meat and drink, as well as from paying them any tribute. But if these laymen are allowed to do their proper work without restriction, what then are the Romanist scribes doing with their own laws, which exempt them from the jurisdiction of the temporal Christian authority? It is just so that they can be free to do evil and fulfil what

St. Peter said, "False teachers will rise up among you who will deceive you, and with their false and fanciful talk, they will take advantage of you" [II Pet. 2:1–3].

For these reasons the temporal Christian authority ought to exercise its office without hindrance, regardless of whether it is pope, bishop, or priest whom it affects. Whoever is guilty, let him suffer. All that canon law has said to the contrary is the invention of Romanist presumption. For thus St. Paul says to all Christians, "Let every soul (I take that to mean the pope's soul also) be subject to the temporal authority; for it does not bear the sword in vain, but serves God by punishing the wicked and benefiting the good" [Rom. 13:1, 4]. St. Peter, too, says, "Be subject to all human ordinances for the sake of the Lord, who so wills it" [I Pet. 2:13, 15]. He has also prophesied in II Peter 2 [:1] that such men would arise and despise the temporal authority. This is exactly what has happened happened through the canon law.

So, then, I think this first paper wall is overthrown. Inasmuch as the temporal power has become a member of the Christian body it is a spiritual estate, even though its work is physical.[20] Therefore, its work should extend without hindrance to all the members of the whole body to punish and use force whenever guilt deserves or necessity demands, without regard to whether the culprit is pope, bishop, or priest. Let the Romanists hurl threats and bans about as they like. That is why guilty priests, when they are handed over to secular law, are first deprived of their priestly dignities.[21] This would not be right unless the secular sword previously had had authority over these priests by divine right. Moreover, it is intolerable that in canon law so much importance is attached to the freedom, life, and property of the clergy, as though the laity were not also as spiritual and as good Christians as they, or did not also belong to the church. Why are your life and limb, your property and honor, so cheap and mine not, inasmuch as we are all Christians and have the same baptism, the same faith, the same Spirit, and all the rest? If a priest is murdered, the whole country is placed under interdict.[22] Why not when a peasant is murdered? How does this great difference come about between two men who are both Christians? It comes from the laws and fabrications of men.

The second wall is still more loosely built and less substantial. The Romanists want to be the only masters of Holy Scripture, although they never learn a thing from the Bible all their life long. They assume the sole authority for themselves, and, quite unashamed, they play about with words before our very eyes, trying to persuade us that the pope cannot err in matters of faith,[23] regardless of whether he is righteous or wicked. Yet they cannot point to a single letter.[24] This is why so many heretical and un-Christian, even unnatural, ordinances stand in the canon law. But there is no need to talk about these ordinances at present. Since these Romanists think the Holy Spirit never leaves them, no matter how ignorant and wicked they are, they become bold and decree only what they want. And if what they claim were true, why have Holy Scripture at all? Of what use is Scripture? Let us burn the Scripture and be satisfied with the unlearned gentlemen at Rome who possess the Holy Spirit! And yet the Holy Spirit can be possessed only by pious hearts. If I had not read the words with my own eyes, I would not have believed it possible for the devil to have made such stupid claims at Rome, and to have won supporters for them.

But so as not to fight them with mere words, we will quote the Scriptures. St. Paul says in I Corinthians 14 [:30], "If something better is revealed to anyone, though he is already sitting and listening to another in God's word, then the one who is speaking shall hold his peace and give place." What would be the point of this commandment if we were compelled to believe only the man who does the talking, or the man who is at the top? Even Christ said in John 6 [:45] that all Christians shall be taught by God. If it were to happen that the pope and his cohorts were wicked and not true Christians, were not taught by God and were without understanding, and at the same time some obscure person had a right understanding, why should the people not follow the obscure man? Has the pope not erred many times? Who would help Christendom when the pope erred if we did not have somebody we could trust more than him, somebody who had the Scriptures on his side?

Therefore, their claim that only the pope may interpret Scripture is an outrageous fancied fable. They cannot produce a single letter [of Scripture] to maintain that the interpretation of Scripture or the confirmation of its interpretation belongs to the pope alone. They themselves have usurped this power. And although they allege that this power was given to St. Peter when the keys were given him, it is clear enough that the keys were not given to Peter alone but to the whole community. Further, the keys were not ordained for doctrine or government, but only for the binding or loosing of sin.[25] Whatever else or whatever more they arrogate to themselves on the basis of the keys is a mere fabrication. But Christ's words to Peter, "I have prayed for you that your faith fail not" [Luke 22:32], cannot be applied to the pope, since the majority of the popes have been without faith, as they must themselves confess. Besides, it is not only for Peter that Christ prayed, but also for all apostles and Christians, as he says in John 17 [:9, 20], "Father, I pray for those whom thou hast given me, and not for these only, but for all who believe on me through their word." Is that not clear enough?

Just think of it! The Romanists must admit that there are among us good Christians who have the true faith, spirit, understanding, word, and mind of Christ. Why, then, should we reject the word and understanding of good Christians and follow the pope, who has neither faith nor the Spirit? To follow the pope would be to deny the whole faith[26] as well as the Christian church. Again, if the article, "I believe in one holy Christian church," is correct, then the pope cannot be the only one who is right. Otherwise, we would have to confess,[27] "I believe in the pope at Rome": This would reduce the Christian church to one man, and be nothing else than a devilish and hellish error.

❋ ❋ ❋ ❋

The third wall falls of itself when the first two are down. When the pope acts contrary to the Scriptures, it is our duty to stand by the Scriptures, to reprove him and to constrain him, according to the word of Christ, Matthew 18 [:15–17], "If your brother sins against you, go and tell it to him, between you and him alone; if he does not listen to you, then take one or two others with you; if he does not listen to them, tell it to the church; if he does not listen to the church, consider him a heathen." Here every member is commanded to care for every other. How much more should we do this when the member that does evil is responsible for the government of the church, and by his evil-doing is the cause of much harm and offense to the rest! But if I am to accuse him before the church, I must naturally call the church together.

The Romanists have no basis in Scripture for their claim that the pope alone has the right to call or confirm a council.[28] This is just their own ruling, and it is only valid as long as it is not harmful to Christendom or contrary to the laws of God. Now when the pope deserves punishment, this ruling no longer obtains, for not to punish him by authority of a council is harmful to Christendom.

Thus we read in Acts 15 that it was not St. Peter who called the Apostolic Council but the apostles and elders. If then that right had belonged to St. Peter alone, the council would not have been a Christian council, but a heretical *conciliabulum*.[29] Even the Council of Nicaea, the most famous of all councils, was neither called nor confirmed by the bishop of Rome, but by the emperor Constantine.[30] Many other emperors after him have done the same, and yet these councils were the most Christian of all.[31] But if the pope alone has the right to convene councils, then these councils would all have been heretical. Further, when I examine the councils the pope did summon, I find that they did nothing of special importance.

Therefore, when necessity demands it, and the pope is an offense to Christendom, the first man who is able should, as a true member of the whole body, do what he can to bring about a truly free council.[32] No one can do this so well as the temporal authorities, especially since they are also fellow-Christians, fellow-priests, fellow-members of the spiritual estate, fellow-lords over all things. Whenever it is necessary or profitable they ought to exercise the office and work which they have received from God over everyone. Would it not be unnatural if a fire broke out in a city and everybody were to stand by and let it burn on and on and consume everything that could burn because nobody had the authority of the mayor, or because, perhaps, the fire broke out in the mayor's house? In such a situation is it not the duty of every citizen to arouse and summon the rest? How much more should this be done in the spiritual city of Christ if a fire of offense breaks out, whether in the papal government, or anywhere else! The same argument holds if an enemy were to attack the city. The man who first aroused the others deserves honor and gratitude. Why, then, should he not deserve honor who makes known the presence of the enemy from hell and rouses Christian people and calls them together?

But all their boasting about an authority which dare not be opposed amounts to nothing at all. Nobody in Christendom has authority to do injury or to forbid the resisting of injury. There is no authority in the church except to promote good. Therefore, if the pope were to use his authority to prevent the calling of a free council, thereby preventing the improvement of the church, we should have regard neither for him nor for his authority. And if he were to hurl his bans and thunderbolts, we should despise his conduct as that of a madman. On the contrary, we should excommunicate him and drive him out as best we could, relying completely upon God. This presumptuous authority of his is nothing. He does not even have such authority. He is quickly defeated by a single text of Scripture, where Paul says to the Corinthians, "God has given us authority not to ruin Christendom, but to build it up" [II Cor. 10:8]. Who wants to leap over the hurdle of this text? It is the power of the devil and of Antichrist which resists the things that serve to build up Christendom. Such power is not to be obeyed, but rather resisted with life, property, and with all our might and main.

❋ ❋ ❋ ❋ ❋

Now, although I am too insignificant a man to make propositions for the improvement of this dreadful state of affairs, nevertheless I shall sing my fool's song through to the end and say, so far as I am able, what could and should be done, either by the temporal authority or by a general council.

1. Every prince, every noble, every city should henceforth forbid their subjects to pay annates to Rome and should abolish them entirely. The pope has broken the agreement and made the annates a robbery to the injury and shame of the whole German nation. He gives them to his friends, sells them for huge sums of money, and uses them to endow offices. In so doing he has lost his right to them and deserves punishment. Consequently the temporal authority is under obligation to protect the innocent and prevent injustice, as Paul teaches in Romans 13, and St. Peter in I Peter 2 [:14], and even the canon law in Case 16, Question 7, in the *de filiis* clause.[33] Thus it has come about that they say to the pope and his crowd, "*Tu ora,* thou shalt pray"; to the emperor and his servants, "*Tu protege,* thou shalt protect"; to the common man, "*Tu labora,* thou shalt work,*" not however as though everyone were not to pray, protect, and work. For the man who is diligent in his work prays, protects, and works in all that he does. But everyone should have his own special work assigned him.

2. Since the pope with his Romanist practices—his commends, coadjutors, reservations, *gratiae expectativae,*[34] papal months, incorporations, unions, pensions, pallia, chancery rules, and such knavery—usurps for himself all the German foundations without authority and right, and gives and sells them to foreigners at Rome who do nothing for Germany in return, and since he robs the local bishops of their rights and makes mere ciphers and dummies of them, and thereby acts contrary to his own canon law, common sense, and reason, it has finally reached the point where the livings and benefices are sold to coarse,

unlettered asses and ignorant knaves at Rome out of sheer greed. Pious and learned people do not benefit from the service or skill of these fellows. Consequently the poor German people must go without competent and learned prelates and go from bad to worse.

For this reason the Christian nobility should set itself against the pope as against a common enemy and destroyer of Christendom for the salvation of the poor souls who perish because of this tyranny. The Christian nobility should ordain, order, and decree that henceforth no further benefice shall be drawn into the hands of Rome, and that hereafter no appointment shall be obtained there in any manner whatsoever, but that the benefices should be dragged from this tyrannical authority and kept out of his reach. The nobility should restore to the local bishops their right and responsibility to administer the benefices in the German nation to the best of their ability. And when a lackey comes along from Rome he should be given a strict order to keep out, to jump into the Rhine or the nearest river, and give the Romish ban with all its seals and letters a nice, cool dip. If this happened they would sit up and take notice in Rome. They would not think that the Germans are always dull and drunk, but have really become Christian again. They would realize that the Germans do not intend to permit the holy name of Christ, in whose name all this knavery and destruction of souls goes on, to be scoffed and scorned any longer, and that they have more regard for God's honor than for the authority of men.

3. An imperial law should be issued that no bishop's cloak[35] and no confirmation of any dignity whatsoever shall henceforth be secured from Rome, but that the ordinance of the most holy and famous Council of Nicaea[36] be restored. This ordinance decreed that a bishop shall be confirmed by the two nearest-bishops or by the archbishop. If the pope breaks the statutes of this and of all other councils, what is the use of holding councils? Who has given him the authority to despise the decisions of councils and tear them to shreds like this?

This is all the more reason for us to depose all bishops, archbishops, and primates and make ordinary parsons of them, with only the pope as their superior, as he now is. The pope allows no proper authority or responsibility to the bishops, archbishops, and primates. He usurps everything for himself and lets them keep only the name and the empty title. It has even gone so far that by papal exemption[37] the monasteries, abbots, and prelates as well are excepted from the regular authority of the bishops. Consequently there is no longer any order in Christendom. The inevitable result of all this is what has happened already: relaxation of punishment, and license to do evil all over the world. I certainly fear that the pope may properly be called "the man of sin" [II Thess. 2:3]. Who but the pope can be blamed for there being no discipline, no punishment, no rule, no order in Christendom? By his usurpation of power he ties the prelates' hands and takes away their rod of discipline. He opens his hands to all those set under him, and gives away or sells their release.[38]

Lest the pope complain that he is being robbed of his authority, it should be decreed that in those cases where the primates or the archbishops are unable to settle a case, or when a dispute arises between them, then the matter should be laid before the pope, but not every little thing. It was done this way in former times, and this was the way the famous Council of Nicaea[39] decreed. Whatever can be settled without the pope, then, should be so settled so that his holiness is not burdened with such minor matters, but gives himself to prayer, study, and the care of all Christendom. This is what he claims to do. This is what the apostles did. They said in Acts 6 [:2–4], "It is not right that we should leave the Word of God and serve tables, but we will hold to preaching and prayer, and set others over that work." But now Rome stands for nothing else than the despising of the gospel and prayer, and for the serving of tables, that is, temporal things. The rule of the apostles and of the pope have as much in common as Christ has with Lucifer, heaven with hell, night with day. Yet the pope is called "Vicar of Christ" and "Successor to the Apostles."

9. The pope should have no authority over the emperor, except the right to anoint and crown him at the altar just as a bishop crowns a king.[40] We should never again yield to that devilish pride which requires the emperor to kiss the pope's feet, or sit at his feet, or, as they say, hold his stirrup or the bridle of his mule when he mounts to go riding. Still less should he do homage and swear faithful allegiance to the pope as the popes brazenly demand as though they had a right to it. The chapter *Solite,*[41] which sets papal authority above imperial authority, is not worth a cent,[42] and the same goes for all those who base their authority on it or pay any deference to it. For it does nothing else than force the holy words of God, and wrest them out of their true meaning to conform to their own fond imaginations, as I have shown in a Latin treatise.[43]

This most extreme, arrogant, and wanton presumption of the pope has been devised by the devil, who under cover of this intends to usher in the Antichrist and raise the pope above God, as many are now doing and even have already done. It is not proper for the pope to exalt himself above the temporal authorities, except in spiritual offices such as preaching and giving absolution. In other matters the pope is subject to the crown, as Paul and Peter teach in Romans 13 [:1–7] and I Peter 2 [:13], and as I have explained above.

The pope is not a vicar of Christ in heaven, but only of Christ as he walked the earth. Christ in heaven, in the form of a ruler, needs no vicar, but sits on his throne and sees everything, does everything, knows everything, and has all power. But Christ needs a vicar in the form of a servant, the form in which he went about on earth, working, preaching, suffering, and dying. Now the Romanists turn all that upside down. They take the heavenly and kingly form from Christ and give it to the pope, and leave the form of a servant to perish completely. He might almost be the Counter-Christ, whom the Scriptures call Antichrist, for all his nature, work, and pretensions run counter to Christ and only blot out Christ's nature and destroy his work.

14. We also see how the priesthood has fallen, and how many a poor priest is overburdened with wife and child, his conscience troubled. Yet no one does anything to help him, though he could easily be helped. Though pope and bishops may let things go on as they are, and allow what is heading for ruin to go to ruin, yet I will redeem my conscience and open my mouth freely, whether it vexes pope, bishop, or anybody else. And this is what I say: according to the institution of Christ and the apostles, every city should have a priest or bishop, as St. Paul clearly says in Titus 1 [:5]. And this priest should not be compelled to live without a wedded wife, but should be permitted to have one, as St. Paul writes in I Timothy 3 [:2, 4] and Titus 1 [:8–7] saying, "A bishop shall be a man who is blameless, and the husband of but one wife, whose children are obedient and well behaved," etc. According to St. Paul, and also St. Jerome,[44] a bishop and a priest are one and the same thing. But of bishops as they now are the Scriptures know nothing. Bishops have been appointed by ordinance of the Christian church, so that one of them may have authority over several priests.

So then, we clearly learn from the Apostle that it should be the custom for every town to choose from among the congregation a learned and pious citizen, entrust to him the office of the ministry, and support him at the expense of the congregation. He should be free to marry or not. He should have several priests or deacons, also free to marry or not as they choose, to help him minister to the congregation and the community with word and sacrament, as is still the practice in the Greek church. Because there was sometimes so much persecution and controversy with heretics after the apostolic age, there were many holy fathers who voluntarily abstained from matrimony that they might better devote themselves to study and be prepared at any moment for death or battle.

But the Roman See has interfered and out of its own wanton wickedness made a universal commandment forbidding priests to marry.[45] This was done at the bidding of the devil, as St. Paul declares in I Timothy 4 [:1, 3], "There shall come teachers who bring the devil's teaching and forbid marriage." Unfortunately so much misery has arisen from this that tongue could never tell it. Moreover, this caused the Greek church to separate,[46] and discord, sin, shame, and scandal were increased no end. But this always happens when the devil starts and carries on. What, then, shall we do about it?

My advice is, restore freedom to everybody and leave every man free to marry or not to marry. But then there would have to be a very different kind of government and administration of church property; the whole canon law would have to be demolished; and few benefices would be allowed to get into Roman hands. I fear that greed is a cause of this wretched, unchaste celibacy. As a result, everyone has wanted to become a priest and everyone wants his son to study for the priesthood, not with the idea of living in chastity, for that could be done outside the priesthood. [Their idea is to] be supported in temporal things without work or worry, contrary to God's command in Genesis 3 [:19] that "in the sweat of your face you shall eat your bread." The Romanists have colored this to mean that their labor is to pray and say mass.

I am not referring here to popes, bishops, canons, and monks. God has not instituted these offices. They have taken these burdens upon themselves, so they will have to bear them themselves. I want to speak only of the ministry which God has instituted, the responsibility of which is to minister word and sacrament to a congregation, among whom they reside. Such ministers should be given liberty by a Christian council to marry to avoid temptation and sin. For since God has not bound them, no one else ought to bind them or can bind them, even if he were an angel from heaven, let alone a pope. Everything that canon law decrees to the contrary is mere fable and idle talk.

Furthermore, I advise anyone henceforth being ordained a priest or anything else that he in no wise vow to the bishop that he will remain celibate. On the contrary, he should tell the bishop that he has no right whatsoever to require such a vow, and that it is a devilish tyranny to make such a demand. But if anyone is compelled to say, or even wants to say, "so far as human frailty permits," as indeed many do, let him frankly interpret these same words in a negative manner to mean "I do not promise chastity." For human frailty does not permit a man to live chastely, but only the strength of angels and the power of heaven. In this way he should keep his conscience free of all vows.

I will advise neither for nor against marrying or remaining single. I leave that to common Christian order and to everyone's better judgment. I will not conceal my real opinion or withhold comfort from that pitiful band who with wives and children have fallen into disgrace and whose consciences are burdened because people call them priests' whores and their children priests' children. As the court-jester[47] I say this openly.

You will find many a pious priest against whom nobody has anything to say except that he is weak and has come to shame with a woman. From the bottom of their hearts both are of a mind to live together in lawful wedded love, if only they could do it with a clear conscience. But even though they both have to bear public shame, the two are certainly married in the sight of God. And I say that where they are so minded and live together, they should appeal anew to their conscience. Let the priest take and keep her as his lawful wedded wife, and live honestly with her as her husband, whether the pope likes it or not, whether it be against canon or human law. The salvation of your soul is more important than the observance of tyrannical, arbitrary, and wanton laws which are not necessary to salvation or commanded by God. You should do as the children of Israel did who stole from the Egyptians the wages they had earned;[48] or as a servant who steals from his wicked master the wages he has earned: steal from the pope your wedded wife and child! Let the man who has faith enough to venture this, boldly follow me. I shall not lead him astray. Though I do not have the authority of a pope, I do have the authority of a Christian to advise and help my neighbor against sins and temptations. And that not without cause or reason!

First, not every priest can do without a woman, not only on account of human frailty, but much more on account of keeping house. If he then may keep a woman, and the pope allows that, and yet may not have her in marriage, what is that but leaving a man and a woman alone together and yet forbidding them to fall? It is just like putting straw and fire together and forbidding them to smoke or burn!

Second, the pope has as little power to command this as he has to forbid eating, drinking, the natural movement of the bowels, or growing fat. Therefore, no one is bound to keep it, but the pope is responsible for all the sins which are committed against this ordinance, for all the souls which are lost, and for all the consciences which are confused and tortured because of this ordinance. he has strangled so many wretched souls with this devilish rope that he has long deserved to be driven out of this world. Yet it is my firm belief that God has been more gracious to many souls at their last hour than the pope was to them in their whole lifetime. No good has ever come nor will come out of the papacy and its laws.

Third, although the law of the pope is against it, nevertheless, when the estate of matrimony has been entered against the pope's law, then his law is already at an end and is no longer valid. For God's commandment, which enjoins that no man shall put husband and wife asunder [Matt. 19:6], is above the pope's law. And the commandments of God must not be broken or neglected because of the pope's commandment. Nevertheless, many foolish jurists, along with the pope, have devised impediments and thereby prevented, broken, and brought confusion to the estate of matrimony so that God's commandment concerning it has altogether disappeared.[49] Need I say more? In the entire canon law of the pope there are not even two lines which could instruct a devout Christian, and, unfortunately, there are so many mistaken and dangerous laws that nothing would be better than to make a bonfire of it.[50]

But if you say that marriage of the clergy would give offense, and that the pope must first grant dispensation, I reply that whatever offense there is in it is the fault of the Roman See which has established such laws with no right and against God. Before God and the Holy Scriptures marriage of the clergy is no offense. Moreover, if the pope can grant dispensations from his greedy and tyrannical laws for money, then every Christian can grant dispensations from these very same laws for God's sake and for the salvation of souls. For Christ has set us free from all man-made laws, especially when they are opposed to

God and the salvation of souls, as St. Paul teaches in Galatians 5 [:1] and I Corinthians 10 [:23].

Endnotes

1. Charles V, who had been elected emperor in 1519 when only twenty years of age, and whom Luther appeared before at the Diet of Worms in 1521.
2. Emperor Frederick Barbarossa (1152 -1190).
3. Frederick II (1212-1250), grandson of Barbarossa and last of the great Hohenstaufen emperors, died under excommunication.
4. Pope Julius II (1503-1513) was notorious for his unscrupulous use of political power. Continually involved in war, he led his armies in person and was "the scourge of Italy."
5. Luther's memory is not accurate here. The Book of Judges speaks of twenty-two thousand.
6. Advocates of papal supremacy.
7. Luther alludes here to the failure of the conciliar movement to reform the church. The movement failed chiefly because the papacy refused to submit to the authority of the council. Furthermore, the papacy refused to co-operate in the convening of councils unless the secular powers first swore not to deprive the pope of his authority. In brief, the papacy refused to submit to the authority of either church or empire. Luther felt that since the church had failed to take the initiative in the matter of reform, the emperor should do so.
8. *Spugnissen*, literally, "ghosts." The sense of the passage is that the Romanists have frightened the world with threats of purgatory and hell.
9. Cf. Josh. 6.20.
10. I.e., confers tonsure.
11. *Olgotzen.*
12. *Ehelich. PE* and other English translations also render this word as "married." It can, however, also mean "legitimately born." Karl Benrath notes that according to canon law only one born in wedlock may receive ordination as a priest. Cf. *An den christlichen Adel deutscher Nation von des christlichen Standes Besserung .... Bearbeitet, sowie mit Einleitung und Erläuterungen versehen von Karl Benrath* (Halle: Verein für Reformationsgeschichte, 1884), p. *83, n. 7.*
13. Canon law, which Luther throughout this treatise and elsewhere calls the "spiritual law," is a general name for the decrees of councils and the decisions of the popes collected in the *Corpus Iuris Canonici.* It comprised the whole body of church law and embodied in legal forms the medieval theory of papal absolutism, which accounts for the bitterness with which Luther speaks of it, especially in this treatise. Cf. PE 2, 67, n. 2.

14. Augustine, bishop of Hippo (395–430).

15. Ambrose, bishop of Milan (374–397), was elected to the office by the people of Milan, even though he was not yet baptized.

16. Cyprian, bishop of Carthage (247–258), was also elected to the episcopate by the laity.

17. The *character indelebilis* or "indelible mark," was given authoritative formulation in the bull *Exultate Deo* (1439). Eugene IV, summing up the decrees of the Council of Florence, wrote: "Among these sacraments there are three—baptism, confirmation, and orders—which indelibly impress upon the soul a character, i.e., a certain spiritual mark which distinguishes them from the rest" (Carl Mirbt, *Quellen zur Geschichte des Papstums* [2nd ed.], No. 150). The Council of Trent, in its twenty-third session, July 15, 1563 (Mirbt, *op. cit.,* No. 312), defined the correct Roman teaching as follows: "Since in the sacrament of orders, as in baptism and confirmation, a character is impressed which cannot be destroyed or taken away, the Holy Synod justly condemns the opinion of those who assert that the priests of the New Testament have only temporary power, and that those once rightly ordained can again be made laymen, if they do not exercise the ministry of the Word of God." Cf *PE* 2, 68, n. 5.

18. *Schwetzen*; literally, "to chatter nonsense."

19. The sharp distinction drawn by the Roman church between clergy and laity made possible the contention that the clergy was exempt from the jurisdiction of the civil courts. This is known as *privilegium fori*, i.e., "benefit of clergy." It was further claimed that the governing of the clergy and the administration of church property were matters for church authorities, and that lay rulers could not make or enforce laws which affected the church in any way. Cf. *PE 2,* 70, n.1.

20. I.e., temporal.

21. Church authorities insisted that clergy charged with infractions of the laws of the state first be tried in ecclesiastical courts. Priests found guilty by such courts were deprived of their priesthood and were surrendered to the temporal authorities. *PE* 2, 71, n.1.

22. The interdict prohibits the administration of the sacraments and the other rites of the church within a given territory. Its use was not uncommon in the Middle Ages, and at the height of papal power it proved an effective means of bringing rulers to terms. Innocent III imposed the interdict upon England in 1208, during the reign of King John. Interdicts of more limited local extent were quite frequent. The use of the interdict for trifling infractions of church law was a subject of complaint at the Diet of Worms in 1521 and of Nürnberg in 1524. Cf. *PE* 2, 72, n.1.

23. The doctrine of papal infallibility was never officially sanctioned in the Middle Ages, but the claim was repeatedly made by the champions of papal power, e.g., Augustinus Triumphus (d. 1328) in his *Summa de potestate Papae*. In his attack

on the *Ninety-five Theses (Dialogus de potestate Papae,* December, 1517) Sylvester Prierias had asserted, "The supreme pontiff cannot err when giving a decision as pontiff, i.e., when speaking officially [*ex officio*]"; and also, "Whoever does not rest upon the teaching of the Roman church and the supreme pontiff as an infallible rule of faith, from which even Holy Scripture draws its vigor and authority, is a heretic" (*EA Var. arg.* 1, 348). In the *Epitome* Prierias had said, "Even though the pope as an individual [*singularis persona*] can do wrong and hold a wrong faith, nevertheless as pope he cannot give a wrong decision" (*WA* 6, 337). Cf. *PE* 2, 73, n. 5.

24. I.e., a single letter of Scripture to support their claim.
25. Matt. 16:19, 18:18, and John 20:23. Throughout his career Luther dealt with the office of the keys. He first mentioned it in 1517 in his *Ninety-five Theses* (*LW* 31, 27, 31) and devoted a substantial portion of his last treatise *Against the Roman Papacy, An Institution of the Devil* (1545) to a discussion of the keys *LW* 41, 315–320 *passim*). His clearest and most extensive treatment was set forth in his 1530 treatise *The Keys* (*LW* 40, 321–377).
26. Literally, "the creed," referring to the Apostles' Creed.
27. *Beten;* literally, "to pray."
28. This is another contention of Prierias. On November 28, 1518, Luther appealed his cause from the decision of the pope, which he could foresee would be adverse, to the decision of a council to be held at some future time. In the *Epitome* Prierias discusses this appeal, asserting among other things that "when there is one undisputed pontiff, it belongs to him alone to call a council," and that "the decrees of councils neither bind nor hold [*nullum ligant vet astringent*] unless they are confirmed by authority of the Roman pontiff." *WA* 6, 335; *PE* 2, 77, n.1.
29. A mere gathering of people as opposed to a *consilium,* i.e., a valid council.
30. The Council of Nicaea (325), the first general council, was convened by Constantine to settle the Arian controversy on the relation of Christ to God. Luther's contention is historically correct.
31. Luther is referring to the first four ecumenical councils: Nicaea, Constantinople (381), Ephesus (432), and Chalcedon (451).
32. A council free of papal control. Cf. note 7.
33. Luther errs here. The clause is not *de filiis,* but *Filiis vel nepotibus.* The clause provides that in case the income from endowments bequeathed to the church is misused, and appeals to the bishop and archbishop fail to correct the misuse, the heirs of the testator may appeal to the royal courts. Luther wants to apply this same principle to the annates. Cf. *PE* 2, 99, n. 3.
34. Promises to bestow livings not yet vacant. Complaints of the evils arising out of the practice were heard continually after 1416, and were made at Worms in 1521. CF *PE* 2,100, n. 4.
35. The pallium.

36. Luther refers to canon 4 of this council. Cf. *PE* 2, 101, n. 3.

37. "Exemption" was the practice by which monastic houses were withdrawn from the jurisdiction of the bishops and made directly subject to the pope. Apparently the practice originated in the tenth century with the famous monastery of Cluny, but it was almost universal in the case of the houses of the mendicant orders. It was a constant subject of complaint by the bishops, and the Fifth Lateran Council passed a decree (1516) abolishing all monastic exemptions. This decree seems not to have been effective. Cf. *PE* 2, 102, n. 1. Cf. also the fuller explanation in Benrath, *op. cit.*, p. 97, n. 42.

38. I.e., release from their lawful superiors.

39. A reference to canon 5 of the Council of Sardica (343), which was later incorporated in canon law as a canon of Nicaea. Cf. *PE* 2, 102, n. 4.

40. Since the coronation of Charlemagne in 800 the German Empire had been regarded as the continuation of the Roman Empire, a fiction fostered by the popes. The right to crown an emperor was held to be the prerogative of the pope. Cf. *PE* 2, 108, n. 2.

41. *Decretalium D. Gregorii Papae IX,* lib. i, tit. XXXIII, C. VI. *CIC* 2, col. 196.

42. *Heller,* a coin of little value.

43. *On the Power of the Pope (de potestate papae)* (1520). *WA* 2, 217.

44. Cf. Luther's understanding of I Cor. 4:1 expressed in *Concerning the Ministry (LW* 40, 35), The reference is to Jerome's *Commentary on Titus* 1:71. *MPL* 26, 562; cf. also 22, 656.

45. The first definitive and documented canon to prescribe and enforce clerical celibacy was that of Pope Siricius in 385. Cf. Henry Charles Lea, *History of Sacerdotal Celibacy in the Christian Church* (revised 3rd ed.; New York: The Macmillan Co., 1907), 1, 64.

46. The controversy over celibacy was involved in the schism between the Greek and Roman churches. Cf. *PE* 2, 120, n. 1.

47. Luther had cast himself in this role in the introduction.

48. Cf. Exod. 12:35–36.

49. The laws that governed marriage were entirely ecclesiastical and prohibited the marriage of blood relatives as far as the seventh degree of consanguinity. In 1204 the prohibition was restricted by the Fourth Lateran Council to the first four degrees; lawful marriage within these degrees was possible only by dispensation, which was not difficult to secure by those willing to pay for it. The relation of godparents to godchildren was looked upon as a "spiritual consanguinity" which might serve as a bar to lawful marriage. Cf. Benrath, *op. cit.*, p. 103, n. 74.

50. This is exactly what Luther did. A copy of the canon law was burned with the papal bull of excommunication on December 10, 1520.

Act in Restraint of Appeals (1533) and the Act of Supremacy (1534)

The Act of Appeals *was a necessary part of Henry VIII's divorce and became an important element of both the English reformation and English identity. Having failed to procure a divorce from Pope Clement VII, Henry moved his case against Catherine of Aragon to the English ecclesiastical courts. In January 1533 he secretly married Anne Boleyn, anticipating a favorable response from the court. Even with a divorce from the English court, however, Catherine could appeal her case back to Rome, and the* Act in Restraint of Appeals *was designed to forestall such a possibility. Its famous opening line declared ringingly that "this realm of England is an empire" and the act went on to proclaim England's independence from any outside power, whether temporal or, more to the point, spiritual. The* Act *therefore recognized the independence of the English church from Rome and laid out the way in which ecclesiastical causes would be dealt with within the kingdom. Apart from its content, the* Act of Appeals *marks the growth of the importance of parliament as a vehicle for change and the beginning of England's reformation through statute.*

While the Act *was making its way through parliament, Convocation found that the pope could not sanction marriage with a brother's widow (the basis of Henry's case) and on May 23, 1533 Henry's marriage to Catherine was declared null and void. A few days later his marriage to Anne Boleyn was declared valid, and on June 1, 1533 she was crowned queen. The following year the* Act of Supremacy *complemented the* Act of Appeals *by confirming the king's position as head of the church in England.*

Chapter Thirteen

4. Prohibition of Appeals to Rome

The prohibition of appeals to Rome grew inevitably out of the Divorce Case. In January, 1533, the King had been secretly married to Anne Boleyn, in anticipation of a judgment in his favour to be pronounced by the English ecclesiastical courts; and it was important in that event to prevent the case of Queen Catharine being carried to Rome by way of appeal.

(1) Act in Restraint of Appeals, 1533

This Act, which was passed through Parliament in spite of some opposition in the Lower House, is an historical landmark of great importance, for the preamble embodies a view of the relations of Church and State on which all subsequent legislation has proceeded, down to modern times. It declares the realm of England to be an empire, and asserts in the most formal manner the insular independence of the nation-church within the nation-state. It should be noted that the word "empire" is not here used in the modern sense, still less in the sense in which we speak of the "empire" of the Caesars. The British Empire and the Roman Empire differ in important respects, but they are alike in this that they were built up from within outwards by means of a great expansion. The "empire" of Henry VIII is the result of the opposite process; it is the nation-state contracting itself upon its insularity. The object of the statute is to deny the subjection of the insular power to any external authority, temporal or spiritual, and it thus embodies the fundamental principle of Henry VIII's Reformation. All spiritual causes concerning wills, marriage, and tithe are to be finally adjudged and determined within the realm, appeals being carried from the archdeacon to the bishop of the diocese, and from the bishop to the archbishop of the province, save in causes touching the King, which might be carried to "the spiritual prelates and other abbots and priors" of the Upper House of Convocation. This Act was subsequently modified by the Act for the Submission of the Clergy of 1534, which provided that a final appeal from the Archbishop's Court should lie to the King in Chancery, who should appoint a special commission, "like as in case of appeal from the Admiral Court," to hear and determine each case; and the same procedure was to be adopted in the case of appeals from monasteries exempt, which had hitherto been entitled to appeal direct to the see of Rome. These special commissions appointed ad hoc were called "Courts of Delegates," the term being taken from the corresponding procedure of the Admiral's Court. While the Act of Appeals was pending, Convocation was persuaded or driven to admit that the Pope could not by dispensation sanction a marriage with a brother's widow, and on May 23, 1533, Cranmer, sitting in his archiepiscopal court at Dunstable, pronounced the marriage with Catharine of Aragon to be null and void. At Lambeth, five days later, after a secret enquiry, he found the marriage already contracted with Anne Boleyn to be valid, and on Whitsunday, June 1, she was crowned queen.

*An Act that the Appeals in such cases as have been used
to be pursued to the See of Rome shall not be from
henceforth had nor used but within this Realm*

Where by divers sundry old authentic histories and chronicles it is manifestly declared and expressed that this realm of England is an empire[1], and so hath been accepted in the world, governed by one Supreme Head and King having the dignity and royal estate of the imperial Crown of the same, unto whom a body politic, compact of all sorts and degrees of people divided in terms and by names of Spiritualty and Temporalty, be bounden and owe to bear next to God a natural and humble obedience; he being also institute and furnished by the goodness and sufferance of Almighty God with plenary, whole, and entire power, preeminence, authority, prerogative, and jurisdiction to render and yield justice and final determination to all manner of folk resiants[2] or subjects within this his realm, in all causes, matters, debates, and contentions happening to occur, insurge, or begin within the limits thereof, without restraint or provocation to any foreign princes or potentates of the world: the body spiritual whereof having power when any cause of the law divine happened to come in question or of spiritual learning, then it was declared, interpreted, and shewed by that part of the said body politic called the Spiritualty, now being usually called the English Church, which always hath been reputed and also found of that sort that both for knowledge, integrity, and sufficiency of number, it hath been always thought and is also at this hour sufficient and meet of itself, without the intermeddling of any exterior person or persons, to declare and determine all such doubts and to administer all such offices and duties as to their rooms spiritual doth appertain; For the due administration whereof and to keep them from corruption and sinister affection the King's most noble progenitors, and the antecessors of the nobles of this realm, have sufficiently endowed the said Church both with honour and possessions: And the laws temporal for trial of propriety of lands and goods, and for the conservation of the people of this realm in unity and peace without ravin or spoil, was and yet is administered, adjudged, and executed by sundry judges and administers[3] of the other part of the said body politic called the Temporalty, and both their authorities and jurisdictions do conjoin together in the due administration of justice the one to help the other: And whereas the King his most noble progenitors, and the Nobility and Commons of this said realm, at divers and sundry Parliaments as well in the time of King Edward the First[4], Edward the Third[5], Richard the Second,[6] Henry the Fourth,[7] and other noble kings of this realm, made sundry ordinances, laws, statutes, and provisions for the entire and sure conservation of the prerogatives, liberties, and preeminences of the said imperial Crown of this realm, and of the jurisdictions spiritual and temporal of the same, to keep it from the annoyance as well of the see of Rome as from the authority of other foreign potentates attempting the diminution or violation thereof as often and from time to time as any such annoyance or attempt might be known or espied: And notwithstanding the said good estatutes and ordinances made in the time of the King's most noble progenitors in preservation of the authority and prerogative of the said imperial Crown as is aforesaid, yet nevertheless since the making of the said good statutes and ordinances divers and sundry inconveniences and dangers not provided for plainly by the said former acts, statutes, and ordinances have risen and sprung by reason of appeals sued out of this realm to the see of Rome, in causes testamentary, causes of matrimony and divorces, right of tithes, oblations, and obventions,[8] not only to the great inquietation, vexation, trouble, costs, and charges of the King's Highness and many of his subjects and resiants in this his realm, but also to the great delay and let to the true and speedy determination of the said causes, for so much as the parties appealing to the said court of Rome most commonly do the same for the delay of justice: And forasmuch as the great distance of way is so far out of this realm, so that the necessary proofs nor the true knowledge of the cause can neither there be so well known nor the witnesses there so well examined as within this realm, so that the parties grieved by means of the said appeals be most times without remedy: In consideration whereof the King's Highness, his Nobles and Commons, considering the great enormities, dangers, long delays, and hurts that as well to his Highness as to his said nobles, subjects, commons, and resiants of this his realm in the said causes testamentary, causes of matrimony and divorces, tithes, oblations, and obventions do daily ensue, doth therefore byhis royal assent and by the assent of the Lords spiritual and temporal and the Commons in this present Parliament assembled and by authority of the same, enact, establish, and ordain that all causes testamentary, causes of matrimony and divorces, rights of tithes, oblations, and obventions, the knowledge whereof by the goodness of princes of this realm and by the laws and customs of the same appertaineth to the spiritual jurisdiction of this realm already commenced, moved, depending, being, happening, or hereafter coming in contention, debate, or question within this realm or within any the King's dominions or marches of the same or elsewhere, whether they concern the King our Sovereign Lord, his heirs or successors, or any other subjects or resiants within the same of what degree soever they be, shall be from henceforth heard, examined, discussed, clearly finally and definitively adjudged and determined, within the King's jurisdiction and authority and not elsewhere, in such courts spiritual and temporal of the same as the natures, conditions, and qualities of the causes and matters aforesaid in contention or hereafter happening in contention shall require, without having any respect to any custom, use, or sufferance in hindrance, let, or prejudice of the same or to any other thing used or suffered to the contrary thereof by any other manner person or persons in any manner of wise; any foreign inhibitions, appeals, sentences, summons, citations, suspensions, interdictions, excommunications, restraints, judgments, or any other process or impediments of what natures, names, qualities, or conditions soever they be, from the see of Rome or any other foreign courts or potentates of the world, or from and out of this realm or any other the King's dominions or marches of the same to the see of Rome or to any other foreign courts or potentates, to the let or impediment thereof in any wise notwithstanding. And that it shall be lawful to the King our Sovereign Lord and to his heirs and successors, and to all other subjects or resiants within this realm or within any the King's dominions or marches of the same, notwithstanding that hereafter it should happen any excommengement,[9] excommunications, interdictions, citations, or any other censures or foreign process out of any outward parties to be fulminate, provulged,[10] declared, or put in execution within this said realm or in any other place or places for any of the causes before rehearsed, in prejudice, derogation, or contempt of this said Act and the very true meaning and execution thereof, may and shall nevertheless as well pursue, execute, have, and enjoy the effects, profits, benefits, and commodities of all such processes, sentences, judgments, and determinations, done or hereafter to be done in any of the said courts spiritual or temporal as the cases shall require, within the limits, power, and authority of this the King's said realm and dominions and marches of the same, and those only and none other to take place and to be firmly observed and obeyed within the same: As also that all spiritual prelates, pastors, ministers, and curates within this realm and the dominions of the same shall and may use, minister, execute, and do, or cause to be used, ministered, executed, and done, all sacraments, sacramentals,[11] divine services, and all other things within the said realm and dominions unto all the subjects of the same as Catholic and Christian men owe to do; Any foreign citations, processes, inhibitions, suspensions, interdictions, excommunications, or appeals for or touching any of the causes aforesaid from or to the see of Rome or any other foreign prince or foreign courts to the let or contrary thereof in any wise notwithstanding. And if any of the said spiritual persons, by the occasion of the said fulminations of any of the same interdictions, censures, inhibitions, excommunications, appeals, suspensions, summons, or other foreign citations for the causes beforesaid or for any of them, do at any time hereafter refuse to minister or to cause to be ministered the said sacraments and sacramentals and other divine services in form as is aforesaid, shall for every such time or times that they or any of them do refuse so to do or to cause to be done, have one year's imprisonment and to make fine and ransom at the King's pleasure.

II. And it is further enacted ... that if any person or persons ... do attempt, move, purchase, or procure, from or to the see of Rome or from or to any other foreign court or courts out of this realm, any manner foreign process, inhibitions, appeals, sentences, summons, citations, suspensions, interdictions, excommunications, restraints, or judgments, of what nature, kind, or quality soever they be, or execute any of the same process, or do any act or acts to the let, impediment, hindrance, or derogation of any process, sentence, judgment, or determination had, made, done, or hereafter to be had, done, or made in any courts of this realm or the King's said dominions or marches of the same for any of the causes aforesaid ... that then every person or persons so doing, and their fautors,[12] comforters, abettors, procurers, executors, and counsellors, and every of them being convict of the same, for every such default shall incur and run in the same pains, penalties, and forfeitures ordained and provided by the statute of provision and praemunire made in the sixteenth year of the reign of ... King Richard the Second[13] ....

III. And furthermore in eschewing the said great enormities, inquietations, delays, charges, and expenses hereafter to be sustained in pursuing of such appeals and foreign process ... do therefore ... ordain and enact that in such cases where heretofore any of the King's subjects or resiants have used to pursue, provoke, or procure any appeal to the see of Rome ... they ... shall from henceforth take, have, and use their appeals within this realm and not elsewhere, in manner and form as hereafter ensueth and not otherwise; that is to say, First from the archdeacon or his official, if the matter or cause be there begun, to the bishop diocesan of the said see ...; And likewise, if it be commenced before the bishop diocesan or his commissary, from the bishop diocesan or his commissary, within fifteen days next ensuing the judgment or sentence thereof there given, to the archbishop of the province of Canterbury, if it be within his province, and if it be within the province of York then to the archbishop of York; and so likewise to all other archbishops in other the King's dominions as the case by the order of justice shall require; and there to be definitively and finally ordered, decreed, and adjudged according to justice, without any other appellation or provocation[14] to any other person or persons, court or courts: And if the matter or contention for any of the causes aforesaid be or shall be commenced ... before the archdeacon of any archbishop or his commissary, then the party grieved shall or may take his appeal, within fifteen days next after judgment or sentence there given, to the Court of the Arches or Audience of the same archbishop or archbishops, and from the said Court of the Arches or Audience, within fifteen days then next ensuing after judgment or sentence there given, to the archbishop of the same province, there to be definitively and finally determined without any other or further process or appeal thereupon to be had or sued.

IV .... And in case any cause, matter, or contention ... which hath, doth, shall, or may touch the King, his heirs or successors kings of this realm, that in all and every such case or cases the party grieved ... shall or may appeal ... to the spiritual prelates and other abbots and priors of the Upper House assembled and convocate by the King's writ in the Convocation being or next ensuing within the province or provinces where the same matter of contention is or shall be begun; so that every such appeal be taken by the party grieved within fifteen days next after the judgment or sentence thereupon given or to be given. And that whatsoever be done or shall be done and affirmed, determined, decreed, and adjudged by the foresaid prelates, abbots, and priors of the

Upper House of the said Convocation as is aforesaid, appertaining, concerning, or belonging to the King, his heirs or successors, in any of these foresaid causes of appeals, shall stand and be taken for a final decree, sentence, judgment, definition, and determination, and the same matter so determined never after to come in question and debate to be examined in any other court or courts: And if it shall happen any person or persons hereafter to pursue or provoke any appeal contrary to the effect of this Act, or refuse to obey, execute, and observe all things comprised within the same ... that then every person and persons so doing, refusing, or offending, ... their procurers, fautors, advocates, counsellors, and abettors, and every of them, shall incur into the pains, forfeitures, and penalties ordained and provided in the said statute made in the said sixteenth year of King Richard the Second[15] ....

> *24 Henr. VIII, c. 12: Statutes of the Realm, iii, 427.*

(2) Act of Supremacy, 1534

If the Act of Appeals declares English independence of all external authority the Act of Supremacy declares the authority of the Crown of England over all persons and all causes within the realm. The idea of the Supremacy was nothing new. It had found expression as early as 1515, when Wolsey had urged the King to allow the case of Standish to be referred to Rome. Henry's reply anticipated his later policy: "We are, by the sufferance of God, King of England; and the Kings of England in times past never had any superior but God. Know, therefore, that we will maintain the rights of the Crown in this matter like our progenitors." The Act now recognises the Supreme Headship as something already existing, and assigns to the Crown the power of ecclesiastical visitation. It has been remarked that Wolsey's legatine autocracy had prepared the way for Henry's Supreme Headship, but the Act itself, except for the clause relating to visitation, is not of the first importance. What the Pope claimed in England was not Supreme Headship, except in virtue of his Supreme Headship of the whole of Christendom, but a practical jurisdiction controlling a large part of the daily life of men. Of this he had been deprived already by the far more important Act of Appeals. The King places on his work an ornamental coping-stone, but the foundations had been already laid and the building erected. The view of the statesmen who supported the Supremacy is indicated by Cranmer. "The Bishop of Rome," he said, "treadeth under foot God's laws and the King's"; and a little later he declared that the clergy maintained the Pope "to the intent they might have as it were a kingdom and laws within themselves, distinct from the laws of the Crown, and wherewith the Crown may not meddle; and so being exempt from the laws of the realm, might live in this realm like lords and kings without damage or fear of any man, so that they please their high and supreme head at Rome."

An Act concerning the King's Highness to be Supreme Head of the Church of England and to have authority to reform and redress all errors, heresies, and abuses in the same

Albeit the King's Majesty justly and rightfully is and ought to be the Supreme Head of the Church of England, and so is recognised by the clergy of this realm in their Convocations; yet nevertheless for corroboration and confirmation thereof, and for increase of virtue in Christ's religion within this realm of England, and to repress and extirp all errors, heresies, and other enormities and abuses heretofore used in the same, Be it enacted by authority of this present Parliament that the King our Sovereign Lord, his heirs and successors kings of this realm, shall be taken, accepted, and reputed the only Supreme Head in earth of the Church of England called *Anglicana Ecclesia,* and shall have and enjoy annexed and united to the imperial Crown of this realm as well the title and style thereof, as all honours, dignities, preeminences, jurisdictions, privileges, authorities, immunities, profits, and commodities, to the said dignity of Supreme Head of the same Church belonging and appertaining: And that our said Sovereign Lord, his heirs and successors kings of this realm, shall have full power and authority from time to time to visit, repress, redress, reform, order, correct, restrain, and amend all such errors, heresies, abuses, offences, contempts, and enormities, whatsoever they be, which by any manner spiritual authority or jurisdiction ought or may lawfully be reformed, repressed, ordered, redressed, corrected, restrained, or amended, most to the pleasure of Almighty God, the increase of virtue in Christ's religion, and for the conservation of the peace, unity, and tranquillity of this realm: any usage, custom, foreign laws, foreign authority, prescription, or any other thing or things to the contrary hereof notwithstanding.

26 Henr. VIII,c.1: Statutes of the Realm, iii, 492.

(3) Act against the Papal Authority, 1536

In connexion with the Act of Supremacy should be studied the rather full-blooded preamble of the Act against the Papal Authority. It marks another stage in the progressive rudeness to the Pope which can be traced throughout the Reformation of Henry VIII[16].

An Act extinguishing the authority of the Bishop of Rome

Forasmuch as notwithstanding the good and wholesome laws, ordinances, and statutes heretofore enacted, made, and established ... for the extirpation, abolition, and extinguishment, out of this realm and other his Grace's dominions, seignories, and countries, of the pretended power and usurped authority of the Bishop of Rome, by some called the Pope, used within the same or elsewhere concerning the same realm, dominions, seignories, or countries, which did obfuscate and wrest God's holy word and testament a long season from the spiritual and true meaning thereof, to his worldly and carnal affections, as pomp, glory, avarice, ambition, and tyranny, covering and shadowing the same with his human and politic devices, traditions, and inventions, set forth to promote and stablish his only dominion, both upon the souls and also the bodies and goods of all Christian people, excluding Christ out of his kingdom and rule of man his soul as much as he may, and all other temporal kings and princes out of their dominions which they ought to have by God's law upon the bodies and goods of their subjects; whereby he did not only rob the King's Majesty, being only the Supreme Head of this his realm of England immediately under God, of his honour, right, and preeminence due unto him by the law of God, but spoiled this his realm yearly of innumerable treasure, and with the loss of the same deceived the King's loving and obedient subjects, persuading to them, by his laws, bulls, and other his deceivable means, such dreams, vanities, and phantasies as by the same many of them were seduced and conveyed unto superstitious and erroneous opinions; so that the King's Majesty, the Lords spiritual and temporal, and the Commons in this realm, being overwearied and fatigated with the experience of the infinite abominations and mischiefs proceeding of his impostures and craftily colouring of his deceits, to the great damages of souls, bodies, and goods, were forced of necessity for the public weal of this realm to exclude that foreign pretended power, jurisdiction, and authority, used and usurped within this realm, and to devise such remedies for their relief in the same as doth not only redound to the honour of God, the high praise and advancement of the King's Majesty and of his realm, but also to the great and inestimable utility of the same; and notwithstanding the said wholesome laws so made and heretofore established, yet it is come to the knowledge of the King's Highness and also to divers and many his loving, faithful, and obedient subjects, how that divers seditious and contentious persons, being imps[17] of the said Bishop of Rome and his see, and in heart members of his pretended monarchy, do in corners and elsewhere, as they dare, whisper, inculce,[18] preach, and persuade, and from time to time instil into the ears and heads of the poor, simple, and unlettered people the advancement and continuance of the said Bishop's feigned and pretended authority, pretending the same to have his ground and original of God's law, whereby the opinions of many be suspended, their judgments corrupted and deceived, and diversity in opinions augmented and increased, to the great displeasure of Almighty God, the high discontentation of our said most dread Sovereign Lord, and the interruption of the unity, love, charity, concord, and agreement that ought to be in a Christian region and congregation: For avoiding whereof, and repression of the follies of such seditious persons as be the means and authors of such inconveniences, Be it enacted, ordained, and established ... That if any person or persons, dwelling, demurring,[19] inhabiting, or resiant[20] within this realm or within any other the King's dominions, seignories, or countries, or the marches of the same, or elsewhere within or under his obeisance[21] and power, of what estate, dignity, preeminence, order, degree, or condition soever he or they be, after the last day of July which shall be in the year of our Lord God 1536 shall, by writing, ciphering, printing, preaching, or teaching, deed, or act, obstinately or maliciously hold or stand with to extol, set forth, maintain, or defend the authority, jurisdiction, or power of the Bishop of Rome or of his see, heretofore used, claimed, or usurped within this realm or in any dominion or country being of, within, or under the King's power or obeisance, or by any pretence obstinately or maliciously invent anything for the extolling, advancement, setting forth, maintenance, or defence of the same or any part thereof, or by any pretence obstinately or maliciously attribute any manner of jurisdiction, authority, or preeminence to the said see of Rome, or to any Bishop of the same see for the time being, within this realm or in any the King's dominions or countries, that then every such person or persons so doing or offending, their aiders, assistants, comforters, abettors, procurers, maintainers, fautors, counsellors, concealors, and every of them, being thereof lawfully convicted according to the laws of this realm, for every such default and offence shall incur and run into the dangers, penalties, pains, and forfeitures ordained and provided by the Statute of Provision and Praemunire made in the sixteenth year of the reign of the noble and valiant prince King Richard the Second against such as attempt, procure, or make provision to the see of Rome or elsewhere for any thing or things to the derogation, or contrary to the prerogative royal or jurisdiction, of the Crown and dignity of this realm.

28 Henr. VIII, c. 10: Statutes of the Realm, iii, 663.

Endnotes

1. The Anglo-Saxon kings from Athelstan to Canute claimed and used imperial titles, such as *imperator* (see Freeman, i, 133–147); and the term "emperor" is used of Edward I, Richard II, and Henry V. See also an article by Professor C. H. Firth in the *Scottish Historical Review*, xv,185, on the use of the phrase "British Empire."
2. Residents.
3. I. e. ministers or administrators.
4. The Statute of Carlisle, 1307 (35 Edw. I, t. 1), an Act against the abuses of papal patronage (Gee and Hardy, p. 92).
5. The First Statute of Provisors, 1351 (25 Edw. III, st. 4) and the First Statute of Praemunire, 1353 (27 Edw. III, st. 1).
6. The Second Statute of Provisors, 1390 (13 Rich. II, st. 2) and the Second Statute of Praemunire, 1393 (16 Rich. II, c. 5).
7. 2 Henr. IV, c. 3, confirmed and extended the Second Statute of Provisors and this was again confirmed by 9 Henr. IV, c. 8; 2 Henr. IV, c. 4, forbade bulls from Rome for exemption from tithe.
8. "Oblations" here include whatever is assigned to pious uses; "obventions" in ecclesiastical law are fees occasionally received.
9. Excommunication.
10. Published.
11. Rites or ceremonies analogous to a sacrament but not reckoned among the sacraments, e.g. the sign of the cross or the use of holy water.
12. favourers, in the sense of adherents or abettors.
13. The Second Statute of Praemunire,1393.
14. "Provocation" is a term technically applied to an appeal from a lower to a higher ecclesiastical court.

15. The Second Statute of Praemunire, 1393.

16. In 1527 Henry, writing to Cardinal Cibo concerning the sack of Rome, refers to the Pope as "our most holy Lord, the true and only Vicar of Jesus Christ upon earth." In the Act of Annates he becomes "the Bishop of Rome, otherwise called the Pope." In the Dispensations Act he is charged with "abusing and beguiling" the King's subjects; and this charge is amplified in the Act against the Papal authority. Finally, in a letter written shortly after the passing of the Act of Supremacy, the Pope is referred to as "the pestilent idol, enemy of all truth, and usurpator of princes."

17. "Imp" is here used in the sense of 'offshoot." The sense of the term is not necessarily bad, as the expression "an imp of Glory" occurs in Quarles, 1621 (*Oxford Dictionary*).

18. A form of "inculk," a word in frequent use in the sense of "inculcate."

19. In the sense of staying or remaining.

20. Resident.

21. Jurisdiction.

Consilium de Emendanda Ecclesia 1537

The Consilium *is one of the earliest documents of the Catholic reform movement. The pontificate of Paul III (1534–1549) marked the beginning of the Church's recognition of the serious need for reform. With a general council of the church scheduled to meet in May 1537, in July of 1536 the pope called together a reform commission to consider the major issues which needed to be addressed. The commission was headed by Cardinal Gasparo Contarini, and was made up of nine of the most prominent Catholic reformers of the period, including Gian Pietro Carafa, the leader of the Theatines, Jacopo Sadoleto, bishop of Carpentras and Reginald Pole. The commission deliberated for three months, and presented its report to the pope in March 1537. It was harshly critical of abuses within the papal curia, and urged the church to respond to the need for more emphasis on pastoral care. Paul III's response to the report can be gauged by his elevation of three of the commissioners—Carafa, Sadoleto and Pole—to the cardinalate.*

Despite the insight of the report, the credentials of the commissioners and the approval of the pope, the Consilium *had a limited impact on the conduct of church business in the short term. Indeed it proved to be something of a liability. Copies of it were soon leaked to the Protestant reformers, who used it as further evidence of the degeneracy of the Catholic church and the rightness of their reforms. Nevertheless it marked the opening of the reform campaign within the Church and identified the directions in which that reform should progress.*

―――――――――――

Chapter Fourteen

Consilium de Emendanda Ecclesia, 1537

Most Holy Father, we are so far from being able to express in words the great thanks the Christian Commonwealth should render to Almighty God because He has appointed you Pope in these times and pastor of His flock and has given you that resolve which you have that we scarcely hope we can do justice in thought to the gratitude we owe God. For that Spirit of God by whom the power of the heavens has been established, as the prophet says, has determined to rebuild through you the Church of Christ, tottering, nay, in fact collapsed, and, as we see, to apply your hand to this ruin, and to raise it up to its original height and restore it to its pristine beauty. We shall hope to make the surest interpretation of this divine purpose—we whom your Holiness has called to Rome and ordered to make known to you, without regard for your advantage or for anyone else's, those abuses, indeed those most serious diseases, which now for a long time afflict God's Church and especially this Roman Curia and which have now led with these diseases gradually becoming more troublesome and destructive to this great ruin which we see.

And your Holiness, taught by the Spirit of God who (as Augustine says) speaks in hearts without the din of words, had rightly acknowledged that the origin of these evils was due to the fact that some popes, your predecessors, in the words of the Apostle Paul, "having itching ears heaped up to themselves teachers according to their own lusts,"[1] not that they might learn from them what they should do, but that they might find through the application and cleverness of these teachers a justification for what it pleased them to do. Thence it came about, besides the fact that flattery follows all dominion as the shadow does the body and that truth's access to the ears of princes has always been most difficult, that teachers at once appeared who taught that the pope is the lord of all benefices and that therefore, since a lord may sell by right what is his own, it necessarily follows that the pope cannot be guilty of simony. Thus the will of the pope, of whatever kind it may be, is the rule governing his activities and deeds: whence it may be shown without doubt that whatever is pleasing is also permitted.

From this source as from a Trojan horse so many abuses and such grave diseases have rushed in upon the Church of God that we now see her afflicted almost to the despair of salvation and the news of these things spread even to the infidels (let your Holiness believe those who know), who for this reason especially deride the Christian religion, so that through us—through us, we say—the name of Christ is blasphemed among the heathens.

But you, Most Holy Father, and truly Most Holy, instructed by the Spirit of God, and with more than that former prudence of yours, since you have devoted yourself fully to the task of curing the ills and restoring good health to the Church of Christ committed to your care, you have seen, and you have rightly seen, that the cure must begin where the disease had its origin, and having followed the teaching of the Apostle Paul you wish to be a steward, not a master, and to be found trustworthy by the Lord, having indeed imitated that servant in the Gospel whom the master set over his household to give them their ration of grain in due time;[2] and on that account you have resolved to turn from what is unlawful, nor do you wish to be able to do what you should not. You have therefore summoned us to you, inexperienced indeed and unequal to so great a task, yet not a little disposed both to the honor and glory of your Holiness and especially to the renewal of the Church of Christ; and you have charged us in the gravest language to compile all the abuses and to make them known to you, having solemnly declared that we shall give an account of this task entrusted to us to Almighty God, if we carelessly or unfaithfully execute it. And you have bound us by oath so that we can discuss all these matters more freely and explain them to you, the penalty of excommunication even having been added lest we disclose anything of our office to anyone.

We have therefore made, in obedience to your command and insofar as it can be briefly done, a compilation of those diseases and their remedies—remedies, we stress, which we were able to devise given the limitations of our talents. But you indeed according to your goodness and wisdom will restore and bring to completion all matters where we have been remiss in view of our limitations. And in order to set ourselves some fixed boundaries, since your Holiness is both the prince of those provinces which are under ecclesiastical authority and the Pope of the universal Church as well as Bishop of Rome, we have not ventured to say anything about matters which pertain to this principality of the Church, excellently ruled, we see, by your prudence. We shall touch however on those matters which pertain to the office of universal Pontiff and to some extent on those which have to do with the Bishop of Rome.

This point, we believed, most Holy Father, must be established before everything else, as Aristotle says in the *Politics*, that in this ecclesiastical government of the Church of Christ just as in every body politic this rule must be held supreme, that as far as possible the laws be observed, nor do we think that it is licit for us to dispense from these laws save for a pressing and necessary reason. For no more dangerous custom can be introduced in any commonwealth than this failure to observe the laws, which our ancestors wished to be sacred and whose authority they called venerable and divine. You know all this, excellent Pontiff; you have long ago read this in the philosophers and theologians. Indeed we think that the following precept is not only most germane to this, but a greater and higher ordinance by far, that it can not be permitted even for the Vicar of Christ to obtain any profit in the use of the power of the keys conferred on him by Christ. For truly this is the command of Christ: "Freely you have received, freely give."[3]

These points having been established at the outset, then [it should be remembered] your Holiness takes care of the Church of Christ with the help of a great many servants through whom he exercises this responsibility. These moreover are all clerics to whom divine worship has been entrusted, priests especially and particularly parish priests and above all bishops. Therefore, if this government is to proceed properly, care must be taken that these servants are qualified for the office which they must discharge.

The first abuse in this respect is the ordination of clerics and especially of priests, in which no care is taken, no diligence employed, so that indiscriminately the most unskilled, men of the vilest stock and of evil morals, adolescents, are admitted to Holy Orders and to the priesthood, to the [indelible] mark, we stress, which above all denotes Christ. From this has come innumerable scandals and a contempt for the ecclesiastical order, and reverence for divine worship has not only been diminished but has almost by now been destroyed. Therefore, we think that it would be an excellent thing if your Holiness first in this city of Rome appointed two or three prelates, learned and upright men, to preside over the ordination of clerics. He should also instruct all bishops, even under pain of censure, to give careful attention to this in their own dioceses. Nor should your Holiness allow anyone to be ordained except by his own bishop or with the permission of deputies in Rome or of his own bishop. Moreover, we think that each bishop should have a teacher in his diocese to instruct clerics in minor orders both in letters and in morals, as the laws prescribe.

Another abuse of the greatest consequence is in the bestowing of ecclesiastical benefices, especially parishes and above all bishoprics, in the matter of which the practice has become entrenched that provision is made for the persons on whom the benefices are bestowed, but not for the flock and Church of Christ. Therefore, in bestowing parish benefices, but above all bishoprics, care must be taken that they be given to good and learned men so that they themselves can perform those duties to which they are bound, and, in addition, that they be conferred on those who will in all likelihood reside. A benefice in Spain or in Britain then must not be conferred on an Italian, or vice versa. This must be observed both in appointments to benefices vacated through death and in the case of resignations, where now only the intention of the person resigning is considered and nothing else. In the case of these resignations we think that it would have good effect if one or several upright men were put in charge of the matter.

Another abuse, when benefices are bestowed or turned over to others, has crept in in connection with the arrangement of payments from the income of these benefices. Indeed, the person resigning the benefice often reserves all the income for himself.[4] In such cases care must be taken that payments can be reserved for no other reason and with no other justification than for alms which ought to be given for pious uses and for the needy. For income is joined to the benefice as the body to the soul. By its very nature then it belongs to him who holds the benefice so that he can live from it respectably according to his station and can at the same time support the expenses for divine worship and for the upkeep of the church and other religious buildings, and so that he may expend what remains for pious uses. For this is the nature of the income of these benefices. But just as in the course of natural events some things occur in particular cases which are contrary to the tendency of nature as a whole, so in the instance of the pope, because he is the universal steward of the goods of the Church, if he sees that that portion of the revenues which should be spent for pious uses or a part of it may more usefully be spent for some other pious purpose, he can without a doubt arrange it. He is able therefore in all justice to set aside payment to aid a person in need, especially a cleric, so that he can live respectably according to his station. For that reason it is a great abuse when all revenues are reserved and everything is taken away which should be allotted to divine service and to the support of him who holds the benefice. And likewise it is certainly a great abuse to make payments to rich clerics who can live satisfactorily and respectably on the income they have. Both abuses must be abolished.

Still another abuse is in the exchanging of benefices which occur under agreements that are all simoniacal and with no consideration except for the profit.

Another abuse must be entirely removed which has now become prevalent in this Curia due to a certain cunning on the part of some experienced persons. For, although the law provides that benefices can not be bequeathed in a will, since they do not belong to the testator but to the Church, and this so that these ecclesiastical properties may be kept in common for the benefit of all and not become the private possession of anyone, human diligence—but not Christian diligence—has discovered a great many ways whereby this law may be mocked. For first the surrender of bishoprics and other benefices are made with the right of regaining them [*cum regressu*]; the reservation of the income is added, then the reservation of conferring benefices; the reservation of the administration is piled on top of this, and by this stipulation they make him bishop who does not have the rights of a bishop, whereas all the episcopal rights are given to him who is not made bishop. May your Holiness see how far this flattering teaching has advanced, where at length it has led, so that what is pleasing is permitted. What, I pray, is this except appointing an heir for oneself to a benefice? Besides this another trick has been devised, when coadjutors are given to bishops requesting them, men less qualified than they are themselves, so that, unless one wishes to close his eyes, he may clearly see that by this means an heir is appointed.

Also, an ancient law was renewed by Clement [VII] that sons of priests may not have the benefices of their fathers, lest in this way the common property [of the Church] become private property. Nevertheless, dispensations are made (so we hear) in the case of this law which ought to be revered. We have not been willing to be silent in the face of that which any prudent man may judge for himself to be absolutely true, namely, that nothing has stirred up more this ill-will toward the clergy, whence so many quarrels have arisen and others threaten, than this diversion of ecclesiastical revenues and income from the general to private advantage. Formerly everyone was hopeful [that such abuses would be corrected]; now led to despair they sharpen their tongues against this See.

Another abuse is in the matter of expectatives and reservations of benefices,[5] and the occasion is given to desire another's death and to hear of it with pleasure. Indeed the more worthy are excluded when there are vacancies, and cause is given for litigations. All these abuses, we think, must be abolished.

Another abuse has been devised with the same cunning. For certain benefices are by right "incompatible," and they are so designated. By virtue of that term our forefathers have wished to remind us that, they should not be conferred on one single person. Now dispensations are granted in these cases, not only for two [such benefices] but for more, and, what is worse, for bishoprics. We feel that this custom which has become so prevalent because of greed must be abolished, especially in the case of bishoprics. What about the lifelong unions of benefices in one man, so that such a plurality of benefices is no obstacle to holding benefices that are "incompatible"? Is that not a pure betrayal of the law?

Another abuse has also become prevalent, that bishoprics are conferred on the most reverend cardinals or that not one but several are put in their charge, an abuse, most Holy Father, which we think is of great importance in God's Church. In the first place, because the offices of cardinal and bishop are "incompatible." For the cardinals are to assist your Holiness in governing the universal Church; the bishop's duty however is to tend his own flock, which he cannot do well and as he should unless he lives with his sheep as a shepherd with his flock.

Furthermore, Holy Father, this practice is especially injurious in the example it sets. For how can this Holy See set straight and correct the abuses of others, if abuses are tolerated in its own principal members? Nor do we think that because they are cardinals they have a greater license to transgress the law; on the contrary, they have far less. For the life of these men ought to be a law for others, nor should they imitate the Pharisees who speak and do not act, but Christ our Savior who began to act and afterwards to teach. This practice is more harmful in the deliberations of the Church, for this license nurtures greed. Besides, the cardinals solicit bishoprics from kings and princes, on whom they are afterwards dependent and about whom they cannot freely pass judgment. Indeed, even if they are able and willing, they are nevertheless led astray, confused in their judgment by their partisanship. Would that this custom be abolished therefore and provision be made that the cardinals can live respectably in accordance with their dignity, each receiving an equal income. We believe that this can easily be done, if we wish to abandon the servitude to Mammon and serve only Christ.

With these abuses corrected which pertain to the appointment of your ministers, through whom as through instruments both the worship of God can be properly directed and the Christian people well instructed and governed in the Christian life, we must now approach those matters which refer to the government of the Christian people. In this regard, most blessed Father, the abuse that first and before all others must be reformed is that bishops above all and then parish priests must not be absent from their churches and parishes except for some grave reason, but must reside, especially bishops, as we have said, because they are the bridegrooms of the church entrusted to their care. For, by the Eternal God, what sight can be more lamentable for the Christian man travelling through the Christian world than this desertion of the churches? Nearly all the shepherds have departed from their flocks, nearly all have been entrusted to hirelings.[6] A heavy penalty, therefore, must be imposed on bishops before the others, and then on parish priests, who are absent from their flocks, not only censures, but also the withholding of the income of absentees, unless the bishops have obtained permission from your Holiness and the parish priests from their bishops to be away for a short period of time. Some laws and the decrees of some Councils may be read in this regard, which provide that the bishop shall not be permitted to be away from his church for more than three Sundays.

It is also an abuse that so many of the most reverend cardinals are absent from this Curia and perform none of the duties incumbent on them as cardinals. Although perhaps not all should reside here, for we think it advantageous that some should live in their provinces—for through them as through some roots spread out into the whole Christian world the peoples are bound together under this Roman See—yet your Holiness therefore should call most to the Curia that they might reside here. For in this way, aside from the fact that the cardinals would be performing their office, provision would also be made for the dignity of the Curia and the gap repaired, if any should occur by the withdrawal of many bishops returning to their own churches.

Another great abuse and one that must by no means be tolerated, whereby the whole Christian people is scandalized, arises from the obstacles the bishops face in the government of their flocks, especially in punishing and correcting evildoers. For in the first place wicked men, chiefly clerics, free themselves in many ways from the jurisdiction of their ordinary. Then, if they have not arranged this exemption, they at once have recourse to the Penitentiary or to the Datary, where they immediately find a way to escape punishment, and, what is worse, they find this in consideration of the payment of money. This scandal, most blessed Father, so greatly disturbs the Christian people that words cannot express it. Let these abuses be abolished, we implore your Holiness by the Blood of Christ, by which He has redeemed for Himself His Church and in which He has bathed her. Let these stains be removed, by which, if any access were given to them in any commonwealth of men or any kingdom, it would at once or very soon fall headlong into ruin, nor could it in any way longer survive. Yet we think that we are at liberty to introduce these monstrosities into the Christian Commonwealth.

Another abuse must be corrected with regard to the religious orders, for many have become so deformed that they are a great scandal to the laity and do grave harm by their example. We think that all conventual orders ought to be done away with, not however that injury be done to anyone, but by prohibiting the admission of novices. Thus they might be quickly abolished without wronging anyone, and good religious could be substituted for them. In fact we now think that it would be best if all boys who have not been professed were removed from their monasteries.

We believe that the appointment of preachers and confessors from among the friars must also be given attention and corrected, first that their superiors take great care that they are qualified and then that they are presented to the bishops, to whom above all others the care of the Church has been entrusted, by whom they may be examined either directly or through capable men. Nor should they be permitted to carry out these tasks without the consent of the bishops.

We have said, most blessed Father, that it is not lawful in any way in the matter of the use of the keys for him exercising this power to obtain any profit. Concerning this there is the firm word of Christ: "Freely you have received, freely give." This pertains not only to your Holiness, but to all who share your power. Therefore we would wish that this same injunction be observed by the legates and nuncios. For just as custom which has now become prevalent dishonors this See and disturbs the people, so, if the contrary were done, this See would win the highest honor and the people would be wonderfully edified.

Another abuse troubles the Christian people with regard to nuns under the care of conventual friars, where in very many convents public sacrilege occurs with the greatest scandal to all. Therefore, let your Holiness take this entire responsibility away from the conventuals and give it either to the ordinaries or to others, whatever will be deemed better.

There is a great and dangerous abuse in the public schools, especially in Italy, where many professors of philosophy teach ungodly things. Indeed, the most ungodly disputations take place in the churches, and, if they are of a religious nature, what pertains to the divine in them is treated before the people with great irreverence. We believe, therefore, that the bishops must be instructed, where there are public schools, to admonish those who lecture that they not teach the young ungodly things, but that they show the weakness of the natural light [of reason] in questions relating to God, to the newness or the eternity of the world, and the like, and guide these youths to what is godly. Likewise, that public disputations on questions of this kind should not be permitted, nor on theological matters either, which disputations certainly destroy much respect among the common people, but that disputations on these matters be held privately and on other questions in the realm of natural science publicly. And the same charge must be imposed on all other bishops, especially of important cities, where disputations of this kind are wont to be held.

The same care must also be employed in the printing of books, and all princes should be instructed by letter to be on their guard lest any books be printed indiscriminately under their authority. Responsibility in this matter should be given to the ordinaries. And because boys in elementary school are now accustomed to read the *Colloquies* of Erasmus, in which there is much to educate unformed minds to ungodly things, the reading of this book and others of this type then must be prohibited in grammar school.[8]

Following these matters which pertain to the instruction of your ministers in the care of the universal Church and in its administration, it must be noted that with regard to privileges granted by your Holiness besides the former abuses other abuses have also been introduced.

The first concerns renegade friars or religious who after a solemn vow withdraw from their order and obtain permission not to wear the habit of their order or even the trace of a habit, but only dignified clerical dress. Let us omit for the moment any reference to gain. For we have already said in the beginning that it is not lawful to make a profit for oneself from the use of the keys and of the power given by Christ, but that one must abstain from this indulgence. For the habit is the sign of profession, whence a dispensation cannot be given even by the bishop to whom these renegades are subject. Therefore this privilege ought not to be granted them, nor should those, when they depart from a vow which binds them to God, be allowed to hold benefices or administrative posts.

Another abuse concerns the pardoners [of the hospital] of the Holy Spirit, [of the hospital] of St. Anthony, and others of this type, who deceive the peasants and simple people and ensnare them with innumerable superstitions.[9] It is our opinion that these pardoners should be abolished.

Another abuse is in connection with dispensing a person established in Holy Orders so that he can take a wife. This dispensation should not be given anyone except for the preservation of a people or a nation, where there is a most serious public reason, especially in these times when the Lutherans lay such great stress on this matter.

There is an abuse in dispensing in the case of marriages between those related by blood or by marriage. Indeed we do not think that this should be done within the second degree [of consanguinity] except for a serious public reason and in other degrees except for a good reason and without any payment of money, as we have already said, unless the parties previously have been united in marriage. In that case it may be permitted in view of the absolution of a sin already committed to impose a money fine after absolution and to allot it to the pious causes to which your Holiness contributes. For just as no money can be demanded when the use of the keys is without sin, so a money fine can be imposed and allotted to pious usage when absolution from sin is sought.

Another abuse concerns the absolution of those guilty of simony. Alas, how this destructive vice holds sway in the Church of God, so that some have no fear of committing simony and then immediately seek absolution from punishment. Indeed they purchase that absolution, and thus they retain the benefice which they have purchased. We do not say that your Holiness is not able to absolve them of that punishment which has been ordained by positive law, but that he ought by no means to do so, so that opposition might be offered to a crime so great that there is none more dangerous or more scandalous.

Also permission should not be given to clerics to bequeath ecclesiastical property except for an urgent reason, lest the possessions of the poor be converted to private pleasure and the enlarging of a person's own estate.

Moreover confessional letters as well as the use of portable altars should not be readily allowed, for this cheapens the devotions of the Church and the most important sacrament of all. Nor should indulgences be granted except once a year in each of the principal cities. And the commutation of vows ought not to be so easily made, except in view of an equivalent good.

It has also been the custom to alter the last wills of testators who bequeath a sum of money for pious causes, which amount is transferred by the authority of your Holiness to an heir or legatee because of alleged poverty, etc., but actually because of greed. Indeed, unless there has been a great change in the household affairs of an heir because of the death of the testator, so that it is likely that the testator would have altered his will in view of that situation, it is wicked to alter the wills of testators. We have already spoken often about greed, wherefore we think that this practice should be entirely avoided.

Having set forth in brief all those matters which pertain to the pontiff of the universal Church as far as we could comprehend them, we shall in conclusion say something about that which pertains to the bishop of Rome. This city and church of Rome is the mother and teacher of the other churches. Therefore in her especially divine worship and integrity of morals ought to flourish. Accordingly, most blessed Father, all strangers are scandalized when they enter the basilica of St. Peter where priests, some of whom are vile, ignorant, and clothed in robes and vestments which they cannot decently wear in poor churches, celebrate mass. This is a great scandal to everyone. Therefore the most reverend archpriest or the most reverend penitentiary must be ordered to attend to this matter and remove this scandal. And the same must be done in other churches.

Also in this city harlots walk about like matrons or ride on mules, attended in broad daylight by noble members of the cardinals' households and by clerics. In no city do we see this corruption except in this model for all cities. Indeed they even dwell in fine houses. This foul abuse must also be corrected.

There are also in this city the hatreds and animosities of private citizens which it is especially the concern of the bishop to compose and conciliate. Therefore, all these animosities must be resolved and the passions of the citizens composed by some cardinals, Romans especially, who are more qualified.

There are in this city hospitals, orphans, widows. Their care especially is the concern of the bishop and the prince. Therefore your Holiness could properly take care of all of these through cardinals who are upright men.

These are the abuses, most blessed Father, which for the present, according to the limitations of our talents, we thought should be compiled, and which seemed to us ought to be corrected. You indeed, in accord with your goodness and wisdom, will direct all these matters. We certainly, if we have not done justice to the magnitude of the task which is far beyond our powers, have nevertheless satisfied our consciences, and we are not without the greatest hope that under your leadership we may see the Church of God cleansed, beautiful as a dove, at peace with herself, agreeing in one body, to the eternal memory of your name. You have taken the name of Paul; you will imitate, we hope, the charity of Paul. He was chosen as the vessel to carry the name of Christ among the nations.[10] Indeed we hope that you have been chosen to restore in our hearts and in our works the name of Christ now forgotten by the nations and by us clerics, to heal the ills, to lead back the sheep of Christ into one fold, to turn away from us the wrath of God and that vengeance which we deserve, already prepared and looming over our heads.

> Gasparo, Cardinal Contarini
> Gian Pietro [Carafa], Cardinal of Chieti
> Jacopo, Cardinal Sadoleto
> Reginald [Pole], Cardinal of England
> Federigo [Fregoso], Archbishop of Salerno
> Jerome [Aleander], Archbishop of Brindisi
> Gian Matteo [Gilberti], Bishop of Verona
> Gregorio [Cortese], Abbot of San Giorgio, Venice
> Friar Tommaso [Badia], Master of the Sacred Palace[11]

Endnotes

1. II Timothy 4,3.
2. Luke 12, 42.
3. Matthew 10,8.
4. Luther's gloss on this particular passage, which is characteristic of his remarks in general on the *Consilium*, reads as follows: "This Romish trick was invented by the popes and cardinals themselves, and it is doubtful that they will be reformed therein." *Luther's* Works, Vol. 34, p. 248.
5. An expectative is the assignment of a benefice before it has become vacant. A reservation of a benefice is the retention of the right of assigning it.
6. "The calamity of our age," says Contarini with reference to such widespread absenteeism and neglect in his *De officio episcopi* (see Chap. VII).
7. The *Consilium* quite clearly is not recommending "the abolition of monasticism," as H. R. Trevor-Roper states it is in his *Historical Essays* (New York, 1966), p. 50. It is simply a matter of doing away with the relaxed or less strict branches of

the mendicant orders, notably the Franciscan Conventuals. In fact the reform of monasticism and the establishment of new orders—the Theatines, the Capuchins, and later the Jesuits—had major support among the authors of the *Consilium*.

8. Erasmus' *Colloquies* was first published in 1518 and saw numerous editions and enlargements in subsequent years. Originally intended as a school text, it became one of Erasmus' most popular works. Because of its ridicule and criticism of many common practices and notably of the monks and friars, it came under frequent attack. Its censure by the Sorbonne in 1526 elicited a defense of it by Erasmus, which may be read in *The Colloquies of Erasmus,* trans. Craig R. Thompson (Chicago, 1965), Appendix I. In view of other condemnations the above prohibition, limited as it is to grammar schools, is rather mild.

9. The pardoners mentioned were attached to two hospitals in Rome. There were many complaints about the kind of indulgence preaching these and similar pardoners conducted. See *Concilium Tridentinum,* XII, 142, n. 1.

10. Acts 9, 15.

11. The question of who actually wrote the *Consilium* has been often discussed, and various attributions have been made (see *Consilium Tridentinum,* XII, 132-33). Given the state of the problem, however, it seems best to attribute it to the nine signatories as a collective work, though perhaps Contarini and Carafa may be viewed as the principal authors. A strong case can be made especially for the latter, in view of his energetic personality and of several important points of similarity between the *Consilium* and a reform memorial sent by Carafa to Clement VII in 1532. This latter document may be found in *ibid.,* XII, 67–77, and is discussed in G. M. Monti, *Ricerche su Papa Paolo IV Carafa* (Benevento, 1925), Part I, where (pp. 41–47) its correspondence with the Consilium is stressed.

John Calvin (1509-1564)

Calvin was born in Noyon, north-east of Paris, in 1509. He began his education in theology, but turned to the law at the direction of his father. Following his father's death he dabbled in the classics, but in the early 1530s he underwent a conversion to Protestantism which changed his life.

In the early 1530s Francis I of France seemed open to the possibilities of reform, until the affair of the Placards (1534) led him to clamp down on religious innovation. This is probably one of the reasons for Calvin's move to Switzerland, where he published the first edition of his major work, the Institutes of the Christian Religion, *in 1536, with a preface addressed to the French king. Expanded and republished several times between 1536 and 1559, the* Institutes *was not only an explication of Calvin's theology, but a plan for constructing the kingdom of God on earth. Calvin had the opportunity to put his plan into action as he worked as a pastor and teacher in both Strasbourg and Geneva. Calvin lived in Geneva from 1536–1538 and again from 1541–1564, when he succeeded in establishing a "godly city." Geneva became a centre of Protestant thought; during Calvin's residence it was filled with Protestant refugees from France, England and northern Italy.*

Calvin held the traditional view that government exists for maintaining order and protecting religion, but he raised the possibility that if the ruler failed in his duties and acted as a barrier to true religion, lesser magistrates might be justified in opposing such tyranny. This idea was developed by many of the Protestant exiles in Geneva and elsewhere into various theories of resistance to constituted authority.

Chapter Fifteen

The Institutes

BOOK ONE
THE KNOWLEDGE OF GOD THE CREATOR

Chapter 1

The Knowledge of God and That of Ourselves are Connected.
How They are Interrelated

1. Without knowledge of self there is no knowledge of God

Nearly all the wisdom we possess, that is to say, true and sound wisdom, consists of two parts: the knowledge of God and of ourselves. But, while joined by many bonds, which one precedes and brings forth the other is not easy to discern. In the first place, no one can look upon himself without immediately turning his thoughts to the contemplation of God, in whom he "lives and moves" (Acts 17:28). For, quite clearly, the mighty gifts with which we are endowed are hardly from ourselves; indeed, our very being is nothing but subsistence in the one God. Then, by these benefits shed, like dew from heaven upon us, we are led as by rivulets to the spring itself. Indeed, our very poverty better discloses the infinitude of benefits reposing in God. The miserable ruin, into which the rebellion of the first man cast us, especially compels us to look upward. Thus, not only will we, in fasting and hungering, seek thence what we lack; but, in being aroused by fear, we shall learn humility. For, as a veritable world of miseries is to be found in mankind, and we are thereby despoiled of divine raiment, our shameful nakedness exposes a teeming horde of infamies. Each of us must, then, be so stung by the consciousness of his own unhappiness as to attain at least some knowledge of God. Thus, from the feeling of our own ignorance, vanity, poverty, infirmity, and—what is more—depravity and corruption, we recognize that the true light of wisdom, sound virtue, full abundance of every good, and purity of righteousness rest in the

Lord alone. To this extent we are prompted by our own ills to contemplate the good things of God; and we cannot seriously aspire to him before we begin to become displeased with ourselves. For what man in all the world would not gladly remain as he is—what man does not remain as he is—so long as he does not know himself, that is, while content with his own gifts, and either ignorant or unmindful of his own misery? Accordingly, the knowledge of ourselves not only arouses us to seek God, but also, as it were, leads us by the hand to find him.

2. Without knowledge of God there is no knowledge of self

Again, it is certain that man never achieves a clear knowledge of himself unless he has first looked upon God's face, and then descends from contemplating him to scrutinize himself. For we always seem to ourselves righteous and upright and wise and holy—this pride is innate in all of us—unless by clear proofs we stand convinced of our own unrighteousness, foulness, folly, and impurity. Moreover, we are not thus convinced if we look merely to ourselves and not also to the Lord, who is the sole standard by which this judgment must be measured. For, because all of us are inclined by nature to hypocrisy, a kind of empty image of righteousness in place of righteousness itself abundantly satisfies us. And because nothing appears within or around us that has not been contaminated by great immorality, what is a little less vile pleases us as a thing most pure—so long as we confine our minds within the limits of human corruption. Just so, an eye to which nothing is shown but black objects judges something dirty white or even rather darkly mottled to be whiteness itself. Indeed, we can discern still more clearly from the bodily senses how much we are deluded in estimating the powers of the soul. For if in broad daylight we either look down upon the ground or survey whatever meets our view round about, we seem to ourselves endowed with the strongest and keenest sight; yet when we look up to the sun and gaze straight at it, that power of sight which was particularly strong on earth is at once blunted and confused by a great brilliance, and thus we are compelled to admit that our keenness in looking upon things earthly is sheer dullness when it comes to the sun. So it happens in estimating our spiritual goods. As long as we do not look beyond the earth, being quite content with our own righteousness, wisdom, and virtue, we flatter ourselves most sweetly, and fancy ourselves all but demigods. Suppose we but once begin to raise our thoughts to God, and to ponder his nature, and how completely perfect are his righteousness, wisdom, and power—the straightedge to which we must be shaped. Then, what masquerading earlier as righteousness was pleasing in us will soon grow filthy in its consummate wickedness. What wonderfully impressed us under the name of wisdom will stink in its very foolishness. What wore the face of power will prove itself the most miserable weakness. That is, what in us seems perfection itself corresponds ill to the purity of God.

3. Man before God's majesty

Hence that dread and wonder with which Scripture commonly represents the saints as stricken, and overcome whenever they felt the presence of God. Thus it comes about that we see men who in his absence normally remained firm and constant, but who, when he manifests his glory, are so shaken and struck dumb as to be laid low by the dread of death—are in fact overwhelmed by it and almost annihilated. As a consequence, we must infer that man is never sufficiently touched and affected by the awareness of his lowly state until he has compared himself with God's majesty. Moreover, we have numerous examples of this consternation both in The Book of Judges and in the Prophets. So frequent was it that this expression was common among God's people: "We shall die, for the Lord has appeared to us" (Judg. 13:22; Isa. 6: 5; Ezek. 2:1; 1:28; Judg. 6:22–23; and elsewhere). The story of Job, in its description of God's wisdom, power, and purity, always expresses a powerful argument that overwhelms men with the realization of their own stupidity, impotence, and corruption (cf. Job 38:1 ff.). And not without cause: for we see how Abraham recognizes more clearly that he is earth and dust (Gen. 18:27) when once he had come nearer to beholding God's glory; and how Elijah, with uncovered face, cannot bear to await his approach, such is the awesomeness of his appearance (I Kings 19:13). And what can man do, who is rottenness itself (Job 13:28) and a worm (Job 7:5; Ps. 22:6), when even the very cherubim must veil their faces out of fear (Isa. 6:2)? It is this indeed of which the prophet Isaiah speaks: "The sun will blush and the moon be confounded when the Lord of Hosts shall reign" (Isa. 24:23); that is, when he shall bring forth his splendor and cause it to draw nearer, the brightest thing will become darkness before it (Isa. 2:10, 19 p.).[1]

Yet, however the knowledge of God and of ourselves may be mutually connected, the order of right teaching requires that we discuss the former first, then proceed afterward to treat the latter.

Chapter II

What it is to Know God, and to what Purpose the Knowledge of Him Tends

1. Piety is requisite for the knowledge of God

Now, the knowledge of God, as I understand it, is that by which we not only conceive that there is a God but also grasp what befits us and is proper to his glory, in fine, what is to our advantage to know of him. Indeed, we shall not say that, properly speaking, God is known where there is no religion or piety. Here I do not yet touch upon the sort of knowledge with which men, in themselves lost and accursed, apprehend God the Redeemer in Christ the Mediator; but I speak only of the primal and simple knowledge to which the very order of nature would have led us if Adam had remained upright. In this ruin of mankind no one now experiences God either as Father or as Author of salvation; or favorable in any way, until Christ the Mediator comes forward to reconcile him to us. Nevertheless, it is one thing to feel that God as our Maker, supports us by his power, governs us by his providence, nourishes us by his goodness, and attends us with all sorts of blessings—and another thing to embrace the grace of reconciliation offered to us in Christ. First, in the fashioning of the universe and in the general teaching of Scripture the Lord shows himself to be the Creator. Then in the face of Christ (cf. II Cor. 4:6) he shows himself to be the Redeemer. Of the resulting twofold knowledge of God[2] we shall now discuss the first aspect; the second will be dealt with in its proper place.[3] Moreover, although our mind cannot apprehend God without rendering some honor to him, it will not suffice simply to hold that there is One whom all ought to honor and adore, unless we are also persuaded that he is the fountain of every good, and that we must seek nothing elsewhere than in him. This I take to mean that not only does he sustain this universe (as he once founded it) by his boundless might, regulate it by his wisdom, preserve it by his goodness, and especially rule mankind by his righteousness and judgment, bear with it in his mercy, watch over it by his protection; but also that no drop will be found either of wisdom and light, or of righteousness or power or rectitude, or of genuine truth, which does not flow from him, and of which he is not the cause. Thus we may learn to await and seek all these things from him, and thankfully to ascribe them, once received, to him. For this sense of the powers of God is for us a fit teacher of piety, from which religion is born. I call "piety" that reverence joined with love of God which the knowledge of his benefits induces. For until men recognize that they owe everything to God, that they are nourished by his fatherly care, that he is the Author of their every good, that they should seek nothing beyond him—they will never yield him willing service. Nay, unless they establish their complete happiness in him, they will never give themselves truly and sincerely to him.

2. Knowledge of God involves trust and reverence

What is God? Men who pose this question are merely toying with idle speculations. If is far better for us to inquire, "What is his natures?" and to know what is consistent with his nature. What good is it to profess with Epicurus some sort of God who has cast aside the care of the world only to amuse himself in idleness? What help is it, in short to know a God with whom we have nothing to do? Rather, our knowledge should serve first to teach us fear and reverence; secondly, with it as our guide and teacher, we should learn to seek every good from him, and, having received it, to credit it to his account. For how can the thought of God penetrate your mind without your realizing immediately that, since you are his handiwork, you have been made over and bound to his command by right of creation, that you owe your life, to him?— that whatever you undertake, whatever you do, ought to be ascribed to him? If this be so, it now assuredly follows that your life is wickedly corrupt unless it be disposed to his service, seeing that his will ought for us to be the law by which we live. Again, you cannot behold him clearly unless you acknowledge him to be the fountainhead and source of every good. From this too would arise the desire to cleave to him and trust in him, but for the fact that man's depravity seduces his mind from rightly seeking him.

For, to begin with, the pious mind does not dream up for itself any god it pleases, but contemplates the one and only true God. And it does not attach to him whatever it pleases, but is content to hold him to be as he manifests himself; furthermore, the mind always exercises the utmost diligence and care not to wander astray, or rashly and boldly to go beyond his will. It thus recognizes God because it knows that he governs all things; and trusts that he is its guide and protector, therefore giving itself over completely to trust in him. Because it understands him to be the Author of every good, if anything oppresses, if anything is lacking, immediately it betakes itself to his protection, waiting for help from him. Because it is persuaded that he is good and merciful, it reposes in him with perfect trust, and doubts not that in his loving-kindness a remedy will be provided for all its ills. Because it acknowledges him as Lord and Father, the pious mind also deems it meet and right to observe his authority in all things, reverence his majesty, take care to advance his glory, and obey his commandments. Because it sees him to be a righteous judge, armed with severity to punish wickedness, it ever holds his judgment seat before its gaze, and through fear of him restrains itself from provoking his anger. And yet it is not so terrified by the awareness of his judgment as to wish to withdraw, even if some way of escape were open. But it embraces him no less as punisher of the wicked than as benefactor of the pious. For the pious mind realizes that the punishment of the impious and wicked and the reward of life eternal for the righteous equally pertain to God's glory. Besides, this mind restrains itself from sinning, not out of dread of punishment alone; but, because it loves and reveres God as Father, it worships and adores him as Lord. Even if there were no hell, it would still shudder at offending him alone.

Here indeed is pure and real religion: faith so joined with an earnest fear of God that this fear also embraces willing reverence, and carries with it such legitimate worship as is prescribed in the law. And we ought to note this fact even more diligently: all men have a vague general veneration for God, but very few really reverence him; and wherever there is great ostentation in ceremonies, sincerity of heart is rare indeed.

BOOK IV

Chapter XX

Civil Government

(How civil and spiritual government are related, 1–2).

1. Differences between spiritual and civil government

Now, since we have established above that man is under a twofold government, and since we have elsewhere discussed at sufficient length the kind that resides in the soul or inner man and pertains to eternal life; this is the place to say something also about the other kind, which pertains only to the establishment of civil justice and outward morality.

For although this topic seems by nature alien to the spiritual doctrine of faith which I have undertaken to discuss, what follows will show that I am right in joining them, in fact, that necessity compels me to do so. This is especially true since, from one side, insane and barbarous men furiously strive to overturn this divinely established order; while, on the other side, the flatterers of princes, immoderately praising their power, do not hesitate to set them against the rule of God himself. Unless both these evils are checked, purity of faith will perish. Besides, it is of no slight importance to us to know how lovingly God has provided in this respect for mankind, that greater zeal for piety, may flourish in us to attest our gratefulness.

First, before we enter into the matter itself, we must keep in mind that distinction which we previously laid down so that we do not (as commonly happens) unwisely mingle these two, which have a completely different nature. For certain men, when they hear that the gospel promises a freedom that acknowledges no king and no magistrate among men, but looks to Christ alone, think that they cannot benefit by their freedom so long as they see any power set up over them. They therefore think that nothing will be safe unless the whole world is reshaped to a new form, where there are neither courts, nor laws, nor magistrates, nor anything which in their opinion restricts their freedom. But whoever knows how to distinguish between body and soul, between this present fleeting life and that future eternal life, will without difficulty know that Christ's spiritual Kingdom and the civil jurisdiction are things completely distinct. Since, then, it is a Jewish vanity to seek and enclose Christ's Kingdom within the elements of this world, let us rather ponder that what Scripture clearly teaches is a spiritual fruit, which we gather from Christ's grace; and let us remember to keep within its own limits all that freedom which is promised and offered to us in him. For why is it that the same apostle who bids us stand and not submit to the "yoke of bondage" (Gal. 5:1) elsewhere forbids slaves to be anxious about their state (I Cor. 7:21), unless it be that spiritual freedom can perfectly well exist along with civil bondage? These statements of his must also be taken in the same sense: In the Kingdom of God "there is neither Jew nor Creek, neither male nor female, neither slaves nor free" (Gal. 3:28, Vg.; order changed). And again, "there is not Jew nor Greek, uncircumcised and circumcised, barbarian, Scythian, slave, freeman; but Christ is all in all" (Col.

3:11 p.). By these statements he means that it makes no difference what your condition among men may be or under what nation's laws you live, since the Kingdom of Christ does not at all consist in these things.

2. The two "governments" are not antithetical

Yet this distinction does not lead us to consider the whole nature of government a thing polluted, which has nothing to do with Christian men. That is what, indeed, certain fanatics who delight in unbridled license shout and boast: after we have died through Christ to the elements of this world (Col. 2:20), are transported to God's Kingdom, and sit among heavenly beings, it is a thing unworthy of us and set far beneath our excellence to be occupied with those vile and worldly cares which have to do with business foreign to a Christian man. To what purpose, they ask, are there laws without trials and tribunals? But what has a Christian man to do with trials themselves? Indeed, if it is not lawful to kill, why do we have laws and trials? But as we have just now pointed out that this kind of government is distinct from that spiritual and inward Kingdom of Christ, so we must know that they are not at variance. For spiritual government, indeed, is already initiating in us upon earth certain beginnings of the heavenly Kingdom, and in this mortal and fleeting life affords a certain forecast of an immortal and incorruptible blessedness. Yet civil government has as its appointed end, so long as we live among men, to cherish and protect the outward worship of God, to defend sound doctrine of piety and the position of the church, to adjust our life to the society of men, to form our social behavior to civil righteousness, to reconcile us with one another, and to promote general peace and tranquillity. All of this I admit to be superfluous, if God's Kingdom, such as it is now among us, wipes out the present life. But if it is God's will that we go as pilgrims upon the earth while we aspire to the true fatherland, and if the pilgrimage requires such helps, those who take these from man deprive him of his very humanity: Our adversaries claim that there ought to be such great perfection in the church of God that its government should suffice for law. But they stupidly imagine such a perfection as can never be found in a community of men. For since the insolence of evil men is so great, their wickedness so stubborn, that it can scarcely be restrained by extremely severe laws, what do we expect them to do if they see that their depravity can go scot-free—when no power can force them to cease from doing evil?

(Necessity and divine sanction of civil government, 3–7)

3. The chief tasks and burdens of civil government

But there will be a more appropriate place to speak of the practice of civil government. Now we only wish it to be understood that to think of doing away with it is outrageous barbarity. Its function among men is no less than that of bread, water, sun, and air; indeed, its place of honor is far more excellent. For it does not merely see to it, as all these serve to do, that men breathe, eat, drink, and are kept warm, even though it surely embraces all these activities when it provides for their living together. It does not, I repeat, look to this only, but also prevents idolatry, sacrilege against God's name, blasphemies against his truth, and other public offenses against religion from arising and spreading among the people; it prevents the public peace from being disturbed; it provides that each man may keep his property safe and sound; that men may carry on blameless intercourse among themselves; that honesty and modesty may be preserved among men. In short, it provides that a public manifestation of religion may exist among Christians, and that humanity be maintained among men.

Let no man be disturbed that I now commit to civil government the duty of rightly establishing religion, which I seem above to have put outside of human decision. For, when I approve of a civil administration that aims to prevent the true religion which is contained in God's law from being openly and with public sacrilege violated and defiled with impunity, I do not here, any more than before, allow men to make laws according to their own decision concerning religion and the worship of God.

But my readers, assisted by the very clarity of the arrangement, will better understand what is to be thought of the whole subject of civil government if we discuss its parts separately. These are three: the magistrate, who is the protector and guardian of the laws; the laws, according to which he governs; the people, who are governed by the laws and obey the magistrate.

Let us, then, first look at the office of the magistrate, noting whether it is a lawful calling approved of God; the nature of the office; the extent of its power; then, with what laws a Christian government ought to be governed; and finally, how the laws benefit the people, and what obedience is owed to the magistrate.

4. The magistracy is ordained by God

The Lord has not only testified that the office of magistrate is approved by and acceptable to him, but he also sets out its dignity with the most honorable titles and marvelously commends it to us. To mention a few: Since those who serve as magistrate are called "gods" (Ex. 22:8, Vg.; Ps. 82:1, 6), let no one think that their being so-called is of slight importance. For it signifies that they have a mandate from God, have been invested with divine authority, and are wholly God's representatives, in a manner, acting as his vicegerents. This is no subtlety of mine, but Christ's explanation. "If Scripture," he says, "called them gods to whom the word of God came..." (John 10:35). What is this, except that God has entrusted to them the business of serving him in their office, and (as Moses and Jehoshaphat said to the judges whom they appointed in every city of Judah) of exercising judgment not for man but for God (Deat. 1:16–17; II Chron. 19:6)? To the same purpose is what God's wisdom affirms through Solomon's mouth, that it is his doing "that kings reign, and counselors decree what is just, that princes exercise dominion, and all benevolent judges of the earth" (Prov. 8:14–16). This amounts to the same thing as to say: it has not come about by human perversity that the authority over all things on earth is in the hands of kings and other rulers, but by divine providence and holy ordinance. For God was pleased so to rule the affairs of men, inasmuch as he is present with them and also presides over the making of laws and the exercising of equity in courts of justice. Paul also plainly teaches this when he lists "ruling" among God's gifts (Rom. 12:8, KJV or RV), which, variously distributed according to the diversity of grace, ought to be used by Christ's servants for the upbuilding of the church. For even though Paul is there speaking specifically of a council of sober men, who were appointed in the primitive church to preside over the ordering of public discipline (which office is called in the letter to the Corinthians, "governments" (I Cor. 12:28)), yet because we see the civil power serving the same end, there is no doubt that he commends to us every kind of just rule.

But Paul speaks much more clearly when he undertakes a just discussion of this matter. For he states both that power is an ordinance of God (Rom. 13:2), and that there are no powers except those ordained by God (Rom. 13:1). Further, that princes are ministers of God, for those doing good unto praise; for those doing evil, avengers unto wrath (Rom. 13:3–4). To this may be added the examples of holy men, of whom some possessed kingdoms, as David, Josiah, and Hezekiah; others, lordships, as Joseph and Daniel; others, civil rule among a free people, as Moses, Joshua, and the judges. The Lord has declared his approval of their offices. Accordingly, no one ought to doubt that civil authority is a calling, not only holy and lawful before God, but also the most sacred and by far the most honorable of all callings in the whole life of mortal men.

5. Against the "Christian" denial or rejection of magistracy

Those who desire to usher in anarchy object that, although in antiquity kings and judges ruled over ignorant folk, yet that servile kind of governing is wholly incompatible today with the perfection which Christ brought with his gospel. In this they betray not only their ignorance but devilish arrogance, when they claim a perfection of which not even a hundredth part is seen in them. But whatever kind of men they may be, the refutation is easy. For where David urges all kings and rulers to kiss the Son of God (Ps. 2:12), he does not bid them lay aside their authority and retire to private life, but submit to Christ the power with which they have been invested, that he alone may tower over all. Similarly, Isaiah, when he promises that kings shall be foster fathers of the church, and queens its nurses (Isa. 49:23), does not deprive them of their honor. Rather, by a noble title he makes them defenders of God's pious worshipers; for that prophecy looks to the coming of Christ. I knowingly pass over very many passages which occur frequently, and especially in the psalms, in which the right of rulers is asserted for them all (Ps: 21; 22; 45; 72; 89; 110; 132). But most notable of all is the passage of Paul where, admonishing Timothy that prayers be offered for kings in public assembly, he immediately adds the reason: "That we may lead a peaceful life under them with all godliness and honesty" (I Tim. 2:2). By these words he entrusts the condition of the church to their protection and care.

6. Magistrates should be faithful as God's deputies

This consideration ought continually to occupy the magistrates themselves, since it can greatly spur them to exercise their office and bring them remarkable comfort to mitigate the difficulties of their task, which are indeed many and burdensome. For what great zeal for uprightness, for prudence, gentleness, self-control, and for innocence ought to be required of themselves by those who know that they have been ordained ministers of divine justice? How will they have the brazenness to admit injustice to their judgment seat, which they are told is the throne of the living God? How will they have the boldness to pronounce an unjust sentence, by that mouth which they know has been appointed an instrument of divine truth? With what conscience will they sign wicked decrees by that hand which they know has been appointed to record the acts of God? To sum up, if they remember that they are vicars of God, they should watch with all care, earnestness, and diligence, to represent in themselves to men some image of divine providence, protection, goodness, benevolence, and justice. And they should perpetually set before themselves the thought that "if all are cursed who carry out in deceit the work of God's vengeance" (Jer. 48:10 p.), much more gravely cursed are they who deceitfully conduct themselves in a righteous calling. Therefore, when Moses and Jehoshaphat wished to urge their judges to do their duty, they had nothing more effective to persuade them than what we have previously mentioned (Deut. 1: 16): "Consider what you do, for you exercise judgment not for man but for the Lord; since he is beside you in judgment. Now then, let the fear of the Lord be upon you. Take heed what you do, for there is no perversity with the Lord our God" (II Chron. 19:6–7 p.). And in another place it is said: "God stood in the assembly of the gods, and holds judgment in the midst of the gods" (Ps. 82:1). This is to hearten them for their task when they learn that they are deputies of God, to whom they must hereafter render account of the administration of their charge. And this admonition deserves to have great weight with them. For if they commit some fault, they are not only wrongdoers to men whom they wickedly trouble, but are also insulting toward God himself, whose most holy judgments they defile (cf. Isa. 3:14–15). Again, they have the means to comfort themselves greatly when they ponder in themselves that they are occupied not with profane affairs or those alien to a servant of God, but with a most holy office, since they are serving as God's deputies.

7. The coercive character of magistracy does not hinder its recognition

Those who, unmoved by so many testimonies of Scripture, dare rail against this holy ministry as a thing abhorrent to Christian religion and piety—what else do they do but revile God himself, whose ministry cannot be reproached without dishonor to himself? And these folk do not just reject the magistrates, but cast off God that he may not reign over them. For if the Lord truly said this of the people of Israel because they refused Samuel's rule (I Sam. 8:7), why with it less truly be said today of these who let themselves rage against all governments ordained by God? The Lord said to his disciples that the kings of the Gentiles exercise lordship over Gentiles, but it is not so among the disciples, where he who is first ought to become the least (Luke 22:25–26); by this saying, they tell us, all Christians are forbidden to take kingdoms or governments. O skillful interpreters! There arose a contention among the disciples over which one would excel the others. To silence this vain ambition, the Lord taught them that their ministry is not like kingdoms, in which one is pre-eminent above the rest. What dishonor, I ask you, does this comparison do to kingly dignity? Indeed, what does it prove at all, except that the kingly office is not the ministry of an apostle? Moreover, among magistrates themselves, although there is a variety of forms, there is no difference in this respect, that we must regard all of them as ordained of God. For Paul also lumps them all together when he says that there is no power except from God (Rom. 13:1). And that which is the least pleasant of all has been especially commended above the rest, that is, the power of one. This, because it brings with it the common bondage of all (except that one man to whose will it subjects all things), in ancient times could not be acceptable to heroic and nobler natures. But to forestall their unjust judgments, Scripture expressly affirms that it is the providence of God's wisdom that kings reign (cf. Prov. 8:15), and particularly commands us to honor the king (Prov. 24:21; I Peter 2:17).

(Obedience, with reverence, due even unjust rulers, 22–29)

22. Deference

The first duty of subjects toward their magistrates is to think most honorably of their office, which they recognize as a jurisdiction bestowed by God, and on that account to esteem and reverence them as ministers and representatives of God. For you may find some who very respectfully yield themselves to their magistrates and desire somebody whom they can obey, because they know that such is expedient for public welfare; nevertheless, they regard magistrates only as a kind of necessary evil. But Peter requires something more of us when he commands that the king be honored (I Peter 2:17); as does Solomon when he teaches that God and king are to be feared (Prov. 24:21). For Peter, in the word "to honor" includes a sincere and candid opinion of the king Solomon, yoking the king with God, shows that the king is full of a holy reverence and dignity. There is also that famous saying in Paul: that we should obey, "not only because of wrath, but because of conscience" (Rom; 13:5, cf. Vg.). By this he means that subjects should be led not by fear alone of princes and rulers to remain in subjection under them (as they commonly yield to an armed enemy who sees that vengeance is promptly taken if they resist), but because they are showing obedience to God himself when they give it to them; since the rulers' power is from God.

I am not discussing the men themselves, as if a mask of dignity covered foolishness, or sloth, or cruelty, as well as wicked morals full of infamous deeds, and thus acquired for vices the praise of virtues; but I say that the order itself is worthy of such honor and reverence that those who are rulers are esteemed among us, and receive reverence out of respect for their lordship.

23. Obedience

From this also something else follows: that, with hearts inclined to reverence their rulers, the subjects should prove their obedience toward them, whether by obeying their proclamations, or by paying taxes, or by undertaking public offices and burdens which pertain to the common defense, or by executing any other commands of theirs. "Let every soul," says Paul, "be subject to the higher powers. . . For he who resists authority, resists what God has ordained" (Rom. 13:1–2; Vg.). "Remind them," he writes to Titus, "to be subject to principalities and powers, to obey magistrates, to be ready for every good work" (Titus 3:1, cf. Vg.). And Peter says, "Be subject to every human creature (or rather, as I translate it, ordinance) for the Lord's sake, whether it be to the king, as supreme, or unto governors who are sent through him, to punish evildoers, but to praise doers of good" (I Peter 2:13–14). Now, in order that they may prove that they are not pretending subjection, but are sincerely and heartily subjects, Paul adds that they should commend to God the safety and prosperity of those under whom they live. "I urge," he says, "that supplications, prayers, intercessions, and thanksgivings be made for all men, for kings, and all that are in authority, that we may lead a quiet and peaceable life, with all godliness and honesty" (I Tim. 2:1–2, cf. Vg.).

Let no man deceive himself here. For since the magistrate cannot be resisted without God being resisted at the same time, even though it seems that an unarmed magistrate can be despised with impunity, still God is armed to avenge mightily this contempt toward himself.

Moreover, under this obedience I include the restraint which private citizens ought to bid themselves keep in public, that they may not deliberately intrude in public affairs, or pointlessly invade the magistrate's office, or undertake anything at all politically. If anything in a public ordinance requires amendment, let them not raise a tumult, or put their hands to the task—all of them ought to keep their hands bound in this respect—but let them commit the matter to the judgment of the magistrate, whose hand alone here is free. I mean, let them not venture on anything without a command. For when the ruler gives his command, private citizens receive public authority. For as the counselors are commonly called the ears and eyes of the prince, so may one reasonably speak of those whom he has appointed by his command to do things, as the hands of the prince.

4. Obedience is also due the unjust magistrate

But since we have so far been describing a magistrate who truly is what he is called, that is, a father of his country, and, as the poet expresses it, shepherd of his people, guardian of peace, protector of righteousness, and avenger of innocence—he who does not approve of such government must rightly be regarded as insane.

But it is the example of nearly all ages that some princes are careless about all those things to which they ought to have given heed, and, far from all care, lazily take their pleasure. Others, intent upon their own business, put up for sale laws, privileges, judgments, and letters of favor. Others drain the common people of their money, and afterward lavish it on insane largesse. Still others exercise sheer robbery, plundering houses, raping virgins and matrons, and slaughtering the innocent.

Consequently, many cannot be persuaded that they ought to recognize these as princes and to obey their authority as far as possible. For in such great disgrace, and among such crimes, so alien to the office not only of a magistrate but also of a man, they discern no appearance of the image of God which ought to have shone in the magistrate; while they see no trace of that minister of God, who had been appointed to praise the good, and to punish the evil (cf. I Peter 2: 14, Vg.). Thus, they also do not recognize as ruler him whose dignity and authority Scripture commends to us. Indeed, this inborn feeling has always been in the minds of men to hate and curse tyrants as much as to love and venerate lawful kings.

25. The wicked ruler a judgment of God

But if we look to God's Word, it will lead us farther. We are not only subject to the authority of princes who perform their office toward us uprightly and faithfully as they ought, but also to the authority of all who by whatever means, have got control of affairs, even though they perform not a whit of the princes' office. For despite the Lord's testimony that the magistrate's office is the highest gift of his beneficence to preserve the safety of men, and despite his appointment of bounds to the magistrates—he still declares at the same time that whoever they may be, they have their authority solely from him. Indeed, he says that those who rule for the public benefit are true patterns and evidences of this beneficence of his; that they who rule unjustly and incompetently have been raised up by him to punish the wickedness of the people; that all equally have been endowed with that holy majesty with which he has invested lawful power.

I shall proceed no farther until I have added some sure testimonies of this thing. Yet, we need not labor to prove that a wicked king is the Lord's wrath upon the earth (Job 34:30, Vg.; Hos. 13:11; Isa. 3:4; 10:5; Deut. 28:29), for I believe no man will contradict me; and thus nothing more would be said of a king than of a robber who seizes your possessions, of an adulterer who pollutes your marriage bed, or of a murderer who seeks to kill you. For Scripture reckons all such calamities among God's curses:

But let us, rather, pause here to prove this, which does not so easily settle in men's minds. In a very wicked man utterly unworthy of all honor, provided he has the public power in his hands, that noble and divine power resides which the Lord has by his Word given to the ministers of his justice and judgment. Accordingly, he should be held in the same reverence and esteem by his subjects, in so far as public obedience is concerned, in which they would hold the best of kings if he were given to them.

26. Obedience to bad kings required in Scripture

First, I should like my readers to note and carefully observe that providence of God, which the Scriptures with good reason so often recall to us, and its special operation in distributing kingdoms and appointing what kings he pleases. In Daniel, the Lord changes times and successions of times, removes kings and sets them up (Dan. 2:21, 37). Likewise: "to the end that the living may know that the Most High rules the kingdom of men, and gives it to whom he will" (Dan. 4:17; cf. ch. 14, Vg.). Although Scripture everywhere abounds with such passages, this prophecy particularly swarms with them. Now it is well enough known what kind of king Nebuchadnezzar was, who conquered Jerusalem—a strong invader and destroyer of others. Nevertheless, the Lord declares in Ezekiel that He has given him the land of Egypt for the service he had done him in devastating it (Ezek. 29:19–20). And Daniel said to him: "You, O king, are a king of kings, to whom the God of heaven has given the kingdom, powerful, mighty, and glorious; to you, I say, he has given also all lands where the sons of men dwell, beasts of the forest and birds of the air: these he has given into your hand and made you rule over them" (Dan. 2:37–38, cf. Vg.). Again, Daniel says to Nebuchadnezzar's son Belshazzar: "The Most High God gave Nebuchadnezzar, your father, kingship and magnificence, honor and glory; and because of the magnificence that he gave him, all peoples, tribes, and tongues were trembling and fearful before him" (Dan. 5:18–19, cf. Vg.). When we hear that a king has been ordained by God, let us at once call to mind those heavenly edicts with regard to honoring and fearing a king; then we shall not hesitate to hold a most wicked tyrant in the place where the Lord has deigned to set him. Samuel, when he warned the people of Israel what sort of things they would suffer from their kings, said: "This shall be the right of the king that will reign over you: he will take your sons and put them to his chariot to make them his horsemen and to plow his fields and reap his harvest, and make his weapons. He will take your daughters to be perfumers and cooks and bakers. Finally, he will take your fields, your vineyards, and your best olive trees and will give them to his servants. He will take the tenth of your grain and of your vineyards, and will give it to his eunuchs and servants. He will take your menservants, maidservants, and asses and set them to his work. He will take the tenth of your flocks and you will be his servants" (I Sam. 8:11–17, with omissions; cf. Hebrew*)*. Surely, the kings would not do this by legal right, since the law trained them to all restraint (Deut. 17:16ff.). But it was called a right in relation to the people, for they had to obey it and were not allowed to resist. It is as if Samuel had said: The willfulness of kings will run to excess, but it will not be your part to restrain it; you will have only this left to you: to obey their commands and hearken to their word.

❋ ❋ ❋ ❋ ❋

29. It is not the part of subjects but of God to vindicate the right

We owe this attitude of reverence and therefore of piety toward all our rulers in the highest degree, whatever they may be like. I therefore the more often repeat this: that we should learn not to examine the men themselves, but take it as enough that they bear, by the Lord's will, a character upon which he has imprinted, and engraved an inviolable majesty.

But (you will say) rulers owe responsibilities in turn to their subjects. This I have already admitted. But if you conclude from this that service ought to be rendered only to just governors, you are reasoning foolishly. For husbands are also bound to their wives, and parents to their children, by mutual responsibilities. Suppose parents and husbands depart from their duty. Suppose parents show themselves so hard and intractable to their children, whom they are forbidden to provoke to anger (Eph. 6:4), that by their rigor they tire them beyond measure. Suppose husbands most despitefully use their wives, whom they are commanded to love (Eph. 5:25) and to spare as weaker vessels (I Peter 3:7). Shall either children be less obedient to their parents or wives to their husbands? They are still subject even to those who are wicked and undutiful.

Indeed, all ought to try not to "look at the bag hanging from their back," that is, not to inquire about another's duties, but every man should keep in mind that one duty which is his own. This ought particularly to apply to those who have been put under the power of others. Therefore, if we are cruelly tormented by a savage prince, if we are greedily despoiled by one who is avaricious or wanton, if we are neglected by a slothful one, if finally we are vexed for piety's sake by one who is impious and sacrilegious, let us first be mindful of our own misdeeds, which without doubt are chastised by such whips of the Lord (cf. Dan. 9:7). By this, humility will restrain our impatience. Let us then also call this thought to mind, that it is not for us to remedy such evils; that only this remains, to implore the Lord's help, in whose hand are the hearts of kings, and the changing of kingdoms (Prov. 21:1 p.). "He is God who will stand in the assembly of the gods, and will judge in the midst of the gods" (Ps. 82:1 p.). Before His face all kings shall fall and be crushed, and all the judges of the earth, that have not kissed his anointed (Ps. 2:10–11), and all those who have written unjust laws to oppress the poor in judgment and to do violence to the cause of the lowly, to pray upon widows and rob the fatherless (Isa. 10:1–2, cf. Vg.).

(Constitutional magistrates, however, ought to check the tyranny of kings; obedience to God comes first; 30-31)

30. When God intervenes, it is sometimes by unwitting agents

Here are revealed his goodness, his power, and his providence. For sometimes he raises up open avengers from among his servants, and arms them with his command to punish the wicked government and deliver his people, oppressed in unjust ways, from miserable calamity. Sometimes he directs to this end the rage of men who intend one thing and undertake another. Thus he delivered the people of Israel from the tyranny of Pharaoh through Moses (Ex. 3:7–10); from the violence of Chusan, king of Syria, through Othniel (Judg. 3:9); and from other servitudes through other kings or judges. Thus he tamed the pride of Tyre by the Egyptians, the insolence of the Egyptians by the Assyrians, the fierceness of the Assyrians by the Chaldeans; the arrogance of Babylon by the Medes and Persians, after Cyrus had already subjugated the Medes. The ungratefulness of the kings of Judah and Israel and their impious obstinancy toward his many benefits, he sometimes by the Assyrians, sometimes by the Babylonians, crushed and afflicted—although not all in the same way.

For the first kind of men, when they had been sent by God's lawful calling to carry out such acts, in taking up arms against kings, did not at all violate that majesty which is implanted in kings by God's ordination; but, armed from heaven, they subdued the lesser power with the greater, just as it is lawful for kings to punish their subordinates. But the latter kind of men, although they were directed by God's hand whither he pleased, and executed his work unwittingly, yet planned in their minds to do nothing but an evil act.

31. Constitutional defenders of the people's freedom

But however these deeds of men are judged in themselves, still the Lord accomplished his work through them alike when he broke the bloody scepters of arrogant kings and when he overturned intolerable governments. Let the princes hear and be afraid.

But we must, in the meantime, be very careful not to despise or violate that authority of magistrates, full of venerable majesty, which God has established by the weightiest decrees even though it may reside with the most unworthy men, who defile it as much as they can with their own wickedness. For, if the correction of unbridled despotism is the Lord's to avenge, let us not at once think that it is entrusted to us, to whom no command has been given except to obey and suffer.

I am speaking all the while of private individuals. For if there are now any magistrates of the people, appointed to restrain the willfulness of kings (as in ancient times the ephors were set against the Spartan kings, or the tribunes of the people against the Roman consuls, or the demarchs against the senate of the Athenians; and perhaps, as things now are, such power as the three estates exercise in every realm when they hold their chief assemblies), I am so far from forbidding them to withstand, in accordance with their duty, the fierce licentiousness of kings, that, if they wink at kings who violently fall upon and assault the lowly common folk I declare that their dissimulation involves nefarious perfidy, because they dishonestly betray the freedom of the people, of which they know that they have been appointed protectors by God's ordinance.

32. Obedience to man must not become disobedience to God

But in that obedience which we have shown to be due the authority of rulers, we are always to make this exception, indeed, to observe it as primary, that such obedience is never to lead us away from obedience to him, to whose will the desires of all kings ought to be subject, to whose decrees all their commands ought to yield, to whose majesty their scepters ought to be submitted. And how absurd would it be that in satisfying men you should incur the displeasure of him for whose sake you obey men themselves! The Lord, therefore, is the King of Kings, who, when he has opened his sacred mouth, must alone be heard, before all and above all men; next to him we are subject to those men who are in authority over us, but only in him. If they command anything against him, let it go unesteemed. And here let us not be concerned about all that dignity which the magistrates possess; for no harm is done to it when it is humbled before that singular and truly supreme power of God. On this consideration, Daniel denies that he has committed any offense against the king when he has not obeyed his impious edict (Dan. 6:22–23, Vg.). For the king had exceeded his limits, and had not only been a wrongdoer against men, but, in lifting up his horns against God, had himself abrogated his power. Conversely, the Israelites are condemned because they were too obedient to the wicked proclamation of the king (Hos. 5:13). For when Jeroboam molded the golden calves, they, to please him, forsook God's Temple and turned to new superstitions (I Kings 12:30). With the same readiness, their descendants complied with the decrees of their kings. The prophet sharply reproaches them for embracing the king's edicts (Hos. 5:11). Far, indeed, is the pretense of modesty from deserving praise, a false modesty with which the court flatterers cloak themselves and deceive the simple while they deny that it is lawful for them to refuse anything imposed by their kings. As if God had made over his right to mortal men, giving them the rule over mankind! Or as if earthly power were diminished when it is subjected to its Authors, in whose presence even the heavenly powers tremble as suppliants! I know with what great and present peril this constancy is menaced, because kings bear defiance with the greatest displeasure, whose "wrath is a messenger of death" (Prov. 16:14), says Solomon. But since this edict has been proclaimed by the heavenly herald Peter "We must obey God rather than men" (Acts 5:29)—let us comfort ourselves with the thought that we are rendering that obedience which the Lord requires when we suffer anything rather than turn aside from piety. And that our courage may not grow faint, Paul pricks us with another goad: That we have been redeemed by Christ at so great a price as our redemption cost him, so that we should not enslave ourselves to the wicked desires of men—much less be subject to their impiety (I Cor. 7:23).

GOD BE PRAISED

Endnotes

1. [p, refers to changes in the text made by Calvin.]
2. *"Duplex... cognitio."* The distinction, "twofold" knowledge, added to the *Institutes* in 1559, is basic to the structure of the completed work. Calvin calls attention to this repeatedly in a striking series of methodological statements, all added in 1559 to clarify the course of the argument. Cf. I. vi, 1, 2; x. 1; xiii. 9, 11 23, 24; xiv. 20, 21, and II, vi. 1. Hence, nothing in Book I belongs to the knowledge of the Redeemer, although everything after ch. v is based in the *special* revelation of Scripture.
3. What is called "the first" makes up the entire remainder of Book I. "The second" broadly corresponds to the whole material of Books II–IV. Strictly speaking, the subject is taken up in II. vi, which is a chapter entirely new in 1559, added to make the transition to the second element of twofold knowledge. The doctrine of sin, II. iv, thus falls between the two books in subject matter, preceding redemption in such a way as to show the occasion for it.

Ignatius Loyola (1491–1556)

Born in 1491 to a noble Basque family, Ignatius Loyola early began a career as a soldier. In 1521 he was gravely wounded during a siege of Pamplona, an event which proved to be the turning point in his career. During his convalescence the only books available to him were Ludolph of Saxony's Life of Christ *and Jacopo de Voragine's* The Golden Legend, *a collection of stories about the saints. As a result of his reading, he determined to turn away from the military life and serve the will of God. Having failed to complete a pilgrimage to Jerusalem in 1522, in 1524 he began an extended programme of study at the universities of Alcalá, Salamanca and Paris.*

Ignatius' Spiritual Exercises *developed during his years at Paris, and it was there that he gathered the group who would become the foundation of the Jesuit order. In 1534 he decided to go with six followers to Jerusalem to work for the conversion of the Turks. Failing to find passage to the east from Venice, the group turned to Rome, where they formed themselves into a formal religious order which received papal approval in 1540.*

The Jesuits combined an intense spirituality with a great emphasis on the importance of education. They have often been portrayed as the shock troops of the Counter-Reformation, but this is a caricature of the order. They were deeply devoted to the church, and to the pope as its leader, and they took a vow of obedience directly to the pope. They were driven, however by a positive desire to reform the church, rather than by a particularly anti-Protestant agenda, and they were one of the most important instruments of Catholic reform. By the time of Ignatius' death in 1556 there were more than a thousand members of his order working as missionaries and educators throughout the known world.

———————

Chapter Sixteen

To the province of Portugal

Letter on Obedience

In this famous Letter St. Ignatius has nothing that is completely new to say about obedience. His teaching is drawn entirely from tradition. He is repeatedly appealing to Scripture, the Fathers, the great monastic legislators. What Ignatius gives is emphasis. His teaching is not his own discovery, if we take discovery in the sense of invention. He may be said to have rediscovered for his own generation, and the generations to follow, the meaning, the weight, the dignity, the merit, the necessity of religious obedience, and to have brought these qualities to the attention of men and women who had for the most part lost sight of them. He did this concisely, coherently, cogently.

Certain explanations of religious obedience as set forth by St. Ignatius have been the occasion of controversy, not because they are inherently unacceptable, but because men have strangely misunderstood them and misinterpreted them. Attention will be called to them as they occur in the Letter.

Ignatius of Loyola sends greetings to his brethren of the Society of Jesus in Portugal, and wishes them the grace and everlasting love of Christ our Lord.

1. It is a cause of deep consolation to me, my dear brothers in Christ, to hear of the eager efforts you are making in your striving after the highest perfection in virtue and in God's service. It is owing to His bounty that, having once called you to this way of life, He keeps you in it, as might be expected of His mercy, and guides you to that happy goal attained by those whom He has chosen.

2. Of course, I wish you to be perfect in all spiritual gifts and adornments. But it is especially in the virtue of obedience, as you have heard from me on other occasions, that I am anxious to see you signalize yourselves. I desire this, not only because of the rare and outstanding blessings connected with obedience, as may be seen from the many distinguished proofs and examples

of it to be found in Holy Scripture, in both the Old and the New Testaments; but also because, as we read in St. Gregory: "Obedience is the only virtue which implants the other virtues in the heart, and preserves them after they have been so implanted" *(Moralium,* xxxv, 14, n. 28. PL 76, col. 765). With this virtue flourishing, the others will surely flourish and bring forth the fruits which I look for in your hearts, and which He requires Who by His saving obedience redeemed the human race which had been laid low and destroyed by the sin of disobedience, "becoming obedient unto death, even to the death of the cross" (Phil, 2:8).

3. We may the more readily allow other religious orders to surpass us in the matter of fasting, watching, and other austerities in their manner of living, which all of them devoutly practice according to their respective Institutes. But in the purity and perfection of obedience and the surrender of our will and judgment, it is my warmest wish, beloved brethren, to see those who serve God in this Society signalize themselves. Indeed, the true and genuine sons of this Society should be recognized by this characteristic, that they never regard the individual himself whom they obey, but in him Christ our Lord for Whose sake they obey. For the superior is not to be obeyed because he is prudent, or kind, or divinely gifted in any other way, but for the sole reason that he holds the place of God and exercises the authority of Him Who says, "He who hears you hears me, and he who despises you despises me" (Luke 10:16). On the other hand, there should not be the least remissness in obedience to him, at least in so far as he is superior, because he happens to be less prudent or less experienced, since he is the representative of Him Whose wisdom cannot be mistaken, and Who will make good whatever is lacking in his representative, even though it be uprightness or other good qualities. Christ our Lord expressly declared this, when He said: "The scribes and Pharisees have sat on the chair of Moses," adding immediately, "all things, therefore, that they command you observe and do, but do not act according to their works" (Matt. 23:2, 3).

4. For this reason it is my desire that you devote yourselves to an unremitting effort, and make it a practice to recognize Christ our Lord in any superior you may have, and with all devotion, reverence and obey the Divine Majesty in Him. This will seem the less surprising if you take note that St. Paul bids us obey our civil and pagan superiors as we would Christ, from Whom flows all legitimate authority. He writes to the Ephesians: "Slaves, obey your masters according to the flesh, with fear and trembling in the sincerity of your heart, as you would Christ: not serving to the eye as pleasers of men, but as

slaves of Christ, doing the will of God from your heart, giving your service with good will as to the Lord and not to man ..." (Eph. 6: 5–7).

From this you yourselves can gather how a religious ought to regard one whom he has chosen not only as a superior, but expressly as Christ's representative, to be his guide and adviser: I mean, whether he should look upon him as a mere man, or as Christ's vicar.

5. Now, this is a point on which you should have a thorough understanding and which I am anxious to see solidly established in your minds, that the first and lowest degree of obedience is exceedingly imperfect, since it does not go beyond the bare execution of a command. In fact, it should not be called obedience at all, unless it rises to the second degree which makes the superior's will the subject's own, and not only conforms it to the superior's will in the actual carrying out of the command, but begets also a conformity of desires. In this way what one wishes the other wishes and what one rejects the other rejects. This is what we read in Holy Scripture: "Obedience is better than sacrifice" (I Kings 15:22), which is thus explained by St. Gregory: "In other sacrifices the flesh of another is slain, but in obedience our own will is sacrificed" (*Moralium*, xxxv, c. 14, n. 28. PL 76, col. 765). Precisely because this faculty of the mind is so precious, the surrender of it to our Lord and Creator in obedience should be held to be of great value.

6. In how great and perilous an error are they involved who, not only in matters pertaining to flesh and blood, but even in those which in other respects are holy and very spiritual, such as fasts, prayers, and other works of devotion, think they are justified in withdrawing from the will and command of their superior! Let them give heed to what Cassian wisely observes in the *Conference of the Abbot Daniel:* "It is one and the same kind of disobedience to break the command of the superior, whether it be done from an interest in work or a desire of ease, and as harmful to disregard the rules of the monastery by going to sleep as by remaining awake. Finally, it would be just as bad to fail to obey the command of the Abbot, whether you did it to read or to sleep" *(Collationes,* lib. IV, c. 20. PL 49, col. 608.). Martha's activity was holy and holy was Magdalen's contemplation, and holy the penitence and tears with which she bathed the feet of Christ our Lord. But these things, it must be noted, were to be done in Bethania, a name which the interpreters say means "House of Obedience." According to St. Bernard, it would seem that our Lord wished to point out to us that neither the zeal of good actions, nor the repose of holy contemplation, nor

the penitent's tears would have been acceptable to Him anywhere but in Bethania (*Sermo ad milites templi,* n. 13. PL 182, col. 939).

7. As far as you can, therefore, my dear brothers, make a complete surrender of your wills. Dedicate as a free gift to your Creator, through His ministers, this liberty which He has bestowed upon you. Be sure of this, that it is no slight benefit to your free will to be allowed to restore it completely to Him from Whom you received it. In doing so, you not only do not lose it, but you even add to it and perfect it, when you conform your own will to that most certain norm of all righteousness, the will of God, which is interpreted for you by him who governs you in God's name.

8. Therefore, you must maintain a watchful guard against ever trying at any time to wrest the superior's will, which you should think of as God's, into agreement with your own. To do this would be not to conform your own will to God's, but to endeavor to rule God's by yours, and thus reverse the order of His Divine Wisdom. Great is the mistake of those whom self-love has blinded into thinking themselves obedient when they have by some stratagem bent the superior's will to their own wishes. Hear what St. Bernard, a man of exceptional experience in this matter, has to say: "Whoever either openly or covertly tries to have his spiritual father enjoin him what he himself desires, deceives himself if he flatters himself into thinking that he is a true follower of obedience. For in this he does not obey his superior, but rather his superior obeys him" *(Sermo de tribus ordinibus Ecclesiae,* n. 4. PL 183, col. 636).

If this is true, whoever wishes to attain the virtue of obedience must rise to this second degree, in which he not only fulfils the superior's commands, but even makes the superior's will his own, or rather strips himself of his own will to clothe himself with God's will as proposed to him by his superior.

9. But he who wishes to make an absolutely complete offering of himself must in addition to his will include his understanding, which is the third and highest degree of obedience. The result will be that he not only identifies his will with that of the superior, but even his thought, and submits his own judgment to the superior's judgment, to the extent that a devout will can bend the understanding. For although this faculty is not endowed with the will's liberty and is naturally borne to assent to whatever is presented to it as true, nevertheless, in many instances, where the evidence of the known truth is not coercive, the intellect under the influence of the will may be inclined to this side rather than to that. In such circumstances everyone who makes profession of obedience must bow to the judgment of the superior.

As a matter of fact, obedience is a whole-burnt offering in which the entire man, without the slightest reserve, is offered in the fire of charity to his Creator and Lord by the hands of His ministers. It is at the same time a complete surrender in which a religious freely yields up his own rights for the purpose of being governed and possessed by Divine Providence through the agency of his superiors. It cannot be denied, therefore, that obedience includes not only the execution, which carries the superior's command into effect, and the will by doing so with a glad heart, but, in addition, it includes also the judgment, so that whatever the superior commands and thinks right ought to appear right and proper to the inferior, to the extent, as I have said, that the will has power to bend the understanding.

10.   Would to God that this obedience of the understanding and judgment were as well understood by men and put into practice as it is pleasing to God and necessary for anyone leading the religious life! This necessity can be seen from a consideration of the heavenly bodies, where, if one is to have any effect upon another, or communicate its movement to it, this body must be subject and subordinate to the first. The same is true among men. If one is to be moved by another's authority, as is done in obedience, he who is in the position of the inferior must accommodate himself to the commands and views of his superior, if the influence of the latter is to reach him and have any effect on him. Now, this subjection and subordination cannot exist unless there be a conformity of will and judgment between the subject and the superior.

11.   Once more then, if we look to the end and purpose of obedience, it is just as possible for the intellect as for the will to be deceived as to what is good for us. And therefore, as the will is united with the superior's will to keep it from error, so the understanding must conform to the judgment of the superior to keep from being misled. "Lean not on thine own prudence," is the warning of Holy Scripture (Prov. 3:5).

Even in the temporal affairs of life, the wise think that the truly prudent man should have little confidence in his own prudence, especially when personal interests are at stake, in which men who are not easy in mind can hardly ever be good judges. Now, if in our own personal affairs we ought to think more of the judgment and advice of another, even when he is not our superior, how much more should we think of that judgment and advice when he is our superior, a man to whom we have surrendered ourselves to be ruled as to God's representative and the interpreter of His holy will!

Certain it is that in men and matters spiritual even greater caution is necessary, seeing that there is greater danger in a spiritual course when one runs along in it without the check of counsel and direction. In the *Conference of Abbot Moses,* Cassian observes: "By no other vice does the devil so lead a monk on in order to hurl him headlong to destruction, as when he persuades him to disregard the counsel of his superiors and trust to his own judgment and decision" (*Collationes,* II, c. 11. PL 49, col. 541).

12.   What is more, without this obedience of the intellect, obedience of the will and execution cannot possibly be what they should. For nature has so arranged matters that what are called the appetitive powers of the soul must follow the apprehensive; and the will cannot long obey without violence when there is disagreement in the judgment. One may obey for some time perhaps, under the common misunderstanding that obey we must even if commanded amiss. But such obedience cannot last, with the resulting failure in perseverance, or at least in the perfection of obedience—which consists in obeying cheerfully and lovingly. And there can be no love or cheerfulness as long as such a conflict exists between action and judgment. We fail in zest and punctuality, when we question whether it is good or not to obey a command. We fail in that glorious simplicity of blind obedience, when we examine a command to see whether it is right or not, and even pass sentence against the superior because he asks us to do something we do not like. We fail in humility, because if from one point of view we obey, from another we prefer ourselves to our superior. We fail in courage in difficult tasks. In a word, all the perfection and dignity of this virtue is lost.

On the other hand, we have instead pain, discontent, delays, weariness, complaints, excuses and other faults which are far from trivial and completely strip obedience of its value and merit. It is this that leads St. Bernard to say, speaking of those who become disgruntled when the commands of the superior are little to their taste: "If you begin to grieve at this, to judge your superior, to murmur in your heart, even though you outwardly fulfil what is commanded, this is not the virtue of patience [obedience], but a cloak over your malice" *(Sermo lll, de Circumcisione,* n, 8. PL 183, col. 140). Peace and tranquillity of soul he certainly shall not enjoy who has in his own heart the cause of his disturbance and unrest, I mean the conflict between his own judgment and the obligations of obedience.

13.   This is why the Apostle, wishing to safeguard the spirit of unity, which is the binding force of every society, is so much in earnest when he

urges all to be of one mind and one heart (Rom. 15:15; I Cor. 1:10; z Cor. 13:11; Phil. 2:2). He knows that if the faithful agree in will and judgment, they will be a mutual and unfailing help to each other. Now if there must be one and the same understanding between the members and the head, it is easy to see whether it is more reasonable for the head to agree with the members, or the members with the head. From all I have thus far said, you can see quite clearly the absolute necessity of this obedience of the understanding.

14. But how perfect is this obedience, and at the same time how pleasing to God, can be seen from this, that what is most excellent in man and beyond all price is consecrated to God. Secondly, because one who thus obeys becomes a living holocaust, most pleasing to His Divine Majesty, seeing that he keeps nothing at all for himself. And finally because of the difficulty which the obedient man experiences in overcoming himself for God's love, since he resists the inclination which is natural to all men: to think for themselves and to follow their own opinion. From these considerations it follows that, although obedience seems to be a perfection of the will, since it makes it prompt and ready at the beck of the superior, yet it has to do also with the understanding itself, as we have pointed out, and should bring it to think what the superior thinks. Thus the whole power of the soul, its will and intelligence, will be brought to bear on a prompt and perfect performance of what is commanded.

15. I think I hear you say, beloved brethren, that you have no doubt about your needing this virtue, and that you would like very much to know how you can acquire it in its perfection. With St. Leo I answer, "To the humble nothing is hard, nothing difficult to the meek" (*Sermo 35,* c. 3. PL 54, col. 252). If you have humility, if you have meekness, God will have the goodness to help you stand by your promise not only cheerfully but even lovingly.

16. In addition to these practices I especially recommend three others which will be a great help to you in your efforts to acquire this obedience of the understanding.

The first is that, as I said in the beginning, you do not take a personal view of your superior and think of him as a mere man, subject to error and adversity, but as Christ Himself Who is Supreme Wisdom, Boundless Goodness and Infinite Charity, Who can neither be deceived nor will deceive you. And since you are well aware that it was out of love for God that you have taken this yoke of obedience upon yourselves, in the thought that in carrying out the superior's will you would be more certain to be carrying out God's will, you should not have the slightest doubt that the most faithful love of God will continue to guide you by the hands of those whom He has placed over you. You should, therefore, listen to their words when they command you, as though they were the very words of Christ Himself. The Apostle, writing to the Colossians and encouraging subjects to be obedient to their superiors, says on this point: "Whatever you do, work at it from the heart as for the Lord and not for men, knowing that from the Lord you will receive the inheritance as your reward. Serve the Lord Christ" (Col. 3:23, 24). And St. Bernard: "Whether it be God or man, His vicar, who commands anything, we must obey with equal diligence and show equal reverence, on the supposition, however, that man commands nothing that is contrary to God" *(Liber de praecepto et dispensatione, c.* 19. PL 182, col. 871). Thus if you behold not man with the eyes of the body, but God with the eyes of the soul, you will surely not find it difficult to conform your will and judgment to that norm of conduct which you yourselves have chosen.

17.   The second practice is that in your own mind you always make a serious effort to defend the superior's command, or even his thought, but never to find fault with it. To do this it will be a help if you are always favorably disposed to any order he may give. You will thus obey, not only without annoyance, but even with a glad heart, because, as St. Leo tells us, "It is not hard to serve when we love what is commanded" *(Sermo de jejunio septimi mensis,* iv. PL 54, col. 444).

18.   There is a third and last way of bringing the judgment into subjection. It is easier and safer and much used by the holy Fathers. Make up your minds that whatever the superior commands is the command and will of God Himself. Just as in accepting a truth which the Catholic Church puts before you, you at once bring into play all the powers of mind and heart, so in carrying out any order whatever of the superior, you should be swept on by a kind of blind passion to obey, without making even the slightest enquiry into the command. It is thus we must believe that Abraham acted when he was told to offer his son, Isaac, in sacrifice (Gen. 22:I–I3). Thus, in the days of the New Testament, some of those holy fathers of whom Cassian speaks, as the abbot John who without a single thought as to whether it would do any good or not, with great and prolonged labor watered a dry stick for a whole year on end, when told to do so: or whether it was possible, when he strove so mightily to move a huge rock which many men with their combined strength could not have budged

(De Institutis Renuntiantium, lib. iv, cc. 25, 26. PL 49, col. 183). We see that heaven sometimes approved this kind of obedience with miracles. Not to mention others, with whom you are well acquainted, Maurus the disciple of St. Benedict, went into a lake on the order of his superior and did not sink (Sancti Gregorii M., *Lib. 2 Dialogorum, Vita Sancti Benedicti,* c. 7. PL 66, col. 146*).* Another, at the word of his superior captured a lioness and brought her home *(De Vitis Patrum,* lib. iii, n. 27. PL 73, col. 755). Now this manner of subjecting one's judgment so as unhesitatingly to approve or praise in one's own mind any command of the superior is not only the practice of holy men, but must be imitated by those who desire to practice perfect obedience in everything, except where sin is clearly involved.

19.   But for all that, you are not forbidden to lay before your superior something that occurs to you and that seems to be at variance with his mind, and which you think might be called to his attention. You should, however, first consult the Lord in prayer. There is, of course, some danger of being deceived by self-love in such instances, and to guard against it and your own judgment you should, both before and after submitting your difficulty, be completely indifferent, not only with regard to undertaking or dropping the proposal itself, but you should be ready even to approve and think best whatever decision the Superior makes.

20.   What I have said of obedience should be the practice of individuals towards their immediate superiors, and of rectors and local superiors towards their provincials, and of provincials towards the general, and of the general, finally, towards him whom God has placed over him, I mean, His vicar on earth. In this way a perfect subordination of authority will be maintained, with the resulting harmony and love, without which neither the proper government of our Society nor of any other congregation whatever could be preserved.

It is in this way that Divine Providence "ordereth all things sweetly" (Wisd. 8:1), leading to their particular ends the lowest by means of the midmost, and the midmost by means of the highest. Among the angels there is likewise this graded subordination of one hierarchy to another, and in the heavenly bodies and all their movements an orderly and close connection and interrelation is kept, all movement coming from the one Supreme Mover in perfect order, step by step, to the lowest.

We see the same thing on earth, not only in every civilized government, but especially in the Church's hierarchy, where officials and their activities draw their authority from the one universal Vicar of Christ our Lord. The better this subordination and gradation is kept, the better and smoother will be the government. But when it is absent, anyone can see how deplorable are the results wherever men are assembled together. It is my earnest desire, therefore, to see this virtue flourish as vigorously in this Society which God has to some extent entrusted to me, as though the well-being and continued existence of our Society depended on it alone.

21. Not to go beyond the limits I set myself at the beginning of this letter, I beg of you in the name of our Lord Jesus Christ, Who gave Himself to us not only as a teacher of obedience, but also as a model of it, to bend every effort to acquire this virtue, and, all athirst for so glorious a victory, to gain complete mastery over yourselves, that is, over the sublimest and most difficult part of your souls, your will, I mean, and understanding. For it is in this way that the true and solid knowledge of God our Lord will draw your souls to Him completely, and rule and govern you throughout the whole course of this mortal pilgrimage, until at last He leads you and many others who have been helped by your efforts and example to that last and most blissful end, which is life everlasting.

I earnestly commend myself to your prayers.

Rome, March 26, 1553.

Teresa of Avila (March 28, 1515–1582)

St. Teresa of Avila was the grand-daughter of a converso, *a converted Jew, who moved his family to Avila after his conversion. She showed early signs of religious piety, setting off at the age of seven with her brother Rodrigo to the land of the Moors to have her head cut off for Christ, though in her early teens she became caught up in the stories of romance and chivalry so popular in Spain. In 1531 her father sent her to school with the Augustinian nuns of Our Lady of Grace in Avila, in the hopes of turning her away from her frivolous interests. While in the convent Teresa began to think of entering the religious life, and over her father's objections, she finally joined the Carmelite monastery of the Incarnation in 1535.*

Teresa made her profession two years later, but by then her health was deteriorating. Attempts to treat her condition almost killed her, and she was paralyzed for three years. After the intercession of St. Joseph, she walked again, but her health remained a constant problem. Her spiritual life was also less than satisfactory, and it was only in the late 1550s that the conversion took place which changed the course of her life. She began to experience both a new level of prayer and new visions, which she feared came from the devil. The inquisition was particularly active in Spain in the late sixteenth century, and Teresa was anxious to ensure that her new experiences were orthodox. In order to explain and understand her new experiences she confided in a series of confessors, whose questions led to the writing of her Life.

Chapter Seventeen

Spiritual Testimonies

33.

(Place uncertain, 1572–1573)
A prophetic vision of victory for her Carmel

I saw a great tempest of trials and that just as the children of Israel were persecuted by the Egyptians, so we would be persecuted; but that God would bring us through dry-shod, and our enemies would be swallowed up by the waves.

34.

(Beas, 1575)
A spiritual token

One day when I was staying at our monastery in Beas, our Lord told me that since I was His bride I should make requests of Him, for He had promised that whatever I asked He would grant me. And as a token He gave me a beautiful ring, with a precious stone resembling an amethyst but with a brilliance very different from any here on earth, and He placed the ring on my finger. I write this with confusion at seeing the goodness of God and my wretched life, for I deserved hell. But, alas, daughters, pray for me and be devoted to St. Joseph who can do a great deal. I'm writing this foolishness ...

35.

(Ecija, Andalusia, May 23, 1575)
The vow of obedience to Father Gratian

1. On the second day after Pentecost, while at Ecija, a person was recalling a great favor she had received from our Lord on the vigil of this feast. Desiring to do something very special in His service, she thought it would be good to promise from that time on not to hide any fault or sin she had committed in her

whole life from the one who stood in God's place. Even though she had made a vow of obedience, this promise seemed to involve something more, because there's no obligation like this toward one's superiors. And she also promised to do all that this confessor might tell her—with regard to serious matters, of course—providing it would not go against her vow of obedience. And even though keeping this promise was hard for her in the beginning, she made it.

2. The first reason why she decided to do so was the thought that she was rendering some service to the Holy Spirit; the second was that she chose a person who was a great servant of God and a learned man, who would help her serve the Lord more.

This learned man knew nothing about the above until some days after she had made the promise. He was Friar Jerome Gratian of the Mother of God.

36.

(Beas, April, 1575)
The vow of obedience to Father Gratian

Material having to do with my conscience and soul. Let no one read it even though I be dead, but give it to the Father Master Gratian.

IHS

1. In 1575, during the month of April, while I was at the foundation in Beas, it happened that the Master Friar Jerome Gratian of the Mother of God came there. I had gone to confession to him at times, but I hadn't held him in the place I had other confessors, by letting myself be completely guided by him. One day while I was eating, without any interior recollection, my soul began to be suspended and recollected in such a way that I thought some rapture was trying to come upon me; and a vision appeared with the usual quickness, like a flash of lightning.

2. It seemed to me our Lord Jesus Christ was next to me in the form in which He usually appears, and at His right side stood Master Gratian himself, and I at His left. The Lord took our right hands and joined them and told me He desired that I take this master to represent Him as long as I live, and that we both agree to everything because it was thus fitting.

3. I remained with very great assurance that the vision was from God. The remembrance of the two confessors I had gone to and followed for a long time and to whom I owed a great deal made me undecided. The remembrance of one

especially made me put up strong resistance, since it seemed to me I was offending him; for I had great respect and love for him. In spite of this I felt assurance from the vision that such an action suited me, and also comfort coming from the thought that this going about consulting different minds with different opinions was now to end. For some, by not understanding me, made me suffer very much; although I never gave up any of them until either they moved away or I did, because I thought the fault was mine. Twice more the Lord returned to tell me in different words not to fear since He gave Master Gratian to me. So I resolved not to do otherwise, and I made the proposal within myself to carry out the Lord's request for the rest of my life, to follow Father Gratian's opinion in everything as long as it wasn't clearly offensive to God— and I was certain it would not be; for, according to some things I have heard, I believe he has made the same promise I have made, of doing the more perfect thing in all matters.

4. I was left with a peace and comfort so great I was amazed, and I felt certain the Lord wanted this, for it doesn't seem to me the devil could give such great peace and comfort of soul. It seems to me I remained outside myself in a way I don't know how to describe, but each time I recall this vision I again praise our Lord and remember that verse which says, *Qui posuit fines suos in pace*; and I want to be consumed in the praises of God.

It seems to me this promise must be for His glory, and so I again propose never to make a change.

5. The second day of Pentecost, after this resolution, while on our way to Seville, we heard Mass in a hermitage in Ecija and remained there for siesta. While my companions were in the hermitage and I was alone in the sacristy there, I began to think of the wonderful favor the Holy Spirit had granted me on the vigil of that feast of Pentecost. Great desires came over me to render Him a special service, but I couldn't find anything that wasn't done. I recalled that although I had made a vow of obedience, it wasn't of a kind I could obey with perfection; and the thought came to me that it would be pleasing to the Holy Spirit to promise what I had proposed in regard to the friar, Father Jerome. On the one hand it seemed to me I wouldn't be doing anything by such a promise, and on the other hand it struck me as something very arduous when I reflected that with superiors you don't reveal your interior state; and that if you don't get along well with one superior, there is finally a change, and another one comes along; and that this promise would mean remaining without any freedom

either interiorly or exteriorly throughout life. And I felt pressed a little, and even very much, not to go through with it.

6. This very resistance that my thoughts caused in my will reproached me. It seemed to me there was already something presenting itself to me that I wasn't doing for God and which I had always fled. The fact is the difficulty so bothered me I don't think I did anything in my life, not even in making profession, over which I felt within myself greater resistance, except when I left my father's house to become a nun. This resistance was the reason I didn't consider my love for this Father; but rather, I then considered the matter as though it regarded a stranger. Nor did I consider his good qualities, but only whether it would be good to make this promise for the Holy Spirit. The doubts that arose as to whether or not it would be of service to God, I believe, caused me to delay.

7. At the end of a period of battle, the Lord gave me great confidence so that it seemed to me I made that promise for the Holy Spirit, and that the Spirit was obliged to give the Father light so that he in turn might give it to me. It also seemed I was to recall that it was our Lord Jesus Christ who had given me the light. And at this point I knelt down and promised that for the rest of my life I would do everything Master Gratian might tell me, as long as there was nothing in opposition to God or my superiors to whom I was obliged. It was my intention that this would apply only in serious matters so as to avoid scruples; for example, when I insist with Father Jerome about some trifling thing in regard to his comfort or mine, and he in turn tells me not to speak of it any more. For such insistence implies no lack of obedience or intention to hide knowingly any of my faults or sins. And not hiding these also involves more than what one is obliged to with superiors. In sum, it was my intention to hold him in the place of God, interiorly and exteriorly.

8. I don't know if I merited, but it seemed to me I did something great for the Holy Spirit, at least all I knew how; and so I remained with great satisfaction and happiness, and I have remained so since then. And although I feared I might be restricted, I was left with greater freedom; and I was more confident our Lord would grant Father Gratian new favors for this service I rendered to God and that I might share in them and receive light in everything.

Blessed be He who created a person who so pleased me that I could dare do this.

❋ ❋ ❋ ❋ ❋

58.

(Seville, 1576)
Account of her spiritual life
for the Inquisitor of Seville

1. Forty years ago this nun took the habit. And from the beginning she has turned her thoughts to the mysteries and the Passion of our Lord and to her sins without ever thinking about supernatural experiences; rather, she has thought about how quickly creatures or things come to an end. And she has spent some periods of the day reflecting on these matters without it even passing through her mind to desire anything more, for her opinion of herself has been such that she has seen that she doesn't deserve even to think about God.

2. She spent about twenty-two years in this way with great dryness, devoting time also to reading good books. It was eighteen years ago that she began to discuss—about three years before the actuality—her first monastery of discalced nuns which she founded in Avila. For, as it seemed to her, she began sometimes to receive interior locutions, and she saw some visions and experienced revelations. She never saw anything, nor has seen anything, of these visions with her bodily eyes. Rather, the representation came like a lightning flash, but it left as great an impression upon her and as many effects as it would if she had seen it with her bodily eyes, and more so.

3. She was terrified, for sometimes she didn't even dare remain alone during the day. Since she couldn't avoid the experiences no matter how much she tried, she went about terribly afflicted, fearing lest she be deceived by the devil. She began to discuss the matter with spiritual persons of the Society of Jesus, among whom were: Father Araoz who happened to go to Avila, for he was the commissary of the Society of Jesus; Father Francis, with whom she spoke twice, who had been duke of Gandia; a provincial of the Society, named Gil González, who is now in Rome and one of the four counselors; also the present provincial of Castile, although she did not speak so much with him; Baltasar Alvarez, who is now rector in Salamanca and who was her confessor for six years; the rector at Cuenca, named Salazar; and, not for long, the rector at Segovia, named Santander; the rector at Burgos, whose name is Ripalda, who was even very unfavorable to her until she talked with him; Doctor Pablo Hernández of Toledo, who was a consultant to the Inquisition; and another,

Ordóñez, who was rector at Avila. In short, wherever she went she sought out those who were most esteemed.

4. She spoke frequently with Friar Peter of Alcántara, and it was he who did a great deal for her.

5. During this time (for more than six years), she was put to the test, shed many tears, and underwent much affliction; and the greater the trials the more favors she received. Often she experienced suspension of the faculties while in prayer, and even outside of it. Many prayers were said and Masses offered that God might lead her by another path, for she had the greatest fear when she was not in prayer, although in all things touching upon the service of God she clearly understood there was improvement, and no vainglory or pride. On the contrary, she felt embarrassed before those who knew about the favors, and regretted speaking about these favors more than she did speaking about her sins; for it seemed to her that her confessors would laugh at her and attribute these favors to the foolish things of women.

6. It was about thirteen years ago, a little more or less, that the Bishop of Salamanca went there, for he was the Inquisitor, I believe, in Toledo and had been here. For the sake of greater assurance she arranged to speak with him and gave him an account of everything. He told her this whole matter was something that didn't belong to his office because all that she saw and understood strengthened her ever more in the Catholic faith. For she always was and is firm in the faith, and she experiences the strongest desires for the honor of God and the good of souls. These desires are such that for one soul she would allow herself to be killed many times. Since he saw she was so concerned, he told her she should write to Master Avila—who was alive—a long account of everything, for he was a man who understood much about prayer; and that with what he would write her, she could be at peace. She did so, and he replied giving her much assurance. Her account was of such a kind that all the learned men who saw it—for they were her confessors—said it was very helpful for information about spiritual things. They ordered her to make a copy and write another little book for her daughters in which she could give some counsels, for she was prioress.

7. In spite of all this, she was not without fears at times, and it seemed to her that spiritual people could be deceived as well as she. She wanted to speak with very learned men, even though they might not be given to prayer, for she only wanted to know whether all her experiences were in conformity with Sacred Scripture. And she was sometimes consoled, thinking that even though

she may have deserved to be deceived because of her sins, God would not permit so many persons to be deceived since they desired to give her light.

8. With this thought in mind she began to discuss these favors with Dominican Fathers because previous to such experiences she often had these Fathers as confessors. The following are the ones whom she consulted. Friar Vicente Barrón was her confessor for a year and a half in Toledo, when she was there for a foundation, for he was consultant to the Inquisition and a very learned man. He gave her much assurance. (And all of them told her that since she didn't offend God and knew she was wretched, she had nothing to fear.) The Master, Friar Domingo Báñez (who is now consultant to the Holy Office in Valladolid) was her confessor for six years, and she always kept in contact with him by letter when something new presented itself. She consulted with Master Chaves. Besides Friar Domingo Báñez, she consulted Friar Pedro Ibáñez, who was then a professor in Avila and a most learned man; and another Dominican whose name was Friar Garcia de Toledo. She consulted the Father Master, Friar Bartolomé de Medina, who has a professor's chair at Salamanca, and who she knew had a very bad opinion of her because he had heard about these experiences. And she thought he better than anyone would tell her if she were being deceived. She consulted him a little more than two years ago when she came to Salamanca. She arranged to go to confession to him and gave him a long account of everything, and she provided that he see what she had written so that he might understand her life better. He assured her very much—more than all of them—and became her close friend. She also made her confession for a time to the Father Master, Friar Felipe de Meneses, when she went to Valladolid for a foundation and he was the prior or rector of that College of St. Gregory. Having heard about these things, he went with great charity to speak to her in Avila, wanting to know if she was being deceived, and pointing out that if she wasn't, there was no reason for so much criticism of her; and he was very satisfied. She also took the matter up with a Dominican provincial, named Salinas, who was a very spiritual man and a great servant of God; and with another professor, now in Segovia, named Friar Diego de Yanguas, who has a truly keen mind.

9. During so many years in which she was subject to those fears, she had the opportunity to consult with others, especially since she went to so many places for foundations. They all tested her because they all wanted to be certain in giving her light; by this light they assured her and were assured themselves.

10. She ever was and ever is subject to all that the holy Catholic faith holds, and all her prayer and the prayer in the houses she has founded is for the increase in the faith. She used to say that if any of her experiences were to induce her to turn against the Catholic faith or the law of God, she would have no need to go in search of proof, for then she would see it was the devil.

11. She never did anything based on what she understood in prayer. Rather, if her confessors told her to do the contrary, she did it immediately, and always informed them about everything. She never believed so decidedly that an experience was from God that, no matter how much they told her it was, she would swear to the fact; although by reason of the effects and great favors that were granted her in some matters, the experience may have seemed to her to be from the good spirit. But she always desired virtues, and this desire she urged upon her nuns, saying that the most humble and mortified would be the most spiritual.

12. What she has written she gave to the Father Master, Friar Domingo Báñez, who is in Valladolid. For it is with him that she more often discusses and has discussed these experiences. She thinks he has presented her written account to the Holy Office in Madrid. In all of it she submits to the correction of the Catholic faith and of the Church. No one has blamed her, for these experiences are not within anyone's power; and our Lord doesn't ask the impossible.

13. Since an account was given to so many because of the great fear she was undergoing, many of these experiences were told around, which was for her an extraordinary torment and cross. She says that this suffering was not caused by humility but by the fear that these things would be attributed to women's fancy. She went to the extreme of not submitting herself to the judgment of any person who she thought believed that everything was from God, for she feared that then the devil would deceive both him and her. She discussed her soul more willingly with anyone who she saw was more fearful, although it also caused her grief to deal with those who completely despised these experiences— they did so to try her—for some of these seemed to her to be very much from God. And she did not want them to give definite condemnation of the experiences simply because they didn't see any reason for them. Nor did she want them to act as though everything were from God, for she understood very well that there could be some deception. For this reason it never seemed to her that she could have complete assurance where there could be danger. She tried as hard as she could not to offend God in anything and always to obey. By

these two means she thought she could free herself even if her experience were from the devil.

14. From the time she began to receive supernatural experiences, her spirit was always inclined to seek what was most perfect, and it almost habitually had great desires for suffering. In persecutions—for she experienced many— she found consolation and a special love for her persecutors. There was a great desire for poverty and solitude, and to leave this exile so as to see God. Because of these effects and other similar ones, she began to grow calm since it seemed to her that a spirit that left these virtues in her would not be bad. And those with whom she discussed this idea agreed. However, this thought didn't make her stop fearing; but it did help her to advance with less worry. Never did her spirit persuade her to hide anything, but always to obey.

15. She never saw anything with her bodily eyes, as has been said. But what she saw was so delicate and intellectual that sometimes at the beginning she thought she had imagined it; at other times she couldn't think such a thing. Nor did she ever hear with her bodily ears—except twice; and these times she didn't hear what was being said, nor did she know.

16. These experiences were not continual, but only came sometimes when there was a need, as once when she endured for some days certain unbearable interior torments and a disturbing inner fear about whether the devil was deceiving her, as is explained more at length in the account of her life and also of her sins, in which her sins were made public as were her other experiences. That time, her fear made her forget her worth. And while in this indescribable state of affliction, merely by hearing the words within, "It is I, do not be afraid," the soul was left so quiet and courageous and confident that it couldn't understand where such a great blessing came from. For neither her confessor nor many learned men with many words sufficed to give her that peace and quiet that were given with these words; nor did these learned men suffice at other times, until she was strengthened by some vision. Without this strength she would have been unable to suffer such great trials, contradictions, and sicknesses, which have been without number. And it happens that she is never without some kind of suffering. There is more and less of it; but ordinarily there are always pains with much other sickness, although since she has been a nun she has been afflicted with more suffering.

17. If some service she renders the Lord or the favors He grants her suddenly come to mind, even though she frequently recalls the favors, she cannot think of them for long as she can of her sins, which are always tormenting

her like foul-smelling mud. That she committed so many sins and served God so little must be the reason she is not tempted to vainglory.

18. She was never persuaded concerning any spiritual experience of hers unless it was completely clean and chaste, and there was above all a great fear of offending God our Lord and the desire to do His will in everything. This latter she begs of Him always. And in her opinion she is so determined not to turn from His will that there is nothing her confessors or superiors might tell her about what they think would be of service to God that she would fail to carry out, confident that the Lord helps those who are resolved to render Him service and glory.

19. Relative to this service, she no more thinks of herself or of her own gain than if she did not exist, insofar as she and her confessors understand concerning herself. Everything on this paper is the full truth, and your Reverence can check with her confessors if you want, and with all the persons who have dealt with her during the past twenty years. Very habitually, her spirit moves her to the praises of God; and she would want everyone to be praising Him even were this to cost her a great deal. That all be praising Him is the source of her desire for the good of souls. And upon seeing how the exterior things of this world are like dung, and how precious the interior are—for the two are incomparable—she has come to have little esteem for the things of the world.

20. The kind of vision your Reverence asked me about is a kind in which nothing is seen, neither interiorly nor exteriorly, because the vision is not an imaginative one. But without seeing anything, the soul understands who it is—and even where the representation is—more clearly than if it saw the person, except that nothing in particular is represented. It's as though we were to feel that another is beside us, and because it is dark don't see that person; yet certainly we know the other is there. However this comparison is insufficient, for one who is in darkness knows in some way, either by hearing a noise or having seen the person before, that someone is there, or knows it from previous knowledge. Here, there is nothing of this; but without any exterior or interior word, the soul understands most clearly who it is and where He is, and sometimes the meaning. Where these visions come from, or how, the soul doesn't know; but they happen in this way, and while they last they cannot be ignored. When one of these visions is taken away, no matter how much the soul wants to imagine it as it was, its efforts are to no avail because what it forms is seen to be something imagined and not a presence; for this presence

is not in its power to produce. And so it is with all the supernatural experiences. This inability to produce them is why individuals to whom God grants such a favor don't consider themselves to be anything, for they see that their experience is a gift and that the soul can neither add nor subtract anything. And this leaves the soul with much more humility and much more love of always serving this Lord, so powerful that He can do what we cannot even understand. However much learning one may have, there are things that cannot be grasped.

May He who grants this vision be blessed forever and ever, amen.

Part Four

The Humanist Imagination

Trial of Mary and Joseph

*This play comes from the N-Town cycle of mystery plays, also known as
the* Ludus Coventriae, *from an early, probably unfounded, association
with Coventry. The cycle seems to have originated in East Anglia, and
was most likely transcribed between about 1468 and the early sixteenth
century. It was written by four scribes on at least seven different kinds of
paper. The cycle opens with the creation of heaven and progresses through
the major stories of the Old Testament through the life of Christ and on to
judgment day. It is an eclectic mixture of plays which seem to have been
put together over a long period of time; the Proclamation which opens
the cycle describes forty pageants, but they do not entirely correspond
with the cycle as it now stands. Besides these problems with the origins
of the material, it is not entirely clear how the pageant was staged, as
scholars have argued for various combinations of processional and fixed-
stage presentations.*

The Trial of Mary and Joseph *is unique to the N-Town cycle among
extant English mysteries. It describes the reaction of the local community,
aware of Mary and Joseph's vow of chastity, to the news of Mary's
pregnancy. By placing the action in a medieval ecclesiastical court the
text gives us a popular view of that institution and its officials, as well as
an insight into issues of religion, sexuality and community.*

Chapter Eighteen

Ludus Coventriae or
The Plaie called Corpus Christi
The Trial of Mary and Joseph

Dramatis Personae:
>First Detractor (Raise Slander)
>Second Detractor (Backbiter)
>First Doctor of Law
>Second Doctor of Law
>Summoner
>Mary
>Joseph
>Bishop Abizacher

Here enters the play of the trial of Mary and Joseph. The first detractor says:

>Ah, sirs, God save you all!
>Here is a fair people, in good faith.
>Good sirs, tell me what men call me.
>I think you can not, by this day.
>Yet I walk wide and many a-way,
>but yet where I come I do no good;
>to raise slander is all my law;
>Backbiter is my brother of blood.
>Did he not come hither at all this day?
>Now, would God that he were here
>and by my troth I dare well say
>that if we two together appear
>more slander we two shall raise
>within an hour, throughout this town,

than ever there was these thousand years,
or else I curse you, both up and down!
Now, by my troth, I have a sight
even of my brother. Lo! Here he is!
Welcome brother, my troth I pledge.
Your gentle mouth let me now kiss.

2nd detractor
Gramercy, brother. So have I bliss,
I am full glad we meet this day!

1st detractor
Right so am I, brother,indeed.
Much gladder than I can say.
But yet, good brother, I pray you,
tell all these people what is your name.
For if they knew it, my life I wager,
they would worship you and speak great fame.

2nd detractor
I am Backbiter, that preaches all game,
both liked and known in many a-place.

1st detractor
By my troth I said the same,
and yet some said you should have evil grace.

2nd detractor
Hark, Raise Slander, can you not tell
of any new thing that has happened of late?

1st detractor
Within a short while a thing befell,
I think you will laugh right well there-at.
For, in truth, a great amount of hate,
if it be known, will grow from it.

2nd detractor
If I may raise, therewith, debate,
I shall not spare the seed to sow.

1st detractor
Sir, in the temple a maid there was
call maid Mary, the truth to tell.
She seemed so holy within that place
men said she was fed by a holy angel.
She made a vow never to lie with a man,
but to live a chaste and clean virgin.
How ever it be, her womb does swell
and is as great as yours or mine!

2nd detractor
Yes, that old shrew Joseph, my troth I pledge,
was so enamoured on that maid
that when he had sight of her beauty
he ceased not until he had her assayed.

1st detractor
Ah, no, no! Well worse she has him paid!
Some fresh young gallant she loves well more
that his legs to her has laid.
And that does grieve the old man sorely!

2nd detractor
By my troth, all may well be!
For fresh and fair she is to sight,
and such a morsel, as it seems to me,
would cause a young man to have delight.

1st detractor
Such a young damsel, of beauty bright,
and of shape so comely, also
of her tail often-times lain by,
and right ticklish under the toe.

2nd detractor
That old cuckold was evilly beguiled
by that fresh wench when he was wed.
Now must he father another man's child
and with his labour he shall be fed.

1st detractor
A young man may do more cheer in bed
to a young wench than may an old:
that is the cause that such law is read,
that many a man is a cuckold!

*Here, the Bishop Abizacher is seated between two doctors of law, and hearing
this defamation, speaks to the detractors, saying:*

Bishop
Hark you fellows! Why speak such shame
of that good virgin fair, maid Mary?
You are cursed, to defame her so!
She that is of life so good and holy,
of her to speak such villainy,
you make my heart very heavy in mood.
I charge you to cease of your false cry
for she is a relation of my own blood!

2nd detractor
Sibling of your kin, though she be,
all great with child her womb does swell.
Do call her hither and yourself shall see
that it is truth, what I you tell.

1st detractor
Sir, for your sake I shall keep counsel.
I am right loath to grieve you.
But listen, sirs, listen to what says the bell,
our fair maid now goes great with child.

First doctor of law
Take good heed, sirs, what you do say.
Advise you well, what you present.
If this be found false another day
full sorely shall you your tale repent.

2nd detractor
Sir, the maid, in truth, is good and gentle,
both comely and gay, and a fair wench,
and craftily with help, she can consent
to set a cuckold on the high bench.

2nd doctor of law
You are too busy in your language!
I hope to God to prove you false!
It would be a great shame if she should behave so
or with such sin to cause mischief.

Bishop
This evil tale does grieve my heart!
Of her to hear such dalliance!
If she is found in such behaviour
she shall sorely rue her governance.

Sym Summonor! In haste wend you your way.
Bid Joseph and his wife by name
to appear at the court this day;
here to purge them of their defame.
Say that I hear of them great shame
and that causes me great heaviness.
If they are clean, without blame,
bid them come hither and show witness.

Summonor
All right sir, I shall them call
here at your court to appear.

And if I may meet them at all
I hope right soon they shall be here.
Away sirs! Let me come near!
A man of worship comes to this place!
It seems to me you need learn of courtesy!
Take off your hoods, with an evil grace!

Do me some worship before my face,
or, by my troth, I'll make you!
If I roll you up in my course,
for fear I shall make your arse quake!
But, yet, if you give me some reward
I will withdraw my great rough tooth.
Gold and silver I will not forsake,
even as all summoners do.

Ah, Joseph, good day with your fair spouse.
My lord, the bishop, has for you sent.
It is told to him that in your house
a cuckold's bow each night is bent.
He that shot the bolt is likely to be brought low.
Fair maid, that is a tale that you can best tell.
Now, by your troth, tell your intent.
Did not the archer please you right well?

Mary
Of God in heaven I take witness
that sinful work was never my thought.
I am yet a maid, of pure cleanness,
just as I was in to this world brought.

Summonor
No other witness shall be sought.
You are with child! Every man may see!
I charge you both. You shall not tarry,
but to the bishop come forth with me.

Joseph
To the bishop with you we go.
Of our vindication we have no doubt.

Mary
Almighty God shall be our friend
when the truth is tried out.

Summonor
Yes, in this way excuse themselves all scoundrels,
when their own sin does defame them.
But they then begin to bow lowly
when they are guilty and found in blame.

Therefore, come forth, cuckold by name,
the bishop shall question your life.
Come forth also goodly dame,
a clean housewife, as I suppose.
I will tell you without any gloss,
if you were mine, without fail
I would each day tweak your nose
if you did bring me such a pack.

My lord the bishop, here have I brought
this goodly couple at your bidding,
and it seems to me by her freight,
"Fair child lallay" soon must she sing.

1st detractor
If you bring a cradle to her
you might save money in her purse.
Because she is your young cousin,
I pray you sir, let her never fare the worse.

Bishop
Alas, Mary, what have you done?
I am ashamed even for your sake.

How have you changed your holy thought?
Did old Joseph, with strength you take?
Or have you chosen another mate
by whom you are thus brought to shame?
Tell me, who has done this injury,
how have you lost your holy name?

Mary
My name, I hope, is safe and sound.
God to witness, I am a maid;
of fleshly lust and ghostly wound
—in deed, nor in thought—I never assayed.

1st doctor of law
How shall your womb thus be arrayed,
so greatly swollen as that it is,
but if some man had you o'er-laid
your womb should never be so great, indeed.

2nd doctor of law
Hark, you, Joseph. I am afraid
that you have worked this open sin.
This woman you have thus betrayed
with great flattering or some false trick.

2nd detractor
Now, by my troth, you hit the pin!
With that purpose in faith I hold.
Tell now how you thus her did win
or acknowledge yourself for a cuckold.

Joseph
She is for me a true clean maid,
and I for her am clean also.
Of fleshly sin I never assayed
since when she was wedded to me.

Bishop

You shall not escape from us yet so.
First you shall tell us another story.
Straight to the altar you shall go,
the drink of vengeance to attempt.

Here is the bottle of God's vengeance.
This drink shall now be your vindication.
This has such virtue, by God's ordinance,
that, whatever man drinks of this potion
and goes certainly in procession
here in this place about this altar,
if he is guilty, some mark
shall show it plainly in his face.

If you are guilty, tell us the cause.
Be not too bold over God's might.
If you presume and are guilty,
God will grieve you many-fold.

Joseph

I am not guilty as I first told.
Almighty God, I take witness!

Bishop

Then drink what you hold in haste
and address yourself to the procession.

Here Joseph drinks and circles the altar seven times, saying:

Joseph

This drink I take with meek intent.
As I am guiltless to God I pray,
Lord, as you are omnipotent,
on me you show the truth this day.
About this altar I take the way,

O gracious God help your servant,
as I am guiltless against yon maid
of your mercy grant me your hand this time.

Summonor
This old shrew may not well go.
Long he tarries to go about.
Lift up your feet, set forth your toes,
or by my troth, you'll get a clout!

2nd detractor
Now sir, evil luck comes to your snout!
What ails your legs, now to be lame?
You did put them right freshly out
when you did play with yon young dame!

1st detractor
I pray to God, give him mischance!
His legs here do fold for age,
but with this damsel, when he did dance,
the old churl had right great courage!

Summonor
The shrew was then set in a dotage
and had good lust that time to play.
Did she not give you broth for a meal,
when you had finished, to comfort your brain?

Joseph
O gracious God, help me at this time,
against these people that do me defame.
As I never more did touch her side,
help me this day from worldly shame.
About this altar, to keep my fame
vii times I have gone round about.
If I am worthy to suffer blame,
O rightful God, my sin show out!

Bishop

Joseph, with heart, thank God the Lord,
whose high mercy does excuse you.
For your vindication we shall record
That you did never muse on sin with her.
But Mary, yourself may not refuse.
All great with child we see you stand.
What mysterious man misused you?
Why have you sinned against your husband?

Mary

I trespassed never with earthly man.
Thereof I hope, through God's dispensation,
here to be purged before your sight
from all sin clean, like as my husband.
Take me the bottle out of your hand.
Here shall I drink before your face.
About this altar then shall I walk
vii times to go by God's grace.

1st doctor of law

See this bold liar would presume
against God to test his might.
Though God's vengeance should her consume
she will not tell her false delight.
You are with child! We see in sight.
To us your womb does you accuse.
There was never woman yet in such plight
that from mankind her could excuse.

1st detractor

In faith, I suppose that this woman slept
outside, all covered while that it snowed.
And a flake thereof into her mouth crept
and thereof the child in her womb does grow.

2nd detractor
Then beware, dame, for this is well known:
when it is born, if that the sun shines
it will turn to water again, as I believe,
for snow unto water does always return.

2nd doctor of law
With God's high might you should not joke!
Advise you well of your purging.
If you are guilty you may not escape.
Beware ever of God, that rightful justice.
If God with vengeance sets on you his eyes,
not only you, but all your kin is shamed.
Better it is to tell the truth, consider,
than to grieve God and anger him.

Mary
I trust in his grace, I shall never grieve him.
His servant I am in word, deed and thought,
a maid undefiled I hope he shall me prove.
I pray you, stop me not.

Bishop
Now, by that good Lord that all this world has wrought,
if God on you shows any manner of token,
vindication, I believe, was never so dearly bought,
if I may, on you, in any way be avenged.

Hold here the bottle and take a large drink
and about the altar go in your procession.

Mary
To God, in this case, my cause I have handed.
Lord, through your help I drink of this potion.

Here the blessed virgin drinks from the potion and afterwards circles the altar saying:

Mary

God, as I never knew of man's stain,
but ever have lived in true virginity,
send me this day your holy consolation
that all these fair people may see my cleanness.

O gracious God, as thou hast chosen me
To be thy mother, to be born of me,
save your tabernacle that is kept clean for you
which now is put at reproof and scorn.
Gabriel told me with words here in my presence
that you, of your goodness, would become my child.
Help now, of your highness, that my worship is not lost.
O dear son, I pray you, help your mother mild.

Bishop

Almighty God, what may this mean?
For all the drink of God's potion,
this woman with child is fair and clean,
without foul spot or stain.
I cannot, by no imagination,
prove her guilty and sinful of life.
It shows openly by her vindication,
she is clean maid, both mother and wife.

1st detractor

By my father's soul, here is a great trick!
Because she is a relation of your kin
the drink is changed by some false scheme
so that she will have no shame this time.

Bishop

Because you think that we do falsehood,
and because you did first them defame,
you shall right here, despite your head,
before all these people, drink of the same!

1st detractor

Sir, in good faith, one draught I pull,
if these two drinkers have not spent it all.

Here he drinks and, feeling a pain in the head, falls and says

Out, out, alas! What ails my skull?
Ah! My head with fire I think is burnt!
Mercy good Mary, I do me repent
of my cursed and false language.

Mary

Now good Lord in heaven omnipotent,
of his great mercy your sickness asuage.

Bishop

We all on our knees fall here on the ground.
You, God's handmaid praying for grace,
all cursed language and shame unsound,
good Mary, forgive us here in this place.

Mary

Now, God forgive you all your trespass
and also forgive you all defamation
that you have said, both more and less,
to my hindrance and stain.

Bishop

Now blessed virgin we thank you all
of your good heart and great patience.
We will go with you home to your hall
to do you service with high reverence.

Mary

I thank you heartily of your benevolence.
On to your own house I pray you go

and take these people home with you hence.
I am not disposed to pass from hence.

Bishop
Then farewell maiden and pure virgin.
Farewell true handmaid of God in bliss.
We all to you lowly incline
and take our leave of you as is worthy.

Mary
Almighty God guide your ways.
For that high Lord is most of might.
May he speed you so that you will not miss
to have of him in heaven a sight.

Joseph
Honoured in heaven by that high Lord,
whose endless grace is so abundant
that he does show the true record
of each man that is his true servant.
That Lord to worship with heart pleasant
we both are bound right on this place,
which our vindication did us grant
and prove us pure by high grace.

Mary
For truth, good spouse, I thank him highly
of his good grace for our vindication.
Our cleanness is known full openly
by virtue of his great consolation.

They exit with joy.

Thomas More (1478-1535)

Thomas More was born in London and educated in the law. He considered taking monastic vows but decided instead to marry and devote himself to the service of the crown, holding among others the offices of speaker of the House of Commons (1523 and Lord Chancellor of England (1529– 1532). The issue of Henry VIII's divorce from Catherine of Aragon resulted in More's resignation; and after his refusal to acknowledge the king as head of the English Church (the Act of Supremacy), he was charged with treason. After an unfair trial, he was executed in July 1535.

More is remembered not only as King Henry's most principled opponent but also as the author of Utopia (1516), one of the great books of the Northern Renaissance. Sharing with his close friends Erasmus and John Colet a strong belief in the need for church reform, he wrote of a previously unknown island where charity, reason, cooperation, and virtue operated. This mythical island of Utopia (No Place) he contrasted to the England he knew. The book is also an evocative expression of the values of northern humanism, a movement More strongly supported both privately and officially.

———————————

Chapter Nineteen

Utopia

BOOK ONE

There was recently a rather serious difference of opinion between that great expert in the art of government, His Invincible Majesty, King Henry the Eighth of England, and His Serene Highness, Prince Charles of Castile. His Majesty sent me to Flanders to discuss and settle the matter, along with my friend Cuthbert Tunstall, an excellent person who has since been appointed Master of the Rolls, much to everyone's satisfaction. Of his learning and moral character I shall say nothing—not because I am afraid of seeming prejudiced in his favour, but because they are too remarkable for me to describe adequately, and too well known to need describing at all. I have no wish to labour the obvious.

We were met at Bruges, as previously arranged, by the envoys from Castile, who were all men of great distinction. Their nominal leader was the Mayor of Bruges, and a splendid fellow he was; but most of the thinking and talking was done by the Provost of Cassel, George de Theimsecke. This man was a born speaker, as well as a highly trained one. He was also a legal expert, and both by temperament and by long experience a first-rate negotiator. After one or two meetings there were still some points on which we had failed to agree, so they said goodbye to us for a few days and set off for Brussels, to consult their royal oracle. In the meantime I went to Antwerp on business of my own.

While I was there, I had several frequent visitors, but the one I liked best was a young native of Antwerp called Peter Gilles. He is much respected by his own people, and holds an important post in that town; but he fully deserves promotion to the highest post of all, for I do not know which impressed me more, his intellectual or his moral qualities. Certainly he is a very fine person, as well as a very fine scholar. He is scrupulously fair to everyone, but towards his friends he shows so much genuine kindness, loyalty, and affection, that he must be almost unique in his all-round capacity for friendship. He is unusually modest, utterly sincere, and has a shrewd simplicity all his own. He is also a delightful talker, who can be witty without hurting anyone's feelings. I was longing to get back to England and see my wife and children, as I had been away for over four months; but my homesickness was to a large extent relieved by the pleasure of his company and the charm of his conversation.

One day I had been to a service at the Cathedral of Notre Dame, a magnificent building which is always packed with people. I was just starting back to my hotel when I happened to see Peter Gilles talking to an elderly foreigner with a sunburnt face, a long beard, and a cloak slung carelessly over one shoulder. From his complexion and costume I judged him to be a sailor. At this point Peter caught sight of me. He immediately came up and said good morning, then before I had time to reply, drew me a little further away.

"Do you see that man over there?" he asked, indicating the one he had been talking to. "I was just bringing him along to visit you."

"If he's a friend of yours," I said, "I'll be very glad to see him."

"When you hear the sort of person he is," said Peter, "you'll be glad to see him anyway—for there's not a man alive today who can tell you so many stories about strange countries and their inhabitants as he can. I know what a passion you have for that kind of thing."

"Then I didn't guess too far wrong," I remarked. "The moment I saw him, I thought he must be a sailor."

"In that case you made a big mistake," he replied. "I mean, he's not a sailor of the Palinurus type. He's really more like Ulysses, or even Plato. You see, our friend Raphael—for that's his name, Raphael Nonseno—is quite a scholar. He knows a fair amount of Latin and a tremendous lot of Greek. He's concentrated on Greek, because he's mainly interested in philosophy, and he found that there's nothing important on that subject written in Latin, apart from some bits of Seneca and Cicero. He wanted to see the world, so he left his brothers to manage his property in Portugal—that's where he comes from—and joined up with Amerigo Vespucci. You know those *Four Voyages* of his that everyone's reading about? Well, Raphael was his constant companion during the last three, except that he didn't come back with him from the final voyage. Instead, he practically forced Amerigo to let him be one of the twenty-four men who were left behind in that fort. So he stayed out there, to indulge his taste for travel, which was all he really cared about. He didn't mind where he eventually died, for he had two favourite quotations, 'The unburied dead are covered by the sky' and 'You can get to heaven from anywhere'—an attitude which, but for the grace of God, might have led to serious trouble. Anyway, when Vespucci had gone, Raphael did a lot of exploring with five other members of the garrison. Finally, by an amazing stroke of luck, they turned up in Ceylon. From there he made his way to Calicut, where he was fortunate enough to find some Portuguese ships, and so, quite unexpectedly, got a passage home."

"Well, thank you very much," I said. "I'll certainly enjoy talking to a man like that. It's most kind of you to give me a chance of doing so."

I then walked up to Raphael and shook hands with him. After making a few stock remarks, as people generally do when first introduced, we adjourned to the garden of my hotel, where we sat down on a bench covered with a layer of turf, and began to talk more freely.

First of all Raphael told us what happened to him and the other men in the fort, from the point where Vespucci left them. By polite and friendly behaviour they gradually started ingratiating themselves with the local inhabitants. Soon relations were not merely peaceful but positively affectionate. They got on particularly well with a certain king, whose name and nationality have slipped my memory. He most generously provided Raphael and his five fellow-explorers with food and money for their journeys, which involved the use of boats as well as carriages. He also supplied a most reliable guide, who was told to put them in touch with various other kings, to whom they were given letters of introduction. Thus after travelling for many days they came to some large towns and densely populated areas, with quite a high standard of political organization.

Apparently, at the equator, and throughout most of the torrid zone, you find vast deserts parched by perpetual heat. Everything looks grim and desolate. There are no signs of cultivation, and no animal life, except for snakes and wild beasts, or equally wild and dangerous human beings. But, if you go on a bit further, things gradually improve. The climate becomes less extreme, the earth grows green and pleasant, human beings and animals are not so fierce. Finally, you come to people living in towns and cities, who are constantly engaged in trade, both by land and by sea, not only with one another or with their immediate neighbours, but even with quite distant countries.

"This gave me the chance," said Raphael, "of travelling about all over the place, for whenever I found a ship just setting sail I asked if my friends and I might go on board, and they were always glad to let us. The first ships we saw were flat-bottomed, with sails made of papyrus leaves stitched together, or else of wicker-work, or in some cases of leather. But the ones we came across later had sharp keels and canvas sails, and were generally just like ours. The sailors out there have a good knowledge of winds and tides, but I made myself extraordinarily popular with them by explaining the use of the magnetic compass.

They'd never heard of it before, and for that reason had always been rather frightened of the sea, and seldom risked going on it except during the summer. But now they put such faith in their compasses that they think nothing of winter voyages—although this new sense of security is purely subjective. In fact their over-confidence threatens to convert an apparently useful invention into a source of disaster."

It would take too long to repeat everything he told us about each place. Besides, that is not the purpose of this book. I may conceivably do so in another one, emphasizing the most instructive parts of his story, such as the sensible arrangements that he noticed in various civilized communities. These were the points on which we questioned him most closely, and he enlarged most willingly. We did not ask him if he had seen any monsters, for monsters have ceased to be news. There is never any shortage of horrible creatures who prey on human beings, snatch away their food, or devour whole populations; but examples of wise social planning are not so easy to find.

Of course, he saw much to condemn in the New World, but he also discovered several regulations which suggested possible methods of reforming European society. These, I say, will have to be dealt with later. My present plan is merely to repeat what he said about the laws and customs of Utopia.

I must start by recording the conversation which led up to the first mention of that republic. After shrewdly pointing out the mistakes that have been made on both sides of the globe—and there are certainly plenty of them—Raphael went on to discuss the more sensible features of Old and New World legislation. He seemed to have the facts about every single country at his finger-tips—as though he had spent a lifetime wherever he had stopped for a night. Peter Gilles was particularly impressed.

PETER: My clear Raphael, I can't think why you don't enter the service of some kind. I'm sure any king would jump at the chance of employing you. With your knowledge and experience, you'd be just the man to supply not only entertainment, but also instructive precedents and useful advice. At the same time you could be looking after your own interests, and being a great help to all your friends and relations.

RAPHAEL: I'm not really worried about them. I feel I've done my duty by them already. Most people hang on to their property until they're too old and ill to do so any longer—and even then they relinquish it with a very ill grace.

But I shared out mine among my friends and relations when I was still young and healthy. I think they should be satisfied with that. They can hardly expect me to go a stage further, and become a king's slave for their benefit.

PETER: God forbid! Service, not servitude, was what I suggested.

RAPHAEL: A few letters don't make all that difference.

PETER: Well, call it what you like, I still think it's our best method of helping other people, both individually and collectively, and also of making life pleasanter for yourself.

RAPHAEL: How can I do that by acting against all my instincts? At present I live exactly as I please, which is more, I suspect, than the vast majority of court officials can say. Besides, kings have quite enough people competing for their friendship already. It won't be any serious hardship for them to do without me, and a handful of others like me.

MORE: My dear Raphael, you're obviously not interested in money or power, and I couldn't respect you more if you were the greatest king on earth. But surely it would be quite in keeping with this admirably philosophical attitude if you could bring yourself, even at the cost of some personal inconvenience, to apply your talents and energies to public affairs? Now the most effective way of doing so would be to gain the confidence of some great King or other, and give him, as I know you would, really good advice. For every king is a sort of fountain, from which a constant shower of benefits or injuries rains down upon the whole population. And you've got so much theoretical knowledge, and so much practical experience, that either of them alone would be enough to make you an ideal member of any privy council.

RAPHAEL: You're quite mistaken, my dear More, first about me and then about the job itself. I'm not so highly qualified as you seem to think, and, even if I were, I still shouldn't do the slightest good to the community by giving myself a lot of extra work. To start with, most kings are more interested in the science of war—which I don't know anything about, and don't want to—than in useful peacetime techniques They're far more anxious, by hook or by crook, to acquire new kingdoms than to govern their existing ones properly. Besides, privy councillors are either too wise to need, or too conceited to take advice from anyone else—though of course they're always prepared to suck up to the King's special favourites by agreeing with the silliest things they say. After all, it's a natural instinct to be charmed by one's own productions. That's why raven chicks are such a delight to their parents, and mother apes find their babies exquisitely beautiful.⌉

⌈So there you have a group of people who are deeply prejudiced against everyone else's ideas, or at any rate prefer their own. Suppose, in such company, you suggest a policy that you've seen adopted elsewhere, or for which you can quote a historical precedent, what will happen? They'll behave as though their professional reputations were at stake, and they'd look fools for the rest of their lives if they couldn't raise some objection to your proposal. Failing all else, their last resort will be: "This was good enough for our ancestors, and who are we to question their wisdom?" Then they'll settle back in their chairs, with an air of having said the last word on the subject—as if it would be a major disaster for anyone to be caught being wiser than his ancestors! And yet we're quite prepared to reverse their most sensible decisions. It's only the less intelligent ones that we cling on to like grim death. I've come across this curious mixture of conceit, stupidity, and stubbornness in several different places. On one occasion I even met it in England.⌉

MORE: Really? Have you been to my country too, then ?

RAPHAEL: Certainly I have. I was there for several months, soon after that disastrous civil war which began with a revolution, in the west country, and ended with a ghastly massacre of the rebels. During my stay, I received a lot of kindness from the Most Reverend John Morton, the Archbishop of Canterbury. He was also a Cardinal, and at that time Lord Chancellor of England. I must tell you about him, Peter—for I can't tell More anything he doesn't know already. He was a person that one respected just as much for his wisdom and moral character as for his great eminence. He was of average height, without a trace of a stoop, although he was fairly old. He had the sort of face that inspires reverence rather than fear. He was quite easy to get on with, though always serious and dignified. Admittedly he was rather inclined to be rude to people who asked him for jobs, but he meant no harm by it. He only did it to test their intelligence and presence of mind, for he found these qualities very congenial, so long as they were used with discretion, and considered them most valuable in public life. He was a polished and effective speaker, with a thorough knowledge of the law. He also had a quite remarkable intellect, and a phenomenal memory— two natural gifts which he'd further developed by training and practice.

Apparently the King had great confidence in his judgement, and at the time of my visit the whole country seemed to depend on him. This was hardly surprising, since he'd been rushed straight from the university to Court, when he was not much more than a boy, and had spent the rest of his life in the public service, learning wisdom the hard way, by having to cope with a long series of crises. And what one learns like that isn't easily forgotten.

I once happened to be dining with the Cardinal when a certain English lawyer was there. I forgot how the subject came up, but he was speaking with great enthusiasm about the stern measures that were then being taken against thieves.

"We're hanging them all over the place," he said, "I've seen as many as twenty on a single gallows. And that's what I find so odd. Considering how few of them get away with it, why are we still plagued with so many robbers?"

"What's odd about it?" I asked—for I never hesitated to speak freely in front of the Cardinal. "This method of dealing with thieves is both unjust and socially undesirable. As a punishment it's too severe, and as a deterrent it's quite ineffective. Petty larceny isn't bad enough to deserve the death penalty, and no penalty on earth will stop people from stealing, if it's their only way of getting food. In this respect you English, like most other nations, remind me of incompetent schoolmasters, who prefer caning their pupils to teaching them. Instead of inflicting these horrible punishments, it would be far more to the point to provide everyone with some means of livelihood, so that nobody's under the frightful necessity of becoming first a thief and then a corpse."

"There's adequate provision for that already," replied the lawyer. "There are plenty of trades open to them. There's always work on the land. They could easily earn an honest living if they wanted to, but they deliberately choose to be criminals."

"You can't get out of it like that," I said. "Let's ignore, for the sake of argument, the case of the disabled soldier, who has lost a limb in the service of King and Country, either at home or abroad—perhaps in that battle with the Cornish rebels, or perhaps during the fighting in France not so long ago. When he comes home, he finds he's physically incapable of practising his former trade, and too old to learn a new one. But as I say, let's forget about him, since war is only an intermittent phenomenon. Let's stick to the type of thing that happens every day.

["Well, first of all there are lots of noblemen who live like drones on the labour of other people, in other words, of their tenants, and keep bleeding them white by constantly raising their rents.]For that's their only idea of practical economy—otherwise they'd soon be ruined by their extravagance. But not content with remaining idle themselves, they take round with them vast numbers of equally idle retainers, who have never been taught any method of earning their living. The moment their master dies, or they themselves fall ill, they're promptly given the sack—for these noblemen are far more sympathetic towards idleness than illness, and their heirs often can't afford to keep up such large establishments. Now a sacked retainer is apt to get violently hungry, if he doesn't resort to violence. For what's the alternative? He can, of course, wander around until his clothes and his body are both worn out, and he's nothing but a mass of rags and sores. But in that state no gentleman will condescend to employ him, and no farmer can risk doing so—for who could be less likely to serve a poor man faithfully, sweating away with mattock and hoe for a beggarly wage and a barely adequate diet, than a man who has been brought up in the lap of luxury, and is used to swaggering about in military uniform, looking down his nose at everyone else in the neighbourhood?"

"But that's exactly the kind of person we need to encourage," retorted the lawyer. "In wartime he forms the backbone of the army, simply because he has more spirit and self-respect than an ordinary tradesman or farm-hand."

["You might as well say," I answered, "that for purposes of war you have to encourage theft.]Well, you"ll certainly never run short of thieves, so long as you have people like that about. And, of course, you're perfectly right—thieves do make quite efficient soldiers, and soldiers make quite enterprising thieves. The two professions have a good deal in common. However, the trouble is not confined to England, although you've got it pretty badly.[It's practically a world-wide epidemic. France, for instance, is suffering from an even more virulent form of it. There the whole country is overrun even in peacetime—if you can call it that—by mercenaries who have been brought in for much the same reasons as you gave for supporting idle retainers.]You see, the experts decided, in the interests of public safety, that they must have a powerful standing army, consisting mostly of veterans—for they put so little faith in raw recruits that they deliberately start wars to give their soldiers practice, and make them cut throats "just to keep their hands in," as Sallust rather nicely puts it.

"So France has learnt by bitter experience how dangerous it is to keep these savage pets, but there are plenty of similar object-lessons in the history of Rome, Carthage, Syria, and many other countries. Again and again standing armies have seized some opportunity of overthrowing the government that employed them, devastating its territory, and destroying its towns. And yet it's quite unnecessary. That's obvious enough from the fact that for all their intensive military training the French can't often claim to have beaten your wartime conscripts—I won't put it more strongly than that, for fear of seeming to flatter present company.

"Besides, it's not generally thought that either of the types you mentioned, the tradesmen in town or the ignorant farmhand in the country, is actually so very frightened of the retainers in question—unless his physical strength isn't equal to his courage, or his spirit has been broken by privations at home. The fact is that though these retainers start off with powerful physiques—for no gentleman would stoop to corrupt an inferior specimen—they soon get soft and flabby by sitting around doing nothing, or nothing that a woman couldn't do. So there's really not much risk of their losing all their manhood, if they were taught useful trades and made to work like men. In any case I don't see how it can possibly be in the public interest to prepare for a war, which you needn't have unless you want to, by maintaining innumerable disturbers of the peace—when peace is so infinitely more important.

"But that's not the only thing that compels people to steal. There are other factors at work which must, I think, be peculiar to your country."

"And what are they?" asked the Cardinal.

"Sheep," I told him. "These placid creatures, which used to require so little food, have now apparently developed a raging appetite, and turned into man-eaters. Fields, houses, towns, everything goes down their throats.

"To put it more plainly, in those parts of the kingdom where the finest, and so the most expensive wool is produced, the nobles and gentlemen, not to mention several saintly abbots, have grown dissatisfied with the income that their predecessors got out of their estates. They're no longer content to lead lazy, comfortable lives, which do no good to society—they must actively do it harm, by enclosing all the land they can for pasture, and leaving none for cultivation. They're even tearing down houses and demolishing whole towns—except, of course, for the churches, which they preserve for use as sheepfolds. As though they didn't waste enough of your soil already on their coverts and game-preserves, these kind souls have started destroying all traces of human habitation, and turning every scrap of farmland into a wilderness.

"So what happens? Each greedy individual preys on his native land like a malignant growth, absorbing field after field, and enclosing thousands of acres with a single fence. Result—hundreds of farmers are evicted. They're either cheated or bullied into giving up their property, or systematically ill-treated until they're finally forced to sell. Whichever way it's done, out the poor creatures have to go, men and women, husbands and wives, widows and orphans, mothers and tiny children, together with all their employees—whose great numbers are not a sign of wealth, but simply of the fact that you can't run a farm without plenty of manpower. Out they have to go from the homes that they know so well, and they can't find anywhere else to live. Their whole stock of furniture wouldn't fetch much of a price, even if they could afford to wait for a suitable offer. But they can't, so they get very little indeed for it. By the time they've been wandering around for a bit, this little is all used up, and then what can they do but steal—and be very properly hanged? Of course, they can always become tramps and beggars, but even then they're liable to be arrested as vagrants, and put in prison for being idle—when nobody will give them a job, however much they want one. For farm-work is what they're used to, and where there's no arable land, there's no farm-work to be done. After all, it only takes one shepherd or cowherd to graze animals over an area that would need any amount of labour to make it fit for corn production.

"For the same reason, corn is much dearer in many districts. The price of wool has also risen so steeply that your poorer weavers simply can't afford to buy it, which means a lot more people thrown out of work. This is partly due to an epidemic of the rot, which destroyed vast numbers of sheep just after the conversion of arable to pasture land began. It almost looked like a judgement on the landowners for their greed—except that *they* ought to have caught it instead of the sheep.

"Not that prices would fall, however many sheep there were, for the sheep market has become, if not strictly a monopoly—for that implies only one seller—then at least an oligopoly. I mean it's almost entirely under the control of a few rich men, who don't need to sell unless they feel like it, and never do feel like it until they can get the price they want. This also accounts for the equally high prices of other types of livestock, especially in view of the shortage of breeders caused by the demolition of farms, and the general decline of agriculture. For the rich men I'm talking about never bother to breed either sheep or cattle themselves. They merely buy scraggy specimens cheap from someone else, fatten them up on their own pastures, and resell them at a large profit. I imagine that's why the full effects of the situation have not yet been felt. So far they've only inflated prices in the areas where they sell, but, if they keep transferring animals from other districts faster than they can be replaced, stocks in the buying areas too will gradually be depleted, until eventually there'll be an acute shortage everywhere.

"Thus a few greedy people have converted one of England's greatest natural advantages into a national disaster. For it's the high price of food that makes employers turn off so many of their servants—which inevitably means turning them into beggars or thieves. And theft comes easier to a man of spirit.

"To make matters worse, this wretched poverty is most incongruously linked with expensive tastes. Servants, tradesmen, even farm-labourers, in fact all classes of society are recklessly extravagant about clothes and food. Then think how many brothels there are, including those that go under the names of wine-taverns or ale-houses. Think of the demoralizing games people play—dice, cards, backgammon, tennis, howls, quoits—what are they but quick methods of wasting a man's money, and sending him straight off to become a thief?

"Get rid of these pernicious practices. Make a law that anyone responsible for demolishing a farm or a country town must either rebuild it himself or else hand over the land to someone who's willing to do so. Stop the rich from cornering markets and establishing virtual monopolies. Reduce the number of people who are kept doing nothing. Revive agriculture and the wool industry, so that there's plenty of honest, useful work for the great army of unemployed—by which I mean not only existing thieves, but tramps and idle servants who are bound to become thieves eventually. Until you put these things right, you're not entitled to boast of the justice meted out to thieves, for it's a justice more specious than real or socially desirable. You allow these people to be brought up in the worst possible way, and systematically corrupted from their earliest years. Finally, when they grow up and commit the crimes that they were obviously destined to commit, ever since they were children, you start punishing them. In other words, you create thieves, and then punish them for stealing."

Long before I'd finished, the lawyer was ready with his answer. He was evidently one of those people whose method of argument consists in repeating what you've said, rather than replying to it—as though having a good memory were all that mattered.

"That was a very fine effort," he said, "especially for a foreigner whose information is bound to be second-hand, and therefore inaccurate— as I'll very briefly demonstrate. I'll begin by running through the points you've made. Then I'll show where you've gone wrong through your ignorance of local conditions. And finally I'll refute all your arguments. Proceeding in that order, I think you've made four—."

"Just a moment," interrupted the Cardinal. "After such an introduction, your reply seems unlikely to be as brief as you suggest. So don't bother to produce it now—keep it fresh for your next meeting. Why not make it tomorrow, if you're both free then? Meanwhile, my dear Raphael, I'd very much like to hear just why you object to capital punishment for theft, and what penalty you think would be more in the public interest. For even you, I take it, feel that stealing should be stopped. And since it goes on merrily in spite of the death penalty, what power on earth could stop it, what possible deterrent could be effective, if the fear of death were removed? Surely any reduction of sentence would be interpreted as a positive invitation to crime?"

"Your Grace," I said, "it seems to me quite unjust to take a man's life because he's taken some money. To my mind no amount of property is equivalent to a human life. If it's argued that the punishment is not for taking the money, but for breaking the law and violating justice, isn't this conception of absolute justice absolutely unjust? One really can't approve of a régime so dictatorial that the slightest disobedience is punishable by death, nor of a legal code based on the Stoic paradox that all offences are equal—so that there's no distinction in law between theft and murder, though in equity the two things are so completely different.

"God said, "Thou shalt not kill"—does the theft of a little money make it quite all right for us to do so? If it's said that this commandment applies only to illegal killing, what's to prevent human beings from similarly agreeing among themselves to legalize certain types of rape, adultery, or perjury? Considering that God has forbidden us even to kill ourselves, can we really believe that purely human arrangements for the regulation of mutual slaughter are enough, without any divine authority, to exempt executioners from the sixth commandment? Isn't that rather like saying that this particular commandment has no more validity than human laws allow it?—in which case the principle can be extended indefinitely, until in all spheres of life human beings decide just how far God's commandments may conveniently be observed.

"Under the law of Moses—which was harsh enough in all conscience, being designed for slaves, and rebellious ones at that—thieves were not hanged, but merely fined. We can hardly suppose that the new dispensation, which expresses God's fatherly kindness towards His children, allows us more scope than the old for being cruel to one another.

"Well, those are my objections on moral grounds. From a practical point of view, surely it's obvious that to punish thieves and murderers in precisely the same way is not only absurd but also highly dangerous for the public. If a thief knows that a conviction for murder will get him into no more trouble than a conviction for theft, he's naturally impelled to kill the person that he'd otherwise merely have robbed. It's no worse for him if he's caught, and it gives him a better chance of not being caught, and of concealing the crime altogether by eliminating the only witness. So in our efforts to terrorize thieves we're actually encouraging them to murder innocent people.

"Now for the usual question—what punishment would be better? I'd have found it much harder to answer, if you'd asked me what would be worse. Well, why should we doubt the value of a system which those expert administrators, the Romans, found satisfactory for so long? They, as we know, sentenced people convicted of major crimes to penal servitude for life in mines or stone quarries.

"However, the best arrangement I know is one I came across while travelling through Persia, in a district generally known as Tallstoria. The Tallstorians form quite a large and well-organized community, which is completely autonomous, except for having to pay taxes to the King of Persia. As they're a long way from the sea, practically encircled by mountains, and content to live on the produce of their own soil, which is extremely fertile, they have little contact with foreigners. They've never had any wish to increase their territory, which is secured against external aggression both by the mountains and by the protection-money that they pay to the Great King. This means that they're exempt from military service, so they're able to live in comfort, if not in luxury, and be happy, if not exactly famous or glorious—for, apart from their immediate neighbours, I doubt if anyone has ever heard of them.

"Well, in Tallstoria a convicted thief has to return what he's stolen to its owner, not, as in most other countries, to the King—who according to the Tallstorians has just about as much right to it as the thief himself. If the stolen goods are no longer in his possession, their value is deducted from his own property, the rest of which is handed over intact to his wife and children. He himself is sentenced to hard labour. Except in cases of robbery with violence, he's not put in prison or made to wear fetters, but left quite free and employed on public works. If he downs tools or goes slow, they don't slow him down still more by loading him with chains—they accelerate his movements with a whip. If he works hard, he's not treated at all badly. He has to answer a roll-call every evening, and he's locked up for the night—but otherwise, apart from having to work very long hours, he has a perfectly comfortable life.

"The food, for instance, is quite reasonable. It's provided at the public expense, since convicts work as servants of the public. The procedure for raising the money varies from place to place. In some districts it's collected from voluntary contributions. This sounds an unreliable method, but in practice it brings in more than any other, for the people there are extraordinarily kind-hearted, Elsewhere, certain public revenues are set aside for the purpose, or a special poll-tax is levied. There are also some places where, instead of being employed on public works, convicts are hired out to private enterprise. Anyone needing their services goes to the market-place and engages them by the day, at a rather lower wage than he would pay for free labour. He's also allowed to whip them if they don't work hard enough. This system ensures that they're never out of work, their meals are provided for them, and each convict makes a daily contribution to public funds.

"They all wear clothes of a special colour which nobody else wears. Their heads aren't actually shaved, but the hair is clipped short just above the ears, and a tiny piece is cut off one of them. Their friends are allowed to give them food and drink, and clothes of the regulation colour, but it's a capital crime for anyone to give them money, or for them to accept it. So it is for free men to accept money on any pretext from slaves—as convicts are usually called—or for slaves to touch any kind of weapon.

"Each slave is given a badge to show which district he belongs to, and it's a capital crime to take one's badge off, to be seen outside one's own district, or to speak to a slave from another district. As for running away, it's just as risky to plan it as to do it. The penalty for being accessory to any such plan is death for a slave, and slavery for a free man—whereas by betraying an escape-project you can earn a reward in cash, if you're a free man, or your freedom, if you're a slave. In either case the informer receives a pardon for his part in the plot, on the principle that it must always be safer to abandon a criminal undertaking than to go ahead with it.

"Well, that's how the system works, and it's obviously most convenient and humane. It comes down heavily on crime, but it saves the lives of criminals, treating them in such a way that they're forced to become good citizens, and spend the rest of their lives making up for the harm they've done in the past.

"In fact there's so little risk of their relapsing into their old habits, that they're generally regarded as the safest possible guides for long-distance travellers, who employ them in relays, one for each district they pass through. You see, slaves have no facilities for highway-robbery. They're not allowed to carry weapons. If money is found on them, it proves that they've committed a crime. If they're caught, punishment is automatic, and they haven't the slightest hope of not being caught—for how can you make an unobtrusive getaway when your clothes are quite different from ordinary people's, unless you decamp in the nude?—and even then your ear will betray you.

"There's still, of course, a theoretical risk that they might start a conspiracy to overthrow the government. But how could the slaves of any one district hope to organize such a large-scale operation, without first sounding and stirring up the slaves in several other districts? And that's physically impossible. They're not even allowed to meet them, or talk to them, or say good morning to them, let alone conspire with them. Besides, can you imagine anyone cheerfully letting the other slaves of his district into a secret which would be so dangerous for them to keep, and so very profitable for them to betray? On the other hand, every slave has some hope of recovering his freedom, simply by doing what he's told and giving the authorities reason to believe that he'll go straight in future—since a certain number of slaves are released every year for good conduct."

I then added that I didn't see why this system shouldn't be adopted in England. It could produce far better results than the so-called "justice" that the lawyer had praised so highly.

At this our learned friend—I mean the lawyer—shook his head.

"Such a system," he announced, with a smile of contempt, "could never be adopted in England, without serious danger to the country."

That was all he said—and practically everyone else agreed with him.

Then the Cardinal gave his opinion.

"It's hard to predict," he said, "without giving it a trial, whether it would work or not. But suppose the king were to postpone the execution of death sentences for an experimental period—having first abolished all rights of asylum. If the results were good, we'd be justified in making the arrangement permanent. If not, the original sentences could still be carried out, with quite as much benefit to society, and quite as much justice, as if they were carried out now. In the meantime no great harm could have been done. As a matter of fact, I don't think it would be at all a bad idea to treat vagrants in the same way. We're always making laws shout them, but so far nothing has had the slightest effect."

This, from the Cardinal, was enough to make everyone wildly in favour of an idea which nobody had taken seriously when *I* produced it, They were particularly keen on the bit about vagrants, since that was his own contribution.

William Caxton (b. 1415–1424, d. 1492)

William Caxton was born between 1415 and 1424 in Kent. His parents apprenticed him to a mercer, Robert Large, who later became mayor of London, suggesting that the Caxtons were a family of some substance. The mercers were heavily involved in overseas trade and Caxton seems to have traveled regularly to Bruges. By 1462 he had settled in that city and was the governor of the English nation of the Merchant Adventurers Company, a prominent position. While in Bruges Caxton probably dealt in the manuscript trade from the Low Countries, and this may have led to his interest in printing. He decided to produce English translations of fashionable Burgundian texts and in 1469 he began a translation of Le Recueil des Histoires de Troye. *In late 1473 or early 1474 he published his translation of the* Recueil, *the* Recuyell of the Histories of Troy, *the first book printed in English. However, Caxton discovered that he could not sell books in English from the continent and in 1476 he moved to England and set up a press near Westminster Abbey. From his shop he sold imported books as well as his own material. Throughout his career he remained a merchant who focused on the book trade, rather than a printer as such. Between 1476 and his death in 1492 he published almost one hundred books, many of which he had translated himself from French. They included romances, saints' lives, medieval versions of the classics and religious treatises. He was careful to ensure that the books he printed would sell, and thus he focused on well-known material, or famous translators. Caxton was both a skilled marketer of books and an insightful critic; many of his prefaces to his translations explain why people should read these particular books, allowing us an unusual insight into the reading taste of the period.*

Chapter Twenty

Prologue to his Translation of Eneydos

After diverse works made, translated and achieved, having no work in hand, I was sitting in my study where many pamphlets and books lay. It happened that a little book in French came to my hand, recently translated out of Latin by some noble clerk of France, which book is called *Eneydos*, written in Latin by that noble poet and great clerk Virgil. In this book I saw and read how, after the general destruction of the great Troy, Aeneas departed bearing his old father Anchises upon his shoulders, his little son Ilus[1] on his hand, his wife with many other people following, and how he took ship and departed, with all the story of his adventures that he had before he came to the achievement of his conquest of Italy, as all along shall be shown in this present book. I had great pleasure in this book because of the fair and honest terms and words in French. I never saw its like before, nor any so pleasant or so well ordered and it seemed to me that this book should be required for noble men to see, as much for the eloquence as the histories, for many hundreds of years ago the said book of *Eneydos*, with many other works, was made and learned daily in schools, especially in Italy and other places, which history the said Virgil made in metre.

And when I had advised me in the said book, I deliberated and concluded to translate it into English. Forthwith I took a pen and ink and wrote a leaf or two, which I looked over again to correct it. And when I saw the fair and strange terms therein, I thought that it should not please some gentlemen who lately blamed me, saying that in my translations I had overcurious terms which could not be understood by the common people, and desired me to use old and homely terms in my translations. I would be glad to satisfy every man, and to do so I took an old book and read it, and certainly the English was so rough and broad that I could not understand it well. And also my lord abbot of Westminster recently showed me certain documents written in old English to reduce it into our English now used. And certainly it was written in such a way that it was more like German than English and I could not reduce or bring it to be understood.

And certainly our language now used varies far from that which was used and spoken when I was born. For we Englishmen are born under the rule of the moon, which is never steadfast but ever wavering, waxing one season and waning and decreasing another season. And the common English that is spoken in one shire varies from another in so much that in my day it happened that certain merchants were in a ship on the Thames to sail over the sea to Zeeland and for lack of wind they waited and went to land to refresh themselves. And one of them called Sheffield, a mercer, came into a house and asked for food and especially he asked for *eggys*. And the good wife answered that she could speak no French. And the merchant was angry, for he also could speak no French, but he would have eggs and she did not understand him. And then at last another said that he would have *eyren* and then the good wife said that she understood him well. Lo, what should a man in these days now write, *egges* or *eyren*, certainly it is hard to please every man because of diversity and change of language. For in these days every man that has any reputation in his country will utter his communication and matters in such manners and terms that few men will understand him. And some honest and great clerks have been with me and desired me to write the most curious terms that I could find. And thus between plain rude and curious I stand abashed, but in my judgment the common terms that are used daily are more easily understood than the old and ancient English.

And for as much as this present book is not for a rude uplandish man to labour therein nor to read it, but only for a clerk and a noble gentleman that experiences and understands feats of arms, love and noble chivalry, therefore in a middle way between both I have reduced and translated this said book into our English, not over rough or curious but in such terms as shall be understood by God's grace according to my copy. And if any man will busy himself in reading it and find terms that he cannot understand, let him go read and learn Virgil or the epistles of Ovid and there he shall easily see and understand all, if he has a good reader and informer. For this book is not for every rude and ignorant man to see, but for clerks and true gentlemen that understand gentleness and science.

Then I pray all those that will read this little treatise to hold me excused for the translating of it. For I acknowledge myself ignorant of cunning to attempt such a high and noble work, but I pray Master John Skelton, late created poet laureate in the university of Oxford, to oversee and correct this said book and to address and expound where fault is found to those that shall require it. For I know that he is able to expound and english every difficulty that is therin, for he has recently translated the epistles of Tully and the book of Diodorus Siculus and divers other works out of Latin into English, not in rough and old language, but in polished and ornate terms with craft, as he that has read Virgil, Ovid, Tully and all the other noble poets and orators unknown to me. And he has also read the ix muses and understands their musical sciences and to which of them each science is appropriate. I suppose he has drunk of Helicon's well. Then I pray him and such other to correct, add or take away where he or they will find fault, for I have only followed my copy in French as nearly as I could. And if any word is said therin well, I am glad, and if otherwise I submit my said book to their correction.

Which book I present unto the high born, my future natural and sovereign lord Arthur, by the grace of God prince of Wales, duke of Cornwall and earl of Chester, first begotten son and heir unto our most dread natural and sovereign lord and most Christian King Henry the VII, by the grace of God king of England and of France and lord of Ireland, beseeching his noble grace to receive it in thank of me his most humble subject and servant. And I shall pray unto almighty God for his prosperous increasing in virtue, wisdom and humanity that he may be equal with the most renowned of all his noble progenitors.

And so to live in this present life that after this transitory life he and we all may come to everlasting life in heaven. Amen.

Endnote

1. Ascanius, called Ilus while Troy stood.

Miguel de Cervantes Saavedra (1547–1616)

Born in 1547 in Alcala de Henares, Cervantes enjoyed a brief humanist education in Madrid under Juan Lopez de Hoyos, but augmented this study with wide reading and travel, visiting Italy, for example, and acquiring a deep appreciation for Italian renaissance culture. He was also a soldier and fought—and was wounded—at the great naval battle of Lepanto in 1571 in which the Christian Holy League defeated the Turkish fleet. Later, however, Cervantes was captured and sold into slavery in Algiers, and not ransomed until 1580.

Returning to Spain he was appointed a collector of taxes to be used to assemble the Armada of Philip II against England, but was imprisoned because of problems with his accounts. In prison on several other occasions for debt, he began to write Don Quixote *while in jail. It is a satire on the tales of chivalry so popular in Spain at the time, following the adventures of its hero, Don Quixote, and his servant, Sancho Panza. This early novel became the most popular work of Spanish literature when printed (part one in 1605, part two in 1615) and made its author's fortune. Cervantes died in Madrid in 1616.*

Chapter Twenty-One

Don Quixote

Dedication To the Duke of Béjar
Marquis of Gibraleón, Count of Benalcázar and Bañares, Viscount of La
Puebla de Alcocer, Lord of the Towns of Capilla, Curiel, and Burguillos[1]

Confident of the courteous reception and honors that Your Excellency bestows
on all sorts of books, as a prince so inclined to favor the fine arts, chiefly those
which by their nobility do not submit to the service and bribery of the vulgar,
I have decided to publish *The Ingenious Gentleman Don Quixote of La Mancha*
in the shelter of Your Excellency's most illustrious name. And with the obeisance
I owe to such grandeur, I beg you to receive it graciously under your protection,
so that in this shadow, though deprived of those precious ornaments of elegance
and erudition that clothe works composed in the houses of those who know, it
may dare appear with assurance before the judgment of some who, trespassing
the bounds of their own ignorance, condemn with more rigor and less justice
the writings of others. It is my earnest hope that Your Excellency's wisdom will
consider my honorable purpose and will not disdain the littleness of so humble
a service.[2]

Prologue

Idle reader: you may believe me, without my having to swear, that I would have
liked this book, as it is the child of my brain, to be the fairest, gayest, and
cleverest that could be imagined. But I could not counteract Nature's law that
everything shall beget its like; and what, then, could this sterile, uncultivated
wit of mine beget but the story of a dry, shriveled, eccentric offspring, full of
thoughts of all sorts and such as never came into any other imagination—just
what might be begotten in a prison, where every misery is lodged and every
doleful sound makes its dwelling?[3] Tranquillity, a cheerful retreat, pleasant
fields, bright skies, murmuring brooks, peace of mind, these are the things that
go far to make even the most barren muses fertile and cause them to bring into
the world offspring that fill it with wonder and delight.

Sometimes when a father has an ugly, unattractive child, the love he bears him so blindfolds his eyes that he does not see its defects; on the contrary, he considers them marks of intelligence and charm and talks of them to his friends as wit and grace. I, however—for though I pass for the father, I am the stepfather of Don Quixote—I have no desire to go with the current of custom or to implore you, dearest reader, almost with tears in my eyes, as others do, to pardon or excuse the defects you may perceive in this child of mine. You are neither its relative nor its friend, your soul is your own and your will as free as any man's, you are in your own house and master of it as much as the king of his taxes, and you know the common saying, "A man's home is his castle"[4]—all of which exempts and frees you from every consideration and obligation. And you can say what you will about the story without fear of being abused for any ill or rewarded for any good you may say of it.

My wish would be simply to present it to you plain and unadorned, without the embellishment of a prologue or the lengthy catalogue of the usual sonnets, epigrams, and eulogies, such as are commonly put at the beginning of books. For I can tell you, though composing it cost me considerable effort, I found nothing harder than the making of this prologue you are now reading. Many times I took up my pen to write it, and many I laid it down again, not knowing what to write. One of these times, as I was pondering with the paper before me, a pen behind my car, my elbow on the desk, and my cheek in my hand, thinking of what I should say, there came in unexpectedly a certain lively, clever friend of mine, who, seeing me so deep in thought, asked the reason; to which I, making no mystery of it, answered that I was thinking of the prologue I had to write for the story of Don Quixote, which so troubled me that I had a mind not to write any at all—nor even publish the achievements of so noble a knight.

"For, how could you expect me not to feel uneasy about what that ancient lawgiver they call the Public will say when it sees me, after slumbering so many year's in the silence of oblivion, coming out now with all my years upon my back, and with a book as dry as a bone, devoid of invention, meager in style, poor in conceits, wholly wanting in learning and doctrine, without quotations in the margin or annotations at the end, after the fashion of other books I see, which, though on fictitious and profane subjects, are so full of maxims from Aristotle and Plato and the whole herd of philosophers that they fill the readers with amazement and convince them that the authors are men of learning, erudition, and eloquence. And then, when they quote the Holy Scriptures, anyone would say they are St. Thomases or other doctors of the Church, observing as they do a decorum so ingenious that in one sentence they describe a distracted lover and in the next deliver a devout little sermon that it is a pleasure and a treat to hear and read. Of all this there will be nothing in my book, for I have nothing to quote in the margin or to note at the end, and still less do I know what authors I follow in it, to place them at the beginning, as all do, under the letters A, B, C, beginning with Aristotle and ending with Xenophon or Zoilus or Zeuxis, though one was a slanderer and the other a painter. Also my book must do without sonnets at the beginning, at least sonnets whose authors are dukes, marquises, counts, bishops, ladies, or famous poets. Though if I were to ask two or three friendly tradesmen, I know they would give me some, and such that the productions of those that have the highest reputation in our Spain could not equal.[5]

"In short, my friend," I continued, "I am determined that Señor Don Quixote shall remain buried in the archives of his own La Mancha until Heaven provides someone to garnish him with all those things he stands in need of; because I find myself, through my incapacity and want of learning, unequal to supplying them, and because I am by nature indolent and lazy about hunting for authors to say what I myself can say without them. Hence, my friend, the cogitation and abstraction you found me in, and what you have heard from me is sufficient cause for it."

Hearing this, my friend, giving himself a slap on the forehead and breaking into a hearty laugh, exclaimed, "Before God, brother, now am I disabused of an error in which I have been living all this long time I have known you, all through which I have taken you to be shrewd and sensible in all you do; but now I see you are as far from that as the heaven is from the earth. Is it possible that things of so little moment and so easy to set right can occupy and perplex a ripe wit like yours, accustomed to break through and crush far greater obstacles? By my faith, this comes, not of any want of ability, but of too much indolence and too little thinking. Do you want to know if I am telling the truth? Well, then, pay attention to me, and you will see how, in the opening and shutting of an eye, I sweep away all your difficulties and supply all those deficiencies which you say check and discourage you from bringing before the world the story of your famous Don Quixote, the light and mirror of all knight-errantry."

"Say on," said I, listening to his talk. "How do you propose to make up for my diffidence and reduce to order this chaos of perplexity I am in?"

To which he answered, "Your first difficulty, about the sonnets, epigrams, or complimentary verses which you lack for the beginning and which ought to be by persons of importance and rank, can be removed if you yourself take a little trouble to write them. You can afterwards baptize them and give them any name you like, fathering them on Prester John of the Indies or the Emperor of Trebizond, who I know were said to have been famous poets. And even if they were not, and any pedants or bachelors should attack you and question the fact, don't let it bother you two *maravedís'* worth, for even if they prove a lie against you, they cannot cut off the hand you wrote it with.

"As to references in the margin to the books and authors from whom you take the maxims and sayings you put into your story, all you have to do is work in any sentence or scraps of Latin you may happen to know by heart, or at any rate that will not give you much trouble to look up. Thus when you speak of freedom and captivity, you can insert *Non bene pro toto libertas venditur auro;*[6] and then refer in the margin to Horace, or whoever said it. Or, if you allude to the power of death, you can bring in *Pallida mors æquo pulsat pede pauperum tabernas,/ Regumque turres.*[7]

"If it is the friendship and the love God commands us to feel towards our enemy, go at once to the Holy Scriptures, which you can do with a very small amount of research, and quote no less than the words of God himself: *Ego autem dico vobis: diligite inimicos vestros.*[8] If you speak of evil thoughts, turn to the Gospel: *De corde exeunt cogitationes malæ.*[9] If of the fickleness of friends, there is Cato, who will give you his couplet: *Donec eris felix muttos numerabis amicos,/Tempora si fuerint nubila, solus eris.*[1] With these and such like bits of Latin they will take you for a grammarian at all events, and that nowadays is no small honor and profit.

"With regard to adding annotations at the end of the book, you may safely do it in this way. If you mention any giant in your book, arrange for it to be the giant Goliath, and with this alone, which will cost you almost nothing, you have a grand note, for you can put *The giant Golias* or *Goliath was a Philistine whom the shepherd David slew by a mighty stone—cast in the Terebinth valley, as is related in the Book of Kings*, in the chapter where you find it written.

"Next, to prove yourself a man of erudition in polite literature and a cosmographer, manage to mention the river Tagus in your story, and there you are at once with another fine annotation, setting forth *The river Tagus was so called after a King of Spain: it has its source in such and such a place and*

falls into the ocean, kissing the walls of the famous city of Lisbon, and it is a
common belief that it has golden sands, etc.

"If you should have anything to do with robbers, I will give you the story
of Cacus, for I know it by heart; if with loose women, there is the Bishop of
Mondoñedo, who will lend you Lamia, Laida, and Flora, any reference to whom
will bring you great credit; if with hardhearted ones, Ovid will furnish you with
Medea; if with witches or enchantresses, Homer has Calypso, and Virgil Circe;
if with valiant captains, Julius Cæsar himself will lend you himself in his own
Commentaries, and Plutarch will give you a thousand Alexanders. If you should
deal with love, and if you have a smattering of Italian, you can go to Leon the
Hebrew, who will supply you to your heart's content; or if you should not care
to go to foreign countries, you have at home Fonseca's *Of the Love of God*, in
which is condensed all that you or the most imaginative mind can want on the
subject.

"In short, all you have to do is to manage to quote these names or refer to
these stories I have mentioned, and leave it to me to insert the annotations and
quotations, and I swear by all that's good to fill your margins and use up four
sheets at the end of the book.

"Now let us come to those references to authors which other books have
and you need for yours. The remedy for this is very simple: you have only to
look up some book that quotes them all, from A to Z as you say yourself, and
then insert the very same list in your book, and though the deception may be
obvious, because you had so little need to make use of them, that is no matter;
there will probably be some stupid enough to believe that you have made use
of them all in this simple, straightforward story of yours. At any rate, if it
answers no other purpose, this long catalogue of authors will serve to give
instant authority to your book.

"Besides, no one will trouble himself to verify whether you have followed
them or whether you have not, since it cannot possibly matter to him; especially
as, if I understand it correctly, this book of yours has no need of any of those
things you say it lacks, for it is, from beginning to end, an attack upon the
books of chivalry, of which Aristotle never dreamed or St. Basil said a word or
Cicero had any knowledge. Nor do the niceties of truth nor the observations of
astrology come within the range of its fanciful nonsense; nor have geometrical
measurements or refutations of the arguments used in rhetoric anything to do
with it; nor does it have any reason to preach to anybody, mixing up things

human and divine, a sort of motley in which no Christian understanding should dress itself. It has only to avail itself of imitation in its writing, and the more perfect the imitation the better the work will be. And as this piece of yours aims at nothing more than to destroy the authority and influence which books of chivalry have in the world and with the public, there is no need for you to go begging for aphorisms from philosophers, precepts from Holy Scripture, fables from poets, speeches from orators, or miracles from saints, but merely to take care that your sentences flow musically, pleasantly, and plainly, with clear, proper, and well-placed words, setting forth your purpose to the best of your power, and putting your ideas intelligibly, without confusion or obscurity.

"Strive, too, that in reading your story the melancholy may be moved to laughter, and the merry made merrier still; that the simple shall not be wearied, that the judicious shall admire the invention, that the grave shall not despise it, or the wise fail to praise it. Finally, keep your aim fixed on the destruction of that ill-founded edifice of the books of chivalry, hated by so many yet praised by many more; for if you succeed in this you will have achieved no small success."

In profound silence I listened to what my friend said, and his observations made such an impression on me that, without attempting to question them, I admitted their soundness, and out of them I determined to make this prologue, in which gentle reader, you will perceive my friend's good sense, my good fortune in finding such an adviser in such a time of need, and why you find— to your relief—the story of Don Quixote of La Mancha so straight-forward and free of extraneous matter. This famous knight is held by all the inhabitants of the district of the Campo de Montiel to have been the chastest lover and the bravest knight that has for many years been seen in that region. I have no desire to magnify the service I am rendering to you in making you acquainted with so renowned and honored a knight, but I do desire your thanks for the acquaintance you will make with the famous Sancho Panza, his squire, in whom, to my thinking, I have given you condensed all the squirely virtues that are scattered throughout the swarm of the vain books of chivalry. And so may God give you health and not forget me. *Vale.*

Endnotes

1. The duke whose patronage is sought in this dedication, Don Alonso de Zúñiga y Sotomayor, was twenty-eight years old at the date of Don Quixote's first edition. By extending a moderate protection to some obscure authors, he had attained a certain reputation as a lover of letters and friend of writers.

2. Cervantes borrowed portions of this dedication from one to the Marquis of Ayamonte with which Fernando de Herrera headed his annotated edition of Garcilaso's works and from the introduction by Francisco de Medina for the same book. The address thus concocted was of little avail, for the duke died in 1619, and no record is preserved of his doing anything in favor of the man who bestowed immortality on his name by attaching it to such a book.

3. Cervantes was in prison in Seville in 1597 and again in 1602. But the language of this sentence is sufficiently ambiguous to allow for both a literal and a purely metaphorical interpretation.

4. Putnam suggests this as an equivalent for the original: "Under my cloak, I kill [*or* I rule] the king."

5. Cervantes, in this portion of the introduction, appears to be criticizing Lope de Vega (1562–1635), Spain's greatest dramatist, whose works often display these pedantic characteristics.

6. Roughly, "One should not sell his liberty for any price." The saying comes from medieval fable collections, not from Horace.

7. "Pale death strikes without distinction the hovels of the poor and the towers of kings." Horace.

8. "But I say unto you, love your enemies…" (Matthew 5:44).

9. "From out of the heart proceed evil thoughts…" (Matthew 15:19)

10. "While you are prosperous, you will have many friends; but when times are troubled, you will be alone.", Ovid, not Dionysius Cato. The substitution of the word *felix* for *sospes* in the original may be another ironical allusion to Lope de Vega, whose full name was Félix Lope de Vega y Carpio.

Marguerite de Navarre (1492–1549)

Marguerite de Navarre was the sister of Francis I of France. She was married in 1509 to Charles, duc d'Alençon. Charles died in 1525, and two years later, Marguerite married Henri d'Albret, king of Navarre. Marguerite was a well-educated woman, and deeply involved in the contemporary literary scene, patron, most famously, of Rabelais. She was also interested in religious reform; not only was she a protector of reforming churchmen, she was also a writer of religious verse. Apart from her intellectual interests, Marguerite also played a role in the ongoing conflict between France and the emperor negotiating her brother's release from captivity in Madrid in 1525 and participating in peace negotiations in 1529 and 1536–8.

Marguerite was not originally identified as the author of the Heptameron, *which was published first in 1558, some years after her death. It was only with the revised edition of 1559 that her name was associated with the collection, and there is still some discussion as to whether the stories were actually composed by the queen, or, as their format suggests, told by a group and gathered by her.*

The Heptameron *displays a notable concern with the question of truth. The prologue tells how the French royal family admired Boccaccio's* Decameron, *and how they wished to produce a French version, with one important difference: the stories were to be true. Although this project was never carried out, the* Heptameron *was a close replacement, and thus carries the implication of veracity, though it is fictionalized. The stories in the collection provide insight into the courtly conventions of the period, gender relations and the author's concerns with corruption in the church, among other issues.*

Chapter Twenty-Two

The Heptameron

STORY FOUR

In Flanders there once lived a lady of high birth, of birth so high, indeed, that there was no one higher in the land. She had no children and had been twice widowed. After her second husband's death she had gone to live with her brother, who was very fond of her. He was himself a noble lord of high estate, married to the daughter of a King. This young Prince was much given to his pleasures, being fond of the ladies, of hunting and generally enjoying himself, just as one would expect of a young man. His wife, however, was rather difficult, and did not enjoy the same things as he did, so he always used to take his sister along as well, because she, while being a sensible and virtuous woman, was also the most cheerful and lively company one could imagine.

Now there was a certain gentleman attached to the household, an extremely tall man, whose charm and good looks made him stand out among his companions. Taking careful note of the fact that his master's sister was a very lively lady who liked to enjoy herself, it occurred to him that it might be worth seeing if an amorous overture from a well-bred gentleman might not be to her taste. So he approached her, only to find that her reply was not what he would have expected. Nevertheless, in spite of the fact that she had given him the sort of answer that becomes an honest woman and a princess, she had had no difficulty in forgiving this good-looking and well-bred man for having been so presumptuous. Indeed, she made it plain that she did not at all mind his talking to her, though she also frequently reminded him that he must be careful what he said. In order to continue to enjoy the honour and pleasure of her company, he was only too glad to promise not to return to his earlier overtures. But as time went by his passion grew stronger, until he forgot his promises altogether. Not that he dared risk opening the subject again verbally—he had already to his cost had a taste of her ability to answer him back with her words of wisdom. No, what he had in mind was this. If he could find the right time and place, then might she not relent and indulge him a little, and indulge herself at the same time? After all, she was a widow and young, healthy and vivacious. To this end he mentioned to his master that he had lands adjoining his home that offered excellent hunting, and assured him that if he came and hunted a stag or two in May he would have the time of his life. Partly because he liked the gentleman and partly because he was addicted to hunting, the Prince accepted this invitation, and went to stay at his house, which was, as one would expect of the richest man in the land, a very fine place and very well maintained. In one wing of the house the gentleman accommodated the Prince and his wife. In the other wing opposite he accommodated the lady whom by now he loved more than he loved life itself. Her room had been luxuriously decorated from top to bottom with tapestries, and the floor was thickly covered with matting—so that it was impossible to see the trap-door by the side of the bed which led down to the room beneath. The gentleman's mother, who normally slept in this room, was old, and her catarrh made her cough in the night, so, in order to avoid disturbing the Princess, she had exchanged rooms with her son. Every evening this old lady took preserves up to the Princess, accompanied by her son, who, being very close to the brother of the Princess, was naturally permitted to attend both her *coucher* and her *lever*. Needless to say, these occasions constantly served to inflame his passion.

So it was that one evening he kept her up very late, and only left her room when he saw she was falling asleep. Back in his own room, he put on the most magnificent and most highly perfumed nightshirt he possessed, and on his head he placed the most beautifully decorated nightcap you ever saw. As he admired himself in his mirror, he was absolutely convinced that there was not a woman in the world who could possibly resist such a handsome and elegant sight. He looked forward with satisfaction to the success of his little plan, and went off to his bed. Not that he expected to stay there long, burning with desire as he was, and quite confident that he was soon to win his place in a bed that was both more pleasurable and more honourable than his own. Once he had dismissed his attendants, he got up to lock the door, and listened carefully for noises in the Princess's room above. When he was sure all was quiet, he turned to the task. Bit by bit he gently lowered the trap-door. It had been well constructed and was so densely covered with cloth, that not a sound was made. He hoisted himself through the aperture and into the room above. The Princess was just falling asleep. Without more ado, without a thought for her rank and station, or for the duty and respect he owed her, without, indeed, so much as a by-your-leave, he jumped into bed with her. Before she knew where she was he was lying there between her arms. But she was a strong woman. Struggling out of his clutches, she demanded to know who he was, and proceeded to lash out, scratching and biting for all she was worth. He was terrified she would call for help, and felt obliged to stuff the bedclothes into her mouth in a vain attempt to prevent her doing so. She realized that he would use all his strength to dishonour her, and fought back with all *her* strength in order to stop him. She shouted at the top of her lungs for her lady-in-waiting, a respectable elderly lady, who was sleeping in the next room, and who, as soon as she heard the shout, rushed to her mistress's rescue, still wearing her night attire.

When the gentleman realized that he had been caught, terrified of being recognized by the Princess, he beat a hasty retreat down through his trap-door. He arrived back in his room in a very sorry state indeed. It was a shattering experience for a man who had set out burning with desire, fully confident that his lady was going to receive him with open arms. He picked up his mirror from the table and examined himself in the candlelight. His face was streaming with blood from the bites and scratches she had inflicted. His beautiful embroidered nightshirt had more streaks of blood in it than it had gold thread.

"So much for good looks!" he groaned. "I suppose you've got what you deserve. I shouldn't have expected so much from my appearance. Now it's made me attempt something that I should have realized was impossible from the start. It might even make my situation worse, instead of making it better! If she realizes that it was I who did this senseless thing, breaking all the promises I had made, I know I shall lose even my privilege of visiting her chastely and openly. That's what my vanity's done for me! To make the most of my charm and good looks, and win her heart and her love. I ought not to have kept it so dark. I ought not to have tried to take her chaste body by force! I ought to have devoted myself to her service, in humility and with patience, accepting that I must wait till love should triumph. For without love, what good to a man are prowess and physical strength?"

And so he sat the whole night through, weeping, gnashing his teeth and wishing the incident had never happened. In the morning he looked at himself again in the mirror, and seeing that his face was lacerated all over, he took to his bed, pretending he was desperately ill and could not bear to go out into the light. There he remained until his visitors had gone home.

Meanwhile, the Princess was triumphant. She knew that the only person at her brother's court who would dare to do such an extraordinary thing was the man who had already once made so bold as to declare his love. In other words, she knew perfectly well that the culprit was her host. With the help of her lady-in-waiting she looked round all the possible hiding-places in the room, without, of course, finding anybody. She was beside herself with rage. "I know very well who it is!" she fumed. "It's the master of the house himself! That's the only person it can be. And mark my words, I shall speak to my brother in the morning, and I'll have the man's head as proof of my chastity!"

Seeing how angry she was, her lady-in-waiting just said: "I am pleased to see that your honour means so much to you, Madame, and that in order to enhance it you have no intention of sparing this man's life—he has already taken too many risks with it because of his violent love for you. But it very often happens that when people try to enhance their honour, they only end up doing the opposite. I would therefore urge you, Madame, to tell me the plain truth about the whole affair."

When she had heard the whole story, she asked: " Do you assure me that all he got from you was blows and scratches?"

"I do assure you," came the reply, "that that was all he got, and unless he manages to find a good doctor indeed, we'll see the marks on his face tomorrow."

"Well, that being so," the old lady went on, "it seems to me that you should be thinking about giving thanks to the Lord, rather than talking about revenge. It must have taken some courage, you know, to make such a daring attempt, and at this moment he must be feeling so mortified by his failure, that death would be a good deal easier for him to bear! If what you want is revenge, then you should just leave him to his passion and his humiliation—he'll torture himself much more than you could. And if you're concerned about your honour, then be careful not to fall into the same trap as he did. He promised himself all kinds of pleasures and delights, and what he actually got was the worst disappointment that any gentleman could ever suffer. So take care, Madame— if you try to make your honour even more impressive, you may only end up doing the opposite. If you make an official complaint against him, you will have to bring the whole thing into the open, whereas at the moment nobody knows anything, and he certainly won't go and tell anybody. What is more, just suppose you did go ahead, and Monseigneur, your brother, did bring the case to justice, and the poor man was put to death—people will say that he *must* have had his way with you. Most people will argue that it's not very easy to accept that a man can carry out such an act, unless he has been given a certain amount of encouragement by the lady concerned. You're young and attractive, you're very lively and sociable in all kinds of company. There isn't a single person at this court who hasn't seen the encouraging way you treat the man you are now suspecting. That could only make people conclude that if he did indeed do what you say, then it couldn't have been without some blame being due to you as well. Your honour, which up till now has been such that you've been able to hold your head high wherever you went, would be put in doubt wherever this story was heard."

As she listened to the wise reasonings of her lady-in-waiting, the Princess knew that what she was saying was true. She would indeed be criticized and blamed, in view of the encouraging and intimate way she had always treated the gentleman, so she asked her lady-in-waiting what she thought she ought to do.

"It is most gracious of you, Madame," the old lady replied, "to heed my advice. You know that I have great affection for you. Well, it seems to me that you should rejoice in your heart that this man—and he is the most handsome and best-bred gentleman I saw in my life—has been completely unable to turn you from the path of virtue, in spite of his love for you, and in spite of using physical violence against you. For this you should humble yourself before God, and acknowledge that it was not your virtue that saved you. For there have been many women, women who have led a far more austere life than you have, who have been humiliated by men far less worthy of affection than the man we are talking of. From now on you should be even more cautious when men make overtures to you, and bear in mind that there are plenty of women who have escaped from danger the first time, only to succumb the second. Never forget that Love is blind, Madame, and descends upon his victims at the very moment when they are treading a path which they think is safe, but which in reality is slippery and treacherous. I think also that you should never allude in any way to what has happened, either to him or anyone else, and even if *he* were to bring it up, I think you should pretend not to understand what he is talking about. In this way there are two dangers that you will be able to avoid. First of all, there's the danger of glorying in your triumph. And then there's the danger that you might enjoy being reminded of the pleasures of the flesh. Even the most chaste of women have a hard time preventing some spark of pleasure being aroused by such things, however much they strive to avoid them. Finally,

Madame, so that he should not get it into his head that you in some way enjoyed what he tried to do, I would advise you to gradually stop seeing so much of him. In that way you will bring home to him what a low opinion you have of his foolish and wicked behaviour. At the same time he will be brought to see what a good person you are to have been satisfied with the triumph that God has already granted you, without seeking any further revenge. May God grant you the grace, Madame, to continue in the path of virtue wherein he has placed you, to continue to love and to serve Him even better than hitherto, in the knowledge that it is from Him alone that all goodness flows."

The Princess made up her mind to follow the wise counsel of her lady-in-waiting, and slept peacefully for the rest of the night, while the wretched gentleman below spent a night of sleepless torment.

The next day the Princess's brother was ready to depart, and asked if he could take his leave of the master of the house. He was astonished to hear that he was ill, could not tolerate the light of day and refused to be seen by anyone. He would have gone to see him, but was told that he was sleeping, and decided not to disturb him. So together with his wife and his sister he left the house without being able to say goodbye. When his sister, the Princess, heard about their host's excuses for not seeing them before they left, she knew for certain that he was the one who had caused her so much distress. Obviously he did not dare to show his face because of the scratches he had received. Indeed, he refused all subsequent invitations to attend court until all his wounds—except, that is, for those he had suffered to his heart and to his pride—had healed. When eventually he did go back to court to face his triumphant enemy, he could not do so without blushing. He, who was the boldest man at court, would completely lose his self-assurance in her presence, and would frequently go quite to pieces. This only made the Princess the more sure that her suspicions had been well-founded. Gently, and little by little, she withdrew her attentions—but not so gently that he failed to appreciate what she was doing. Scared lest anything worse befell him, he dared not breathe a word. He simply had to nurse his passion in the depths of his heart, and put up with a rebuff that had been justly deserved.

❁ ❁ ❁

"And that, Ladies, is a story that should strike fear into the hearts of any man who thinks he can help himself to what doesn't belong to him. The Princess's virtue and the good sense of her lady-in-waiting should inspire courage in the hearts of all women. So if anything like this should ever happen to any of you, you now know what the remedy is!"

"In my opinion," said Hircan, "the tall lord of your story lacked nerve, and didn't deserve to have his memory preserved. What an opportunity he had! He should never have been content to eat or sleep till he'd succeeded. And one really can't say that his love was very great, if there was still room in his heart for the fear of death and dishonour."

"And what," asked Nomerfide, "could the poor man have done with two women against him?"

"He should have killed the old one, and when the young one realized there was no one to help her, he'd have been half-way there!"

"Kill her!" Nomerfide cried. "You wouldn't mind him being a murderer as well, then? If that's what you think, we'd better watch out we don't fall into *your* clutches!"

"If I'd gone that far," he replied, "I'd consider my honour ruined if I didn't go through with it!"

Then Geburon spoke up: "So you find it strange that a princess of high birth who's been brought up in the strict school of honour should be too much for one man? In that case you'd find it even stranger that a woman of poor birth should manage to get away from *two* men!"

"I invite you to tell the fifth story, Geburon," said Ennasuite, "because it sounds as if you have one about some poor woman that will be far from dull."

"Since you've chosen me [to speak]," he began, "I shall tell a story that I know to be true because I conducted an inquiry into it at the very place where it happened. As you'll see, it isn't only princesses who've got good sense in their heads and virtue in their heart. And love and resourcefulness aren't always to be found where you'd expect them, either."

STORY ELEVEN

In the household of Madame de La Trémoille there was a lady by the name of Roncex. One day she was visiting the Franciscan house at Thouars, and felt a sudden need to go where you can't send your servant for you. For company she asked a girl called La Mothe to go with her, but for the sake of privacy and modesty she left her in a room nearby, and went on her own into the privy, which was very dark. It was the place used by all the Franciscans, and all over the seat and everywhere else there was ample evidence that Franciscan bellies had been doing justice to the fruits of Bacchus and Ceres. Well, this poor lady, who was already in such a hurry that she scarcely had time to lift her skirts, went and sat down on the filthiest and dirtiest seat in the whole place. She stuck to it as if held on by glue! Her poor buttocks, her clothes, her feet, everything was in such a disgusting mess that she didn't dare take a step to one side or the other, for fear of even worse. So she started to scream for all she was worth.

"La Mothe! La Mothe!" she cried, "I am undone, I am dishonoured!" The poor girl, who had heard plenty of stories about the vile behaviour of the Franciscans, thought that some of them must have been lying in wait, and that they must be trying to rape Madame de Roncex. So she ran to her aid as fast as her legs would carry her, shouting to everyone she met: "Help! Help! The friars are trying to rape Madame de Roncex in the privy!"

Everyone dashed to the scene, only to find the wretched Madame de Roncex standing there, bottom bare lest her gown should be soiled, and shrieking for one of her women to come and clean her up. A splendid spectacle for the men who had come running to her rescue! And the only trace of a Franciscan was the filth stuck to the poor lady's behind! Needless to say it was all very amusing for the gentlemen, but somewhat humiliating for the lady, who after all had been expecting her women to run along to help her get clean. Instead there was a crowd of men to do her bidding, and there was she, exposed in the worst condition a woman could ever appear in! Immediately she saw them she let her skirts fall to cover herself up, thereby dirtying what little of her attire had remained clean. She quite forgot the filthy state she was in, so ashamed was she at the sight of the men. When she eventually managed to get out of the disgusting place, she had to be stripped naked and have all her clothes changed before she could leave the monastery. She felt very much inclined to be angry with La Mothe for bringing assistance in the way she had, but when she heard that the girl had thought there had been even worse things afoot, she forgot her anger, and laughed with the rest.

❊ ❊ ❊

"Well, Ladies, I don't think that my story was either very long or very melancholy! So you've had what you expected!"

Thereupon her audience burst into peals of laughter, and Oisille said: "It was a rather dirty story, but when one knows the people involved, one cannot really object to it. How I would have loved to see La Mothe's face—and the face of the lady she tried to rescue! Anyway, as you've finished so quickly, Nomerfide, will you choose us a new storyteller—someone perhaps who won't be quite so frivolous?"

"If you want me to make up for my naughtiness," said Nomerfide, "I think I shall choose Dagoucin, who's so wise and good that he would never for the life of him allow anything bad or foolish to pass his lips!"

Dagoucin thanked her for her high opinion of his good sense, and began.

"The story I have decided to tell you is to show you how love can blind even the greatest and most honourable of men, and how hard it is to overcome wickedness by means of kindness and generosity."

STORY TWENTY

There once lived in the Dauphiné a gentleman named the Seigneur de Riant. He belonged to the household of King Francis I, and was as handsome and honourable a man as you could possibly wish to see. For a long time he had devoted himself to the service of a certain lady, a widow. So much did he love and revere her that, for fear of losing her good graces altogether, he did not dare demand from her that which above all things he desired. Feeling that he was a fine figure of a man and not unworthy of a lady's love, he firmly believed her whenever she solemnly swore, as she often did, that she loved him more than any other man in all the world. If ever she were obliged to do anything for a gentleman, she would declare, she would do it for him alone, for he was the most perfect gentleman she had ever known. Then she would beg and beseech that he would content himself with this, and not go beyond the bounds of respectable friendship. If she ever found him dissatisfied with what was reasonable and good, if she ever found him laying claim to other favours, then, she assured him, he would lose her for ever. Well, not only was the poor man satisfied with his lot, he deemed himself fortunate indeed to have won the heart of a lady who seemed so full of honour and virtue!

It would take me a long time to give you the whole account of his love for this lady, to tell you of all the time he spent with her, and how he made many a long journey to see her. To cut a long story short, suffice it to say that this wretched martyr to the sweet fire of love constantly went in search of ways of making his martyrdom worse—for the more you burn in such a fire, the more you want to burn. One day he was suddenly taken by a desire to see the one whom he loved more dearly than life itself, this fair one whom he adored above all other women in the world. So he went with all possible speed by post-horse to her house. On asking where she was, he was told that she had only just come in from vespers, and that she had gone into the game park to finish off her devotions. So he got down from his horse, and went straight to the park, where he found her women attendants, who said that she had gone for a walk on her own down a broad tree-lined path that ran through the grounds. This made him all the more hopeful that he was going to be in luck. So off he went to seek out his fair lady, treading ever so carefully so as not to make the slightest noise, and hoping above hope that he was going to find her alone. Then he came to a leafy bower, in the most delightful spot you ever did see, and, unable to contain himself any longer, he went bursting straight in. What does he find but his beloved stretched out on the grass in the arms of one of her stable-boys! A stable-boy as dirty, common and ugly as de Riant was handsome, gallant and refined! I shan't attempt to describe his feelings—enough to say that his indignation was sufficient to extinguish instantaneously the fire of a passion that had endured time and circumstance.

"Do as you please, Madame, and much good may it do you!" he cried, as impassioned with rage as he had been with love. "This day I am cured by your wickedness and delivered from the perpetual suffering which was occasioned by what once I took to be your noble virtue!"

Without waiting to say goodbye, he turned, and went somewhat more quickly than he had come. The poor woman did not know what to reply. As she could not hide her shame, she covered up her eyes, so as not to see the man who in spite of her long dissimulation, could now see *her* all too clearly!

❋ ❋ ❋

"And so, Ladies, if you don't intend to love perfectly, kindly do not try to deceive men of honour, or try to cross them for the sake of your pride and glory. Hypocrites get their just deserts, and God is good to those who love openly!"

"Well, indeed!" exclaimed Oisille. "You certainly did keep a fine story to finish off the day! If it were not for the fact that we have all sworn to tell the truth, I could not believe that a woman of such station could be so corrupt—

corrupt in her soul, corrupt in the sight of God and corrupt in her body. To leave an upright gentleman for a vulgar stable-boy!"

"Ah! Madame, if you only knew," said Hircan, "what a great difference there is between a gentleman who spends his whole life in armour on active service and a well-fed servant who never budges from home, you'd excuse the poor widow in this story!"

"You may say what you like, Hircan," replied Oisille, "but I do not think *you* would be capable of accepting excuses from her!"

"I've heard it said," began Simontaut, "that there are some women who like to have their 'evangelists' to preach abroad their virtue and chastity! They treat them in the most encouraging and intimate way possible and assure them that if only they were not held back by honour and conscience they would grant them their heart's desire. Then when the poor fools get together with their friends, they start talking about their ladies, and swear that to uphold their beloved's virtue they'd stick their fingers in the fire and not feel a thing, because they believe they've personally tried and tested their love to the farthest extreme! That's the way women manage to get honourable men to spread their good name. But they show themselves in their true colours to those of their own kind. They pick men who would never be so bold as to talk about what they knew, and who, if they did happen to talk, wouldn't be believed in any case, because they're so base and common."

"That," said Longarine, "is a point of view I've heard expressed before by men who are particularly jealous and suspicious. But it's all sheer fantasy. Just because something like that happens to some miserable wretch of a woman, there's no reason to go round suspecting all women of the same thing."

"The more we pursue this subject," said Parlamente, "the more these fine gentlemen here will embroider on what Simontaut has already said, at the expense of us ladies. We had better go to vespers, so that we don't keep the monks waiting as long as we did yesterday."

They were all in agreement, and, as they got up to go, Oisille said: ["May each and every one of us give thanks to God that we have today told the truth in the stories we have told. As for you, Saffredent, you ought to pray for forgiveness for having told one so insulting to women."]

"Upon my oath, Ladies," replied Saffredent, "although my story is a [curious] one, I heard it [from reliable people, and it is true.] If I were to tell you one about women that I know from first-hand experience, I'd have you making more signs of the cross than they do to consecrate churches!"

To this Geburon replied: "You're a long way from repentance when your confession only makes your sin the worse!"

And Parlamente said: "If that's your opinion of women, then they ought to deprive you of their refined conversation and cease to have anything to do with you."

But Saffredent retorted: "There are some women who have followed your recommendation and have banished me from all that is decent, good and refined, and have been so thorough about it that if I could say anything worse, or *do* anything worse to [each and every one of them, and to one in particular who does me considerable wrong,] then I wouldn't hesitate to do so and take my revenge!"

On hearing these words Parlamente raised her mask to her face, and went into the church. They found that although the bell had been ringing heartily for vespers, not a single monk had yet appeared. The fact was that they had heard that the ladies and gentlemen were meeting together in the meadow to recount all manner of amusing tales and, preferring their pleasures to their prayers, they had been hiding in a ditch behind a thick hedge flat on their bellies, so that they could overhear. So attentively had they been listening, they had not even heard their own monastery bell ringing. The consequence was that they came scurrying to their places in such a hurry that they hardly had enough breath left to start singing the service! When vespers were over and they were asked why they had been so late and their chanting so out of tune, they confessed, and admitted that it was because they had been listening to the stories. When it was realized that they were so favourably disposed towards the proceedings, they were given permission to go along every day and listen from behind the hedge for as long as they wished. At supper everyone enjoyed themselves. The conversations that had remained unfinished in the meadow were continued and went on the whole evening, until Oisille urged them all to retire for the night. If they had a good long rest, their minds would be all the fresher the next day, for, as she said, an hour before midnight is worth three after. And so, taking their leave of one another, they went each to their respective rooms, and brought the second day to its close.

Part Five

The Voyages
of Discovery

Bernal Díaz (1492–1581)

Bernal Díaz was born in 1492 in Medina del Campo in Spain, and he died at the age of eighty nine on his estates in Guatemala. He was over seventy when he began writing his story of the conquest, and at one point almost gave up on it, before finishing it at about the age of eighty four. Díaz was the last survivor of the conquest of Mexico, and his narrative has the value of an eye-witness account. Díaz himself recognized that he was no great stylist, and this embarrassment at his lack of polish was largely responsible for his almost abandoning the project. However, his concern at his own shortcomings was outweighed by his annoyance at the inaccuracy of other accounts of the conquest, and his desire to present the true version of events eventually drove him to finish his narrative.

Díaz's account has not only the vivid detail of the personal account, but is imbued with his own awareness of the magnitude of the conquerors' accomplishment. He was no idealist, and he recognized the greed of the soldiers and their cruelty to the Aztecs. However, he was also aware of their sense of mission, and convinced that the success of such a small and isolated group could only be attributed to the intervention of God, who, in Díaz's eyes, clearly wished New Spain and its inhabitants to be ruled by Charles V and the Catholic church.

Chapter Twenty-Three

The Expedition of
Francisco Hernandez de Cordoba

I, Bernal Díaz del Castillo, citizen and governor of the most loyal city of Santiago de Guatemala, one of the first discoverers and conquerors of New Spain and its provinces, and of the Cape of Honduras and Higueras, native of the most noble and famous city of Medina del Campo, and son of its former governor Francisco Díaz del Castillo, known as the Courteous—and his legal wife Maria Díaz Rejon—may their souls rest in glory!—tell you the story of myself and my comrades; all true conquerors, who served His Majesty in the discovery, conquest, pacification, and settlement of the provinces of New Spain; one of the finest regions of the New World yet discovered, this expedition being undertaken by our own efforts, and without His Majesty's knowledge.

My ancestors having always been servants of the Crown, and my father and one of my brothers being in the service of the Catholic Kings, Don Ferdinand and Doñia Isabella, I wished in some sort to emulate them. When, therefore, in the year 1514 a gentleman named Pedrarias Davila went out as Governor of Tierra Firme,[1] I agreed to accompany him to the newly conquered country, and after an uneventful voyage we arrived at Nombre de Dios, as it was called. Some three or four months, however, after the settlement was made, there came an epidemic from which many soldiers died, and all the rest of us were ill with bad ulcers on the legs. In addition, there were disputes between the Governor and a rich gentleman named Vasco Nuñez de Balboa, who had conquered the province and was then commander of the army. Pedrarias Davila had given him his daughter in marriage but had afterwards been suspicious that his son-in-law might raise a rebellion and lead a body of soldiers towards the Southern Sea. He had therefore given orders that Balboa should be beheaded and certain of his soldiers disciplined.

As we were witnesses of these events, and of other revolts among the captains, and as news had reached us that the island of Cuba had lately been conquered and settled, under the governorship of a kinsman of mine named

Diego Velazquez, some of us gentlemen and persons of quality who had come out with Pedrarias Davila decided to ask his permission to go there. This he readily gave us, since he did not require all the soldiers he had brought out from Spain, the province being a small one and now entirely conquered.

Once we had received permission we boarded a good ship, and with fair weather reached the island of Cuba. On landing we paid our respects to the Governor, who was pleased to see us and promised to give us Indians as soon as there were any to spare. I was at that time twenty-four.

After spending three fruitless years in Tierra Firme and Cuba, about a hundred and ten of us, settlers from Tierra Firme or Spaniards who had come to Cuba but received no grant of Indians, decided to make an expedition to seek new lands in which to try our fortunes and find occupation. We arranged with Francisco Hernandez de Cordoba, a rich man who owned a village on the island, that he should be our leader, and he was well fitted for the post.

With this expedition in view, we purchased three ships, two of them a good capacity and the third a barque bought on credit from the Governor Diego Velazquez, who let us have it on condition that all three vessels should go to some islands, lying between Cuba and Honduras, and now called the Guanaxes Islands, and there fight the natives, whom we could then sell to him for slaves and thus pay for the barque. Realizing the wickedness of the Governor's demand, we answered that it would be against the laws of God and the king for us to turn free men into slaves; and when he learnt our plans, he decided they were better than his. So he helped us with provisions for our voyage in quest of new lands. Certain interested persons have asked me why I have recorded this proposal of Diego Velazquez, since it is discreditable to him and has nothing to do with my story. My answer is that it is in keeping with his subsequent persecution of us, in alliance with Juan Rodriguez de Fonseca, Bishop of Burgos.

We found ourselves in possession of three ships loaded with cassava bread, which is made from a root, and we bought pigs, which cost us three pesos each. At that time there were no sheep or cattle in the island of Cuba, for it was only beginning to be settled. We added a supply of oil and some inexpensive articles for barter. We then sought out three pilots of whom the chief, who took charge of our fleet, was Anton de Alaminos, a native of Palos. We also engaged the necessary sailors, and the best supply we could get of ropes, cordage, cables, and anchors, of casks for water, and everything else we needed for our voyage, and all this at our own cost on credit.

When we had collected all our soldiers we set out for a port on the northern coast which the Indians call Axaruco, twenty-four miles away from San Cristobal, where there was then a settlement which was transferred two years later to the present town of Havana. In order that our fleet should take the right course, we asked a priest of San Cristobal called Alonso Gonzalez to come with us. We also chose for the office of Inspector a soldier named Bernaldino Iñiguez of Santo Domingo de la Calzada so that, should we by God's will come upon rich lands, or peoples possessed of gold or silver or pearls or any other kind of wealth, there should be someone to guard the royal fifth.

When all this was arranged and we had heard mass, we commended ourselves to God and His blessed Mother, and began our voyage.

On the eighth of February 1517 we sailed for Axaruco, and twelve days later doubled Cape San Antonio. Then, once in the open sea, we steered at a venture towards the west, without knowledge of the depths or currents, or of the winds that prevail in those latitudes. So we were in great hazard of our lives when a storm struck us which lasted two days and two nights and had such force that we were nearly wrecked. When the weather moderated we resumed our course, and twenty-one days after leaving port to our great joy we sighted land, for which we gave thanks to God. This land was as yet undiscovered, and we had received no report of it. From the ships we could see a large town, which appeared to lie six miles back from the coast, and as we had never seen one as large in Cuba or Hispaniola we named it the Great Cairo.

We decided that the two vessels of shallowest draught should go in as near as possible to see if there was any anchorage close to the shore; and on the morning of 4 March we saw ten large canoes called pirogues, full of the inhabitants of that town, approaching us with oars and sail. These pirogues are shaped like troughs. They are large and hollowed out of huge single logs, and many of them will hold forty Indians.

These canoes came close to our ships, and we made signs of peace, waving our hands and our cloaks as an invitation to them to come and speak to us. For at that time we had no interpreters who knew the languages of Yucatan and Mexico. They approached quite fearlessly, and more than thirty men came aboard our flagship. We gave each of them a string of green beads, and they spent some time examining the ships. Then the principal man among them, who was the *Cacique*,[2] told us by signs that they wanted to board their canoes and go back to the town. He indicated that they would return another day with more canoes, in which we could go ashore.

These Indians wore cotton shirts made in the shape of jackets, and covered their private parts with narrow cloths which they called *masteles*. We considered them a more civilized people than the Cubans. For they went about naked, except for the women, who wore cotton cloths that came down to their thighs.

Next morning the same *Cacique* came back bringing twelve large canoes with Indian oarsmen. With a smiling face and every appearance of friendliness, he made signs that we should go to his town, where they would give us food and everything else we needed, and to which they would take us in their canoes. As he invited us aboard he repeated in his language: "*Cones catoche, cones catoche*," which means: "Come to our houses." For this reason we called the place Cape Catoche, and so it is still named on the charts.

When our captain and the soldiers saw these friendly demonstrations, it was agreed that we should lower our ships' boats, and all go ashore together in the smallest of them and the twelve canoes. We saw the whole coast crowded with Indians who had come from the town, and therefore decided that we would all land at the same moment. When the *Cacique* saw us land but make no move towards the town, he again made signs to our captain that we should go with him to the houses. He gave so much evidence of peaceful intentions that after some discussion most of us soldiers agreed that we should go forward, taking all the arms that we could carry. We took fifteen crossbows and ten muskets, and started to follow the road along which the *Cacique* was going with his great company of Indians.

We advanced in this way until we came to some brushcovered hillocks. Then the *Cacique* started shouting to some bands of warriors whom he had placed in ambush to kill us. In response to the *Cacique*'s call these bands quickly fell on us with great fury, and began to shoot with such accuracy that the first flight of arrows wounded thirteen soldiers. The Indians wore armour made of cotton which reached down to their knees. They carried lances and shields, bows and arrows, slings, and many stones; and after the arrow-flights, with their feathered crests waving, they attacked us hand to hand. Wielding their lances in both hands, they did us great damage. But, thanks be to God, when they felt the sharp edge of our swords and the effect of our crossbows and muskets, they quickly took to their heels, leaving fifteen dead on the field.

A little beyond this place where they attacked us was a small square with three houses built of masonry, which served as *cues* or prayer-houses. These contained many idols of baked clay, some with demons' faces, some with women's, and others equally ugly which seemed to represent Indians committing sodomy with one another. Inside the houses were some small wooden chests containing other idols and some disks made partly of gold but mainly of copper, also some pendants, three diadems, and other small objects in the shape of fishes and of the local ducks, all made of poor-quality gold. When we saw the gold and the masonry houses we were very pleased to have found such a country. For Peru had not yet been discovered, nor was it to be discovered for another twenty years.

Whilst we were fighting the Indians, the priest Gonzalez took possession of the chests, the idols, and the gold, and carried them to the ship. In this skirmish we captured two Indians, who when they were afterwards baptized received the names of Julian and Melchior. Both were cross-eyed. Once this surprise attack was over we returned to our ships and after attending to the wounded set sail along the coast in a westerly direction.

Believing this to be an island, as our pilot assured us it was, we went forward very cautiously, sailing by day and anchoring at night. And after fifteen days we sighted what appeared to be a large town beside a great inlet or bay. Here we thought there might be a river or stream at which we could take water, of which we were very short, since the casks and other vessels we had brought were not watertight. The reason for this was that we were too poor to buy good ones. The day of our landing was St Lazarus' Sunday, and so we called the place Lazaro, by which name it is still marked on the charts. The proper Indian name for it is Campeche.

So that we could all disembark at once and not be caught as we had been at Cape Catoche, we decided to go in the smallest ship and the three boats, and to carry all our arms.

In these bays or inlets the water drops very considerably at low tide. So we had to leave our ships anchored more than three miles off shore. We disembarked near the town, where there was a pool of good water, at which the inhabitants were accustomed to drink. For as far as we could see, there were no rivers in this country. We landed the casks, intending to fill them and re-embark. But when we were ready to go a company of about fifty Indians, dressed in good cotton cloaks, who looked like *Caciques*, came peacefully out of the town, and asked us by signs what we were looking for. We gave them to understand that we had come for water, and were going straight back to our ships. They asked us by gesture whether we came from the east, and repeated the word "*Castilan, Castilan*." But we did not understand what they meant.

Then they invited us to go with them to their town, and after some discussion among ourselves we decided to go, but in good formation and very cautiously.

They led us to some very large buildings of fine masonry which were the prayer-houses of their idols, the walls of which were painted with the figures of great serpents and evil-looking gods. In the middle was something like an altar, covered with clotted blood, and on the other side of the idols were symbols like crosses, and all were coloured. We stood astonished, never having seen or heard of such things before.

It appears that they had just sacrificed some Indians to their idols, so as to ensure victory over us. However, many Indian women were strolling about most peacefully, as it seemed, laughing and amusing themselves. But as the men were gathered in such numbers, we were afraid that there might be another ambush, like that at Catoche. At this point many more Indians came up, wearing very ragged cloaks, and carrying dried reeds, which they put down on the ground. These were followed by two bands of Indian archers in cotton armour, carrying lances, shields, slings, and stones, and each of these bands was drawn up by its captain at a short distance from us. At that moment there came from another house, which was the temple of their idols, ten Indians wearing long white cotton cloaks which fell to their feet. Their hair was very long, and so clotted with blood that it would have needed cutting before it could be combed or parted. These were the priests of their gods, who in New Spain are generally called *papas*. They brought us incense of a sort of resin which they call *copal*, and began to burn it over us in earthenware braziers full of live coals. By means of signs they gave us to understand that we must leave their land before the firewood that they had piled there burnt out. Otherwise they would attack us and kill us. The *papas* then ordered the reeds to be set alight, and departed without more words, and the warriors who were drawn up to attack us began to whistle and sound their trumpets and drums.

When we saw these great bands of Indians threatening us so boldly we were afraid. For we had not yet recovered from the wounds received at Cape Catoche, and had just thrown overboard the bodies of two soldiers who had died. So we decided to retire to the coast in good order, and began to march along the shore towards a large rock which rose out of the sea, while the boats and the small ship laden with the water-casks coasted along close to the shore. We had not dared to embark near the town, where we had landed, since a great number of Indians were waiting for us there, and we were sure they would attack as we did so.

Once we had embarked and got the casks on board, we sailed on for six days and nights in good weather. Then we were struck by a *norther*, which is a cross-wind on that coast. It lasted four days and nights, and was so strong that it almost drove us ashore, and forced us to anchor. In doing so we broke two cables, and one ship began to drag. Our danger was very great, for if the last cable had broken we should have been driven ashore and destroyed. But, thank God, we were able to ease the strain by lashing it with ropes and hawsers.

When the weather had improved, we continued to follow the coast, going ashore as often as we could, to take fresh water. For, as I have said, our casks were not watertight. They gaped and we could not repair them. But as we were following the coast we trusted that we should find water wherever we landed, either in *jagueyes* (pools) or by digging for it.

As we sailed on our course we sighted another town about three miles back from an inlet which looked like the mouth of a river or stream. So we decided to anchor; and because the tide falls so far on this coast and ships are liable to be stranded, we stood three miles off. Then we went ashore in our boats and the smallest ship, carrying all our casks and well provided with weapons. We landed a little after midday three miles from the town, where there were some pools, some maize plantations, and a few small stone houses. As we were filling our casks, many bands of Indians came along the coast from the town of Champoton, as it is called, wearing cotton armour to the knees, and carrying bows and arrows, lances and shields, swords which appeared to be two-handed, slings and stones. They wore the habitual feathered crests, their faces were painted black and white and rust-red, and they approached us silently. They came straight towards us, as if in peace, and asked us by signs whether we came from the east. We replied also by signs that we did. We were puzzled by the words that they then called out to us, which were the same as the Indians at Lazaro had used. But we could not make out what they meant. All this happened about nightfall, and the Indians then went off to some nearby village. We posted sentinels as a precaution, for we mistrusted these great assemblies of Indians.

As we watched through the night, we heard a great band of warriors approaching from the farms and the town, and we well knew that this boded us no good. We discussed what we should do, and some were for embarking immediately. As is usual in such cases, there was no agreement. The majority thought, however, that if we attempted to do so the Indians would attack us at once, and since they were so many we should be in danger of our lives. But a few of us were for attacking them in the night, for, as the proverb goes, the first blow is half the battle.

While we were still debating, the dawn broke, and we saw that we were outnumbered by two hundred to one. So wishing one another a stout heart for the fight, we commended ourselves to God and did our best to save our lives.

Once it was daylight we could see many more warriors advancing along the coast with banners raised and plumes and drums, to join the others who had gathered during the night. After forming up in squadrons and surrounding us on all sides, they assailed us with such a shower of arrows and darts and stones from their slings that more than eighty of our soldiers were wounded. Then they attacked us hand to hand, some with lances and some shooting arrows, and others with their two-handed cutting swords. Though we fought back with swords and muskets and crossbows they brought us to a bad pass. At last, feeling the effects of our sword-play, they drew back a little, but not far, and only to shoot at us from greater safety. During the fighting, the Indians shouted to one another "*Al calachuni, calachuni*, which means in their language, "Attack and kill the captain." Our captain was hit by ten arrows, and I by three, one of which gave me a dangerous wound in the left side, piercing between my ribs. All the rest received severe lance wounds, and two of our men were captured alive.

Our captain saw that good fighting did not help us, since so many bands surrounded us and so many more were coming up fresh from the town, bringing food and drink with them and a large supply of arrows. All our soldiers had received two or three arrows, three of them had their throats pierced by lance-thrusts, and our captain was bleeding from many wounds. Already fifty of our men had been killed, and we knew that we had no more strength to resist. So we determined with stout hearts to break through the Indian battalions and seek shelter in our boats, which lay off shore, not far away. Thus we saved ourselves. Forming ourselves up in a close squadron, we broke through the enemy, who with fearful yells, whistles, and cries showered arrows upon us, and hurled their lances with all their might, wounding still more of us.

Then we ran into another danger. As we all jumped into the boats at the same time, and there were many of us, they began to sink. Clinging to the sides of the waterlogged craft as best we could, and half swimming, we reached the vessel of shallowest draught, which came in haste to our assistance. Many of our men were wounded again as we embarked, especially those who were clinging to the stern of the boats, for they presented a good target. The Indians even waded into the sea with their lances, and attacked us with all their might. But, thank God, by a great effort we escaped with our lives from these people's clutches.

The battle had lasted an hour, and in addition to the fifty men or more killed and the two prisoners we threw five men overboard a few days later, who had died of their wounds and of the great thirst we suffered. As I said, the town was called Champoton, and the pilots and sailors named this coast on their charts La Costa de Mala Pelea.[3]

When it was all safely over we thanked God for our escape. But as the soldiers' wounds were being dressed some of them complained of pains, for they were beginning to grow cold and the salt water caused considerable swelling. Some of them also cursed the pilot and his voyage to this island that we had discovered. For he was always insisting that it was an island, and not the mainland.

After attending to our wounds, we decided to return to Cuba. But as almost all the sailors were wounded we had not enough men to tend the sails. So we abandoned our smallest vessel and set fire to her after removing her sails, cables, and anchors and dividing her unwounded crew among the two larger vessels. But we had even worse trouble in our lack of fresh water. Owing to the attack at Champoton and our hurried retreat to the boats, we had not been able to fetch off the casks and barrels we had filled, but had left them on shore. We had such a thirst that our mouths and tongues were cracked, and there was nothing to give us relief. Such are the hardships to be endured when discovering new lands in the manner that we set about it! No one can imagine their severity who has not himself endured them.

We kept our course very close to the land in the hope of finding some river or bay where we could get fresh water; and after three days we sighted an inlet in which we thought there might be a stream or a freshwater creek. Fifteen of the sailors who had stayed aboard and were unwounded and three soldiers whose wounds were no longer dangerous landed with pickaxes and some barrels. The creek was salty and they dug some holes on the shore. But there the water was as salty and bitter as in the creek. However, bad as the water was, they filled the casks and brought them aboard. But no one could drink it, and it pained the mouths and stomachs of the few soldiers who tried. In this creek there were so many large alligators that it has always been called El Estero de los Lagartos, by which name it is marked on the charts.

While the boats were ashore taking water, a north-east gale arose, so violent that the ships dragged their anchors and were driven towards the beach. Seeing this danger, the sailors who had gone ashore hastily brought the boats back, and had just time to throw out additional anchors and cables, so that the ships rode in safety for two days and nights. Then we raised anchor and set sail, continuing our voyage towards Cuba. The pilot Alaminos discussed our course with the two other pilots, and it was agreed that we should now make for Florida which, according to his readings of the chart, was only two hundred miles away. Once we had reached Florida, he said, the crossing would be shorter than the course by which we had come.

[The ships sailed to Florida, and there took water just in time to save the lives of the parched adventurers. There was a sharp skirmish with the Indians, after which the expedition returned to Cuba, where its leader Francisco Hernandez de Cordoba and three of the soldiers died of their wounds. A report was made to the Governor Diego Velazquez that a thickly populated country had been discovered, whose inhabitants built stone houses, wore cotton clothes, possessed gold, and cultivated maize. The objects taken from the temple at Catoche appeared much superior to anything so far found in the New World. The idols aroused particular interest, and some attributed them to the Jews who were exiled by Titus and Vespasian and sent overseas.

The Governor examined the two prisoners, Melchior and Julian, as to the existence of gold-mines in their country. They replied that there were some, but Bernal Díaz considered this to be untrue. The Spaniards understood the newly discovered country to be called "Yucatan." In fact the prisoners were explaining that they cultivate the Yuca or cassava, the plant of which they make their bread.

Diego Velazquez reported to the Royal Council for the Indies that he had made the discoveries himself at very great expense; and the President of the Council, Fonseca, Bishop of Burgos, advised the King—the Emperor Charles V—who was in Flanders, that this was so.

Bernal Díaz was reduced to poverty, and after a disastrous trading expedition asked for the help of the Governor, who was, as we have heard, his relative. Velazquez asked him if he would be prepared to return to Yucatan, and Bernal Díaz, after twitting him on the mistaken name and expatiating on the hardships of Hernandez' expedition, was told that such hardships are to be expected by those who set out to discover new lands and gain honour. Bernal then agreed to serve in the next expedition.]

Endnotes

1. The Spanish Main, a settlement on the coast of Panama.
2. The Carib word for military chief. The *Cacique*'s privileges and duties varied from nation to nation.
3. The Coast of the Evil Battle.

Gonzalo Fernandez de Oviedo (1478–1557)

Gonzalo Fernandez de Oviedo was born in Madrid in 1478 and educated at the royal court. He was present at the return of Columbus from his first voyage to the New World and he knew the admiral's sons. In 1514 he took his first trip to the New World, in the same expedition as Bernal Diaz, acting as inspector of gold smelting. He spent many years there in various administrative and military positions, crossing the Atlantic twelve times. He died in Valladolid in 1557.

Most of Oviedo's output was historical. In 1526 he wrote a short natural history of the Indies, describing the flora and fauna, customs and mineral wealth of the new discovery. His work was well-received at the Spanish court, and he was appointed General Chronicler of the Indies. In 1535 he published the first part of the General and Natural History of the Indies, *and he continued to work on the project until 1548, though the complete text was not published in his lifetime. Much of the history is an eye-witness account, but as chronicler of the Indies, Oviedo was given the authority to require accounts from all royal officials in the conquest. Oviedo uses this information, but makes it clear to his reader when he is not speaking from personal knowledge, and indeed indicates any reservations he has as to the accuracy of his source. Oviedo was acutely aware of the intellectual problems posed by the discovery of the New World, and of the growing tension between the knowledge acquired by experience and the venerated learning of the ancients. He emphatically chooses experience, reminding the reader of his intimate familiarity with his subject material, though his broad education in the classics is also clear from his writing.*

Chapter Twenty-Four

General and Natural History of the Indies by Captain Gonzalo Fernandez de Oviedo

BOOK II

CHAPTER 2

The origin and character of Christopher Columbus,
first Admiral of the Indies, and common opinions
of his motives in embarking on his discoveries

Some say that these lands were first known many centuries ago, and that their situation was written down and the exact latitudes noted in which they lay, but their geography and the sea routes by which they were to be reached were forgotten, and that Christopher Columbus, a learned man well read in the science of cosmography, set out to make a fresh discovery of these islands. I am inclined to believe this theory for reasons that I will explain in later chapters. But it is right to accept this man, to whom we owe so much, as the prime mover of this great enterprise, which he initiated for the benefit of all now living and those who shall live after us.

I will say that Christopher Columbus, as I've heard from men of his nation, was a native of the province of Liguria, in which lies the city and lordship of Genoa. Some give his birthplace as Savona, or a small town or village called Nervi, on the Levant coast two leagues from Genoa, but the most reliable story is that he came from Cugureo, which is also near Genoa. He was a man of decent life and parentage, handsome and well-built, and of more than average height and strength. His eyes were lively and his features well proportioned. His hair was chestnut brown and his complexion rather ruddy and blotchy; he was well spoken, cautious and extremely intelligent. He had good Latin and great cosmographical knowledge; he was charming when he wished to be and very testy when annoyed. His ancestors came from the city of Piacenza in

Lombardy, which lies on the banks of the Po, and were members of the ancient family of Pelestrel. In the lifetime of his father Dominico, Christopher Columbus, now a well-educated young man who had attained his majority, left Italy for the Levant and travelled over the greater part of the Mediterranean, where he learnt navigation and put it to practical use. After several voyages in these restricted waters, having a mind for greater enterprises and wider prospects, he decided to see the great ocean and left for Portugal. Here he lived for some time in the city of Lisbon. From there, or wherever else he was, as a grateful son he sent some part of all he earned to his old father, whom he helped to support and who lived in some poverty with hardly enough money for his bare needs.

There is a story that a caravel sailing from Spain to England with a cargo of merchandise and provisions, wines and other goods, not to be found in England and generally sent there from Spain, was overwhelmed by such violent contrary winds that it was forced to run west for many days, in the course of which it sighted one or more of the Indies. A landing was made on one of these islands and naked people were seen like those found here today. When the winds, which had brought them here against their will, died down, they took aboard water and wood and sailed back on to their previous course. The story goes on to say that as the greater part of the ship's cargo consisted of food and wine the crew had sufficient to keep them alive on this long and arduous voyage and to make the return passage, meeting with favourable weather. They reached Europe safely and made for Portugal. The voyage had been extremely long and dangerous and they had all the time been greatly afraid. Moreover, though the winds had driven them swiftly on their course, the journey there and back had lasted four or five months, or possible even more. In the course of that time almost all the ship's crew died. The only men to land in Portugal were the pilot and three or four of the sailors, and all these were so ill that they also died a short time after their arrival.

The story goes that this pilot was a close friend of Christopher Columbus and had some knowledge of the quadrant, and that he marked the position of this land he had discovered. He is said to have given this information very privately to Columbus, asking him to make a map and place upon it this land which he had seen. Columbus is said to have welcomed him into his house as a friend and got him medical treatment, for by now he was very sick. Nevertheless he died like the others; thus Columbus remained with sole knowledge of these islands, and this he kept to himself. According to some accounts, this pilot was an Andalusian, others make him Portuguese, others a Basque. Some accounts say that Columbus was at that time in the island of Madeira, others in the Cape

Verde Islands and that it was at this or that place the caravel arrived and there that Columbus heard of these lands. Whether these events took place or not cannot be decided with certainty, but this romantic story is in common circulation in the form that I have set down. In my opinion it is a fiction. As St. Augustine says: "When the facts are obscure, it is better to exercise doubt than to argue an uncertain case." It is better to doubt what we do not know than to insist on facts that are not proven.

CHAPTER 3

*The author's opinions concerning the alleged discovery
and description of the islands by the Ancients*

In the last chapter I gave a common story concerning the previous discovery of the Indies. Now I will set down my beliefs concerning Christopher Columbus's motives and the knowledge which emboldened him, as a man of some learning, to undertake this great enterprise, so memorable to the men of his and future times. He rightly recognized that these lands had been forgotten, for he had found them described—and of this I am in no doubt at all—as one-time possessions of kings of Spain. I should like to quote Aristotle on this matter. On leaving the Straits of Gibraltar for the Atlantic ocean, he said, some Carthaginian merchants discovered a large island which had never been discovered before and was inhabited only by wild animals. It was therefore entirely wild and covered with large trees. It had great rivers on which ships could sail and was very fertile; everything that was planted there germinated and produced an abundant crop. This island was very remote, lying far off the coast of Africa at a distance of several days' sailing. On reaching it, these Carthaginian merchants, inspired by the fertility of the soil and the mildness of the climate, began to settle and build farms and villages. On learning this the Carthaginians in their senate proclaimed under pain of death that thenceforth none should sail for this land and that all those who had been there should be put to death. For the fame of this island was so high that if any other nation or empire were to hear of it it would conquer it and thus become a very formidable enemy to Carthage and its liberties.

This story is included in the repertory of Brother Theophilus de Ferrariis of Cremona, in his *Vitae regularis sacri ordinis predicatorum* which cites Aristotle's *De admirandis in natura auditis*.

[Oviedo now tells the story of the legendary Hesperus, twelfth king of Spain in descent from Tubal Cain, who was present at the fall of the Tower of Babel. He bases a long and fanciful argument on the fabulous histories of Beroso and Isidore of Seville, and on the evidence of various early geographers proves that the Fortunate Islands, known as the Hesperides after King Hesperus, were not the Canaries, as was generally assumed, but the Indies themselves. From this he develops an argument that, while admitting Columbus's courage, minimizes his achievement and suggests that he was not discovering but rediscovering the New World.]

The islands known as the Hesperides mentioned by Sebosus and Solinus, Pliny and Isidore must undoubtedly be the Indies and must have belonged to the Kingdom of Spain ever since Hesperus's time, who, according to Beroso, reigned 1,650 years before the birth of Our Lord. Therefore, if we add the 1,535 years since Our Saviour came into the world, the kings of Spain have been lords of the Hesperides for 3,193 years in all. So by the most ancient rights on this account and for other reasons that will be stated during the description of Christopher Columbus's voyages, God has restored this realm to the kings of Spain after many centuries. It appears therefore that divine justice restored to the fortunate and Catholic Kings Ferdinand and Isabel, conquerors of Granada and Naples, what had always been theirs and belongs to their heirs in perpetuity. In their time and by their commands, the admiral Christopher Columbus discovered this New World (or a very large part of it), which had been completely forgotten: during the reign of his Imperial Majesty, our Lord Charles V, these regions have been more widely explored and his empire thus largely extended.

All the authors whom I have mentioned indicate that these Hesperides were in fact the Indies, and I believe that Columbus followed their authority (or perhaps that of others that were known to him) when he set out on his long voyage, boldly risking so many dangers in search of the lands that he found. Whether or not he was guided by this knowledge, he undertook a journey into these seas which none had undertaken before him and which neither he nor any other sailor would have risked without the authority of these early geographers.

CHAPTER 4

That Christopher Columbus was the first to teach the Spaniards to
navigate by taking the altitudes of the sun and the North Star.
He goes to Portugal and other lands, seeking help and support
for his project of discovering the Indies. The Catholic sovereigns,
Ferdinand and Isabela, receive information about him, and at
their command he makes his discovery

Many are of the opinion (which is well supported by convincing arguments) that Christopher Columbus was the first in Spain to teach the art of navigating the wide ocean seas by measuring the height in degrees of the sun and the North Star. He was the first to practise the art, for, before his time, though it was taught in the schools, few (in fact none) had dared to try it out at sea. For this is a science which cannot be translated into actual knowledge unless it is practised in very large stretches of sea far from the coasts. Till then steersmen, pilots and seamen had exercised their craft by trial and error, relying on the knowledge of the captain or pilot, but not scientifically as is done today with our present knowledge of the seas. They steered as in the Mediterranean, along the shores of Spain and Flanders, the rest of Europe and Africa, and everywhere else, by hugging the coast. But in order to sail in search of provinces as distant as the Indies are from Spain, the pilot must make use of the science of the quadrant, which is practicable only in such vast expanses of sea as those lying between here[1] and Europe or our possessions in the Spicelands at the western end of the mainland of these Indies.

Impelled by his desire for discovery and having achieved practical mastery of the secret of navigation (touching the plotting of the course), Columbus set about seeking support. Perhaps he relied on this scientific mastery, perhaps on information received from the pilot, who is said to have given him an account of these unknown lands, either in Portugal, or in the Azores (supposing this story to be true), perhaps on the authorities mentioned in my last chapter or perhaps he was impelled in some other way. In any case, Columbus worked through his brother Bartholomew on King Henry VII of England (father of the present King Henry VIII) to support him and equip him with ships in which to discover these western seas, offering to give him great wealth and to increase his realm and estates with new kingdoms and lordships. After consulting his counsellors and certain men whom he had asked to examine Columbus's proposals, the King laughed at the idea, considering all that Columbus said to be nonsense.

In no way disconcerted when Columbus saw that his services would not be accepted in England, he began to open negotiations of the same kind with King John II of Portugal. King John was no more convinced by Columbus, although he was living and had married in that kingdom and by his marriage had become a subject of Portugal. Uninfluenced by this, King John refused either to support or aid Columbus in his project and put no trust in him.

He decided therefore to go to Castile, and on arriving at Seville made the acquaintance of the illustrious and brave Don Enrique Guzman, Duke of Medina-Sidonia. Not finding in him the support that he was seeking, he moved on to open new negotiations with the illustrious Don Luis de la Cerda, first Duke of Medina Celi, who also found his proposals fantastic, though some say that this duke agreed to equip Columbus in his city of Puerto de Sancta Maria, but was refused a licence to do so by the Catholic sovereigns. Therefore, since theirs was the highest authority, Columbus went to their most serene Catholic Majesties—King Ferdinand and Queen Isabela, and spent some time at their court in great poverty, meeting with no response from those to whom he spoke.

Remaining there in great straits he endeavoured to persuade those fortunate sovereigns to support him and equip some caravels, in which he might discover this new world (or regions unknown to him at this time) in their royal name. But this project was alien to the ideas of those to whom he proposed it. It did not please them, nor did they share the hopes of its great success in which Columbus alone believed. Not only did they attach little credit to his ideas; they actually considered that he was talking nonsense. He persisted in his suit for almost seven years, repeatedly holding out great prospects of wealth and riches for the crown of Castile. But as his cloak was poor and ragged, he was considered a dreamer and everything he said was taken to be fantastic. Being an unknown foreigner he found none to back him. What is more, the projects which he laid before them were great and unheard of. But see God's care in giving the Indies to their rightful owners! The offer had been made to the mighty kings of England and of Portugal and to those two rich dukes I have mentioned. He did not permit any of them to risk the small sum that Columbus asked. Disappointed by all these princes, Columbus went in search of the Catholic sovereigns, whom he found occupied at that time in their holy war against the Moors of the Kingdom of Granada.

It is no marvel that such Catholic princes should be more concerned with winning souls for salvation than with treasure and new estates which would only increase their royal cares and responsibilities, nor that they decided to back this project of discovery. But let no one believe that this alone could account for their good fortune, for eye had never seen, nor ear heard, nor human heart dreamed of the rewards prepared by God for those who love Him. These and many other blessings fell to our good sovereigns for their faithful service to Jesus Christ and their fervent desire for the spread of His holy faith. It was for this purpose that the Lord brought Christopher Columbus to their notice, for He sees the ends of the earth and all that happens beneath the sky. And when in due season this great business was concluded, it was God's purpose that was to be fulfilled.

During the time when Columbus was at court he lodged at the house of Alonso de Quintanilla, chief accountant to the Catholic sovereigns, a man of importance greatly devoted to their service and anxious for the extension of their power. Pitying Columbus's poverty he gave him food and money for his needs. In him Columbus found more support and understanding than in anyone else in Spain. On this gentleman's introduction, Columbus was received by the most reverend and illustrious Pedro Gonzalez de Mendoza, Cardinal of Spain and Archbishop of Toledo, who, on giving Columbus a first hearing, recognized him as a man of fair speech and learning who argued his case well. Realizing that he had a good intelligence and great knowledge he formed a favourable impression of Columbus and took pain to back him.

Thanks to the support of the cardinal and of Quintanilla, Columbus was received by the King and Queen and they immediately attached some credit to his written proposals and petitions. The business was finally concluded while the sovereigns were besieging the great and famous city of Granada,[2] in the year 1492. From their royal camp which they had built in the midst of their army and had named Santa Fé the blessed sovereigns concluded their agreement with Columbus; there, in the camp-city of the Holy Faith and in the holy faith that lay in their Highnesses' hearts, this discovery had its beginnings.

Not content with the holy and victorious enterprise which they had in hand, and by which they finally subdued all the Moors in Spain, who had insulted and maltreated Christians since the year 720 (as many chroniclers agree), these blessed princes, in addition to bringing the whole of Spain to our Catholic religion, decided to send an expedition in search of this new world and propagate the Christian faith there, for they devoted every hour to the service of God. For this holy purpose they ordered Columbus to be dispatched, giving him authority under the royal seal to hire three caravels of the type he required in Andalusia, with all necessary crews and provisions, for this long voyage whose only hope of success lay in the pious zeal and holy purpose of these Christian princes, under whose auspices and by whose commands this great adventure began. And since he needed money for his expedition, sufficient to prepare his ships and set out on the first discovery of the Indies, on account of the costly war this was lent him by Luis de Santangel, the financial secretary. A first grant and agreement was made by the sovereigns to Columbus in the city of Santa Fé, in the Kingdom of Granada, on 18 April 1492, before secretary Juan de Coloma. And the agreement was confirmed by a royal appointment given to him thirteen days later in the city of Granada on 30 April of the same year 1492, and with this authority Columbus departed, as has been said, and went to the city of Palos de Moguer, where he prepared for his voyage.

Endnotes

1. The last Moorish city in Spain.
2. Santo Domingo, where Oviedo was writing.

Part Six

Education, Learning
and the Occult

Malleus Maleficarum (1486)

The Malleus Maleficarum *was published in 1486 by the Dominicans Jacob Sprenger and Heinrich Kramer (Institoris). It appeared in the middle of the era of witch-hunting: witchcraft prosecutions had begun in the thirteenth century, with the development of the inquisitorial procedure. The essence of the inquisitorial procedure was that cases against suspected offenders were brought by the authorities, based on information provided by the public. Once the suspect had been denounced, the judge could begin the investigation, or "inquisition." The accused was rarely allowed a lawyer, and the main aim of the procedure was to convince the accused to confess and be reconciled to the church, rather than to determine guilt or innocence. Such a confession could be obtained by torture.*

The idea of the witch was fully developed by the early fifteenth century; familiar ideas such as the witch's sabbath and nocturnal flight, which were entirely absent from early prosecutions, were common by the 1430s. The Malleus Maleficarum *comes from this period, before the mass persecutions of the witch-craze in the sixteenth and seventeenth centuries. Although it is one of the most famous of the witch-hunting manuals of the period, it does not feature some of the more graphic elements of the witch's habits, such as the witch's sabbath. However, it is notable for its virulent misogyny. It also shares one of the central problems of the source material for witchcraft in that it gives us the perceptions of the learned persecutors of witches, rather than witches themselves or their victims.*

Chapter Twenty-Five

Malleus Maleficarum
Part 1
Question 6

Concerning Witches who copulate with Devils.
Why it is that Women are chiefly addicted to Evil Superstitions.

There is also, concerning witches who copulate with devils, much difficulty in considering the methods by which such abominations are consummated. On the part of the devil: first, of what element the body is made that he assumes; secondly, whether the act is always accompanied by the injection of semen received from another; thirdly, as to time and place, whether he commits this act more frequently at one time than at another; fourthly, whether the act is invisible to any who may be standing by. And on the part of the women, it has to be inquired whether only they who were themselves conceived in this filthy manner are often visited by devils; or secondly, whether it is those who were offered to devils by midwives at the time of their birth; and thirdly, whether the actual venereal delectation of such is of a weaker sort. But we cannot here reply to all these questions, both because we are only engaged in a general study, and because in the second part of this work they are all singly explained by their operations, as will appear in the fourth chapter, where mention is made of each separate method. Therefore let us now chiefly consider women; and first, why this kind of perfidy is found more in so fragile a sex than in men. And our inquiry will first be general, as to the general conditions of women; secondly, particular, as to which sort of women are found to be given to superstition and witchcraft; and thirdly, specifically with regard to midwives, who surpass all others in wickedness.

Why Superstition is chiefly found in Women.

As for the first question, why a greater number of witches is found in the fragile feminine sex than among men; it is indeed a fact that it were idle to contradict, since it is accredited by actual experience, apart from the verbal testimony of credible witnesses. And without in any way detracting from a sex in which God has always taken great glory that His might should be spread abroad, let us say that various men have assigned various reasons for this fact, which nevertheless agree in principle. Wherefore it is good, for the admonition of women, to speak of this matter; and it has often been proved by experience that they are eager to hear of it, so long as it is set forth with discretion.

For some learned men propound this reason; that there are three things in nature, the Tongue, an Ecclesiastic, and a Woman, which know no moderation in goodness or vice; and when they exceed the bounds of their condition they reach the greatest heights and the lowest depths of goodness and vice. When they are governed by a good spirit, they are most excellent in virtue; but when they are governed by an evil spirit, they indulge the worst possible vices.

This is clear in the case of the tongue, since by its ministry most of the kingdoms have been brought into the faith of Christ; and the Holy Ghost appeared over the Apostles of Christ in tongues of fire. Other learned preachers also have had as it were the tongues of dogs, licking the wounds and sores of the dying Lazarus. As it is said: With the tongues of dogs ye save your souls from the enemy.

For this reason S. Dominic,[1] the leader and father of the Order of Preachers, is represented in the figure of a barking dog with a lighted torch in his mouth, that even to this day he may by his barking keep off the heretic wolves from the flock of Christ's sheep.

It is also a matter of common experience that the tongue of one prudent man can subdue the wrangling of a multitude; wherefore not unjustly Solomon sings much in their praise, in *Proverbs* x: In the lips of him that hath understanding wisdom is found. And again, The tongue of the just is as choice silver: the heart of the wicked is little worth. And again, The lips of the righteous feed many; but fools die for want of wisdom. For this cause he adds in chapter xvi, The preparations of the heart belong to man; but the answer of the tongue is from the Lord.

But concerning an evil tongue you will find in *Ecclesiasticus* xxviii: A backbiting tongue hath disquieted many, and driven them from nation to nation: strong cities hath it pulled down, and overthrown the houses of great men. And by a backbiting tongue it means a third party who rashly or spitefully interferes between two contending parties.

Secondly, concerning Ecclesiastics, that is to say, clerics and religious of either sex, S. John Chrysostom[2] speaks on the text, He cast out them that bought and sold from the temple. From the priesthood arises everything good, and everything evil. S. Jerome in his epistle to Nepotian says: Avoid as you would the plague a trading priest, who has risen from poverty to riches, from a low to a high estate. And Blessed Bernard in his 23rd Homily *On the Psalms* says of clerics: If one should arise as an open heretic, let him be cast out and put to silence; if he is a violent enemy, let all good men flee from him. But how are we to know which ones to cast out or to flee from? For they arc confusedly friendly and hostile, peaceable and quarrelsome, neighbourly and utterly selfish.

And in another place: Our bishops are become spearmen, and our pastors shearers. And by bishops here is meant those proud Abbots who impose heavy labours on their inferiors, which they would not themselves touch with their little finger. And S. Gregory says concerning pastors: No one does more harm in the Church than he who, having the name or order of sanctity, lives in sin; for no one dares to accuse him of sin, and therefore the sin is widely spread, since the sinner is honoured for the sanctity of his order. Blessed Augustine also speaks of monks to Vincent the Donatist: I freely confess to your charity before the Lord our God, which is the witness of my soul from the time I began to serve God, what great difficulty I have experienced in the fact that it is impossible to find either worse or better men than those who grace or disgrace the monasteries.

Now the wickedness of women is spoken of in *Ecclesiasticus* xxv: There is no head above the head of a serpent and there is no wrath above the wrath of a woman. I had rather dwell with a lion and a dragon than to keep house with a wicked woman. And among much which in that place precedes and follows about a wicked woman, he concludes: All wickedness is but little to the wickedness of a woman. Wherefore S. John Chrysostom says on the text, It is not good to marry (*S. Matthew* xix):[3] What else is woman but a foe to friendship, an unescapable punishment, a necessary evil, a natural temptation, a desirable calamity, a domestic danger, a delectable detriment, an evil of nature, painted with fair colours! Therefore if it be a sin to divorce her when she ought to be kept, it is indeed a necessary torture; for either we commit adultery by divorcing her, or we must endure daily strife. Cicero in his second book of *The Rhetorics* says: The many lusts of men lead them into one sin, but the one lust of women leads them into all sins; for the root of all woman's vices is avarice. And Seneca says in his *Tragedies*: A woman either loves or hates; there is no third grade. And the tears of a woman are a deception, for they may spring from true grief, or they may be a snare. When a woman thinks alone, she thinks evil.

But for good women there is so much praise, that we read that they have brought beatitude to men, and have saved nations, lands, and cities; as is clear in the case of Judith, Debbora, and Esther. See also I *Corinthians vii*: If a woman hath a husband that believeth not, and he be pleased to dwell with her, let her not leave him. For the unbelieving husband is sanctified by the believing wife. And *Ecclesiasticus* xxvi: Blessed is the man who has a virtuous wife, for the number of his days shall be doubled. And throughout that chapter much high praise is spoken of the excellence of good women; as also in the last chapter of *Proverbs* concerning a virtuous woman.

And all this is made clear also in the New Testament concerning women and virgins and other holy women who have by faith led nations and kingdoms away from the worship of idols to the Christian religion. Anyone who looks at Vincent of Beavais (in *Spe. Histor.*, XXVI. 9) will find marvellous things of the conversion of Hungary by the most Christian Gilia[4] and of the Franks by Clotilda,[5] the wife of Clovis. Wherefore in many vituperations that we read against women, the word woman is used to mean the lust of the flesh. As it is said: I have found a woman more bitter than death, and a good woman subject to carnal lust.

Others again have propounded other reasons why there are more superstitious women found than men. And the first is, that they are more credulous; and since the chief aim of the devil is to corrupt faith, therefore he rather attacks them. See *Ecclesiasticus* xix: He that is quick to believe is light-minded, and shall be diminished. The second reason is, that women are naturally more impressionable, and more ready to receive the influence of a disembodied spirit; and that when they use this quality well they are very good, but when they use it ill they are very evil.

The third reason is that they have slippery tongues, and are unable to conceal from their fellow-women those things which by evil arts they know; and, since they are weak, they find an easy and secret manner of vindicating themselves by witchcraft. Sec *Ecclesiasticus* as quoted above: I had rather dwell with a lion and a dragon than to keep house with a wicked woman. All wickedness is but little to the wickedness of a woman. And to this may be added that, as they are very impressionable, they act accordingly.

There are also others who bring forward yet other reasons, of which preachers should be very careful how they make use. For it is true that in the Old Testament the Scriptures have much that is evil to say about women, and this because of the first temptress, Eve, and her imitators; yet afterwards in the New Testament we find a change of name, as from Eva to Ave (as S. Jerome says), and the whole sin of Eve taken away by the benediction of MARY. Therefore preachers should always say as much praise of them as possible.

But because in these times this perfidy is more often found in women than in men, as we learn by actual experience, if anyone is curious as to the reason, we may add to what has already been said the following: that since they are feebler both in mind and body, it is not surprising that they should come more under the spell of witchcraft.

For as regards intellect, or the understanding of spiritual things, they seem to be of a different nature from men; a fact which is vouched for by the logic of the authorities, backed by various examples from the Scriptures. Terence[6] says: Women are intellectually like children. And Lactantius (Institutiones, III): No woman understood philosophy except Temeste. And *Proverbs* xi, as it were describing a woman, says: As a jewel of gold in a swine's snout, so is a fair woman which is without discretion.

But the natural reason is that she is more carnal than a man, as is clear from her many carnal abominations. And it should be noted that there was a defect in the formation of the first woman, since she was formed from a bent rib, that is, a rib of the breast, which is bent as it were in a contrary direction to a man. And since through this defect she is an imperfect animal, she always deceives. For Cato says: When a woman weeps she weaves snares. And again: When a woman weeps, she labours to deceive a man. And this is shown by Samson's wife, who coaxed him to tell her the riddle he had propounded to the Philistines, and told them the answer, and so deceived him. And it is clear in the case of the first woman that she had little faith; for when the serpent asked why they did not eat of every tree in Paradise, she answered: Of every tree, etc.—lest perchance we die. Thereby she showed that she doubted, and had little faith in the word of God. And all this is indicated by the etymology of the word; for *Femina* comes from *Fe* and *Minus,* since she is ever weaker to hold and preserve the faith. And this as regards faith is of her very nature; although both by grace and nature faith never failed in the Blessed Virgin, even at the time of Christ's Passion, when it failed in all men.

Therefore a wicked woman is by her nature quicker to waver in her faith, and consequently quicker to abjure the faith, which is the root of witchcraft.

And as to her other mental quality, that is, her natural will; when she hates someone whom she formerly loved, then she seethes with anger and impatience in her whole soul, just as the tides of the sea are always heaving and boiling. Many authorities allude to this cause. *Ecclesiasticus* xxv: There is no wrath above the wrath of a woman. And Seneca (*Tragedies*, VIII): No might of the flames or of the swollen winds, no deadly weapon, is so much to be feared as the lust and hatred of a woman who has been divorced from the marriage bed (*Medea*).

This is shown too in the woman who falsely accused Joseph, and caused him to be imprisoned because he would not consent to the crime of adultery with her (*Genesis* xxx). And truly the most powerful cause which contributes to the increase of witches is the woeful rivalry between married folk and unmarried women and men. This is so even among holy women, so what must it be among the others? For you see in *Genesis* xxi how impatient and envious Sarah was of Hagar when she conceived: how jealous Rachel was of Leah because she had no children (*Genesis* xxx): and Hannah, who was barren, of the fruitful Peninnah (I. *Kings* i): and how Miriam (*Numbers* xii) murmured and spoke ill of Moses, and was therefore stricken with leprosy: and how Martha was jealous of Mary Magdalen, because she was busy and Mary was sitting down *(S. Luke* x). To this point is *Ecclesiasticus* xxxvii: Neither consult with a woman touching her of whom she is jealous. Meaning that it is useless to consult with her, since there is always jealousy, that is, envy, in a wicked woman. And if women behave thus to each other, how much more will they do so to men.

Valerius Maximus tells how, when Phoroneus, the king of the Greeks, was dying, he said to his brother Leontius that there would have been nothing lacking to him of complete happiness if a wife had always been lacking to him. And when Leontius asked how a wife could stand in the way of happiness, he answered that all married men well knew. And when the philosopher Socrates was asked if one should marry a wife, he answered: If you do not, you are lonely, your family dies out, and a stranger inherits; if you do, you suffer perpetual anxiety, querulous complaints, reproaches concerning the marriage portion, the heavy displeasure of your relations, the garrulousness of a mother-in-law, cuckoldom, and no certain arrival of an heir. This he said as one who knew. For S. Jerome in his *Contra Iouinianum*[6] says: This Socrates had two wives, whom he endured with much patience, but could not be rid of their contumelies and clamorous vituperations. So one day when they were complaining against him, he went out of the house to escape their plaguing, and sat down before the house; and the women then threw filthy water over him. But the philosopher was not disturbed by this, saying, "I knew that the rain would come after the thunder."

There is also a story of a man whose wife was drowned in a river, who, when he was searching for the body to take it out of the water, walked up the stream. And when he was asked why, since heavy bodies do not rise but fall, he was searching against the current of the river, he answered: "When that woman was alive she always, both in word and deed, went contrary to my commands;—therefore I am searching in the contrary direction in case even now she is dead she may preserve her contrary disposition."

And indeed, just as through the first defect in their intelligence they are more prone to abjure the faith; so through their second defect of inordinate affections and passions they search for, brood over, and inflict various vengeances, either by witchcraft, or by some other means. Wherefore it is no wonder that so great a number of witches exist in this sex.

Women also have weak memories; and it is a natural vice in them not to be disciplined, but to follow their own impulses without any sense of what is due; this is her whole study, and all that she keeps in her memory. So Theophrastus says: If you hand over the whole management of the house to her, but reserve some minute detail to your own judgement, she will think that you are displaying a great want of faith in her, and will stir up strife; and unless you quickly take counsel, she will prepare poison for you, and consult seers and soothsayers; and will become a witch.

But as to domination by women, hear what Cicero says in the *Paradoxes*. Can he be called a free man whose wife governs him, imposes laws on him, orders him, and forbids him to do what he wishes, so that he cannot and dare not deny her anything that she asks? I should call him not only a slave, but the vilest of slaves, even if he comes of the noblest family. And Seneca, in the character of the raging Medea, says: Why do you cease to follow your happy impulse; how great is that part of vengeance in which you rejoice? Where he adduces many proofs that a woman will not be governed, but will follow her own impulse even to her own destruction. In the same way we read of many women who have killed themselves either for love or sorrow because they were unable to work their vengeance.

S. Jerome, writing of Daniel, tells a story of Laodice, wife of Antiochus king of Syria; how, being jealous lest he should love his other wife, Berenice, more than her, she first caused Berenice and her daughter by Antiochus to be slain, and then poisoned herself. And why? Because she would not be governed, but would follow her own impulse. Therefore S. John Chrysostom says not without reason: O evil worse than all evil, a wicked woman, whether she be poor or rich. For if she be the wife of a rich man, she does not cease night and day to excite her husband with hot words, to use evil blandishments and violent importations. And if she have a poor husband she does not cease to stir him also to anger and strife. And if she be a widow, she takes it upon herself everywhere to look down on everybody, and is inflamed to all boldness by the spirit of pride.

If we inquire, we find that nearly all the kingdoms of the world have been overthrown by women. Troy, which was a prosperous kingdom, was, for the rape of one woman, Helen, destroyed, and many thousands of Greeks slain. The kingdom of the Jews suffered much misfortune and destruction through the accursed Jezebel, and her daughter Athaliah, queen of Judah who caused her son's sons to be killed, that on their death she might reign herself; yet each of them was slain. The kingdom of the Romans endured much evil through Cleopatra, Queen of Egypt, that worst of women. And so with others. Therefore it is no wonder if the world now suffers through the malice of women.

And now let us examine the carnal desires of the body itself, whence has arisen unconscionable harm to human life. Justly may we say with Cato of Utica: If the world could be rid of women, we should not be without God in our intercourse. For truly, without the wickedness of women, to say nothing of witchcraft, the world would still remain proof against innumerable dangers. Hear what Valerius said to Rufinus: You do not know that woman is the Chimaera, but it is good that you should know it; for that monster was of three forms; its face was that of a radiant and noble lion, it had the filthy belly of a goat, and it was armed with the virulent tail of a viper And he means that a woman is beautiful to look upon, contaminating to the touch, and deadly to keep.

Let us consider another property of hers, the voice. For as she is a liar by nature, so in her speech she stings while she delights us. Wherefore her voice is like the song of the Sirens, who with their sweet melody entice the passers-by and kill them. For they kill them by emptying their purses, consuming their strength, and causing them to forsake God. Again Valerius says to Rufinus: When she speaks it is a delight which flavours the sin; the flower of love is a rose, because under its blossom there are hidden many thorns. See *Proverbs* v, 3–4: Her mouth is smoother than oil; that is, her speech is afterwards as bitter as absinthium. [Her throat is smoother than oil. But her end is as bitter as wormwood.]

Let us consider also her gait, posture, and habit, in which is vanity of vanities. There is no man in the world who studies so hard to please the good God as even an ordinary woman studies by her vanities to please men. An example of this is to be found in the life of Pelagia,[7] a worldly woman who was wont to go about Antioch tired and adorned most extravagantly. A holy father, named Nonnus, saw her and began to weep, saying to his companions, that never in all his life had he used such diligence to please God; and much more he added to this effect, which is preserved in his orations.

It is this which is lamented in *Ecclesiastes* vii, and which the Church even now laments on account of the great multitude of witches. And I have found a woman more bitter than death, who is the hunter's snare, and her heart is a net, and her hands are bands. He that pleaseth God shall escape from her; but he that is a sinner shall be caught by her. More bitter than death, that is, than the devil: *Apocalypse* vi, 8, His name was Death. For though the devil tempted Eve to sin, yet Eve seduced Adam. And as the sin of Eve would not have brought death to our soul and body unless the sin had afterwards passed on to Adam, to which he was tempted by Eve, not by the devil, therefore she is more bitter than death.

More bitter than death, again, because that is natural and destroys only the body; but the sin which arose from woman destroys the soul by depriving it of grace, and delivers the body up to the punishment for sin.

More bitter than death, again, because bodily death is an open and terrible enemy, but woman is a wheedling and secret enemy.

And that she is more perilous than a snare does not speak of the snare of hunters, but of devils. For men are caught not only through their carnal desires, when they see and hear women: for S. Bernard says: Their face is a burning wind, and their voice the hissing of serpents: but they also cast wicked spells on countless men and animals. And when it is said that her heart is a net, it speaks of the inscrutable malice which reigns in their hearts. And her hands are as bands for binding; for when they place their hands on a creature to bewitch it, then with the help of the devil they perform their design.

To conclude. All witchcraft comes from carnal lust, which is in women insatiable. See *Proverbs* xxx: There are three things that are never satisfied, yea, a fourth thing which says not, It is enough; that is, the mouth of the womb.

Wherefore for the sake of fulfilling their lusts they consort even with devils. More such reasons could be brought forward, but to the understanding it is sufficiently clear that it is no matter for wonder that there are more women than men found infected with the heresy of witchcraft. And in consequence of this, it is better called the heresy of witches than of wizards, since the name is taken from the more powerful party. And blessed be the Highest Who has so far preserved the male sex from so great a crime: for since He was willing to be born and to suffer for us, therefore He has granted to men this privilege.

Endnotes

1. "S. Dominic." Before the birth of S. Dominic, his mother, Blessed Joanna d'Aza, dreamed that she had brought forth a black-and-white dog carrying in his mouth a lighted torch. The dog with the torch is accordingly the pictorial attribute of the Saint. Nor must the play upon the name of his sons be forgotten—Dominicani, Domini canes, Hounds of the Lord.

2. "S. John Chrysostom." Born at Antioch 347; died at Comana in Pontus, 1 September, 407. His fifty-nine homilies "On the Psalms" (iv-xii, xli, xliii–xlix, cviii–cxvii, cxix–cl) are very famous.

3. "S. Matthew." The ninety Homilies on S. Matthew were written about the year 390.

4. "Gilia." Rather Gisela, the devout sister of Duke Henry of Bavaria (the future Emperor S. Henry II); in 995 married S. Stephen of Hungary, who succeeded to the throne in 997. She was untiring in her efforts to spread the Faith throughout the kingdom. The coronation mantle of Hungary, a purple damask cope, embroidered in silk and gold by Queen Gisela, dated 1031, is preserved at Budapest.

5. "Clotilda." Born probably at Lyons about 474; died at Tours, 3 June, 545. The feast of S. Clotilda is celebrated 3 June. From the sixth century onwards, the marriage of Clovis I, King of the Salic Franks, and Clotilda, which took place in 492 or 493, was made the theme of epic narratives and many legends. Clotilda soon acquired a great ascendancy over her husband, and she availed herself of this influence to win him to the Catholic Faith. For a time her efforts seemed unavailing, but Clovis, who in a great battle against the Alemanni saw his men on the point of defeat, invoked the God of his wife, promising to become a Christian if only victory should be granted to the Franks. The tide instantly turned, and, true to his word, he was baptized at Reims by S. Remigius at Christmas, 496. His sister and three thousand of his noblest warriors at the same time embraced the Faith. Thus S. Clotilda was the instrument in the conversion of a mighty people.

6. "*Contra louinianum.*" This treatise was written 392–93.

7. "Pelagia." "Pelagia meretrix"or "Pelagia mima," a beautiful actress who led the life of a prostitute at Antioch. She was converted by the holy bishop Nonnus, and disguised as a man went on pilgrimage to Jerusalem, where for many years she led a life of extremest mortification and penance in a grotto on the Mount of Olives. This "bienheureuse pécheresse" attained to such heights of sanctity that she was canonized, and in the East, where her cult was long very popular, her festival is kept on 8 October, which is also the day of her commemoration in the Roman Martyrology.

Nostradamus (1503–1566)

Michel de Nostradame was born in 1503. Both of his grandfathers were medical doctors and philosophers, and they saw to his early education. He enrolled in the university of Avignon, where he pursued his early interest in astronomy and astrology, but he eventually decided to pursue the family tradition in medicine. In 1522 he went to Montpellier, one of the best medical schools of the period. In 1525 the university was closed as a wave of plague rolled through southern France. Nostradamus decided to fight the plague, and met with a remarkable degree of success. His fame led to the offer of a teaching position when the university re-opened. Nostradamus felt restricted by the academic routine, however, and he took up an offer from Joseph Scaliger, one of the best-known scholars in Europe, to come to Agen and study with him. He settled there, but after another wave of plague killed his wife and two small children, his reputation suffered, he fought with Scaliger, and he had a brush with heresy charges.

In 1538 he left Agen and began to travel through France and Italy. It was at this time that his interest in astrology seems to have broadened into an interest in prophecy. Through this period he continued to practice medicine with some success, but he was regarded with suspicion both by fellow doctors and the inquisition. In 1547 he finally settled in Salon, where he married again. In 1550 he began to publish his almanacs and in 1554 his Presages appeared. Following their success he began to rely more heavily on his prophetic powers and between 1554 and 1565 he produced his Centuries—collections of 100 quatrains of prophetic verse. He died a famous man in 1566.

Chapter Twenty-Six

Nostradamus to
King Henri II of France

Salon, 27 June, 1558

To the most invincible, very puissant, and most Christian Henry King of France the Second: Michael Nostradamus, his most humble, most obedient servant and subject, wishes victory and happiness.

For that sovereign observation that I had, O most Christian and very victorious King, since that my face, long obscured with cloud, presented itself before the deity of your measureless Majesty, since that in that I have been perpetually dazzled, never failing to honour and worthily revere that day, when first before it, as before a singularly humane majesty, I presented myself. I searched for some occasion by which to manifest good heart and frank courage, by the means of which I might grow into greater knowledge of your serene Majesty. I soon found in effect it was impossible for me to declare it, considering the contrast of the solitariness of my long obnubilation and obscurity, and my being suddenly thrust into brilliancy, and transported into the presence of the sovereign eye of the first monarch of the universe. Likewise I have long hung in doubt as to whom I ought to dedicate these three *Centuries*, the remainder of my Prophecies amounting now to a thousand. I have long meditated on an act of such audacity. I have at last ventured to address your Majesty, and was not daunted from it as Plutarch, that grave author, relates in the life of Lycurgus, that, seeing the gifts and presents that were made in the way of sacrifice at the temples of the immortal gods in that age, many were staggered at the expense, and dared not approach the temple to present anything.

Notwithstanding this, I saw your royal splendour to be accompanied with an incomparable humanity, and paid my addresses to it, not as to those Kings of Persia whom it was not permissible to approach. But to a very prudent and very wise Prince I have dedicated my nocturnal and prophetic calculations, composed out of a natural instinct, and accompanied by a poetic fervour, rather than according to the strict rules of poetry. Most part, indeed, has been composed and adjusted by astronomical calculation corresponding to the years, months, and weeks, of the regions, countries, and for the most part towns and cities, throughout Europe, Africa, and a part of Asia, which nearest approach [or resemble] each other in all these climates, and this is composed in a natural manner. Possibly some may answer—who, if so, had better blow his nose [that he may see the clearer by it]—that the rhythm is as easy to be understood, as the sense is hard to get at. Therefore, O most gracious King, the bulk of the prophetic quatrains are so rude, that there is no making way through them, nor is there any interpreter of them. Nevertheless, being always anxious to set down the years, towns, and regions cited, where the events are to occur, even from the year 1585, and the year 1606, dating from the present time, which is the 14th of March, 1557.

Then passing far beyond to things which shall happen at the commencement of the seventh millenary, deeply calculated, so far as my astronomic calculus, and other knowledge, has been able to reach, to the time when the adversaries of Jesus Christ and of His Church shall begin to multiply in great force. The whole has been composed and calculated on days and hours of best election and disposition, and with all the accuracy I could attain to at a moment [blessed] *"Minerva libera et non invita,"*[1] my calculations looking forward to events through a space of time to come that nearly equals that of the past even up to the present, and by this they will know in the lapse of time and in all regions what is to happen, all written down thus particularly, immingled with nothing superfluous.

Notwithstanding that some say, *"Quod de futuris non est determinata omnino veritas,"*[2] I will confess, Sire, that I believed myself capable of presage from the natural instinct I inherit of my ancestors, adjusted and regulated by elaborate calculation, and the endeavour to free the soul, mind, and heart from all care, solicitude, and anxiety, by resting and tranquilizing the spirit, which finally has all to be completed and perfected in one respect *tripode oeneo* [by the brazen tripod]. With all this there will be many to attribute to me as mine, things no more mine than nothing. The Almighty alone, who strictly searches the human heart, pious, just, and pitiful, is the true Judge; to Him I pray to defend me from the calumny of wicked men. Such persons, with equal calumny, will bring into question how all your ancient progenitors the Kings of France have cured the evil; how those of other nations have cured the bite of serpents;

others have had a certain instinct in the art of divination, and other faculties that would be too long to recount here. Notwithstanding such as cannot be restrained from the exercise of the malignancy of the evil spirit, [there is hope that] by the lapse of time, and after my extinction here on earth, my writings will be more valued than during my lifetime.

However, if I err in calculation of ages, or find myself unable to please all the world, may it please your Imperial Majesty to forgive me, for I protest before God and His saints, that I purpose to insert nothing whatever in writing this present Epistle that shall militate against the true Catholic Faith, whilst consulting the astronomical calculations to the very best of my knowledge. For the stretch of time of our forefathers [i.e. the age of the world] which has gone before is such, submitting myself to the direction of the soundest chronologists, that the first man, Adam, was about one thousand two hundred and forty years before Noah, not computing time by Gentile records, such as Varro has committed to writing, but taking simply the Sacred Scriptures for the guide in my astronomic reckonings, to the best of my feeble understanding. After Noah, from him and the universal deluge, about one thousand and fourscore years, came Abraham, who was a sovereign astrologer according to some; he first invented the Chaldaean alphabet. Then came Moses, about five hundred and fifteen or sixteen years later. Between the time of David and Moses five hundred and seventy years elapsed. Then after the time of David and the time of our Saviour and Redeemer, Jesus Christ, born of a pure Virgin, there elapsed (according to some chronographers) one thousand three hundred and fifty years ….

I fully confess that all proceeds from God, and for that I return Him thanks, honour, and immortal praise, and have mingled nothing with it of the divination which proceeds *à fato*, but *à Deo, à natura*,[3] and for the most part accompanied with the movement of the celestial courses. Much as, if looking into a burning mirror [we see], as with darkened vision, the great events, sad or portentous, and calamitous occurrences that are about to fall upon the principal worshippers. First upon the temples of God, secondly upon such as have their support from the earth [i.e. by the kings], this decadence draweth nigh, with a thousand other calamitous incidents that in the course of time will be known to happen.

For God will take notice of the long barrenness of the great Dame, who afterwards will conceive two principal children. But, she being in great danger, the girl she will give birth to with risk at her age of death in the eighteenth year, and not possible to outlive the thirty-sixth, will leave three males and one female, and he will have two who never had any of the same father. The three brothers will be so different, though united and agreed, that the three and four parts of Europe will tremble. By the youngest in years will the Christian monarchy be sustained and augmented; heresies spring up and suddenly cast down, the Arabs driven back, kingdoms united, and new laws promulgated. Of the other children the first shall possess the furious crowned Lions, holding their paws upon the bold escutcheon. The second, accompanied by the Latins, shall penetrate so far that a second trembling and furious descent shall be made, descending Mons Jovis [at Barcelona] to mount the Pyrenees, shall not be translated to the antique monarchy, and a third inundation of human blood shall arise, and March for a long while will not be found in Lent. The daughter shall be given for the preservation of the Christian Church, the dominator falling into the Pagan sect of new infidels, and she will have two children, the one fidelity, the other infidelity, by the confirmation of the Catholic Church. The other, who to his great confusion and tardy repentance wished to ruin her, will have three regions over a wide extent of leagues, that is to say, Roumania, Germany, and Spain, which will entail great intricacy of military handling, stretching from the 50th to the 52nd degree of latitude. And they will have to respect the more distant religions of Europe and the north above the 48th degree of latitude, which at first in a vain timidity will tremble, and then the more western, southern, and eastern will tremble. Their power will become such, that what is brought about by union and concord will prove insuperable by warlike conquest. By nature they will be equal, but exceedingly different in faith.

After this the sterile Dame, of greater power than the second, shall be received by two nations, by the first made obstinate by him who had power over all, by the second, and third, that shall extend his forces towards the circuit of the east of Europe; [arrived] there his standards will stop and succumb, but by sea he will run on to Trinacria and the Adriatic with his mirmidons. The Germans will succumb wholly and the Barbaric sect will be disquieted and driven back by the whole of the Latin race. Then shall begin the grand Empire of Antichrist in the Atila and Xerxes, [who is] to descend with innumerable multitudes, so that the coming of the Holy Spirit, issuing from the 48th degree, shall make a transmigration, chasing away the abomination of Antichrist, that made war upon the royal person of the great vicar of Jesus Christ, and against

His Church, and reign *per tempus, et in occasione temporis* [for a time, and to the end of time]. This will be preceded by an eclipse of the sun, more obscure and tenebrose than has ever been since the creation of the world, up to the death and passion of Jesus Christ, and from thence till now. There will be in the month of October a grand revolution [translation] made, such that one would think that the librating body of the earth had lost its natural movement in the abyss of perpetual darkness. There will be seen precursive signs in the spring-time, and after extreme changes ensuing, reversal of kingdoms, and great earthquakes [i.e. wars]. All this accompanied with the procreations of the New Babylon [Paris], a miserable prostitute big with the abomination of the first holocaust [death of Louis XVI]. It will only continue for seventy-three years seven months.

Then there will issue from the stock so long time barren, proceeding from the 50th degree, [one] who will renovate the whole Christian Church. A great peace, union, and concord will then spring up between some of the children of races [long] opposed to each other and separated by diverse kingdoms. Such a peace shall be set up, that the instigator and promoter of military faction by means of the diversity of religions, shall dwell attached to the bottom of the abyss, and united to the kingdom of the furious, who shall counterfeit the wise. The countries, towns, cities, and provinces that had forsaken their old customs to free themselves, enthralling themselves more deeply, shall become secretly weary of their liberty, and, true religion lost, shall commence by striking off to the left, to return more than ever to the right.

Then replacing holiness, so long desecrated by their former writings [circulating slanders], afterwards the result will be that the great dog will issue as an irresistible mastiff [Napoleon?] who will destroy everything, even to all that may have been prepared in time past, till the churches will be restored as at first, and the clergy reinstated in their pristine condition; till it lapses again into whoredom and luxury, to commit and perpetrate a thousand crimes. And drawing near to another desolation, then, when she shall be at her highest and sublimest point of dignity, the kings and generals [*mains militaires*] will come up [against her], and her two swords will be taken from her, and nothing will be left her but the semblance of them. [The following paragraph I can make nothing of, so I give it in the words of Garencières;[4] and in inverted commas.] "From which by the means of the crookedness that draweth them, the people causing it to go straight, and not willing to submit unto them by the end opposite to the sharp hand that toucheth the ground they shall provoke." Until there shall be born unto the branch a long time sterile, one who shall deliver the French people from the benign slavery that they voluntarily submitted to, putting himself under the protection of Mars, and stripping Jupiter [Napoleon I] of all his honours and dignities, for the city constituted free and seated in another narrow Mesopotamia. The chief and governor shall be cast from the midst, and set in a place of the air, ignorant of the conspiracy of the conspirators [Fouché, Duc d' Otranto, etc.] with the second Thrasibulus, who for a long time had prepared all this. Then shall the impurities and abominations be with great shame set forth and manifested to the darkness of the veiled light, shall cease towards the end of his reign, and the chiefs of the Church shall evince but little of the love of God, whilst many of them shall apostatize from the true faith.

Of the three sects [Lutheran, Catholic, and Mahometan], that which is in the middle, by the action of its own worshippers, will be thrown a little into decadence. The first totally throughout Europe, and the chief part of Africa exterminated by the third, by means of the poor in spirit, who by the madness engendered of libidinous luxury, will commit adultery [i.e. apostatize]. The people will pull down the pillar, and chase away the adherents of the legislators, and it shall seem, from the kingdoms weakened by the Orientals, that God the Creator has loosed Satan from the infernal prisons, to make room for the great Dog and Dohan [Gog and Magog],[5] which will make so great and injurious a breach in the Churches, that neither the reds nor the whites, who are without eyes and without hands [meaning the latter Bourbons, "who learn nothing and forget nothing"], cannot judge of the situation, and their power will be taken from them. Then shall commence a persecution of the Church such as never was before. Whilst this is enacting, such a pestilence shall spring up that out of three parts of mankind two shall be removed. To such a length will this proceed that one will neither know nor recognize the fields or houses, and grass will grow in the streets of the cities as high as a man's knees. To the clergy there shall be a total desolation, and the martial men shall usurp what shall come back from the City of the Sun [Rome], and from Malta and the Islands of Hières [off Marseilles], and the great chain of the port shall be opened that takes its name from the marine ox [Bosphorus] ....

Had I wished to give to every quatrain its detailed date, it could easily have been done, but it would not have been agreeable to all, and still less to interpret them, Sire, until your Majesty should have fully sanctioned me to do this, in order not to furnish calumniators with an opportunity to injure me. Always reckoning the years since the creation of the world to the birth of Noah as being 1506 years, and from that to the completion of the building of the ark at the period of the universal deluge 600 years elapsed (let them be solar years, or lunar, or mixed), I hold that the Scripture takes them to be solar. At the conclusion of this 600 years, Noah entered the ark to escape the deluge. The deluge was universal over the earth, and lasted one year and two months. From the conclusion of the deluge to the birth of Abraham there elapsed 295 years, and 100 years from that to the birth of Isaac. From Isaac to Jacob 60 years. From the time he went into Egypt until his coming out of it was 130 years, and from the entry of Jacob into Egypt to his exit was 436 years; and from that to the building of the Temple by Solomon in the fortieth year of his reign, makes 480 years. From the building of the Temple to Jesus Christ, according to the supputation of the Hierographs, there passed 490 years. Thus by this calculation that I have made, collecting it out of the sacred writings, there are about 4173 years and eight months less or more. Now, from Jesus Christ, in that there is such a diversity of opinion, I pass it by, and having calculated the present prophecies in accordance with the order of the chain which contains the revolution, and the whole by astronomical rule, together with my own hereditary instinct. After some time, and including in it the period Saturn takes to turn between the 7th of April up to the 25th of August; Jupiter from the 14th of June to the 7th of October; Mars from the 17th of April to the 22nd of June; Venus from the 9th of April to the 22nd of May; Mercury from the 3rd of February to the 24th of the same; afterwards from the 1st of June to the 24th of the same; and from the 25th of September to the 16th of October, Saturn in Capricorn, Jupiter in Aquarius, Mars in Scorpio, Venus in Pisces, Mercury within a month in Capricorn, Aquarius, and Pisces; the moon in Aquarius, the Dragon's head in Libra, the tail in her sign opposite. Following the conjunction of Jupiter to Mercury, with a quadrin aspect of Mars to Mercury, and the head of the Dragon shall be with a conjunction of Sol with Jupiter, the year shall be peaceful without eclipse.

Then will be the commencement [of a period] that will comprehend in itself what will long endure [i.e. the vulgar advent of the French Revolution], and in its first year there shall be a great persecution of the Christian Church, fiercer than that in Africa [by the Vandals from 1439 to 1534], and this will burst out [*durera*] the year one thousand seven hundred and ninety-two; they will think it to be a renovation of time. After this the people of Rome will begin to reconstitute themselves [in 1804, when Napoleon is emperor], and to chase away the obscurity of darkness, recovering some share of their ancient brightness, but not without much division and continual changes. Venice after that, in great force and power, shall raise her wings very high, not much short of the force of ancient Rome. At that time great Byzantine sails, associated with the Piedmontese by the help and power of the North, will so restrain them that the two Cretans will not be able to maintain their faith. The arks built by the ancient warriors will accompany them to the waves of Neptune. In the Adriatic there will be such permutations, that what was united will be separated, and that will be reduced to a house which before was a great city, including the Pampotan and Mesopotamia of Europe, to 45, and others to 41, 43, and 47. And in that time and those countries the infernal power will set the power of the adversaries of its law against the Church of Jesus Christ. This will constitute the second Antichrist, which will persecute that Church and its true vicar, by means of the power of the temporal kings, who in their ignorance will be reduced by tongues that will cut more than any sword in the hands of a madman ....

After that Antichrist will be the infernal prince. Then at this last epoch, all the kingdoms of Christianity, as well as of the infidel world, will be shaken during the space of twenty-five years, and the wars and battles will be more grievous, and the towns, cities, castles, and all other edifices will be burnt, desolated, and destroyed with much effusion of vestal blood, married women and widows violated, sucking children dashed and broken against the walls of town; and so many evils will be committed by means of Satan, the prince infernal, that nearly all the world will become undone and desolated. Before the events occur certain strange birds [imperial eagles] will cry in the air, "*To-day! to-day!*" and after a given time will disappear [June, 1815]. After this has endured for a certain length of time [twenty-five years he has said before, 1790 to 1815], there will be almost renewed another reign of Saturn, the age of gold [this might be the discovery of California, but for what follows]. God the Creator shall say, hearing the affliction of His people, Satan shall be precipitated and bound in the bottomless abyss, and then shall commence between God and men a universal peace. There he shall abide for the space of a thousand years, and shall turn his greatest force against the power of the Church, and shall then be bound again.

How justly are all these figures adapted by the divine letters to visible celestial things, that is to say, by Saturn, Jupiter, and Mars, and others in conjunction with them, as may be seen more at large by some of the quatrains! I would have calculated it more deeply, and adapted the one to the other; but, seeing, O most serene King, that some who are given to censure will raise a difficulty, I shall take the opportunity to retire my pen and seek my nocturnal repose "*Multa etiam, O Rex potentissime proeclara, et sane to brevi ventura, sed omnia in hâc tuâ Epistola, innectere non possumus, nec volumus, sed ad intellegenda quoedam facta, horrida fata pauca libanda sunt, quamvis tanta sit in omnes tua amplitudo et humanitas homines, deosque pietas, ut solos amplissimo et Christianissimo Regis nomine, et ad quem summa totius religionis auctoritas deferatur dignus esse videare.*" But I shall only beseech you, O most clement King, by this your singular and most prudent goodness, to understand rather the desire of my heart, and the sovereign wish I have to obey your most excellent Majesty, ever since my eyes approached so nearly to your solar splendour, than the grandeur of my work can attain to or acquire.

Faciebat Michael Nostradamus.

Endnotes

1. "When Minerva was free and favourable."
2. "There can be no truth entirely determined for certain which concerns the future."
3. Which proceeds from fate, but from God, and nature.
4. Théophile de Garencières was a seventeenth-century interpreter of Nostradamus, several of whose notes occur here within brackets with those of Charles Ward.
5. *Gog and Magog*: the two nations pitted by Satan at the Battle of Armageddon against the Kingdom of God (*Revelations* 20:8)

Fugger Newsletters (1568–1604)

The Fugger family began to build their banking fortune in the late fifteenth century. Through the sixteenth century they loaned money to various European rulers, most importantly the house of Habsburg which ruled central Europe, the Netherlands, Spain, Italy and much of the New World. As security for the money, the Habsburgs gave the Fuggers interests in their mines, their lands and their administration. By the middle of the sixteenth century the bankers had business interests which covered the empire and stretched beyond to the New World and the Far East.

In 1655 the Emperor Ferdinand III bought the Fugger family library, of which the newsletters were a part. The newsletters originated with Count Philip Edward Fugger (1546–1618), who had a voracious appetite for news. Aware of his interests, the employees of the branch offices added news of current events in their various parts of the world to routine dispatches sent to the head office. The count seems to have added to this collection from news sources available in his home city of Augsburg. As the collection grew, the count had the unwieldy mass of material copied, and it was this collection which entered the imperial library. It is difficult to tell which of the items are actually from Fugger correspondents and which from the news sheets of the time, though this item on the witch Walpurga Hausmann is probably of the latter variety.

Chapter Twenty-Seven

The Fugger Newsletters

105. The Famous Alchemist Bragadini

From Venice, the 1st day of November 1589.

Your Grace will no doubt have learnt from the weekly reports of one Marco Antonio Bragadini, called Mamugnano. He is the bastard son of a nobleman here and was born in Cyprus. He is reported to be able to turn base metal into gold. Our government has had him conveyed hither under safe escort because the Inquisition has put him under ban. He is forty years old and was formerly possessed of no mean fortune, but spent it in riotous living. Then for a time he was mint-master to the Grand Duke Francis. From thence he came to the late Pope Gregory, who held him in great esteem. He thus obtained several thousand ducats. But when these too had been spent, he became a Capuchin and had taken his second vows. But since he could not subject himself to the strict rule of the order, he absconded without dispensation (hence the excommunication bar by the Holy Office) and betook himself to France. There he served several princes incognito. Latterly he has returned again to Bergamo in Italy and has exhibited his art in Valcamonica and in a short time increased his fortune to over and above two hundred thousand crowns. He has expounded his craft to several persons and it had got so far that he was prevailed upon to come here of his free will. Such a host of princes and lords beleaguered him that he was scarcely safe, although he had a bodyguard of fifty archers. This man is now here in this city, holds banquet daily for five hundred people and lives in princely style in the Palazzo Dandolo on the Giudecca. He literally throws gold about in shovelfuls. This is his recipe: he takes ten ounces of quicksilver, puts it into the fire and mixes it with a drop of liquid, which he carries in an ampulla. Thus it promptly turns into good gold. He has no other wish but to be of good use to his country, the Republic. The day before yesterday he presented to the Secret Council of Ten two ampullas with this liquid, which have been tested in his absence. The first test was found to be successful and it is said to have resulted in six million ducats. I doubt not but that this will appear mighty strange to Your Grace. It verily sounds like a fairy tale, but Your Grace will surely believe us, for everything is so obvious that it cannot be doubted. The confectioning of this liquid is, however, his secret, for in his letter of safe conduct he made express demand that he be not be forced to divulge this. He also craves nothing more from this our Government but that it may exercise good watch over his life and his person. In return he will provide them with gold in sufficiency according to their demands. He has already made known that he is greatly amazed at the ignorance of the world, in not discovering this art before, considering that little is requisite for this achievement. This is truly marvellous and quite novel to all of us. The alchemists have taken heart of grace again and are working night and day. One hears of nothing but of this excellent man who, as already stated, has no other wish but to serve his country.

From Venice, the 8th day of December 1589.

You have learnt latterly that the craft of the alchemist Marco Bragadini after being tested has been approved of. The tests have shown this sufficiently. The most noble personages here address him by the title "Illustrissimo" and feast with him daily. The Duke speaks to him in the second person. By day noblemen attend upon him, by night he is guarded by armed barges. Whereas so many strange people have arrived here, the Government holds in readiness three fully equipped galleys.

From Venice, the 16th day of December 1589.

The alchemist is said to be at work now in making five thousand sequins per month at the request of our rulers. Thereafter he will make fifteen or sixteen millions more which he has promised to hand over to it. Day by day he shows himself in great pomp. He makes his friends presents of twenty thousand and more ducats at a time. Monday last he gave a banquet in honour of the Duc de Luxembourg, the French Catholic Ambassador in Rome, which, without counting all kinds of special confectionery, cost near upon six hundred crowns.

From Rome, the 16th day of December 1589.

The Venetian Ambassador has solemnly besought the Pope that Mamugnano, the alchemist, who now resides in Venice, may remain there without molestation by the Holy Office, on account of his being a former Capuchin. Thereupon the Pope made answer that he was not a little surprised at the afore-mentioned Rulers putting so much faith in that man. Though his art might be found to be successful, yet it only could accrue unto him by the help of Satan.

From Venice, the 4th day of January 1590.

It is said of our Mamugnano that his craft for transforming quicksilver into gold does suffice for small quantities, but fails to produce larger ones. It is reported that the night before last he made two ingots in the presence of some of our patrician aldermen, each one of the weight of one pound. There no longer exists any doubt in the matter. Discussion, however, is rife amongst some of this city's philosophers as to whether Mamugnano can renew the material wherewith he has made his gold, once it is used up. Some say yes, and others say no, so that it is doubtful what they really think about it.

106. Gold from New Spain

From Venice, the 12th day of January 1590.

News reaches us from Lyons that letters from Lisbon of the 18th day of December of the past year report the arrival in Seville from New Spain of the fleet with eight millions in gold. More ships are expected to arrive shortly, which had to remain behind on account of storms. They are bringing a further four millions. This cause for the delay in the arrival of the first ships is the fact that they took their course several degrees higher than is their wont in order to escape the English cruisers who were waiting for them on the usual degree. The other ships have probably taken their course along other degrees for the same reason.

107. Bragadini works on

From Venice, the 19th day of January 1590.

Mamugnano changed a pound of quicksilver into gold some days ago. But he is not satisfied with this weight, because he has been asked by several persons to produce a larger sum.

109. Further Successes by Bragadini

From Venice, the 26th day of January 1590.

Concerning the alchemist, Mamugnano, no one harbours doubts any longer about his daily experiments in changing quicksilver into gold. It was realized that his craft did not go beyond one pound of quicksilver, however much various persons begged him to produce more. Thus the belief is now held that his allegations to produce a number of millions have been a great fraud, in which he caused people to believe. For he who can make a small amount of gold should also be able to produce a large quantity. This is the question upon which learned professors hold dispute. Meanwhile he has cut down his expenses, also reduced his banqueting, and is seen about with a smaller suite than formerly. It is reported from Spain that the King has concluded an agreement with the Genoese for a loan of five millions towards the end of the months of March and April, one million during the middle of July and the last during the middle of September.

From Venice, the 26th day of January 1590.

The alchemist Mamugnano is making gold here for his needs. He is intending this Shrovetide to hold a joyous masque in the Square of St. Stephen, for which purpose he is having sent hither six fine stallions from Mantua.

110. Printing of the Bible for the Heathen

From Rome, the 26th day of January 1590.

The Pope has learned with particular satisfaction that the Grand Duke of Florence is willing to have the books of the Bible printed here at his expense in the Chaldean, Arabic, Syrian and Ethiopian languages, and to have them expedited to these countries. These people have complained that hitherto they had to live in blindness for the lack of biblical writings and they demand to be instructed in the Christian Faith.

111. Adultery at the Court of Saxe-Coburg

From Strasburg, the 7th day of February
of the year 1590 of the old calendar.

John Casimir is said to be in sore trouble concerning his consort, for she has committed adultery with a Pole. The latter has had intercourse with her seven or eight times, and upon each occasion she presented him with a hundred crowns. When these things became bruited abroad, he was taken into strict custody to the Palace of Mannheim, about two miles distant from the city of Worms. Not long ago he escaped, but was caught again in the Palatinate. By order of the said Duke, several hundredweight of iron were fastened to his person, so that he may not be able to flee again. May God console him and all such as are afflicted!

The Princess has been divested of all her princely apparel and raiment. She is reported to be wearing the clothing of one of her former tiring women and to be in durance no less hard than her lover. Only an old woman is let in to her.

Otherwise information has been received that the alchemist of Venice has been instigated by the Grand Vizier to pass himself off as an alchemist and an artist in order thus to gain admittance to the city of Venice. This scheme has been, however, discovered, and the alchemist will not escape punishment.

112. Genoese Money for the League

From Venice, the 9th day of February 1590.

Tidings come from France that the Spinolas, wealthy Genoese merchants who did a large business in Paris, have collected a goodly part of the moneys owing to them from such countries as France, England and the Netherlands. Finding themselves possessed in Paris of so large a sum in cash as near on four hundred thousand crowns, they dared not remove it, because they were afeared that it might be taken from them. Still less did they wish to take it to Italy or Spain because trade there is at a standstill. They are now offering this sum to the League, and His Royal Majesty of Spain has promised its repayment in Spain.

In Rouen there are other Spanish merchants, who possess a still larger fortune, which they also wish to offer to the League.

It is said that Mamugnano has won near on ten thousand ducats gambling with several noblemen, so that rumour hath it that he is as clever at gambling as at making gold. He is reported to have produced in these latter days ten thousand gold crowns at one sitting, which fact is confirmed by a credible witness, who was present on that occasion.

113. Attempt to Poison Philip II

From Venice, the 6th day of April 1590.

A terrifying miracle, so they say, has occurred in Spain. One morning, as the King after praying in his oratory before a crucifix, which he held in great devotion, as was his daily custom, wished to kiss the image of Christ, the latter turned away from him. This greatly horrified and frightened the King and he once more began to pray that God might forgive him his sins. He thereupon once more tried to kiss the image of Christ, which again withdrew from him. When the King had perceived this with great concern and affliction, he sent for his Father Confessor, to whom he related this miracle. The latter then began praying to God that He might reveal this secret unto him. When he had concluded his prayers, he told the King to send for two of his most eminent councillors and bid them kiss the crucifix. They did so and soon thereafter fell sick and died. Some aver that the crucifix was poisoned so that the King might lose his life thereby.

114. Execution of Two Children

From Vienna, the 24th day of April 1590.

Yesterday two boys, the one thirteen and the other seventeen years of age, were put to death by fire and sword. For some time they had caused much damage through setting fire to property. May God guard henceforth all the children of pious parents!

115. Another Burning of Witches

From Schwab-München, the 4th day of May 1590.

Last Wednesday the innkeeper's wife of Möringen and the baker's wife of Bobingen were tried here for their misdeeds in witchcraft. Mine hostess is a short, stout, seventy-year-old doxy, who had taken to her accursed witchery when eighteen years of age. This she has practised fifty-two years, and it is easy to imagine what havoc she has wrought in such a long time. As the result of fervent petitioning, her sentence has been lightened inasmuch as she was first strangled and then only burned.

The other was only seduced to this work of the Devil by Ursula Krämer, who was the first to be executed here. So far, she has not perpetrated any sore misdeeds, but so much has she owned to, that her life is forfeit. Even on her day of judgment she still thought she could vindicate herself, and even at the place of execution I myself heard her say that she was dying innocent. Most unwillingly did she submit to her fate. But in the end she was reconciled to it and prayed long to God that He might pardon her misdeeds.

This morn another woman was brought hither from Möringen. Only half a year ago she married off one of her sons to a widow, who is said to be of the same craft. Thus it is hoped that it may incriminate others here. To-morrow or next week some more are to be brought here, but no one knows from whence. There is much discussion here about the hostess of Göggingen. May the Lord grant that this be but idle talk.

116. Fresh Deeds of the Alchemist of Venice

From Venice, the 11th day of May 1590.

Whereas Mamugnano, the alchemist, passed some time in a village a certain distance from here, and several persons suspected him of making gold for other people, his rooms were sealed at the request of his creditors. By order of the Signori Capitani, however, one room was unsealed again.

During the last days a large fish was caught by the fishers near Malamocco. It weighs more than a thousand pounds, according to our weights, and measures twenty spans. It has two wide wings, eyes as large as those of an ox, and a round, small mouth with two teeth, one in the upper and one in the lower jaw They are almost as thick as a finger and the fish has a strange colour. What kind of a fish it is the fishermen are as yet unable to say.

We have just learned that Mamugnano, the alchemist, has returned here. The Pope is said to have granted him absolution, but he had to make a donation of five thousand crowns and enter the Order of the Knights of Malta.

Roger Ascham (1515–1568)

Ascham was educated at Cambridge where he studied Greek and became a strong proponent of humanistic studies. He received his degree in 1534 and was subsequently elected a fellow of St John's College, Cambridge. He later served as secretary to the English ambassador to the Emperor Charles V and as Latin secretary to Queen Mary and tutor and later reader to Queen Elizabeth.

In addition to his work on archery, Toxophilus *(1545), he is known for his treatise on education* The Scholemaster, *printed posthumously in 1570. This book examines the best methods for learning classical Latin and constitutes in many ways a guide to the development of students both as scholars and as moral and ethical individuals in the highest traditions of northern, Christian humanism.*

Chapter Twenty-Eight

R. Ascham, to John Asteley.

Salutem Plurimam in Christo Iesu. That part of your letters from *Hatfield, decimo nono Octob.* renewing a most pleasaunt memory of our frēdly fellowship together, & full of your wonted good will towardes me: I aunswered immediatly from *Spires* by *Fraunces* the post: whiche letter if it be not yet come to your hand, ye might haue heard tell of it in M. Secretary *Cicels* chamber in the Court.

As concernyng the other part of your letter, for your wish, to haue bene with me, in this mine absence from my countrey: and for your request, to be made partaker by my letters of the sturre of these times here in *Germany.* Surely I would you had your wish: for then should not I now nede to bungle vp yours so great a request, when presently you should haue sene with much pleasure, which now peraduēture you shall read with some doubt, lesse thynges may encrease by writyng which were so great in doyng, as I am more afrayd to leaue behind me much of the matter, then to gather vp more then hath sprong of the trouth.

Your request conteineth few wordes but cōprehendeth both great and diuers matters. As first the causes of the open inuasion by the *Turke:* of the secret workyng for such soddeyne brechesse in *Italy,* and *Germany:* of the fine fetches in the *French* practises: of the double dealyng of *Rome* with all partes: thē more particularly why Duke *Octauio,* the Prince of *Salerne,* Marches *Albert,* and Duke *Maurice* brake so out with the Emperour, which were all so fast knit vnto hym as the bondes of affinitie, loyaltie, bloud, and benefites could assure him of them: *Octauio* being his sonne in law, the Prince one of hys priuy chamber, Marches *Albert* hys kynsman, and Duke *Maurice* so inhaunsed with honor and enriched with benefites by hym, as the Duke could not haue wished greater in hope, then the Emperour performed in deede. Here is stuffe plenty to furnish well vp a trimme history if a workeman had it in handlyng. When you and I read *Liuie* together if you do remember, after some reasonyng we cōcluded both what was in our opinion to be looked for at his hand that would well and aduisedly write an history: First point was, to write nothyng false: next, to be bold to say any truth, wherby is auoyded two great faultes, flattery and hatred: For which two pointes *Caesar* is read to his great prayse, and *Iouius* the *Italian* to hys iust reproch. Then to marke diligently the causes, coūsels, actes, and issues in all great attemptes: And in causes, what is iust or vniust: in coūsels, what is purposed wisely or rashly: in actes, what is done couragiously or fayntly: And of euery issue, to note some generall lesson of wisedome & warines, for lyke matters in time to come: wherin *Polibius* in *Greeke* and *Phillip Comines* in *French* haue done the duties of wyse and worthy writers. Diligence also must be vsed in kepyng truly the order of tyme: and describyng lyuely, both the site of places and nature of persons not onely for the outward shape of the body: but also for the inward dispositiō of the mynde as *Thucidides* doth in many places very trimly, and *Homer* euery where and that alwayes most excellently, which observation is chiefly to be marked in hym. And our *Chaucer* doth the same, very praise worthely: marke hym well and conferre hym with any other that writeth of our tyme in their proudest toung whosoever lyst. The stile must be alwayes playne and open: yet sometime higher and lower as matters do ryse and fall: for if proper and naturall wordes, in well ioyned sentences do lyuely expresse the matter, be it troublesome, quyet, angry or pleasant, A man shal thincke not to be readyng but present in doyng of the same. And herein *Liuie* of all other in any toung, by myne opiniō carieth away the prayse.

Syr *Thomas More* in that pamphlet of *Richard* the thyrd, doth in most part I beleue of all these pointes so content all men, as if the rest of our story of England were so done, we might well compare with *Fraunce, Italy,* or *Germany,* in that behalfe. But see how the pleasant remembraunce of our old talke together hath caried me farther then I thought to go. And as for your request to know the cause and maner of these late sturres here ye shall not looke for such precise order now in writyung, as we talked on then. No it is not all one thing to know perfectly by reading and to performe perfectly in doyng I am not so vnaduised to take so much vpō me, nor you so vnfrendly to looke for so much from me. But that you may know that I haue not bene altogether idle in this my absence, and that I will not come home as one that can say nothing of that he hath sene and heard abroad: I will homely and rudely (yet not altogether disorderly) part priuately vnto you such notes of affaires as I priuately marked for my selfe: which I either felt and saw, or learned in such place and of such persōs as had willes to seeke for, and wayes to come by, and wittes to way the greatest matters that were to be marked in all these affaires. For no wieke almost hath past in the which there hath not commonly come to my hand for the most part of the notable thynges that haue bene attempted in *Turky, Hungary, Italy, Fraunce,* and *Germany.* In declaryng to you these thyngs I will obserue onely the first two pointes of our wont communication: that is to my writyng I will set forward nothyng that is false, nor yet keepe backe any thyng that is true. For I playing no part of no one side, but sittyng downe as indifferent looker on, neither Imperiall nor Frēch, but flat English do purpose with troth to report the matter. And seyng I shall lyue vnder such a Prince, as kyng *Edward* is, and in such a countrey as Englād is (I thanke God) I shall haue neither neede to flatter the one side for profite, nor cause to feare the other side for displeasure. Therefore let my purpose of reportyng the troth as much content you, as the meane handlyng of the matter may mislike you. Yet speakyng thus much of trouth, I meane not such a hid trouth as was onely in the brest of Monsieur *d'Arras* on the Emperours side, or in Baron *Hadeck* on Duke *Maurice* side, with whom and with on other of his counsell he onely conferred all his purposes three yeares before he brake out with ye Emperour: but I meane such a troth as by conference and common cōsent amongest all the Ambassadors and Agentes in this Court and other witty & indifferent heades beside was generally conferred and agreed vpō. What better cōmoditie to know the trouth any writer in *Greeke Latine* or other toung hath had, I can not perceiue, except onely *Xenophon, Caesar,* and *Phillip Comines:* which two first worthy writers wrote their owne actes so wisely, and so without all suspicion of parcialitie, as no mā hetherto by mine opinion hath borne him selfe so vprightly in writyng the histories of others: The thyrd hauyng in a maner ye like oportunitie hath not deserued lyke commendations, at least as I suppose. Englād hath matter & Englād hath mē furnished with all abilitie to write: who if they would might bryng both lyke prayse vnto them selues, & like profite to others, as these two noble mē haue done. They lay for their excuse the lacke of leysure which is true in deede: But if we cōsider the great affaires of *Caesar* we may judge hee was worthy to winne all praise that was so willing & wittie to winne such time when his head & his handes night and day were euer most full, would to God that these our mē as they are ready to prayse hym were euen as willyng to follow hym, and so to wynne like prayse them selues.

And to keepe you no longer with my priuate talke from the matter it selfe, I will begyn at the spryng of the matter from whence all these mischiefes dyd flow, the which now hath so ouerflowed the most part of Christendome, as God onely from heauen must make an end of this miserable tragedie, wherein these two great Princes take such pleasure still to play. In Religion & libertie were sayd to be of many men in the very causes of all these sturres: yet in myne opinion & as the matter it selfe shall well proue it, vnkyndnes was the very sede, whereof all these troubles dyd grow. A Knight of England of worthy memorie for wit learnyng and experience old Syr *Thomas Wiat* wrote to his sonne that the greatest mischief amongest men and least punished is vnkyndnes: the greatest mischief truly & least punished also by any ordinary law & sentence, yet as I haue sene here by experience, vnkyndnes hath so wrought with men, as the meane were not affrayd to attempt their reuēge, nor the Emperour able to withstand their displease. Yea vnkyndnes was onely the hoke, which *Henry* the *French* kyng hath vsed these late yeares to plucke from the Emperour and draw to hym selfe, so many Princes and great cōmodities as he hath: with this hoke bayted with money the bayte of all mischief; the *French* kyng hath not ceased to angle at as many harts in *Italy* and *Germany* as he knew any matter of vnkyndnes to bee ministred vnto, by the Emperour. There be few princes in all the Empire but if I had leysure, I could particularly proue, and when I come home in our priuate talke I wil fully declare that some good big matter of vnkindnes hath bene offred vnto them by the Emperour. Yea *Ferdinando* his brother, *Maximilian* his nephew and sonne in law, the Dukes of *Bauarie* and *Cleues* which haue maried his nieces haue bene shrewdly touched therwith. Also yᵉ Papisticall Byshops as *Mentz, Pamburge, Herbipolis, Saltzburge,* and diuers others haue felt their part herein. Few Princes or states, Protestantes or Papistes, but haue bene troubled therwith. But euen as a quaterne in the begynnyng is a wanderyng disease in the body vnknowne what it wil turne vnto, and yet at last it draweth to certaine dayes & houres: euen so these grieues in the whole body of the Empire dyd first worke secretly and not appeare openly, vntill this melancholy vnkyndnes did so swell in mens stomaches that at length in *Insburgh* it brast out into a shrewd sicknes, whereof the first fit was felt to be so daūgerous, that if the Emperour and we had not more spedely chaunged the ayre, I am affrayed and sure I am we were wel affrayd then, the sickenes would haue proued also to us that were present with hym very contagious. Well this grief growyng this to certaine fittes, and I my selfe beyng not greatly greued at yᵉ hart with it but had leysure enough with small ieoperdy (I thanke God) to looke quietly vpon them that were sicke, because I would not be idle amongst them I began dayly to note the workyng of this sickenes, and namely from the xix. of May. 1552. when we ranne from *Insburgh* till the first of next January whē the siege of *Metz* was abādoned.

Neuertheles before I come to these ordinary dayes I will shortly touch how the Emperour beyng in peace with all the world .1550. when we came to his Court, had soone after so many enemyes as hee knew not which way to turne hym.

19. The Turke.

The date of peace betwixt the Emperor and the *Turke* had to expire an .1551. The Emperour hearyng what preparation the *Turke* had made the yeare before for warr and specially by Sea, which must needes agaynst Christendome, thought it better for him to ende the peace with some aduauntage, thē that the *Turke* should begyn the warr with too much strength & therfore in sommer. 1550. he sent *John de Vega* Viceroy of *Cicile* & *Andrea Dorea* into *Barbaria,* who wan the strong towne of *Affrica* from *Dragut Raies* sometyme a Pirate, and now the *Turkes* chief doer in all the affaires of *Affrike* and *mare mediteraneo.* This Court raised vp other rumors of this brech with the *Turke* how that this enterprice was made for *Seripho* sake a hethen kyng. But the Emperours frend in *Barbaria* to whom *Dragat Rayes* had done great wrong, yet men that knew the troth, and are wont also to say it, haue told me that the towne of *Affrica* stode so fit to annoy *Spayne* for the *Turke* when he list, that the Emperour was compelled to seeke by all meanes to obtaine it, much fearyng, lest when he was absent in *Germany,* the *Turke* would be too nigh and to homely a gest with hym in *Spayne* whensoeuer the peace should be expired. The whole story of winnyng *Affrica* ye may read whē you list beyng wel written in *Latin* by a *Spaniard* that was present at it.

 Affrica was earnestly required agayne by the *Turke,* and fayre promised agayne by the Emperour, but beyng in deede not deliuered, the *Turke* for a reuenge the next yeare, first assaulted *Malta* and after wan *Tripoly* from whence the *Turke* may easely and soddenly whensoeuer hee list set vpon *Cicelie, Naples*, or any cost of *Italie* or *Spayne* and most commodiously, what soeuer the Emperour doth hold in *Barbary*: so that the gayne of *Affrica* is thought nothyng comparable with the losse of *Tripoly.*

 When *Tripoly* was besieged by the *Turkes, Monsieur Daramont* was sent Ambassadour to *Constantinople* from the *French* kyng: and ariuyng by the way at *Malta,* hee was desired by the great master of the order to go to *Tripoly,* and for the frendshyp that was betwene *Fraunce* and the *Turke* to treat for the Christians there. *Daramont* did so and had leaue of the *Turkes* generall to enter the towne and talke with the Captaine. And by this meanes they within yelded on this condition to part safe with bag and baggage which was graunted by the generall. But assoone as the *Turkes* entred the towne they put old & yong, man, woman, and child to the sword sauing two hundred of the strongest men to be their Galley slaues for euer. The generall beyng asked why he kept no promise made this aunswere: If the Emperour had kept faith with my master for *Affrica* I would not haue broken with them of *Tripoly,* and therfore (sayth he) with Christen men which care for no trothe promises play iustly be broken. This *Turkish* crueltie was reuenged this last yeare in *Hungary,* when lyke promise of lyfe was made, and yet all but to the sword the Christians biddyng the *Turkes* remember *Tripoly.* To such beastly crueltie the noble feates of armes be come vnto betwixt the Christen men and the *Turkes.* And one fact of either side is notable to bee knowen, yet horrible to be told and fouler to be followed: and it is pitie that mās nature is such as will commonlie commend good thynges in readyng and yet will as commonly follow ill thynges in doyng.

The *Bassa* of *Buda,* tooke in a skirmish a gētleman of the kyng of *Romanes:* for whose deliuery men for entreaty and money for hys raunsome were sent to *Buda.* The *Bassa* appointed a day to geue them aunswere, and at time and place assigned, called forthem and sent for the gentleman likewise. And soddenly came out two hangmen bare armed with great butchers kniues in theyr handes bringing with them certaine bandogges musled kept hungry without meate of purpose: the *Bassa* bad them do their feate: who commyng to the gentleman stripped him naked, and bound him to a piller, after with their kniues they cut of his flesh by gobbets and flang it to the dogges. Thus yᵉ poore gentlemā suffred grief great for yᵉ payne, but greater for the spight: nor so tormēted in feelyng his fleshe mangled with kniues, as in seyng him selfe peece meale deuoured by dogges. And thus as long as he felt any payne they cut him in collops, and after they let their dogges lose vpon him to eate vp the residue of him, that yᵉ brief which was ended in him being dead might yet continue in his frendes lookyng on. They were bad depart and tell what they saw, who ye may be sure were in care enough to cary home with them such a cruell message.

Not long after this, three *Turkes* of good estimation and place, were taken by the Christen men: for whose raunsome great summes of gold were offred. Aunswere was made to the messenger that all the gold in *Turky* should not saue thē. And because yᵉ *Turkes* will eate no swines flesh, you shall see if swine will eate any *Turkish* fleshe. And so likewise great bores were kept hungry, & in sight of the messenger the three *Turkes* were cut in collops and throwne amongest them.

For these foule deedes I am not so angry with the *Turkes* that began them as I am sory for the Christen men that follow them. I talked with a worthy gentleman this day both for his great experience and excellent learnyng *Marc Anthonio d'Anula* Ambassadour of *Venice* with the Emperour: who told me that the great *Turke* him selfe (Religion excepted) is a good and mercyfull, iust and liberall Prince, wise in makyng and true in performyng any couenant, and as sore a reuenger of troth not kept. He prayed God to kepe him long aliue: for his eldest sonne *Mustapha* is cleane contrary, geuē to all mischief cruell, false, gettyng he careth nut how vniustly, and spendyng he careth not how vnthriftely what socuer he may lay hand on, wilye in makyng for his porpose, & ready to breake for his profite all couenantes, he is wery of quietnes and peace, a seeker of strife and warre, a great mocker of meane men, a sore oppressor of poore men, openly contemnyng God, and a bent enemy agaynst Christes name and Christen men. But to go forward with my purpose. The *Turke* beyng onest disclosed an open enemy to the Emperour, many meane men begā to be the bolder to put out their heades to see some open remedy for theyr priuate iniuries: *Fraunce* beyng at euery mans elbow to harten and to helpe, whosoever had cause to be aggreued with the Emperour. And first *Octauio* Duke of *Parma,* much agreued as nature well required with his fathers death & besides that fearing the losse not onely of his state, but also of his lyfe, fell from the Emperour in the end of the yeare. 1550.

Pietro Aloysio Farnesio sonne to *Papa Paulo tercio* Duke of *Placētia:* father to this Duke *Octauio* Duke of *Parma* which maried the Emperors base daughter, and to *Horatio* Duke of *Castro,* who of late hath maried also the *French* kynges base daughter, and the two Cardinals *Alexandro* and *Ramusio Farnesy,* was slaine men say by the meanes of *Ferranto Gonzaga* gouernour of *Millan* by whose death the state of *Placentia* belōging then to the house of *Fernesia* came into the Emperour handes. The whole processe of this mans death is at length set out in the stories of *Italie:* my purpose is only to touch it, because hereby rose such a heate betwixt the whole famely of *Fernesia* and *Don Ferranto Gonzaga* as hath stirred vp such a smoke in *Italy* betwixt the Emperour and *Fraunce,* as is not like to be quenched but with many a poore mans bloud, as *Horace* noteth wittely out of *Homer,* saying:

What follies so euer great Princes make:
The people therfore go to wrake.

Octauio beyng sorest greeued with his fathers death and beyng best able
to reuenge it was so feared of *Gonzaga* that he thought hym selfe neuer
assured for *Petro Luis* death as long as *Octauio* his sonne should lyue: for
men neuer loue whē they haue iust cause to feare, but must nedes still mistrust
without all hope of reconcilyng whom they haue before hurt beyōd all remedy
of amendes. And yet I heard a gentlemā of *Millan* say (who was sent hether to
the Emperour by *Gonzatga)* that *Octauio* is such a Prince for good nature and
gentle behauiour that he supposed there was not one in *Italy* but did loue hym
except it were his maister *Gonzaga*. These two Princes beyng neighbours the
one at *Millan* the other at *Parma* shewed smal frendshyp the one to the other.
But *Octauio* was euermore wrong to the worse by many and sundry spites, but
chiefly with dayly feare of hys life by poysoning: for the which fact certain
persons in *Parma* were taken and layd fast. Neuertheles *Octauios* nature is so
farre from seekyng bloud and revenge and so geuen to pitie and gentlenes,
that although they went about not onely to geue away his state by treason, but
also to take away his life by poysonyng, yea, and after that the deede was
proued playnly on them, and sentence of death pronounced openly agaynst
them, yet he gaue them lyfe and libertie which would haue taken both from
hym.

And when *Monsieur Thermes* earnestly told him that where the euill were
not kept in with feare of Iustice, the good should neuer lyue in suretie and
quietnes: his aunswere was that he so abhorred the sheddyng of bloud in
others as he would neuer wash his handes in any: let his enemies do to him the
worst they could. Addyng, that he thought it his most honor to he vnlykest
such for his gentlenes which were misliked of all mē for their crueltie: wherby
he hath wonne that he which of good nature can hurt none, is now of right
loued of all and onely hated of him whō no man in *Italy* for his cruelty doth
loue. And this talke is so true that it was told in an other language but in the
selfe same termes at an honorable table here in *Bruxels* by a gentleman of
Millan an agent in the Court, a doer for *Gonzaga,* who the same tyme was
prisoner in *Parma.*

And although *Octauio* by good nature was harmeles in not seekyng
reuenge, yet he was not careles by good reason in seekyng hys remedy but
made oft & great cōplaintes of his grieues to the Emperour, which were not so

hotely made, but they were as coldly heard, that at lēgth *Octauio* findyng least comfort, where of right he looked for most ayde. & seyng that displeasures could not be ended in *Gonzaga* nor could not be amended by the Emperour: then he compelled agaynst his nature turned his hate due to *Gonzaga* to reuenge this vndeserued vnkyndnes in the Emperour, euen as *Pausanias* dyd with *Phillip* kyng of *Macedonie,* who conqueryng with pollicie and power all outward enemyes, was slayne when and where, he thought him selfe most sure of his dearest frēd, for vnkindnes because *Phillip* ought and would not reuēge *Pausanias* on him that had done him a foule displeasure.

Octauio seyng what was done to his father euen when hys graundfather was Byshop of *Rome,* thought, that now as his house decayed, so his ieopardy encreased. And therfore agaynst a desperate euill began to seeke for a desperate remedie, which was fet from *Rome* a shop alwayes open to any mischief as you shall perceiue in these few leaues if you marke them well.

Octauio cōplained to *Iulio tercio* of the wrōges *of Gonzaga* & of the vnkindnes of the Emperour, desiryng that by his wisedome and authoritie, he would now succor him or els not onely he should leese his life but also the church of *Rome* should lose her right in *Parma,* as she had done before in *Placentia.* The Byshop gaue good eare to this talke, for he spied that hereby should be offred vnto him, a fit occasion to set the Emperour and *Fraunce* together by the eares. He thought the Emperour was to bigge in *Italy* hauyng on ye one side of *Rome Naples* vnder his obedience, on the other side *Siena, Florence* and *Genoa* at his commaundement, besides *Placentia, Millan, Monteferrato,* and a great part of *Piemount.*

The Emperour beyng thus strong in *Italy*, the Byshop thought his own state to be his so lōg as it pleased the Emperour to let him haue it: & therfore if *Parma* were not left an entry for *Fraunce* to come into *Italy,* he might ouersoone be shut vp in present miserie when all outward ayde should be shut out from him.

The Popes counsel was that *Octauio* should put him selfe vnder the *French* kynges protection whom he knew would most willingly receiue him: *Parma* lying so fit for the *French* kyng when soeuer he would set upon the enterprice of *Millan.* This practise of the Pope *Monsieur de Thermes* the *French* kynges Ambassadours dyd vtter before the consistorie of Cardinals at *Rome:* prouing that the Pope, not the kyng his master was the occasion of that warre.

When *Octauio* with the whole house *of Farnesia* became thus *Frēch,* the Emperour more fearyng the state of *Millan* then lamentyng the losse of *Octauio* persuaded on his side the Byshop of *Rome* to require *Parma* as the Churches right, & to punish *Octauio* as the Churches rebell, promising that he him selfe as an obedient sonne of the Church would stretch out his arme and open his purse in that recouery of the Churches right: neuertheles the Byshop must beare the name of the warre because hee might not breake peace with *Fraunce*. Thus Princes openly cōtenācing quietnes & priuily brewyng debate although they got others to broch it, yet God commōly suffreth thē selves to drinke most of the misery thereof in the end. The Byshop seyng that he must either begyn the mischief or els it would not on so fast as he wished to haue it, set lustely vpon it: and first cited *Octauio,* after excommunicated him, and shortly after besieged *Parma* ayded both with mē and money by the Emperour: which thyng the *French* kyng began to stomach, thinckyng that yᵉ Emperour dyd offer him both wrong & dishonor in not suffring him beyng a kyng to helpe a poore man that fled to his ayde. And thus these two Princes first helpyng others began by litle and litle to fall out them selues. And that the Pope dyd set these two Princes together, a *Pasquill* made at *Rome* and sent to this Court doth well declare. And seyng that you so well vnderstand the *Italian* toung and that if it were turned into English it would leese the whole grace therof, I will recite it in the toung that it was made in.

Interlocutori Pasquillo et Romano.

> Pᴀsǫ. *Hanno vn bel gioco il Re, e l'Imperatore*
> *per terzo el Papa,et giocano à Primera.*
> Rom. *che v' e d' invito?*
> Pᴀsǫ. *Italia tutta intera.*
> Rom. *Chi vi l' ha messa?*
> Pᴀsǫ. *il coglion del pastore.*
> Rom. *Che tien in mano il Re?*
> Pᴀsǫ. *Ponto magiore. e'l Papa ha cinquant' vno, e se despera.*
> Rom. *Caesar che Ponto s'a?*
> Pᴀsǫ. *lui sta a Primera.*
> Rom. *che gli manca?*
> Pᴀsǫ. *danari a far fauore.*
> *Il Papa dice,à vol,e vuol Partito:*
> *Caesar Pensoso sta Sopra di questo,*
> *teme à Scoprir di [non] trouar moneta*

Il Re dice, no, no, Scoprite Presto,
che io tengo Ponto, a guadagnar l' invito
I' ho li danari, et Caesar se gli aspeta.

Tutti stanno a vedetta

Chi di lor due guadagni.
Rom. *il Papa?*
Pasq. *è fuora, vinca chi vuol, lui Perde, in sua mal' hora.*

L' Imperatore anchora

Teme, e tien stretto, e Scopre Pian le carte,
e quì la sorte gioca, più che l'Arte.

Metta questi in disparte.

Stabilito è nel Ciel quello, che esser dè,
ne gioua 'l nostro dir, questo Sarà questo è.

The *French* king in the summer .1551. proclaimed warre against *Charles* kyng of *Spayne,* abusing that name for a sottlety to separate ye whole quarrell from the Empire: when the Emperour would not be persuaded at *Augusta* that either the *Turke* would, or the *French* kyng durst make him open warre, or that any Prince in *Italy* or *Germany* could be entised to breake out with him.

Monsieur Mariliacke the *French A*mbassadour at *Augusta* euer bare the Emperour in hand that such rumors of war were raysed of displeasure & that his master intended nothyng so much as the continuance of amitie, yea this he durst do, when many in y[e] Emperours court knew that the war was already proclaimed in *Fraunce.*

The Emperour blinded with the ouer good opinion of his own wisedome, likyng onely what him selfe listed, and contemnyng easely all aduise of others (which selfe will condition doth commonly follow, and as commonly doth hurt all great wittes) dyd not onely at this tyme suffer him selfe thus to be abused: but also afterward more craftely by the Pope for the continuaunce of warre at *Parma,* & more boldly by Duke *Maurice* for his repayre to *Inspruke,* and not the least of all, now lately at *Metz* by some of his owne counsellours for the recouery of that towne.

But Princes and great personages which will heare but what and whom they list, at the length fayle when they would not, and commonly blame whom they should not: But it is well done that as great men may by authoritie contemne the good aduise of others: so God doth prouide by right iudgement that they have leaue in the ende to beare both the losse and shame therof them selues.

Thus ye see how the Pope was both the brewer and brocher and also bringer of ill lucke to both these Princes, and as it came wel to passe dranke well of it him selfe both with expences of great treasures, and with the losse of many lyues and specially of two noble gentlemen, the Prince of *Macedonia* and *Il Seign. Giouan Baptista di Monte* his owne nephew: but the Popes care was neither of money nor men, so that he might set the two Princes surely together. And therfore was not onely content (as a man might say) to hasard *Parma* on the meyne chauce: but to make the two Princes better sporte & fresher game, set also euē then *Mirandula* on a bye chaunce that mischief enough might come together.

When the Princes were well in and the one so lusty with good lucke that hee had no lust to leaue, aud the other so chafed with leesyng, that still he would venture. Besides their playing in sporte for the Pope at *Parma* and *Mirandula,* they fell to it a good them selues in *Piemoūt, Loraigne, Flaunders* and *Picardy*, the French kyng robbyng by Sea and spoyling by land, with calling in the *Turke,* and sturryng vp all Princes and states that had any occasion to beare any grudge to the Emperour. Of all their neighbours onely our noble kyng, and the wise senate *of Venize* would be lookers on.

And when the Pope saw they were so hote at it as he well knew as the one would not start in so great good lucke: so ye other could not leaue by so much shame of losse. And although it did him good to see them cope so lustely together: neuertheles he thought it scarce his surety that they should play so nere his elbow so earnestly, least if they fell to farre out and the one should winne to much of the other, then he peraduenture would compell at length the Pope him selfe which begā the play to kepe him sport afterward for that that he had in *Italy*. And therefore very craftely he gat them to play in an other place, and tooke vp the game for *Parma* and *Mirandula* taking truce with *Fraunce* for certaine yeares, and bad them make what sport they would farther of in *Loraigne & Picardy.* And that there should lacke neither iniurie nor spite in the Popes doynges, whē the Emperour saw that whether hee would or no, the Pope would needes fall in with *Fraunce,* then he desired the Pope that such bastilians and fortes of fence as were made about *Mirandula* when it was besieged might either be deliuered to hys mens handes or els defaced that the *Frenchmen* might not haue them, which request was very reasonable seyng the Emperour had bene at all the charge in makyng of them: But they were neither deliuered nor defaced, nor left indifferēt, but so put into the *French mens* handes, that *Mirandula* now is made very strong to the *French* faction by Emperours money and the Popes falsehode.

This fact was very wrongfull of the Pope for the deede: but more spitefull for the tyme: for euen when Duke *Maurice* had wonne A*ugusta,* euen then the Pope gaue vp the siege *of Mirandula* and fell in with *Fraunce* that care enough might come vppon the Emperour together both out of *Germany,* and out of *Italy* at once. And evē this day .25. June .1553. when I was writyng this place, commeth newes to *Bruxells,* that the Pope hath of new played with the Emperour more foule play at *Siena,* then he dyd before at *Mirandula:* For whē the Emperour had bene at passing charges in kepyng a great host, for the recovery of *Sierra* from December last vnto June: the Pope would needes become stickler in that matter betwene the Emperour, the *French* kyng and *Siena* promising such conditions to all, as neither of the Princes should lose honour and yet *Siena* should haue had liberties. The Emperour good man yet agayne trustyng him who so spightfully had deceaued hym before dismissed hys hoste, which done *Siena* was left still in the *French* mēs hādes: who therby haue such oportunitie to fortifie it, as yᵉ Emperor is not like by force to recouer it. *Piramus* Secretary to yᵉ Emperor told this tale to Syr *Phillip Hobby* & the Byshop of Westminster openly at yᵉ table: which *Piramus* is a Papist for his life: & beyng asked how he could excuse the Popes vnkyndnes agaynst his master yᵉ Emperour! Hee aunswered smilyng *Iulius tercius* is a knaue but yᵉ Pope is an honest mā, which saying is cōmō in this court. And although they wil vnderstād both yᵉ spight of yᵉ pope, & ye shame of their master, yet are they cōtent stil to speake of yᵉ pope though he neuertheles still do ill to yᵉ Emperour.

And thus to returne to my purpose how the Pope set the two Princes together, & shift his owne necke a while out of the halter, leauyng most vnfrendly the Emperour when he was farthest behynd hand: and how *Octauio* for feare of *Gonzaga,* and vnkyndnes of the Emperour fell with all hys famely to be *French,* I haue briefly passed over for the bast I haue to come to the matters of *Germany.*

William Harvey (1578-1657)

Harvey was born in Folkestone, England, in 1578 and was educated at Canterbury before beginning the study of medicine at Gonville and Caius College, Cambridge (1593). In 1600 he migrated to the University of Padua in Italy to study with Fabricius, the celebrated professor of anatomy. In 1602 Harvey graduated as a Doctor of Medicine. Having returned to England, he was admitted to the Royal College of Physicians in 1604, the same year in which he married.

By 1616 he was developing his theory, based largely on dissection, that the blood flows in a circular manner through the body, an idea that challenged accepted opinion derived from the ancient physician, Galen. His famous Essay on the Motion of the Heart and Blood in Animals *appeared in 1628. The following year Harvey was appointed royal physician and later attended on the royal family during the Civil War; but eventually he settled in Oxford. In 1645 he was named warden of Merton College, Oxford. William Harvey died on 3 June 1657.*

Chapter Twenty-Nine

Motion of the Heart and Blood

Chapter 1

The author's motives for writing

When I first gave my mind to vivisections, as a means of discovering the motions and uses of the heart, and sought to discover these from actual inspection, and not from the writings of others, I found the task so truly arduous, so full of difficulties, that I was almost tempted to think, with Fracastorius, that the motion of the heart was only to be comprehended by God. For I could neither rightly perceive at first when the systole and when the diastole took place, nor when and where dilatation and contraction occurred, by reason of the rapidity of the motion, which in many animals is accomplished in the twinkling of an eye, coming and going like a flash of lightning; so that the systole presented itself to me now from this point, now from that; the diastole the same; and then everything was reversed, the motions occurring, as it seemed, variously and confusedly together. My mind was therefore greatly unsettled, nor did I know what I should myself conclude, nor what believe from others; I was not surprised that Andreas Laurentius should have said that the motion of the heart was as perplexing as the flux and reflux of Euripus had appeared to Aristotle.

At length, and by using greater and daily diligence, having frequent recourse to vivisections, employing a variety of animals for the purpose, and collating numerous observations, I thought that I had attained to the truth, that I should extricate myself and escape from this labyrinth, and that I had discovered what I so much desired, both the motion and the use of the heart and arteries; since which time I have not hesitated to expose my views upon these subjects, not only in private to my friends, but also in public, in my anatomical lectures, after the manner of the Academy of old.

These views, as usual, pleased some more, others less; some chid and calumniated me, and laid it to me as a crime that I had dared to depart from the precepts and opinion of all anatomists; others desired further explanations of the novelties, which they said were both worthy of consideration, and might perchance be found of signal use. At length, yielding to the requests of my friends, that all might be made participators in my labours, and partly moved by the envy of others, who receiving my views with uncandid minds and understanding them indifferently, have essayed to traduce me publicly, I have been moved to commit these things to the press, in order that all may be enabled to form an opinion both of me and my labours. This step I take all the more willingly, seeing that Hieronymus Fabricius of Aquapendente, although he has accurately and learnedly delineated almost every one of the several parts of animals in a special work, has left the heart alone untouched. Finally, if any use or benefit to this department of the republic of letters should accrue from my labours, it will, perhaps, be allowed that I have not lived idly, and, as the old man in the comedy says:

> *For never yet has any one attained*
> *To such perfection, but that time, and place,*
> *And use, have brought addition to his knowledge;*
> *Or made correction, or admonished him,*
> *That he was ignorant of much which he*
> *Had thought he knew; or led him to reject*
> *What he had once esteemed of highest price.*

So will it, perchance, be found with reference to the heart at this time; or others, at least, starting from hence, the way pointed out to them, advancing under the guidance of a happier genius, may make occasion to proceed more fortunately, and to inquire more accurately.

Chapter 2

Of the motions of the heart, as seen in the dissection of living animals

In the first place, then, when the chest of a living animal is laid open and the capsule that immediately surrounds the heart is slit up or removed, the organ is seen now to move, now to be at rest; there is a time when it moves, and a time when it is motionless.

These things are more obvious in the colder animals, such as toads, frogs serpents, small fishes, crabs, shrimps, snails, and shell-fish. They also become more distinct in warm-blooded animals, such as the dog and hog, if they be attentively noted when the heart begins to flag, to move more slowly, and, as it were, to die: the movements then become slower and rarer, the pauses longer, by which it is made much more easy to perceive and unravel what the motions really are, and how they are performed. In the pause, as in death, the heart is soft, flaccid, exhausted, lying, as it were, at rest.

In the motion, and interval in which this is accomplished, three principal circumstances are to be noted:

1. That the heart is erected, and rises, upwards to a point so that at this time it strikes against the breast and the pulse is felt externally.

2. That it is everywhere contracted, but more especially towards the sides, so that it looks narrower, relatively longer, more drawn together. The heart of an eel taken out of the body of the animal and placed upon the table or the hand, shows these particulars; but the same things are manifest in the heart of small fishes and of those colder animals where the organ is more conical or elongated.

3. The heart being grasped in the hand, is felt to become harder during its action. Now this hardness proceeds from tension, precisely as when the forearm is grasped, its tendons are perceived to become tense and resilient when the fingers are moved.

4. It may further be observed in fishes, and the colder blooded animals, such as frogs, serpents, etc., that the heart, when it moves, becomes of a paler colour, when quiescent of a deeper blood-red colour.

From these particulars it appeared evident to me that the motion of the heart consists in a certain universal tension—both contraction in the line of its fibres, and constriction in every sense. It becomes erect, hard, and of diminished size during its action; the motion is plainly of the same nature as that of the muscles when they contract in the line of their sinews and fibres; for the muscles, when in action, acquire vigour and tenseness, and from soft become hard, prominent, and thickened: in the same manner the heart.

We are therefore authorized to conclude that the heart at the moment of its action, is at once constricted on all sides, rendered thicker in its parietes and smaller in its ventricles, and so made apt to project or expel its charge of blood. This, indeed, is made sufficiently manifest by the fourth observation preceding, in which we have seen that the heart, by squeezing out the blood it contains becomes paler, and then when it sinks into repose and the ventricle is filled anew with blood, that the deeper crimson colour returns. But no one need remain in doubt of the fact, for if the ventricle be pierced the blood will be seen to be forcibly projected outwards upon each motion or pulsation when the heart is tense.

These things, therefore, happen together or at the same instant: the tension of the heart, the pulse of its apex, which is felt externally by its striking against the chest, the thickening of its parietes, and the forcible expulsion of the blood it contains by the constriction of its ventricles.

Hence the very opposite of the opinions commonly received, appears to be true; inasmuch as it is generally believed that when the heart strikes the breast and the pulse is felt without, the heart is dilated in its ventricles and is filled with blood; but the contrary of this is the fact, and the heart, when it contracts [and the shock is given], is emptied. Whence the motion which is generally regarded as the diastole of the heart, is in truth its systole. And in like manner the intrinsic motion of the heart is not the diastole but the systole; neither is it in the diastole that the heart grows firm and tense, but in the systole, for then only, when tense, is it moved and made vigorous.

Neither is it by any means to be allowed that the heart only moves in the line of its straight fibres, although the great Vesalius, giving this notion countenance, quotes a bundle of osiers bound into a pyramidal heap in illustration; meaning, that as the apex is approached to the base, so are the sides made to bulge out in the fashion of arches, the cavities to dilate, the ventricles to acquire the form of a cupping-glass and so to suck in the blood. But the true effect of every one of its fibres is to constringe the heart at the same time that they render it tense; and this rather with the effect of thickening and amplifying the walls and substance of the organ than enlarging its ventricles. And, again, as the fibres run from the apex to the base, and draw the apex towards the base, they do not tend to make the walls of the heart bulge out in circles, but rather the contrary; inasmuch as every fibre that is circularly disposed, tends to become straight when it contracts; and is distended laterally and thickened, as in the case of muscular fibres in general, when they contract, that is, when they are shortened longitudinally, as we see them in the bellies of the muscles of the body at large. To all this, let it be added, that not only are the ventricles contracted in virtue of the direction and condensation of their walls, but farther, that those fibres, or bands, styled nerves by Aristotle, which are so conspicuous in the ventricles of the larger animals, and contain all the straight fibres, (the parietes of the heart containing only circular ones), when they contract simultaneously, by an admirable adjustment all the internal surfaces are drawn together, as if with cords, and so is the charge of blood expelled with force.

Neither is it true, as vulgarly believed, that the heart by any dilatation or motion of its own has the power of drawing the blood into the ventricles; for when it acts and becomes tense, the blood is expelled; when it relaxes and sinks together it receives the blood in the manner and wise which will by and by be explained.

Chapter 3
Of the motions of arteries,
as seen in the dissection of living animals

In connection with the motions of the heart these things are further to be observed having reference to the motions and pulses of the arteries:

1. At the moment the heart contracts, and when the breast is struck, when in short the organ is in its state of systole, the arteries are dilated, yield a pulse, and are in the state of diastole. In like manner, when the right ventricle contracts and propels its charge of blood, the arterial vein [the pulmonary artery] is distended at the same time with the other arteries of the body.

2. When the left ventricle ceases to act, to contract, to pulsate, the pulse in the arteries also ceases further, when this ventricle contracts languidly, the pulse in the arteries is scarcely perceptible. In like manner, the pulse in the right ventricle failing, the pulse in the vena arteriosa [pulmonary artery] ceases also.

3. Further, when an artery is divided or punctured, the blood is seen to be forcibly propelled from the wound at the moment the left ventricle contracts; and, again, when the pulmonary artery is wounded, the blood

will be seen spouting forth with violence at the instant when the right ventricle contracts.

So also in fishes, if the vessel which leads from the heart to the gills be divided, at the moment when the heart becomes tense and contracted, at the same moment does the blood flow with force from the divided vessel.

In the same way, finally, when we see the blood in arteriotomy projected now to a greater, now to a less distance, and that the greater jet corresponds to the diastole of the artery and to the time when the heart contracts and strikes the ribs, and is in its state of systole, we understand that the blood is expelled by the same movement.

From these facts it is manifest, in opposition to commonly received opinions, that the diastole of the arteries corresponds with the time of the heart's systole; and that the arteries are filled and distended by the blood forced into them by the contraction of the ventricles; the arteries, therefore, are distended, because they are filled like sacs or bladders, and are not filled because they expand like bellows. It is in virtue of one and the same cause, therefore, that all the arteries of the body pulsate, viz. the contraction of the left ventricle; in the same way as the pulmonary artery pulsates by the contraction of the right ventricle.

Finally, that the pulses of the arteries are due to the impulses of the blood from the left ventricle, may be illustrated by blowing into a glove, when the whole of the fingers will be found to become distended at one and the same time, and in their tension to bear some resemblance to the pulse. For in the ratio of the tension is the pulse of the heart, fuller, stronger, more frequent as that acts more vigorously, still preserving the rhythm and volume and order of the heart's contractions. Nor is it to be expected that because of the motion of the blood the time at which the contraction of the heart takes place and that at which the pulse in an artery (especially a distant one) is felt, shall be otherwise than simultaneous: it is here the same as in blowing up a glove or bladder; for in a plenum (as in a drum, a long piece of timber, etc.) the stroke and the motion occur at both extremities at the same time. Aristotle too, has said, "the blood of all animals palpitates within their veins, (meaning the arteries), and by the pulse is sent everywhere simultaneously." And further,[2] "thus do all the veins pulsate together and by successive strokes because they all depend upon the heart; and, as it is always in motion, so are they likewise always moving together, but by successive movements." It is well to observe with Galen, in this place, that the old philosophers called the arteries veins.

I happened upon one occasion to have a particular case under my care, which plainly satisfied me of this truth: A certain person was affected with a large pulsating tumour on the right side of the neck, called an aneurism, just at that part where the artery descends into the axilla, produced by an erosion of the artery itself, and daily increasing in size; this tumour was visibly distended as it received the charge of blood brought to it by the artery, with each stroke of the heart: the connexion of parts was obvious when the body of the patient came to be opened after his death. The pulse in the corresponding arm was small, in consequence of the greater portion of the blood being diverted into the tumour and so intercepted.

Whence it appears that wherever the motion of the blood through the arteries is impeded, whether it be by compression or infarction, or interception, there do the remote divisions of the arteries beat less forcibly, seeing that the pulse of the arteries is nothing more than the impulse or shock of the blood in these vessels.

Endnotes
1. De Animal. iii, cap. 9.
2. De Respirat. cap. 20.

François Rabelais (c.1483–1553)

Rabelais was born sometime between 1483 and 1490 near Chinon, the son of a lawyer and landowner. Sent to a Franciscan monastery, Rabelais took priest's orders by 1521, but spent much time and energy studying Greek. His superiors objected so Rabelais left the Franciscans and entered a Benedictine monastery where he became secretary to the abbot, who shared his interest in humanism.

Leaving the monastery at some time before 1530, Rabelais travelled to Paris perhaps to study medicine. He matriculated in medicine at Montpellier in 1530 and accepted the position of physician in a hospital in Lyon in 1532. His doctorate in medicine was granted by Montpellier in 1537.

Rabelais travelled to Rome on two occasions (1533, 1535) in the suite of Cardinal Jean du Bellay. He subsequently entered another Benedictine monastery in France, St Maur, but accepted in 1537 an appointment as a physician in Metz. Although he remained in the Roman Church, Rabelais had several illegitimate children, knew a number of French Protestants and satirized the theologians of the Sorbonne. The faculty of theology retaliated in 1543 by condemning his work. Rabelais died in 1553.

1532 saw the publication of Pantagruel *followed soon after by* Gargantua. *These works tell the story of the giants, Gargantua and Pantagruel, following their adventures and celebrating their love of eating, drinking and the other pleasures of the flesh. Informed by a brilliant satiric wit and deep sympathy with the human condition, this large, rollicking collection of stories has remained among the most popular of all Renaissance books.*

Chapter Thirty

From *Gargantua* and *Pantagruel*

Few intellectuals have puzzled historians so much as has François Rabelais, for they have described him as a skeptical free-thinker, a forerunner of Voltaire, as a crypto-Protestant, a truly pious Catholic, or as an Erasmian humanist. Born around 1495, as a child he was placed with the Franciscans and spent his youth as a Franciscan. He studied the Greek and Latin classics in his spare time. Not happy with the unintellectual mendicants, he joined the Benedictine order, which had a longer tradition of learning. Still dissatisfied he became a secular priest in order to travel about. In 1530 he enrolled in the school of medicine at Montpellier and the following year he lectured on Hippocrates and Galen. In 1532 he moved to Lyon, where a lively circle of writers and publishers were at work. There he began to write *Gargantua* and *Pantagruel* to which he was to return in his leisure time for many years thereafter. He journeyed to Rome in 1533 and 1535 with Jean du Bellay, who was made a cardinal. He rejoined the Benedictines and became a canon of St. Maur. He took his doctorate in medicine at Montpellier in 1537 and served as a physician in Metz, a city in the Empire, during the last repressive years at the end of the reign of Francis I. His major work was, in fact, censured by the Sorbonne and the Parlement forbade its sale. He died in the year 1553.

The plot of his yarn can be simply told. Rabelais borrowed the names Gargantua and Pantagruel from some stories already in circulation at the time. Gargantua's giant parents celebrate the birth of their gigantic infant with a fantastic feast at which the guests gorge themselves with food and drink. As a young man Gargantua founded the Abbey of Thélème, which is the ideal monastery, welcoming both sexes. Its inhabitants are pure spirits who shun evil and cultivate the good, and learn freely, without restraint. The motto of Thélème is "Do what thou wouldst!" Gargantua's son, Pantagruel, while a student at Paris learns to know Panurge, a lecherous fellow, a hard drinker, and a coward. Panurge declares his intention of marrying, but seeks oracular advice. He and Pantagruel set sail for the Land of the Lanterns to consult the Oracle of the Bottle. When they at last arrive the Oracle instructs Panurge to "Drink a Toast!" This he takes as a sanction for marriage, but the book ends at this point. The entire yarn is full of digressions, satires, seemingly irrelevant incidents, puzzles, and mysterious poems. It reflects the intellectual currents of French humanist society during Rabelais's life. "To laugh is proper to man" wrote Rabelais. He is the best-known of the French vernacular writers of the early sixteenth century.

How Gargantua Had the Abbey of Thélème Built for the Monk

There remained the monk to provide for. Gargantua wanted to make him Abbot of Seuilly, but the friar refused. He wanted to give him the Abbey of Bourguêil or that of Saint-Florent, whichever might suit him best, or both, if he had fancy for them. But the monk gave a peremptory reply to the effect that he would not take upon himself any office involving the government of others.

"For how," he demanded, "could I govern others, who cannot even govern myself? If you are of the opinion that I have done you, or may be able to do you in the future, any worthy service, give me leave to found an abbey according to my own plan."

This request pleased Gargantua, and the latter offered his whole province of Thélème, lying along the River Loire, at a distance of two leagues from the great Forest of Port-Huault. The monk then asked that he be permitted to found a convent that should be exactly the opposite of all other institutions of the sort.

"In the first place, then," said Gargantua, "you don't want to build any walls around it; for all the other abbeys have plenty of those."

"Right you are," said the monk, "for where there is a wall (*mur*) in front and behind there is bound to be a lot of *murmur*—ing, jealousy and plotting on the inside."

Moreover, in view of the fact that in certain convents in this world there is a custom, if any woman (by which, I mean any modest or respectable one) enters the place, to clean up thoroughly after her wherever she has been—in view of this fact, a regulation was drawn up to the effect that if any monk or nun should happen to enter this new convent, all the places they had set foot in were to be thoroughly scoured and scrubbed. And since, in other convents, everything is run, ruled, and fixed by hours, it was decreed that in this one there should not be any clock or dial of any sort, but that whatever work there was should be done whenever occasion offered. For, as Gargantua remarked, the greatest loss of time he knew was to watch the hands of the clock. What good came of it? It was the greatest foolishness in the world to regulate one's conduct by the tinkling of a time-piece, instead of by intelligence and good common sense.

Another feature: Since in those days women were not put into convents unless they were blind in one eye, lame, hunchbacked, ugly, misshapen, crazy, silly, deformed, and generally of no account, and since men did not enter a monastery unless they were snotty-nosed, underbred, dunces, and troublemakers at home—

"Speaking of that," said the monk, "of what use is a woman who is neither good nor good to look at?"

"Put her in a convent," said Gargantua.

"Yes," said the monk, "and set her to making shirts."

And so, it was decided that in this convent they would receive only the pretty ones, the ones with good figures and sunny dispositions, and only the handsome, well set-up, good-natured men.

Item: Since in the convents of women, men never entered, except underhandedly and by stealth, it was provided that, in this one, there should be no women unless there were men also, and no men unless there were also women.

Item: Inasmuch as many men, as well as women, once received into a convent were forced and compelled, after a year of probation, to remain there all the rest of their natural lives—in view of this, it was provided that, here, both men and women should be absolutely free to pick up and leave whenever they happened to feel like it.

Item: Whereas, ordinarily, the religious take three vows, namely, those of chastity, poverty and obedience, it was provided that, in this abbey, one might honorably marry, that each one should be rich, and that all should live in utter freedom.

With regard to the lawful age for entering, the women should be received from the age of ten to fifteen years, the men from the age of twelve to eighteen.

How the Abbey of the Thelemites Was Built and Endowed

For the building and furnishing of the abbey, Gargantua made a ready-money levy of two-million-seven-hundred-thousand-eight-hundred-thirty-one of the coins known as "big woolly sheep"; and for each year, until everything should be in perfect shape, he turned over, out of the toll-receipts of the Dive River, one-million-six-hundred-sixty-nine-thousand "sunny crowns" and the same number of "seven-chick pieces." For the foundation and support of the abbey, he made a perpetual grant of two-million-three-hundred-sixty-nine-thousand-five-hundred-fourteen "rose nobles," in the form of ground-rent, free and exempt of all encumbrances, and payable every year at the abbey gate, all of this being duly witnessed in the form of letters of conveyance.

As for the building itself, it was in the form of a hexagon, so constructed that at every corner there was a great round tower sixty paces in diameter, all these being of the same size and appearance. The River Loire flowed along the north elevation. Upon the bank of this river stood one of the towers, named Arctic, while, proceeding toward the east, there was another, named Calaer, following it another, named Anatole, then another, named Mesembrine, another after it, named Hesperia, and finally, one named Cryere. Between every two towers, there was a distance of three-hundred-twelve paces. To the building proper, there were six stories in all, counting the underground cellars as one. The second story was vaulted, in the form of a basket handle. The rest were stuccoed with plaster of Paris, in the manner of lamp bottoms, the roof being covered over with a fine slate, while the ridge-coping was lead, adorned with little mannikins and animal figures, well grouped and gilded. The eaves-troughs, which jutted out from the walls, between the mullioned windows, were painted with diagonal gold and blue figures, all the way down to the ground, where they ended in huge rainspouts, all of which led under the house to the river.

This building was a hundred times more magnificent than the one at Bonivet, at Chambord, or at Chantilly; for in it there were nine-thousand-three-hundred-thirty-two rooms, each equipped with a dressing-room, a study, a wardrobe, and a chapel, and each opening into a large hall. Between the towers, in the center of the main building, was a winding stair, the steps of which were partly of porphyry, partly of Numidian stone, and partly of serpentine marble, each step being twenty-two feet long and three fingers thick, with an even dozen between each pair of landings. On each landing were two fine antique arches, admitting the daylight, while through these arches, one entered a loggia of the width of the stair, the chair itself running all the way to the roof and ending in a pavilion. From this stair one could enter, from either side, a large hall, and from this hall the rooms.

From the tower known as Arctic to the one called Cryere, there were fine large libraries, in Greek, Latin, Hebrew, French, Tuscan, and Spanish, separated from each other according to the different languages. In the middle of the building was another and marvelous stairway, the entrance to which was from outside the house, by way of an arch thirty-six feet wide. This stair was so symmetrical and capacious that six men-at-arms, their lances at rest, could ride up abreast, all the way to the roof. From the tower Anatole to Mesembrine, there were large and splendid galleries, all containing paintings representative of deeds of ancient prowess, along with historical and geographical scenes. In the center of this elevation was still another gateway and stair, like the one on the river-side. Over this gate, there was inscribed, in large old-fashioned letters, the following poem:

Inscription Over the Great Portal of Thélème

You hypocrites and two-faced, please stay out:
Grinning old apes, potbellied snivelbeaks,
Stiffnecks and blockheads, worse than Goths, no doubt,
Magogs and Ostrogoths we read about;
You hairshirt whiners and you slippered sneaks;
You fur-lined beggars and you nervy freaks;
You bloated dunces, trouble-makers all;

> *Go somewhere else to open up your stall,*
> *Your cursed ways*
> *Would fill my peaceful days*
> *With nasty strife;*
> *With your lying life,*
> *You'd spoil my roundelays—*
> *With your cursed ways.*

Stay out, you lawyers, with your endless guts,
You clerks and barristers, you public pests,
You Scribes and Pharisees, with your "if's" and "buys,"
You hoary judges (Lord, how each one struts!):
You feed, like dogs, on squabbles and bequests;
You'll find your salary in the hangman's nests;
Go there and bray, for here there is no guile
That you can take to court, to start a trial.

> *No trials or jangles*
> *Or legal wrangles:*

We're here to be amused.
If your jaws must be used,
You've bags full of tangles,
Trials and jangles.

Stay out, you usurers and misers all,
Gluttons for gold, and how you hoard the stuff!
Greedy windjammers, with a world of gall,
Hunchbacked, snubnosed, your money-jars full, you bawl
For more and more; you never have enough;
Your stomachs never turn, for they are tough,
As you heap your piles, each miser-faced poltroon:
I hope Old Death effaces you, right soon!

That inhuman mug
Makes us shrug:
Take it to another shop,
And please don't stop,
But elsewhere lug
That inhuman mug!

Stay out of here, at morning, noon and night,
Jealous old curs, dotards that whine and moan,
All trouble-makers, full of stubborn spite,
Phantom avengers of a Husband's plight,
Whether Greek or Latin, worst wolves ever known;
You syphilitics, mangy to the bone,
Go take your wolfish sores, and let them feed at ease—
Those cakey crusts, signs of a foul disease.

Honor, praise, delight
Rule here, day and night;
We're gay, and we agree;
We're healthy, bodily;
And so, we have a right
To honor, praise, delight.

But welcome here, and very welcome be,
And doubly welcome, all noble gentlemen.
This is the place where taxes all are free,
And incomes plenty, to live merrily,
However fast you come—I shan't "say when":
Then, be my cronies in this charming den;
Be spruce and jolly, gay and always mellow,
Each one of us a very pleasant fellow.

> *Companions clean,*
> *Refined, serene,*
> *Free from avarice;*
> *For civilized bliss,*
> *See, the tools are keen,*
> *Companions clean.*

And enter here, all you who preach and teach
The living Gospel, though the heathen raves:
You'll find a refuge here beyond their reach,
Against the hostile error you impeach,
Which through the world spreads poison, and depraves
Come in, for here we found a faith that saves;
By voice and letter, let's confound the herd
Of enemies of God's own Holy Word.

> *The word of grace*
> *We'll not efface*
> *From this holy place;*
> *Let each embrace,*
> *And himself enlace*
> *With the word of grace.*

Enter, also, ladies of high degree!
Feel free to enter and be happy here,
Each face with beauty flowering heavenly,
With upright carriage, pleasing modesty:

This is the house where honor's held most dear,
Gift of a noble lord whom we revere,
Our patron, who's established it for you,
And given us his gold, to see it through.

> *Gold given by gift*
> *Gives golden shrift—*
> *To the giver a gift,*
> *And very fine thrift,*
> *A wise man's shift,*
> *Is gold given by gift.*

What Kind of Dwelling the Thelemites Had

In the middle of the lower court was a magnificent fountain of beautiful alabaster, above which were the three Graces with cornucopias, casting out water through their breasts, mouths, ears, eyes, and the other openings of their bodies.

The interior of the portion of the dwelling that opened upon this court rested upon great pillars of chalcedony and of porphyry, fashioned with the finest of antique workmanship. Above were splendid galleries, long and wide, adorned with paintings, with the horns of deer, unicorns, rhinoceroses, and hippopotamuses, as well as with elephants' teeth and other objects interesting to look upon.

The ladies' quarters extended from the tower Arctic to the Mesembrine gate. The men occupied the rest of the house. In front of the ladies' quarters, in order that the occupants might have something to amuse them, there had been set up, between the first two outside towers, the lists, the hippodrome, the theatre, and the swimming-pools, with wonderful triple-stage baths, well provided with all necessary equipment and plentifully supplied with water of myrrh.

Next the river was a fine pleasure-garden, in the center of which was a handsome labyrinth. Between the towers were the tennis courts and the ball-grounds. On the side by the tower Cryere was the orchard, full of all sorts of fruit trees, all of them set out in the form of quincunxes. Beyond was the large park, filled with every sort of savage beast. Between the third pair of towers were the targets for arquebus, archery, and crossbow practice. The servants' quarters were outside the tower Hesperia and consisted of one floor only, and beyond these quarters were the stables. In front of the latter stood the falcon-house, looked after by falconers most expert in their art. It was furnished annually by the Canadians, the Venetians, and the Sarmatians, with all kinds of out-of-the-ordinary birds: eagles, gerfalcons, goshawks, sakers, lanners, falcons, sparrow-hawks, merlins, and others, all so well trained and domesticated that, when these birds set out from the castle for a little sport in the fields, they would take everything that came in their way. The hunting kennels were a little farther off, down toward the park.

All the halls, rooms and closets were tapestried in various manners, according to the season of the year. The whole floor was covered with green cloth. The bedding was of embroidered work. In each dressingroom was a crystal mirror, with chasings of fine gold, the edges being trimmed with pearls; and this mirror was of such a size that—it is the truth I am telling you—it was possible to see the whole figure in it at once. As one came out of the halls into the ladies' quarters, he at once encountered the perfumers and the hair-dressers, through whose hands the gentlemen passed when they came to visit the ladies. These functionaries each morning supplied the women's chambers with rose, orange, and "angel" water; and in each room a precious incense-dish was vaporous with all sorts of aromatic drugs.

How the Monks and Nuns of Thélème Were Clad

The ladies, when the abbey was first founded, dressed themselves according to their own fancy and good judgment. Later they of their own free will introduced a reform. In accordance with this revised rule, they went clad as follows:

They wore scarlet or kermes-colored stockings, and these extended above their knees for a distance of three inches, to be precise, the borders being of certain fine embroideries and pinkings. Their garters were of the same color as their bracelets, and clasped the leg above and below the knee. Their shoes, pumps, and slippers were of brilliant-colored velvet, red or violet, shaped in the form of a lobster's barbel.

Above the chemise, they wore a fine bodice, of a certain silk-camlet material, and a taffeta petticoat, white, red, tan, gray, etc. Over this went a skirt of silver taffeta, made with embroideries of fine gold or elaborate needlework, or, as the wearer's fancy might dictate, and depending upon the weather, of satin, of damask, or of velvet, being orange, tan, green, ash-gray, blue, bright yellow, brilliant red, or white in color, and being made of cloth-of-gold, silver tissue, thread-work, or embroidery, according to the feast-days. Their gowns, which were in keeping with the season, were of gold tissue or silver crisping, and were made of red satin, covered with gold needle-work, or of white, blue, black, or tan taffeta, silk serge, silk-camlet, velvet, silver-cloth, silver-tissue, or of velvet or satin with gold facings of varying design.

In summer, on certain days, in place of gowns they wore cloaks of the above-mentioned materials, or sleeveless jackets, cut in the Moorish fashion and made of violet-colored velvet, with crispings of gold over silver needlework, or with gold knots, set off at the seams with little Indian pearls. And they always had a fine plume, matching the color of their sleeves and well trimmed with golden spangles.

In winter, they wore taffeta gowns of the colors mentioned, trimmed with the fur of lynxes, black-spotted weasels, Calabrian or Siberian sables, and other precious skins. Their chaplets, rings, gold-chains, and goldwork necklaces contained fine stones: carbuncles, rubies, balas rubies, diamonds, sapphires, emeralds, turquoises, garnets, agates, beryls, and pearls great and small.

Their head-dress, likewise, depended upon the weather. In winter, it was after the French fashion; in spring, after the Spanish style; in summer, after the Tuscan. That is, excepting feast-days and Sundays, when they wore the French coiffure, for the reason that it is more respectable and better in keeping with matronly modesty.

The men dressed after a fashion of their own. Their stockings were of broadcloth or of serge, and were scarlet, kermes-hued, white, or black in color. Their hose were of velvet and of the same colors, or very nearly the same, being embroidered and cut to suit the fancy. Their doublets were of cloth-of-gold, silver-cloth, velvet, satin, damask, or taffeta, of the same shades, all being cut, embroidered, and fitted in a most excellent fashion. Their girdles were of the same-colored silk, the buckles being of well enameled gold. Their jackets and vests were of cloth-of-gold, gold-tissue, silver-cloth, or velvet. Their robes were as precious as the ladies' gowns, the girdles being of silk, of the same color as the doublet. Each one carried a fine sword at his side, with a gilded handle, the scabbard being of velvet, of the same shade as the stockings, while the tip was of gold or goldsmith-work, with a dagger to match. Their bonnets were of black velvet, trimmed with a great many berry-like ornaments and gold buttons, and the white plume was most prettily divided by golden spangles, from the ends of which dangled handsome rubies, emeralds, etc.

Such a sympathy existed between the men and women that each day they were similarly dressed; and in order that they might not fail on this point, there were certain gentlemen whose duty it was to inform the men each morning what livery the ladies proposed to wear that day, for everything depended upon the will of the fair ones. In connection with all these handsome garments and rich adornments, you are not to think that either sex lost any time whatsoever, for the masters of the wardrobe had the clothing all laid out each morning, and the ladies of the chamber were so well trained that in no time at all their mistresses were dressed and their toilets completed from head to foot.

In order to provide the more conveniently for these habiliments, there was, near the wood of Thélème, a large group of houses extending for half a league, houses that were well lighted and well equipped, in which dwelt the goldsmiths, lapidaries, embroiderers, tailors, gold-thread-workers, velvet-makers, tapestry-makers, and upholsterers; and there each one labored at his trade and the whole product went for the monks and nuns of the abbey. These workmen were supplied with material by my Lord Nausicltus, who every year sent them seven ships from the Pearl and Cannibal Islands, laden with gold-nuggets, raw silk, pearls, and precious stones. And if certain pearls showed signs of aging and of losing their native luster, the workmen by their art would renew these, by feeding them to handsome cocks, in the same manner in which one gives a purge to falcons.

How the Thelemites Were Governed in Their Mode of Living

Their whole life was spent, not in accordance with laws, statutes, or rules, but according to their own will and free judgment. They rose from bed when they felt like it and drank, ate, worked, and slept when the desire came to them. No one woke them, no one forced them to drink or to eat or do any other thing. For this was the system that Gargantua had established. In the rule of their order there was but this one clause:

Do what thou wouldst

for the reason that those who are free born and well born, well brought up, and used to decent society possess, by nature, a certain instinct and spur, which always impels them to virtuous deeds and restrains them from vice, an instinct which is the thing called honor. These same ones, when, through vile subjection and constraint, they are repressed and held down, proceed to employ that same noble inclination to virtue in throwing off and breaking the yoke of servitude, for we always want to come to forbidden things; and we always desire that which is denied us.

In the enjoyment of their liberty, the Thelemites entered into a laudable emulation in doing, all of them, anything which they thought would be pleasing to one of their number. If anyone, male or female, remarked: "Let us drink," they all drank. If anyone said: "Let us play," they all played. If anyone suggested: "Let us go find some sport in the fields," they all went there. If it was hawking or hunting, the ladies went mounted upon pretty and easy-paced nags or proud-stepping palfreys, each of them bearing upon her daintily gloved wrist a sparrowhawk, a lanneret, or a merlin. The men carried the other birds.

They were all so nobly educated that there was not, in their whole number, a single one, man or woman, who was not able to read, write, sing, play musical instruments, and speak five or six languages, composing in these languages both poetry and prose.

In short, there never were seen knights so bold, so gallant, so clever on horse and on foot, more vigorous, or more adept at handling all kinds of weapons than were they. There never were seen ladies so well groomed, so pretty, less boring, or more skilled at hand and needlework and in every respectable feminine activity. For this reason, when the time came that any member of this abbey, either at the request of his relatives or from some other cause, wished to leave, he always took with him one of the ladies, the one who had taken him for her devoted follower, and the two of them were then married. And if they had lived at Thélème in devotion and friendship, they found even more of both after their marriage, and remained as ardent lovers at the end of their days, as they had been on the first day of their honeymoon.

The Letter Which Pantagruel at Paris Received from His Father Gargantua

Pantagruel studied very hard, you may be sure of that, and profited greatly from it; for he had a two-fold understanding, while his memory was as capacious as a dozen casks and flagons of olive oil. And while he was residing there, he received one day a letter from his father, which read as follows:

My very dear Son:

Among all the gifts, graces, and prerogatives with which that sovereign plastician, Almighty God, has endowed and adorned human nature in its beginnings, it seems to me the peculiarly excellent one is that by means of which, in the mortal state, one may acquire a species of immortality, and in the course of a transitory life be able to perpetuate his name and his seed. This is done through that line that issues from us in legitimate marriage. By this means, there is restored to us in a manner that which was taken away through the sin of our first parents, of whom it was said that, inasmuch as they had not been obedient to the commandment of God the Creator, they should die, and that, through their death, the magnificent plastic creation which man had been should be reduced to nothingness. By this means of seminal propagation, there remains for the children that which was lost to the parents, and for the grandchildren that which, otherwise, would have perished with the children; and so, successively, down to the hour of the last judgment when Jesus Christ shall have rendered to God the Father His specific realm, beyond all danger and contamination of sin; for then shall cease all begettings and corruptions, and the elements shall forego their incessant transmutations, in view of the fact that the peace that is so desired shall then have been consummated and perfected, and all things shall have been brought to their period and their close.

It is not, therefore, without just and equitable cause that I render thanks to God, my Saviour, for having given me the power to behold my hoary old age flowering again in your youth: for when, by the pleasure of Him who rules and moderates all things, my soul shall leave this human habitation, I shall not feel that I am wholly dying in thus passing from one place to another, so long as, in you and through you, my visible image remains in this world, living, seeing, and moving among men of honor and my own good friends, as I was wont to do. My own conduct has been, thanks to the aid of divine grace—not, I confess, without sin, for we are all sinners, and must be continually beseeching God to efface our sins—but at least, without reproach.

For this reason, since my bodily image remains in you, if the manners of my soul should not likewise shine there, then you would not be held to have been the guardian and the treasury of that immortality which should adhere to our name; and the pleasure I should take in beholding you would accordingly be small, when I perceive that the lesser part of me, which is the body, remained, while the better part, which is the soul, through which our name is still blessed among men, had become degenerate and bastardized. I say this, not out of any doubt of your virtue, of which you have already given me proof, but to encourage you, rather, to profit still further, and to go on from good to better. And I am now writing you, not so much to exhort you to live in this virtuous manner, as to urge you to rejoice at the fact that you are so living and have so lived, that you may take fresh courage for the future. In order to perfect and consummate that future, it would be well for you to recall frequently the fact that I have spared no expense on you, but have aided you as though I had no other treasure in this world than the joy, once in my life, of seeing you absolutely perfect in virtue, decency, and wisdom, as well as in all generous and worthy accomplishments, with the assurance of leaving you after my death as a mirror depicting the person of me, your father—if not altogether as excellent and as well formed an image as I might wish you to be, still all that I might wish, certainly, in your desires.

But while my late father of blessed memory, Grandgousier, devoted all his attention to seeing that I should profit from and be perfected in political wisdom, and while my studious labors were equal to his desires and perhaps even surpassed them, nevertheless, as you can readily understand, the times were not so propitious to letters as they are at present and I never had an abundance of such tutors as you have. The times then were dark, reflecting the unfortunate calamities brought about by the Goths who had destroyed all fine literature; but through divine goodness, in my own lifetime light and dignity have been restored to the art of letters, and I now see such an improvement that at the present time I should find great difficulty in being received into the first class of little rowdies—I who, in the prime of my manhood, and not wrongly so, was looked upon as the most learned man of the century. I do not say this in any spirit of vain boasting, even though I might permissibly do so—you have authority for it in Marcus Tullius, in his book on Old Age, as well as in that maxim of Plutarch's that is to be found in his book entitled How One May Praise One's Self Without Reproach—but I make the statement, rather, to give you the desire of climbing higher still.

Now all the branches of science have been reestablished and languages have been restored: Greek, without which it is a crime for any one to call himself a scholar, Hebrew, Chaldaic, and Latin; while printed books in current use are very elegant and correct. The latter were invented during my lifetime, through divine inspiration, just as, on the other hand, artillery was invented through the suggestion of the devil. The world is now full of scholarly men, learned teachers, and most ample libraries; indeed, I do not think that in the time of Plato, of Cicero, or of Papinian, there ever were so many advantages for study as one may find today. No one, longer, has any business going out in public or being seen in company, unless he has been well polished in the workshop of Minerva. I see brigands, hangmen, freebooters, and grooms nowadays who are more learned than were the doctors and preachers of my time. What's this I'm saying? Why, even the women and the girls have aspired to the credit of sharing this heavenly manna of fine learning. Things have come to such a pass that, old as I am, I have felt it necessary to take up the study of Greek, which I had not contemned, like Cato, but which I never had had the time to learn in my youth. And I take a great deal of pleasure now in reading the Morals of Plutarch, the beautiful Dialogues of Plato, the Monuments of Pausanias, and the Antiquities of Athenaeus, as I wait for the hour when it shall please God, my Creator, to send for me and to command me to depart this earth.

For this reason, my son, I would admonish you to employ your youth in getting all the profit you can from your studies and from virtue. You are at Paris and you have your tutor, Epistemon; the latter by word-of-mouth instruction, the former by praiseworthy examples, should be able to provide you with an education.

It is my intention and desire that you should learn all languages perfectly: first, the Greek as Quintilian advises; secondly, the Latin; and finally, the Hebrew, for the sake of the Holy Scriptures, along with the Chaldaic and the Arabic, for the same purpose. And I would have you form your style after the Greek, in imitation of Plato, as well as on the Latin, after Cicero. Let there be no bit of history with which you are not perfectly familiar. In this you will find the various works which have been written on cosmography to be of great help.

As for the liberal arts, geometry, arithmetic, and music, I gave you some taste for these while you were still a little shaver of five or six; keep them up; and as for astronomy, endeavor to master all its laws; do not bother about divinatory astrology and the art of Lully, for they are mere abuses and vanities.

As for civil law, I would have you know by heart the best texts and compare them with philosophy.

As for a knowledge of the facts of nature, I would have you apply yourself to this study with such curiosity that there should be no sea, river, or stream of which you do not know the fish; you should likewise be familiar with all the birds of the air, all the trees, shrubs, and thickets of the forest, all the grasses of the earth, all the metals hidden in the bellies of the abysses, and the precious stones of all the East and South: let nothing be unknown to you.

Then, very carefully, go back to the books of the Greek, Arabic, and Latin physicians, not disdaining the Talmudists and the Cabalists, and by means of frequent dissections, see to it that you acquire a perfect knowledge of that other world which is man. And at certain hours of the day, form the habit of spending some time with the Holy Scriptures. First in Greek, the New Testament and the Epistles of the Apostles; and then, in Hebrew, the Old Testament.

In short, let me see you an abysm of science, for when you shall have become a full-grown man, you will have to forsake your quiet life and leisurely studies, to master the art of knighthood and of arms, in order to be able to defend my household and to succor my friends in all their undertakings against the assaults of evildoers.

In conclusion, I would have you make a test, to see how much profit you have drawn from your studies; and I do not believe you can do this in any better fashion than by sustaining theses in all branches of science, in public and against each and every comer, and by keeping the company of the learned, of whom there are as many at Paris as there are anywhere else.

But since, according to the wise Solomon, wisdom does not enter the malevolent soul, and since science without conscience is but the ruin of the soul, it behooves you to serve, love, and fear God and to let all your thoughts and hopes rest in Him, being joined to Him through a faith formed of charity, in such a manner that you can never be sundered from Him by means of sin. Look upon the scandals of the world with suspicion. Do not set your heart upon vain things, for this life is transient but the word of God endures eternally. Be of service to all your neighbors and love them as yourself. Respect your teachers, shun the company of those whom you would not want to be like, and do not receive in vain the graces which God has bestowed upon you. And when you feel that you have acquired all the knowledge that is to be had where you now are, come back to me, so that I may see you and give you my blessing before I die.

My son, may the peace and grace of Our Lord be with you! Amen.

From Utopia, this seventeenth day of the month of March.

Your Father,
Gargantua

When he had received and read this letter, Pantagruel took fresh courage, and was inflamed to profit more than ever from his studies; to such a degree that, seeing him so study and profit, you would have said that his mind among his books was like a fire among brushwood, so violent was he and so indefatigable.

Miguel de Cervantes Saavedra (1547–1616)

Born in 1547 in Alcala de Henares, Cervantes enjoyed a brief humanist education in Madrid under Juan Lopez de Hoyos, but augmented this study with wide reading and travel, visiting Italy, for example, and acquiring a deep appreciation for Italian renaissance culture. He was also a soldier and fought—and was wounded—at the great naval battle of Lepanto in 1571 in which the Christian Holy League defeated the Turkish fleet. Later, however, Cervantes was captured and sold into slavery in Algiers, and not ransomed until 1580.

Returning to Spain he was appointed a collector of taxes to be used to assemble the Armada of Philip II against England, but was imprisoned because of problems with his accounts. In prison on several other occasions for debt, he began to write Don Quixote *while in jail. It is a satire on the tales of chivalry so popular in Spain at the time, following the adventures of its hero, Don Quixote, and his servant, Sancho Panza. This early novel became the most popular work of Spanish literature when printed (part one in 1605, part two in 1615) and made its author's fortune. Cervantes died in Madrid in 1616.*

Chapter Thirty-One

Don Quixote

The station in life and the pursuits of the famous gentleman,
Don Quixote de la Mancha

In a village of La Mancha the name of which I have no desire to recall, there lived not so long ago one of those gentlemen who always have a lance in the rack, an ancient buckler, a skinny nag, and a greyhound for the chase. A stew with more beef than mutton in it, chopped meat for his evening meal, scraps for a Saturday, lentils on Friday, and a young pigeon as a special delicacy for Sunday, went to account for three-quarters of his income. The rest of it he laid out on a broadcloth greatcoat and velvet stockings for feast days, with slippers to match, while the other days of the week he cut a figure in a suit of the finest homespun. Living with him were a housekeeper in her forties, a niece who was not yet twenty, and a lad of the field and market place who saddled his horse for him and wielded the pruning knife.

This gentleman of ours was close on to fifty, of robust constitution but with little flesh on his bones and a face that was lean and gaunt. He was noted for his early rising, being very fond of the hunt. They will try to tell you that his surname was Quijada or Quesada—there is some difference of opinion among those who have written on the subject—but according to the most likely conjectures we are to understand that it was really Quejana. But all this means very little so far as our story is concerned, providing that in the telling of it we do not depart one iota from the truth.

You may know, then, that the aforesaid gentleman, on those occasions when he was at leisure, which was most of the year around, was in the habit of reading books of chivalry with such pleasure and devotion as to lead him almost wholly to forget the life of a hunter and even the administration of his estate. So great was his curiosity and infatuation in this regard that he even sold many acres of tillable land in order to be able to buy and read the books that he loved, and he would carry home with him as many of them as he could obtain.

Of all those that he thus devoured none pleased him so well as the ones that had been composed by the famous Feliciano de Silva, whose lucid prose style and involved conceits were as precious to him as pearls; especially when he came to read those tales of love and amorous challenges that are to be met with in many places, such a passage as the following, for example: "The reason of the unreason that afflicts my reason, in such a manner weakens my reason that I with reason lament me of your comeliness." And he was similarly affected when his eyes fell upon such lines at these: "… the high Heaven of your divinity divinely fortifies you with the stars and renders you deserving of that desert your greatness doth deserve."

The poor fellow used to lie awake nights in an effort to disentangle the meaning and make sense out of passages such as these, although Aristotle himself would not have been able to understand them, even if he had been resurrected for that sole purpose. He was not at ease in his mind over those wounds that Don Beliants gave and received; for no matter how great the surgeons who treated him, the poor fellow must have been left with his face and his entire body covered with marks and scars. Nevertheless, he was grateful to the author for closing the book with the promise of an interminable adventure to come; many a time he was tempted to take up his pen and literally finish the tale as had been promised, and he undoubtedly would have done so, and would have succeeded at it very well, if his thoughts had not been constantly occupied with other things of greater moment.

He often talked it over with the village curate, who was a learned man, a graduate of Sigüenza, and they would hold long discussions as to who had been the better knight, Palmerin of England or Amadis of Gaul; but Master Nicholas, the barber of the same village, was in the habit of saying that no one could come up to the Knight of Phoebus, and that if anyone *could* compare with him it was Don Galaor, brother of Amadis of Gaul, for Galaor was ready for anything—he was none of your finical knights, who went around whimpering as his brother did, and in point of valor he did not lag behind him.

In short, our gentleman became so immersed in his reading that he spent whole nights from sundown to sunup and his days from dawn to dusk in poring over his books, until, finally, from so little sleeping and so much reading, his brain dried up and he went completely out of his mind. He had filled his imagination with everything that he had read, with enchantments, knightly encounters, battles, challenges, wounds, with tales of love and its torments, and all sorts of impossible things, and as a result had come to believe that all these fictitious happenings were true; they were more real to him than anything else in the world. He would remark that the Cid Ruy Díaz had been a very good knight, but there was no comparison between him and the Knight of the Flaming Sword, who with a single backward stroke had cut in half two fierce and monstrous giants. He preferred Bernardo del Carpio, who at Roncesvalles had slain Roland despite the charm the latter bore, availing himself of the stratagem which Hercules employed when he strangled Antaeus, the son of Earth, in his arms.

He had much good to say for Morgante who, though he belonged to the haughty, overbearing race of giants, was of an affable disposition and well brought up. But, above all, he cherished an admiration for Rinaldo of Montalbán, especially as he beheld him sallying forth from his castle to rob all those that crossed his path, or when he thought of him overseas stealing the image of Mohammed which, so the story has it, was all of gold. And he would have liked very well to have had his fill of kicking that traitor Galalón, a privilege for which he would have given his housekeeper with his niece thrown into the bargain.

At last, when his wits were gone beyond repair, he came to conceive the strangest idea that ever occurred to any madman in this world. It now appeared to him fitting and necessary, in order to win a greater amount of honor for himself and serve his country at the same time, to become a knight-errant and roam the world on horseback, in a suit of armor; he would go in quest of adventures, by way of putting into practice all that he had read in his books; he would right every manner of wrong, placing himself in situations of the greatest peril such as would redound to the eternal glory of his name. As a reward for his valor and the might of his arm, the poor fellow could already see himself crowned Emperor of Trebizond at the very least; and so, carried away by the strange pleasure that he found in such thoughts as these, he at once set about putting his plan into effect.

The first thing he did was to burnish up some old pieces of armor, left him by his great-grandfather, which for ages had lain in a corner, moldering and forgotten. He polished and adjusted them as best he could, and then he noticed that one very important thing was lacking: there was no closed helmet, but only a morion, or visorless headpiece, with turned-up brim of the kind foot soldiers wore. His ingenuity, however, enabled him to remedy this, and he proceded to fashion out of cardboard a kind of half-helmet, which, when attached to the morion, gave the appearance of a whole one. True, when he went to see if it was strong enough to withstand a good slashing blow, he was somewhat disappointed; for when he drew his sword and gave it a couple of thrusts, he succeeded only in undoing a whole week's labor. The ease with which he had hewed it to bits disturbed him no little, and he decided to make it over. This time he placed a few strips of iron on the inside, and then, convinced that it was strong enough, refrained from putting it to any further test; instead, he adopted it then and there as the finest helmet ever made.

After this, he went out to have a look at his nag; and although the animal had more cuartos, or cracks, in its hoof than there are quarters in a real, and more blemishes than Gonela's steed which *tantum pellis et ossa fuit*, it nonetheless looked to its master like a far better horse than Alexander's Bucephalus or the Babicca of the Cid. He spent all of four days in trying to think up a name for his mount; for—so he told himself—seeing that it belonged to so famous and worthy a knight, there was no reason why it should not have a name of equal renown. The kind of name he wanted was one that would at once indicate what the nag had been before it came to belong to a knight-errant and what its present status was; for it stood to reason that, when the master's worldly condition changed, his horse also ought to have a famous, high-sounding appellation, one suited to the new order of things and the new profession that it was to follow.

After he in his memory and imagination had made up, struck out, and discarded many names, now adding to and now subtracting from the list, he finally hit upon "Rocinante," a name that impressed him as being sonorous and at the same time indicative of what the steed had been when it was but a hack, whereas now it was nothing other than the first and foremost of all the hacks in the world.

Having found a name for his horse that pleased his fancy, he then desired to do as much for himself, and this required another week, and by the end of that period he had made up his mind that he was henceforth to be known as Don Quixote, which, as has been stated, has led the authors of this veracious history to assume that his real name must undoubtedly have been Quijada, and not Quesada as others would have it. But remembering that the valiant Amadis was not content to call himself that and nothing more, but added the name of his kingdom and fatherland that he might make it famous also, and thus came to take the name of Amadis of Gaul, so our good knight chose to add his place of origin and become "Don Quixote de la Mancha"; for by this means, as he saw it, he was making very plain his lineage and was conferring honor upon his country by taking its name as his own.

And so, having polished up his armor and made the morion over into a closed helmet, and having given himself and his horse a name, he naturally found but one thing lacking still: he must seek out a lady of whom he could become enamored; for a knight-errant without a lady-love was like a tree without leaves or fruit, a body without a soul.

"If," he said to himself, "as a punishment for my sins or by a stroke of fortune I should come upon some giant hereabouts, a thing that very commonly happens to knights-errant, and if I should slay him in a hand-to-hand encounter or perhaps cut him in two, or, finally, if I should vanquish and subdue him, would it not be well to have someone to whom I may send him as a present, in order that he, if he is living, may come in, fall upon his knees in front of my sweet lady, and say in a humble and submissive tone of voice, 'I, lady, am the giant Caraculiambro, lord of the island Malindrania, who has been overcome in single combat by that knight who never can be praised enough, Don Quixote de la Mancha, the same who sent me to present myself before your Grace that your Highness may dispose of me as you see fit'?"

Oh, how our good knight reveled in this speech, and more than ever when he came to think of the name that he should give his lady! As the story goes, there was a very good-looking farm girl who lived near by, with whom he had once been smitten, although it is generally believed that she never knew or suspected it. Her name was Aldonza Lorenzo, and it seemed to him that she was the one upon whom he should bestow the title of mistress of his thoughts. For her he wished a name that should not be incongruous with his own and that would convey the suggestion of a princess or a great lady; and, accordingly, he resolved to call her "Dulcinea del Toboso," she being a native of that place. A musical name to his ears, out of the ordinary and significant, like the others he had chosen for himself and his appurtenances.

The first sally that the ingenious Don Quixote made from his native heath

Having, then, made all these preparations, he did not wish to lose any time in putting his plan into effect, for he could not but blame himself for what the world was losing by his delay, so many were the wrongs that were to be righted, the grievances to be redressed, the abuses to be done away with, and the duties to be performed. Accordingly, without informing anyone of his intention and without letting anyone see him, he set out one morning before daybreak on one of those very hot days in July. Donning all his armor, mounting Rocinante, adjusting his ill-contrived helmet, bracing his shield on his arm, and taking up his lance, he sallied forth by the back gate of his stable yard into the open countryside. It was with great contentment and joy that he saw how easily he had made a beginning toward the fulfillment of his desire.

No sooner was he out on the plain, however, than a terrible thought assailed him, one that all but caused him to abandon the enterprise he had undertaken. This occurred when he suddenly remembered that he had never formally been dubbed a knight, and so, in accordance with the law of knighthood, was not permitted to bear arms against one who had a right to that title. And even if he had been, as a novice knight he would have had to wear white armor, without any device on his shield, until he should have earned one by his exploits. These thoughts led him to waver in his purpose, but, madness prevailing over reason, he resolved to have himself knighted by the first person he met, as many others had done if what he had read in those books that he had at home was true. And so far as white armor was concerned, he would scour his own the first chance that offered until it shone whiter than any ermine. With this he became more tranquil and continued on his way, letting his horse take whatever path it chose, for he believed that therein lay the very essence of adventures.

And so we find our newly fledged adventurer jogging along and talking to himself. "Undoubtedly," he is saying, "in the days to come, when the true history of my famous deeds is published, the learned chronicler who records them, when he comes to describe my first sally so early in the morning, will put down something like this: 'No sooner had the rubicund Apollo spread over the face of the broad and spacious earth the gilded filaments of his beauteous locks, and no sooner had the little singing birds of painted plumage greeted with their sweet and mellifluous harmony the coming of the Dawn, who, leaving the soft couch of her jealous spouse, now showed herself to mortals at all the doors and balconies of the horizon that bounds La Mancha—no sooner had this happened than the famous knight, Don Quixote de la Mancha, forsaking his own downy bed and mounting his famous steed, Rocinante, fared forth and began riding over the ancient and famous Campo de Montiel.'"

And this was the truth, for he was indeed riding over that stretch of plain.

"O happy age and happy century," he went on, "in which my famous exploits shall be published, exploits worthy of being engraved in bronze, sculptured in marble, and depicted in paintings for the benefit of posterity. O wise magician, whoever you be, to whom shall fall the task of chronicling this extraordinary history of mine! I beg of you not to forget my good Rocinante, eternal companion of my wayfarings and my wanderings."

Then, as though he really had been in love: "O Princess Dulcinea, lady of this captive heart! Much wrong have you done me in thus sending me forth with your reproaches and sternly commanding me not to appear in your beauteous presence. O lady, deign to be mindful of this your subject who endures so many woes for the love of you."

And so he went on, stringing together absurdities, all of a kind that his books had taught him, imitating insofar as he was able the language of their authors. He rode slowly, and the sun came up so swiftly and with so much heat that it would have been sufficient to melt his brains if he had had any. He had been on the road almost the entire day without anything happening that is worthy of being set down here; and he was on the verge of despair, for he wished to meet someone at once with whom he might try the valor of his good right arm. Certain authors say that his first adventure was that of Puerto Lápice, while others state that it was that of the windmills; but in this particular instance I am in a position to affirm what I have read in the annals of La Mancha; and that is to the effect that he went all that day until nightfall, when he and his hack found themselves tired to death and famished. Gazing all around him to see if he could discover some castle or shepherd's hut where he might take shelter and attend to his pressing needs, he caught sight of an inn not far off the road along which they were traveling, and this to him was like a star guiding him not merely to the gates, but rather, let us say, to the palace of redemption. Quickening his pace, he came up to it just as night was falling.

By chance there stood in the doorway two lasses of the sort known as "of the district"; they were on their way to Seville in the company of some mule drivers who were spending the night in the inn. Now, everything that this adventurer of ours thought, saw, or imagined seemed to him to be directly out of one of the storybooks he had read, and so, when he caught sight of the inn, it at once became a castle with its four turrets and its pinnacles of gleaming silver, not to speak of the drawbridge and moat and all the other things that are commonly supposed to go with a castle. As he rode up to it, he accordingly reined in Rocinante and sat there waiting for a dwarf to appear upon the battlements and blow his trumpet by way of announcing the arrival of a knight.

The dwarf, however, was slow in coming, and as Rocinante was anxious to reach the stable, Don Quixote drew up to the door of the hostelry and surveyed the two merry maidens, who to him were a pair of beauteous damsels or gracious ladies taking their ease at the castle gate.

And then a swineherd came along, engaged in rounding up his drove of hogs—for, without any apology, that is what they were. He gave a blast on his horn to bring them together, and this at once became for Don Quixote just what he wished it to be: some dwarf who was heralding his coming; and so it was with a vast deal of satisfaction that he presented himself before the ladies in question, who, upon beholding a man in full armor like this, with lance and buckler, were filled with fright and made as if to flee indoors. Realizing that they were afraid, Don Quixote raised his pasteboard visor and revealed his withered, dust-covered face.

"Do not flee, your Ladyships," he said to them in a courteous manner and gentle voice. "You need not fear that any wrong will be done you, for it is not in accordance with the order of knighthood which I profess to wrong anyone, much less such highborn damsels as your appearance shows you to be."

The girls looked at him, endeavoring to scan his face, which was half-hidden by his ill-made visor. Never having heard women of their profession called damsels before, they were unable to restrain their laughter, at which Don Quixote took offense.

"Modesty," he observed, "well becomes those with the dower of beauty, and, moreover, laughter that has not good cause is a very foolish thing. But I do not say this to be discourteous or to hurt your feelings; my only desire is to serve you."

The ladies did not understand what he was talking about, but felt more than ever like laughing at our knight's unprepossessing figure. This increased his annoyance, and there is no telling what would have happened if at that moment the innkeeper had not come out. He was very fat and very peaceably inclined; but upon sighting this grotesque personage clad in bits of armor that were quite as oddly matched as were his bridle, lance, buckler, and corselet, mine host was not at all indisposed to join the lasses in their merriment. He was suspicious, however, of all this paraphernalia and decided that it would be better to keep a civil tongue in his head.

"If, Sir Knight," he said, "your Grace desires a lodging, aside from a bed—for there is none to be had in this inn—you will find all else that you may want in great abundance."

When Don Quixote saw how humble the governor of the castle was—for he took the innkeeper and his inn to be no less than that—he replied, "For me, Sir Castellan, anything will do, since

> *Arms are my only ornament,*
> *My only rest the fight, etc."*

The landlord thought that the knight had called him a castellan because he took him for one of those worthies of Castile, whereas the truth was, he was an Andalusian from the beach of Sanlúcar, no less a thief than Cacus himself, and as full of tricks as a student or a page boy.

"In that case," he said,

> *"Your bed will be the solid rock,*
> *Your sleep: to watch all night.*

This being so, you may be assured of finding beneath this roof enough to keep you awake for a whole year, to say nothing of a single night."

With this, he went up to hold the stirrup for Don Quixote, who encountered much difficulty in dismounting, not having broken his fast all day long. The knight then directed his host to take good care of the steed, as it was the best piece of horseflesh in all the world. The innkeeper looked it over, and it did not impress him as being half as good as Don Quixote had said it was. Having stabled the animal, he came back to see what his guest would have and found the latter being relieved of his armor by the damsels, who by now had made their peace with the new arrival. They had already removed his breastplate and backpiece but had no idea how they were going to open his gorget or get his improvised helmet off. That piece of armor had been tied on with green ribbons which it would be necessary to cut, since the knots could not be undone, but he would not hear of this, and so spent all the rest of that night with his headpiece in place, which gave him the weirdest, most laughable appearance that could be imagined.

Don Quixote fancied that these wenches who were assisting him must surely be the chatelaine and other ladies of the castle, and so proceeded to address them very gracefully and with much wit:

Never was knight so served
By any noble dame
As was Don Quixote
When from his village he came,
With damsels to wait on his every need
While princesses cared for his hack ...

"By hack," he explained, "is meant my steed Rocinante, for that is his name, and mine is Don Quixote de la Mancha. I had no intention of revealing my identity until my exploits done in your service should have made me known to you; but the necessity of adapting to present circumstances that old ballad of Lancelot has led to your becoming acquainted with it prematurely. However, the time will come when your Ladyships shall command and I will obey and with the valor of my good right arm show you how eager I am to serve you."

The young women were not used to listening to speeches like this and had not a word to say, but merely asked him if he desired to eat anything.

"I could eat a bite of something, yes," replied Don Quixote. "Indeed, I feel that a little food would go very nicely just now."

He thereupon learned that, since it was Friday, there was nothing to be had in all the inn except a few portions of codfish, which in Castile is called *abadejo*, in Andalusia *bacalao*, in some places *curadillo*, and elsewhere *truchuella* or small trout. Would his Grace, then, have some small trout, seeing that was all there was that they could offer him?

"If there are enough of them," said Don Quixote, "they will take the place of a trout, for it is all one to me whether I am given in change eight reales or one piece of eight. What is more, those small trout may be like veal, which is better than beef, or like kid, which is better than goat. But however that may be, bring them on at once, for the weight and burden of arms is not to be borne without inner sustenance."

Placing the table at the door of the hostelry, in the open air, they brought the guest a portion of badly soaked and worse cooked codfish and a piece of bread as black and moldy as the suit of armor that he wore. It was a mirth-provoking sight to see him eat, for he still had his helmet on with his visor fastened, which made it impossible for him to put anything into his mouth with his hands, and so it was necessary for one of the girls to feed him. As for giving him anything to drink, that would have been out of the question if the innkeeper had not hollowed out a reed, placing one end in Don Quixote's mouth while through the other end he poured the wine. All this the knight bore very patiently rather than have them cut the ribbons of his helmet.

At this point a gelder of pigs approached the inn, announcing his arrival with four or five blasts on his horn, all of which confirmed Don Quixote in the belief that this was indeed a famous castle, for what was this if not music that they were playing for him? The fish was trout, the bread was of the finest, the wenches were ladies, and the innkeeper was the castellan. He was convinced that he had been right in his resolve to sally forth and roam the world at large, but there was one thing that still distressed him greatly, and that was the fact that he had not as yet been dubbed a knight; as he saw it, he could not legitimately engage in any adventure until he had received the order of knighthood.

Of the amusing manner in which Don Quixote had himself dubbed a knight

Wearied of his thoughts, Don Quixote lost no time over the scanty repast which the inn afforded him. When he had finished, he summoned the landlord and, taking him out to the stable, closed the doors and fell on his knees in front of him.

"Never, valiant knight," he said, "shall I arise from here until you have courteously granted me the boon I seek, one which will redound to your praise and to the good of the human race."

Seeing his guest at his feet and hearing him utter such words as these, the innkeeper could only stare at him in bewilderment, not knowing what to say or do. It was in vain that he entreated him to rise, for Don Quixote refused to do so until his request had been granted.

"I expected nothing less of your great magnificence, my lord," the latter then continued, "and so I may tell you that the boon I asked and which you have so generously conceded me is that tomorrow morning you dub me a knight. Until that time, in the chapel of this your castle, I will watch over my armor, and when morning comes, as I have said, that which I so desire shall then be done, in order that I may lawfully go to the four corners of the earth in quest of adventures and to succor the needy, which is the chivalrous duty of all knights-errant such as I who long to engage in deeds of high emprise."

The innkeeper, as we have said, was a sharp fellow. He already had a suspicion that his guest was not quite right in the head, and he was now convinced of it as he listened to such remarks as these. However, just for the sport of it, he determined to humor him; and so he went on to assure Don Quixote that he was fully justified in his request and that such a desire and purpose was only natural on the part of so distinguished a knight as his gallant bearing plainly showed him to be.

He himself, the landlord added, when he was a young man, had followed the same honorable calling. He had gone through various parts of the world seeking adventures, among the places he had visited being the Percheles of Malága, the Isles of Riarán, the District of Seville, the Little Market Place of Segovia, the Olivera of Valencia, the Rondilla of Granada, the beach of Sanlúcar, the Horse Fountain of Cordova, the Small Taverns of Toledo, and numerous other localities where his nimble feet and light fingers had found much exercise. He had done many wrongs, cheated many widows, ruined many maidens, and swindled not a few minors until he had finally come to be known in almost all the courts and tribunals that are to be found in the whole of Spain.

At last he had retired to his castle here, where he lived upon his own income and the property of others; and here it was that he received all knights-errant of whatever quality and condition, simply out of the great affection that he bore them and that they might share with him their possessions in payment of his good will. Unfortunately, in this castle there was no chapel where Don Quixote might keep watch over his arms, for the old chapel had been torn down to make way for a new one; but in case of necessity, he felt quite sure that such a vigil could be maintained anywhere, and for the present occasion the courtyard of the castle would do; and then in the morning, please God, the requisite ceremony could be performed and his guest be duly dubbed a knight, as much a knight as anyone ever was.

He then inquired if Don Quixote had any money on his person, and the latter replied that he had not a cent, for in all the storybooks he had never read of knights-errant carrying any. But the innkeeper told him he was mistaken on this point; supposing the authors of those stories had not set down the fact in black and white, that was because they did not deem it necessary to speak of things as indispensable as money and a clean shirt, and one was not to assume for that reason that those knights-errant of whom the books were so full did not have any. He looked upon it as an absolute certainty that they all had well-stuffed purses, that they might be prepared for any emergency; and they also carried shirts and a little box of ointment for healing the wounds that they received.

For when they had been wounded in combat on the plains and in desert places, there was not always someone at hand to treat them, unless they had some skilled enchanter for a friend who then would succor them, bringing to them through the air, upon a cloud, some damsel or dwarf bearing a vial of water of such virtue that one had but to taste a drop of it and at once his wounds were healed and he was as sound as if he had never received any.

But even if this was not the case, knights in times past saw to it that their squires were well provided with money and other necessities, such as lint and ointment for healing purposes; and if they had no squires—which happened very rarely—they themselves carried these objects in a pair of saddle bags very cleverly attached to their horses' croups in such a manner as to be scarcely noticeable, as if they held something of greater importance than that, for among the knights-errant saddlebags as a rule were not favored. Accordingly, he would advise the novice before him, and inasmuch as the latter was soon to be his godson, he might even command him, that henceforth he should not go without money and a supply of those things that have been mentioned, as he would find that they came in useful at a time when he least expected it.

Don Quixote promised to follow his host's advice punctiliously; and so it was arranged that he should watch his armor in a large barnyard at one side of the inn. He gathered up all the pieces, placed them in a horse trough that stood near the well, and bracing his shield on his arm, took up his lance and with stately demeanor began pacing up and down in front of the trough even as night was closing in.

The innkeeper informed his other guests of what was going on, of Don Quixote's vigil and his expectation of being dubbed a knight; and, marveling greatly at so extraordinary a variety of madness, they all went out to see for themselves and stood there watching from a distance. For a while the knight-to-be, with tranquil mien, would merely walk up and down; then, leaning on his lance, he would pause to survey his armor, gazing fixedly at it for a considerable length of time. As has been said, it was night now, but the brightness of the moon, which well might rival that of Him who lent it, was such that everything the novice knight did was plainly visible to all.

At this point one of the mule drivers who were stopping at the inn came out to water his drove, and in order to do this it was necessary to remove the armor from the trough.

As he saw the man approaching, Don Quixote cried out to him, "O bold knight, whoever you may be, who thus would dare to lay hands upon the accouterments of the most valiant man of arms that ever girded on a sword, look well what you do and desist if you do not wish to pay with your life for your insolence!"

The muleteer gave no heed to these words—it would have been better for his own sake had he done so—but, taking it up by the straps, tossed the armor some distance from him. When he beheld this, Don Quixote rolled his eyes heavenward and with his thoughts apparently upon his Dulcinea exclaimed, "Succor, O lady mine, this vassal heart in this my first encounter; let not your favor and protection fail me in the peril in which for the first time I now find myself."

With these and other similar words, he loosed his buckler, grasped his lance in both his hands, and let the mule driver have such a blow on the head that the man fell to the ground stunned; and had it been followed by another one, he would have had no need of a surgeon to treat him. Having done this, Don Quixote gathered up his armor and resumed his pacing up and down with the same calm manner as before. Not long afterward, without knowing what had happened—for the first muleteer was still lying there unconscious—another came out with the same intention of watering his mules, and he too was about to remove the armor from the trough when the knight, without saying a word or asking favor of anyone, once more adjusted his buckler and raised his lance, and if he did not break the second mule driver's head to bits, he made more than three pieces of it by dividing it into quarters. At the sound of the fracas everybody in the inn came running out, among them the innkeeper; whereupon Don Quixote again lifted his buckler and laid his hand on his sword.

"O lady of beauty," he said, "strength and vigor of this fainting heart of mine! Now is the time to turn the eyes of your greatness upon this captive knight of yours who must face so formidable an adventure."

By this time he had worked himself up to such a pitch of anger that if all the mule drivers in the world had attacked him he would not have taken one step backward. The comrades of the wounded men, seeing the plight those two were in, now began showering stones on Don Quixote, who shielded himself as best he could with his buckler, although he did not dare stir from the trough for fear of leaving his armor unprotected. The landlord, meanwhile, kept calling to them to stop, for he had told them that this was a madman who would be sure to go free even though he killed them all. The knight was shouting louder than ever, calling them knaves and traitors. As for the lord of the castle, who allowed knights-errant to be treated in this fashion, he was a lowborn villain, and if he, Don Quixote, had but received the order of knighthood, he would make him pay for his treachery.

"As for you others, vile and filthy rabble, I take no account of you; you may stone me or come forward and attack me all you like; you shall see what the reward of your folly and insolence will be."

He spoke so vigorously and was so undaunted in bearing as to strike terror in those who would assail him; and for this reason, and owing also to the persuasions of the innkeeper, they ceased stoning him. He then permitted them to carry away the wounded, and went back to watching his armor with the same tranquil, unconcerned air that he had previously displayed.

The landlord was none too well pleased with these mad pranks on the part of his guest and determined to confer upon him that accursed order of knighthood before something else happened. Going up to him, he begged Don Quixote's pardon for the insolence which, without his knowledge, had been shown the knight by those of low degree. They, however, had been well punished for their impudence. As he had said, there was no chapel in this castle, but for that which remained to be done there was no need of any. According to what he had read of the ceremonial of the order, there was nothing to this business of being dubbed a knight except a slap on the neck and one across the shoulder, and that could be performed in the middle of a field as well as anywhere else. All that was required was for the knight-to-be to keep watch over his armor for a couple of hours, and Don Quixote had been at it more than four. The latter believed all this and announced that he was ready to obey and get the matter over with as speedily as possible. Once dubbed a knight, if he were attacked one more time, he did not think that he would leave a single person in the castle alive, save such as he might command be spared, at the bidding of his host and out of respect to him.

Thus warned, and fearful that it might occur, the castellan brought out the book in which he had jotted down the hay and barley for which the mule drivers owed him, and, accompanied by a lad bearing the butt of a candle and the two aforesaid damsels, he came up to where Don Quixote stood and commanded him to kneel. Reading from the account book—as if he had been saying a prayer—he raised his hand and, with the knight's own sword, gave him a good thwack upon the neck and another lusty one upon the shoulder, muttering all the while between his teeth. He then directed one of the ladies to gird on Don Quixote's sword, which she did with much gravity and composure; for it was all they could do to keep from laughing at every point of the ceremony, but the thought of the knight's prowess which they had already witnessed was sufficient to restrain their mirth.

"May God give your Grace much good fortune," said the worthy lady as she attached the blade, "and prosper you in battle."

Don Quixote thereupon inquired her name, for he desired to know to whom it was he was indebted for the favor he had just received, that he might share with her some of the honor which his strong right arm was sure to bring him. She replied very humbly that her name was Tolosa and that she was the daughter of a shoemaker, a native of Toledo who lived in the stalls of Sancho Bienaya. To this the knight replied that she would do him a very great favor if from then on she would call herself Doña Tolosa, and she promised to do so. The other girl then helped him on with his spurs, and practically the same conversation was repeated. When asked her name, she stated that it was La Molinera and added that she was the daughter of a respectable miller of Antequera. Don Quixote likewise requested her to assume the "don" and become Doña Molinera and offered to render her further services and favors.

These unheard-of ceremonies having been dispatched in great haste, Don Quixote could scarcely wait to be astride his horse and sally forth on his quest for adventures. Saddling and mounting Rocinante, he embraced his host, thanking him for the favor of having dubbed him a knight and saying such strange things that it would be quite impossible to record them here. The innkeeper, who was only too glad to be rid of him, answered with a speech that was no less flowery, though somewhat shorter, and he did not so much as ask him for the price of a lodging, so glad was he to see him go.

Of the good fortune which the valorous Don Quixote had in the terrifying and never-before-imagined adventure of the windmills, along with other events that deserve to be suitably recorded

At this point they caught sight of thirty or forty windmills which were standing on the plain there, and no sooner had Don Quixote laid eyes upon them than he turned to his squire and said, "Fortune is guiding our affairs better than we could have wished; for you see there before you, friend Sancho Panza, some thirty or more lawless giants with whom I mean to do battle. I shall deprive them of their lives, and with the spoils from this encounter we shall begin to enrich ourselves; for this is righteous warfare, and it is a great service to God to remove so accursed a breed from the face of the earth."

"What giants?" said Sancho Panza.

"Those that you see there," replied his master, "those with the long arms some of which are as much as two leagues in length."

"But look, your Grace, those are not giants but windmills, and what appear to be arms are their wings which, when whirled in the breeze, cause the millstone to go."

"It is plain to be seen," said Don Quixote, "that you have had little experience in this matter of adventures. If you are afraid, go off to one side and say your prayers while I am engaging them in fierce, unequal combat."

Saying this, he gave spurs to his steed Rocinante, without paying any heed to Sancho's warning that these were truly windmills and not giants that he was riding forth to attack. Nor even when he was close upon them did he perceive what they really were, but shouted at the top of his lungs, "Do not seek to flee, cowards and vile creatures that you are, for it is but a single knight with whom you have to deal!"

At that moment a little wind came up and the big wings began turning.

"Though you flourish as many arms as did the giant Briareus," said Don Quixote when he perceived this, "you still shall have to answer to me."

He thereupon commended himself with all his heart to his lady Dulcinea, beseeching her to succor him in this peril; and, being well covered with his shield and with his lance at rest, he bore down upon them at a full gallop and fell upon the first mill that stood in his way, giving a thrust at the wing, which was whirling at such a speed that his lance was broken into bits and both horse and horseman went rolling over the plain, very much battered indeed. Sancho upon his donkey came hurrying to his master's assistance as fast as he could, but when he reached the spot, the knight was unable to move, so great was the shock with which he and Rocinante had hit the ground.

"God help us!" exclaimed Sanclio, "did I not tell your Grace to look well, that those were nothing but windmills, a fact which no one could fail to see unless he had other mills of the same sort in his head?"

"Be quiet, friend Sancho," said Don Quixote. "Such are the fortunes of war, which more than any other are subject to constant change. What is more, when I come to think of it, I am sure that this must be the work of that magician

Frestón, the one who robbed me of my study and my books, and who has thus changed the giants into windmills in order to deprive me of the glory of overcoming them, so great is the enmity that he bears me; but in the end his evil arts shall not prevail against this trusty sword of mine."

"May God's will be done," was Sancho Panza's response. And with the aid of his squire the knight was once more mounted on Rocinante, who stood there with one shoulder half out of joint. And so, speaking of the adventure that had just befallen them, they continued along the Puerto Lápice highway; for there, Don Quixote said, they could not fail to find many and varied adventures, this being a much traveled thoroughfare. The only thing was, the knight was exceedingly downcast over the loss of his lance.

"I remember," he said to his squire, "having read of a Spanish knight by the name of Diego Pérez de Vargas, who, having broken his sword in battle, tore from an oak a heavy bough or branch and with it did such feats of valor that day, and pounded so many Moors, that he came to be known as Machuca, and he and his descendants from that day forth have been called Vargas y Machuca. I tell you this because I too intend to provide myself with just such a bough as the one he wielded, and with it I propose to do such exploits that you shall deem yourself fortunate to have been found worthy to come with me and behold and witness things that are almost beyond belief."

"God's will be done," said Sancho. "I believe everything that your Grace says; but straighten yourself up in the saddle a little, for you seem to be slipping down on one side, owing, no doubt, to the shaking-up that you received in your fall."

"Ah, that is the truth," replied Don Quixote, "and if I do not speak of my sufferings, it is for the reason that it is not permitted knights-errant to complain of any wound whatsoever, even though their bowels may be dropping out."

"If that is the way it is," said Sanclio, "I have nothing more to say; but, God knows, it would suit me better if your Grace did complain when something hurts him. I can assure you that I mean to do so, over the least little thing that ails me—that is, unless the same rule applies to squires as well."

Don Quixote laughed long and heartily over Sancho's simplicity, telling him that he might complain as much as he liked and where and when he liked, whether he had good cause or not; for he had read nothing to the contrary in the ordinances of chivalry. Sancho then called his master's attention to the fact that it was time to eat. The knight replied that he himself had no need of food at the moment, but his squire might eat whenever he chose. Having been granted this permission, Sancho seated himself as best he could upon his beast, and, taking out from his saddlebags the provisions that he had stored there, he rode along leisurely behind his master, munching his victuals and taking a good, hearty swig now and then at the leather flask in a manner that might well have caused the biggest-bellied tavernkeeper of Málaga to envy him. Between draughts he gave not so much as a thought to any promise that his master might have made him, nor did he look upon it as any hardship, but rather as good sport, to go in quest of adventures however hazardous they might be.

The short of the matter is, they spent the night under some trees, from one of which Don Quixote tore off a withered bough to serve him as a lance, placing it in the lance head from which he had removed the broken one. He did not sleep all night long for thinking of his lady Dulcinea; for this was in accordance with what he had read in his books, of men of arms in the forest or desert places who kept a wakeful vigil, sustained by the memory of their ladies fair. Not so with Sancho, whose stomach was full, and not with chicory water. He fell into a dreamless slumber, and had not his master called him, he would not have been awakened either by the rays of the sun in his face or by the many birds who greeted the coming of the new day with their merry song.

Upon arising, he had another go at the flask, finding it somewhat more flaccid than it had been the night before, a circumstance which grieved his heart, for he could not see that they were on the way to remedying the deficiency within any very short space of time. Don Quixote did not wish any breakfast; for, as has been said, he was in the habit of nourishing himself on savorous memories. They then set out once more along the road to Puerto Lápice, and around three in the afternoon they came in sight of the pass that bears that name.

"There," said Don Quixote as his eyes fell upon it, "we may plunge our arms up to the elbow in what are known as adventures. But I must warn you that even though you see me in the greatest peril in the world, you are not to lay hand upon your sword to defend me, unless it be that those who attack me are rabble and men of low degree, in which case you may very well come to my aid; but if they be gentlemen, it is in no wise permitted by the laws of chivalry that you should assist me until you yourself shall have been dubbed a knight."

"Most certainly, sir," replied Sancho, "Your Grace shall be very well obeyed in this; all the more so for the reason that I myself am of a peaceful disposition and not fond of meddling in the quarrels and feuds of others. However, when it comes to protecting my own person, I shall not take account of those laws of which you speak, seeing that all laws, human and divine, permit each one to defend himself whenever he is attacked."

"I am willing to grant you that," assented Don Quixote, "but in this matter of defending me against gentlemen you must restrain your natural impulses."

"I promise you I shall do so," said Sancho. "I will observe this precept as I would the Sabbath day."

As they were conversing in this manner, there appeared in the road in front of them two friars of the Order of St. Benedict, mounted upon dromedaries— for the she-mules they rode were certainly no smaller than that. The friars wore travelers' spectacles and carried sunshades, and behind them came a coach accompanied by four or five men on horseback and a couple of muleteers on foot. In the coach, as was afterwards learned, was a lady of Biscay, on her way to Seville to bid farewell to her husband, who had been appointed to some high post in the Indies. The religious were not of her company although they were going by the same road.

The instant Don Quixote laid eyes upon them he turned to his squire. "Either I am mistaken or this is going to be the most famous adventure that ever was seen; for those black-clad figures that you behold must be, and without any doubt are, certain enchanters who are bearing with them a captive princess in that coach, and I must do all I can to right this wrong."

"It will be worse than the windmills," declared Sancho. "Look you, sir, those are Benedictine friars and the coach must be that of some travelers. Mark well what I say and what you do, lest the devil lead you astray."

"I have already told you, Sancho," replied Don Quixote, "that you know little where the subject of adventures is concerned. What I am saying to you is the truth, as you shall now see."

With this, he rode forward and took up a position in the middle of the road along which the friars were coming, and as soon as they appeared to be within earshot he cried out to them in a loud voice, "O devilish and monstrous beings, set free at once the highborn princesses whom you bear captive in that coach, or else prepare at once to meet your death as the just punishment of your evil deeds."

The friars drew rein and sat there in astonishment, marveling as much at Don Quixote's appearance as at the words he spoke. "Sir Knight," they answered him, "we are neither devilish nor monstrous but religious of the Order of St. Benedict who are merely going our way. We know nothing of those who are in that coach, nor of any captive princesses either."

"Soft words," said Don Quixote, "have no effect on me. I know you for what you are, lying rabble!" And without waiting for any further parley he gave spur to Rocinante and, with lowered lance, bore down upon the first friar with such fury and intrepidity that, had not the fellow tumbled from his mule of his own accord, he would have been hurled to the ground and either killed or badly wounded. The second religious, seeing how his companion had been treated, dug his legs into his she-mule's flanks and scurried away over the countryside faster than the wind.

Seeing the friar upon the ground, Sancho Panza slipped lightly from his mount and, falling upon him, began stripping him of his habit. The two mule drivers accompanying the religious thereupon came running up and asked Sancho why he was doing this. The latter replied that the friar's garments belonged to him as legitimate spoils of the battle that his master Don Quixote had just won. The muleteers, however, were lads with no sense of humor, nor did they know what all this talk of spoils and battles was about; but, perceiving that Don Quixote had ridden off to one side to converse with those inside the coach, they pounced upon Sancho, threw him to the ground, and proceeded to pull out the hair of his beard and kick him to a pulp, after which they went off and left him stretched out there, bereft at once of breath and sense.

Without losing any time, they then assisted the friar to remount. The good brother was trembling all over from fright, and there was not a speck of color in his face, but when he found himself in the saddle once more, he quickly spurred his beast to where his companion, at some little distance, sat watching and waiting to see what the result of the encounter would be. Having no curiosity as to the final outcome of the fray, the two of them now resumed their journey, making more signs of the cross than the devil would be able to carry upon his back.

Meanwhile Don Quixote, as we have said, was speaking to the lady in the coach.

"Your beauty, my lady, may now dispose of your person as best may please you, for the arrogance of your abductors lies upon the ground, overthrown by this good arm of mine; and in order that you may not pine to know the name of your liberator, I may inform you that I am Don Quixote de la

Mancha, knight-errant and adventurer and captive of the peerless and beauteous Doña Dulcinea del Toboso. In payment of the favor which you have received from me, I ask nothing other than that you return to El Toboso and on my behalf pay your respects to this lady, telling her that it was I who set you free."

One of the squires accompanying those in the coach, a Biscayan, was listening to Don Quixote's words, and when he saw that the knight did not propose to let the coach proceed upon its way but was bent upon having it turn back to El Toboso, he promptly went up to him, seized his lance, and said to him in bad Castilian and worse Biscayan, "Go, *caballero*, and bad luck go with you; for by the God that created me, if you do not let this coach pass, me kill you or me no Biscayan."

Don Quixote heard him attentively enough and answered him very mildly, "If you were a *caballero*, which you are not, I should already have chastised you, wretched creature, for your foolhardiness and your impudence."

"Me no *caballero*?" cried the Biscayan. "Me swear to God, you he like a Christian. If you will but lay aside your lance and unsheath your sword, you will soon see that you are carrying water to the cat! Biscayan on land, gentleman at sea, but a gentleman in spite of the devil, and you lie if you say otherwise."

"'You shall see as to that presently,' said Agrajes,'" Don Quixote quoted. He cast his lance to the earth, drew his sword, and, taking his buckler on his arm, attacked the Biscayan with intent to slay him. The latter, when he saw his adversary approaching, would have liked to dismount from his mule, for she was one of the worthless sort that are let for hire and he had no confidence in her; but there was no time for this, and so he had no choice but to draw his own sword in turn and make the best of it. However, he was near enough to the coach to be able to snatch a cushion from it to serve him as a shield; and then they fell upon each other as though they were mortal enemies. The rest of those present sought to make peace between them but did not succeed, for the Biscayan with his disjointed phrases kept muttering that if they did not let him finish the battle then he himself would have to kill his mistress and anyone else who tried to stop him.

The lady inside the carriage, amazed by it all and trembling at what she saw, directed her coachman to drive on a little way; and there from a distance she watched the deadly combat, in the course of which the Biscayan came down with a great blow on Don Quixote's shoulder, over the top of the latter's shield, and had not the knight been clad in armor, it would have split him to the waist.

Feeling the weight of this blow, Don Quixote cried out, "O lady of my soul, Dulcinea, flower of beauty, succor this your champion who out of gratitude for your many favors finds himself in so perilous a plight!" To utter these words, lay hold of his sword, cover himself with his buckler, and attack the Biscayan was but the work of a moment; for he was now resolved to risk everything upon a single stroke.

As he saw Don Quixote approaching with so dauntless a bearing, the Biscayan was well aware of his adversary's courage and forthwith determined to imitate the example thus set him. He kept himself protected with his cushion, but he was unable to get his she-mule to budge to one side or the other, for the beast, out of sheer exhaustion and being, moreover, unused to such childish play, was incapable of taking a single step. And so, then, as has been stated, Don Quixote was approaching the wary Biscayan, his sword raised on high and with the firm resolve of cleaving his enemy in two; and the Biscayan was awaiting the knight in the same posture, cushion in front of him and with uplifted sword. All the bystanders were trembling with suspense at what would happen as a result of the terrible blows that were threatened, and the lady in the coach and her maids were making a thousand vows and offerings to all the images and shrines in Spain, praying that God would save them all and the lady's squire from this great peril that confronted them.

But the unfortunate part of the matter is that at this very point the author of the history breaks off and leaves the battle pending, excusing himself upon the ground that he has been unable to find anything else in writing concerning the exploits of Don Quixote beyond those already set forth. It is true, on the other hand, that the second author of this work could not bring himself to believe that so unusual a chronicle would have been consigned to oblivion, nor that the learned ones of La Mancha were possessed of so little curiosity as not to be able to discover in their archives or registry offices certain papers that have to do with this famous knight. Being convinced of this, he did not despair of coming upon the end of this pleasing story, and Heaven favoring him, he did find it, as shall be related in the second part.

Juan Luis Vives (1492–1540)

Vives was born in Valencia in 1492, and studied Latin and Greek in Spain and scholastic philosophy at the University of Paris (1509–12). Unhappy with the rigid scholasticism of Paris, he moved to Bruges where he became tutor to the young Cardinal de Croy, Archbishop of Toledo. Moving in 1517 to Louvain with his pupil, Vives began teaching at the university until the death of his patron, de Croy, required a more secure income.

In 1522 Vives was offered a chair at the Spanish University of Alcala but stopped en route in England where he was invited to teach Greek at Oxford. He also received the patronage of King Henry VIII and Queen Catherine of Aragon, serving as tutor to Princess Mary in 1527–8, and enjoying the company of leading English humanists. His support of Queen Catherine during the divorce proceedings resulted in his leaving England permanently. Vives, like his friend Thomas More, was much concerned with the plight of the poor. His 1526 On The Help of the Poor *recommended a system of poor relief and criticizes the church for not attending sufficiently to the problem. He was, though, best known as an educator whose treatises stressed not only Christian virtue and classical studies but also vernacular languages as the foundations of knowledge, as well as specifically addressing the education of women. Vives died in Bruges in 1540.*

Chapter Thirty-Two

On the writing of letters

To Senor Idiáquez, Secretary of Charles V

1. When I was setting about, my dear Idiáquez,[1] to publish a brief work on the composition of letters, which are of great utility in every walk of life, it seemed proper to me to inscribe it with a dedication to your name. It is not that you have need of these prescriptions of mine. since in the acquisition of this skill, you have Cicero and Pliny as mentors and guides, in whose footsteps you tread with singular success, winning the admiration of all those who know how quickly you have realized your goals in the study of Latin. But it is rather that this treatise seems ideally suited to one who must daily, write a great number of Latin epistles (both in your own name and in that of the Emperor Charles) on matters of great importance. Finally, in view of our close friendship and mutual goodwill, whatever comes from one of us cannot fail to bring great pleasure to the other.

2. A letter[2] is a conversation by means of the written word between persons separated from each other. It was invented to convey the mental concepts and thoughts of one person to another as a faithful intermediary and bearer of a commission. "The purpose of the letter," said Saint Ambrose to Sabinus, "is that though physically separated we may be united in spirit. In a letter the image of the living presence emits its glow between persons distant from each other, and conversation committed to writing unites those who are separated. In it we also share our feelings with a friend and communicate our thoughts to him." The Greeks called it an epistle from the verb "to send," as if one were to say in Latin *missoria*,[3] a word not found in established usage. Among those present to each other there is no need of a letter unless perhaps you intend to deal with something in definite and explicit language, as Suetonius recounts of Caesar Augustus, who in private conversation of some importance, even with his wife Livia, would speak from written notes, for fear of saying too much or too little if he were to speak *ex tempore*, and we read in Tacitus of that arrogant master of Rome[4] who never had any dealings with his slaves except by gesture or in writing.

3. Likewise, writing tablets[5] were invented for the use of those who lived in the same city and neighborhood, but either had little desire or opportunity to see each other, or in any case could more conveniently commit the matter to writing. There is frequent mention of these writing tablets in Cicero, Tacitus and others. Letters in early antiquity were employed for the sole purpose of conveying news of public or private affairs to an absent party, reporting what had been done, what was likely to happen, what was going on, what they wished would be done or not done. We see that Cicero's letters, especially those to Titus Atticus, are of this type. Later, everything that could be said or written fell into the confines of the letter. Cicero wrote to Curio: "You are well aware that there are many kinds of letters, but one thing is beyond doubt: the reason why letter-writing was invented was to inform those not present of anything that it would be to our interest or theirs for them to know. For the rest there are two kinds of letters that I particularly enjoy: one is the familiar, humorous letter, the other austere and serious." Thus the true genuine letter is that by which we signify to someone what it is important for him or for us to know in the conduct of one's affairs, such as, in general, letters of information, petition, recommendation, advice, admonishment and any others of this kind which make up for the absence of the writer.

4. Afterwards there were added letters of consolation, reconciliation, instruction, and letters of discussion that treated of every argument of philosophy, law, ancient history, in short, of all branches of learning and of all those topics which would be committed to writing even among those who often frequent each other's company. Thus Plato writes to Dionysius[6] and others on philosophy; Seneca writes to Lucilius; Jerome, Ambrose, Augustine and Cyprian write to various persons on sacred subjects. The books of Cato the Censor[7] and of many jurisconsults[8] on queries and responses in the form of a letter may be cited. I do not wish for the present to discuss how widely the name letter should be applied, but certainly if we agree that whatever bears a salutation is to be called a letter, what is to prevent us from calling the *Tusculan Disputations* or the *De finibus* letters to Brutus, the essays *De senectute* and *De amicitia* letters to Atticus, the *De officiis* a letter to his son Marcus, or if you were to preface the salutation "To the jury" to the *Pro Milone* or the *In Verrem*, would they then qualify as letters?" But as a woman who puts on cuisses or girds herself with a sword does not by that token become a man, so not every book to which a salutation is prefixed becomes a letter, unless it takes

on the nature and qualities of a letter, as we shall demonstrate immediately. Pliny put it well when he said "It is one thing to write history, but another to write a letter," signifying that they are distinct in nature.

On Invention

5. We shall combine invention in letters with a part of the disposition of the subject matter, especially in the exordium of the letter, because often these cannot readily be separated. Indeed the rules concerning both of them are the same in several respects. Many people who are about to write a letter struggle over the introduction as if they were navigating among reefs, and they would easily complete the rest of the journey if they had only escaped the treachery of the harbour. At the outset it must be said that all invention, not only in the letter but in any other kind of speech or discourse, as also in what we are saying now, is not at all a matter of skill, but of proficiency. It is the product of ability, memory, judgment and experience. In the transmission of skills we can be of help but we do not make perfect: recommendations are given, but not a complete training. Consequently, no one should expect to acquire a full comprehension of the art of letter-writing or of any other type of literary skill either in this section or in others, or from myself or any other writer or teacher. There are some who condemn as useless rules that do not immediately make a stupid man brilliant or one with no training an expert. Therefore, let this stand as the first rule, that we facilitate and further invention by these formulas, but that they will have no effect of themselves unless thet are joined with experience and practice. With this premise I come now to the main subject.

6. One who sets about to write a letter should consider who the writer is and to whom he is writing and on what subject; who we are to him, and who he is in his own right. As to ourselves, we may be either strangers or acquaintances, friends or enemies, casual or dubious friends, or open and close friends, equals or unequals, from various points of view: family, social station, learning, age. Then, concerning the addressee, we must consider his family background: plebeian or patrician, well-born or of lowly origins: his personal resources—opulent, conspicuous, moderate, humble, non-existent; his legal status, free or slave. We must determine whether he is outspoken or secretive, of good or bad reputation, leisurely or occupied, cobbler or tailor; we must consider his learning: great, poor, average; whether he is a theologian, doctor, philosopher, lawyer,

experienced or otherwise; his character and morals—stern or good-natured, lax or severe, mild-mannered or irascible, affable or haughty, easy or difficult, sharp-writted or dull. All these things may easily be surveyed in a single mental reflection, in a moment's time. Frequently you must plead in excuse that you write as a complete stranger or as a mere casual acquaintance, or that you are writing to a person of great importance, or to one who may think you are of unfriendly disposition. This must be made clear from the beginning, for it is a natural tendency that once the letter is opened and the writer's name is read, the recipient of the letter will wonder whether it is sent by a stranger or by someone not especially endeared to him, or by an enemy. And so in his mind he condemns the writer right from the start for impudence, temerity, arrogance or insanity, with the result that he does not so much repudiate the letter as conceive a dislike for its author, all the more intensely if he is haughty or ill-tempered and inclined to feelings of antipathy. Therefore one must make allowance for this eventuality, for, even in the forum new orators were compelled before proceeding to plead their case to give some personal background explaining why they were speaking: as Cicero did in the *Pro Roscio Amerino*,[9] the first speech he delivered before a jury, and in the *Pro lege Manilia*,[10] his first speech before the people.

7. The opening therefore must be drawn either from yourself or from things pertaining to you, or from the recipient or things pertaining to him, or from the subject itself on which you are writing, in the form of a short introduction. Concerning yourself, somewhat in the following manner: that you have always loved and cherished him; that you have on every occasion held him in the highest esteem and spoken well of him; that you regret that you have remained unknown to him for so long or were only slightly acquainted with a man whom you have always so admired for his talent and virtue; or that you regret that this suspicion presented itself to his mind concerning your good will towards him, since you continue to count that friendship as one of your principal blessings. You will adduce, if you can, some proof of your friendly sentiments towards him; you will cast blame on those who were envious of your friendship, or even on the addressee himself, but in a restrained manner and without any harshness, or on your own imprudence and inexperience; or you will openly confess your guilt, if the circumstances require it, indicating your repentance and your resolution to give some concrete demonstration of how well-disposed you now are towards him. If you begin with things pertaining to yourself, you

will point out some friendship that you have in common with him, or was shared by your fathers. If you open the letter with references to him, you will say, as in letters of reconciliation, that you were induced to write to him by the talent, literary accomplishments, humane character, and moral excellence that you admired in him; that although you were a stranger to him, in his extraordinary kindness and zeal for doing good he welcomes all into his friendship. Moreover, owing to his literary reputation and wisdom, it was impossible either that he could be unknown to anyone or think that anyone was unknown to him or not his concern. The same could be said of power, for a prince or a king, to whom one must resort as if for sanctuary, cannot make any distinction between those who are known or unknown; all those who have entrusted themselves to his care have sufficient recognition.

8. We must take particular care to make it appear that we have been more influenced by his virtues than attracted by his good fortune, but in the enumeration of his virtues there should be no semblance of flattery. Rather we shall show that we have either discovered it for ourselves, if we have benefitted from some good action of his, or have heard it from others, who have experienced it, or have learned of it or witnessed it of ourselves. Accordingly we shall adduce some concrete evidence of his accomplishments, as in the case of men of learning, from books published by him, speeches delivered, lectures or disputations. And we shall mention especially those good qualities of his that are most appropriate to the substance of our letter, as his clemency, if we are seeking pardon; his friendly nature, if we seek his friendship; his generosity, if we solicit a favor; his wisdom and uprightness, if it is counsel that we desire.

9. If the letter begins with things pertaining to him, allusion may be made to some common friendship or friendship between your fathers. From the subject matter of the letter, that it is a noble, learned and subtle argument, and therefore worthy of our writing to him about it; or an urgent matter, and therefore we were compelled to take refuge in him, as to a sacred altar, just as in connection with wealth one has recourse to a rich man, or in matters of justice to a judge, a king, or a magistrate. It may be stated that we preferred to undergo suspicion of any vice whatever, even if it would have grave consequences for us, at least in the mind of the person whom we esteem so highly, rather than not write. You may recall to him that necessity is a very powerful weapon, which none can resist, that it is more honorable when something is done for another; or that the matter is of such a nature that when he becomes thoroughly acquainted with it, he will not consider you rash or presumptuous in writing about it, but a man completely

without guile and vigorous in the pursuit of good. On the contrary he would have considered you remiss had you neglected it. One must also apologize to a friend for writing about something which you could have dealt with personally. Cicero wrote to Lucceius: "Often, when I attempted to discuss this subject with you privately, I was inhibited by a kind of almost backward bashfulness, but now that I am not in your presence I shall set forth my thoughts more confidently, for a letter does not blush."

10. This is the first encounter, which, as the character in the comedy says, is the hardest; after this the rest is more effortless and easier to manage. Therefore in the first letter we must take great pains that in the eyes of this new acquaintance we do not come under suspicion of some vice, like impudence or arrogance or loquacity or ostentation or cunning or pedantic affectation or excessive and parasitical flattery or scurrility or ignorance or imprudence. For there is much at stake in the first contact, as in cases that are still fragile and delicate before they fuse. Nor do I think that I need remind anyone that not everything is suitable for all persons. You must determine to whom you can express your admiration, to whom you can mention parental ties of hospitality, or the care of subordinates. But if you have no need of giving any reason for your writing to him, then you will take into consideration who it is to whom you are writing, for this will set the tone for the whole letter.

11. To a prosperous, haughty person the letter must be more respectful, but without flattery: to one who is stern and disagreeable, use a more mild and reserved style: to one who is unsophisticated or dull-witted, a more lucid style is called for: to a clever person, the style must be more studied and ornate, if he takes pleasure in that and regards it as an expression of respect: to a learned man, use a style more consonant with that of the ancient writers: to a busy man, be brief: to a man of leisure, be more expansive, if you think he will appreciate it: to a jovial person, write in a sprightly manner: to a kindly person, be less anxious about detail: to a severe person, be somewhat solemn: to one who is easy-going, be light-hearted: to a gloomy person, gloomy: to a faithful friend, express yourself openly and with great confidence: to an uncertain friend, be more cautious, but in such a manner that he thinks he is loved and that you truly love him. This is the law of nature, this is what Christ commands, more valid than the law of nature, with the result that one who does not love in return will be deservedly condemned for ingratitude. You should write to an enemy in such a way that you expect that he may become your friend and that a return to

your favor remains always possible and feasible. All harshness should be absent and you should demonstrate a certain gentleness even towards an enemy. And it will be best to remember our profession of faith, whereby we are forbidden to hate anyone. Thus you will show him that you wish that he be corrected, not damned, and that you hate the vice, but love the person. To one of equal rank and one who is dear to you you will write in a simple and familiar manner: to one less intimate, more cautiously, but courteously and without condescension: to one beneath your rank, in a kindly manner, so that you do not appear to speak down to him, but on an equal footing, even to people of very humble circumstances. Good morals recommend this, and religious piety commands it. Examples will be readily at hand from experience.

12. To be banned altogether from all human experience is that deceitful, insipid, inept type of letter, in which all indications of intentions are blurred. So insincere and flattering are such letters that there is no way of discerning the writer's intent, e.g., those letters that go by the name of courtly and polite. For human thought, enveloped by the ponderous mass of the body, is impenetrable; it is made manifest to a certain extent in speech. But if this too is completely feigned and disguised, what do we have left to understand our fellow man? What kind of communication and fellowship will exist among mankind when no one will be able to distinguish a well-wisher from an ill-wisher, will give welcome to the wolf instead of the sheep, or will flee from the sheep in fear of the wolf's ferocity? But this is the object of another program of learning. Now to the subject matter of letters.

Endnotes

1. Idiáquez: Alonso de Idiáquez, secretary together with Francisco de los Cobos of the Emperor Charles V.
2. A letter: This definition, a free reminiscence of a fragment of the comic writer Turpilius, a contemporary of Terence, is often quoted in antiquity. Angell Day in *The English Secretorie*, published in 1586, defined the letter as "the Messenger of the Absent."
3. *missoria*: The word is not found elsewhere in this sense. In ordinary usage the adjective *missiva* was used to describe a letter that initiated a correspondence, as opposed to an *epistola responsiva*. Cf. Demetrio Marzi, *La cancelleria della republica fiorentina* (Rocca S. Casciano, 1910) p. 356.

4. Arrogant master: Pallas, freedman of Antonia and financial secretary of her son, Claudius. His wealth, success and arrogant temper made him deservedly unpopular. He fell into disfavor after the accession of Nero and was put to death.

5. Writing tablets: These were wooden tablets with wax coating, which could be sealed or opened at need, and were thus useful for brief messages.

6. Plato writes to Dionysius: Letters 1–3 and 13 of the correspondence attributed to Plato.

7. Cato the Censor: None of these books survive. Cicero testified to Cato's knowledge of juridical science.

8. jurisconsults: Jurists often gave their opinions on questions of law in writing, called *responsa*, which were then sent under seal to the judge.

9. *Pro Roscio Amerino*: Delivered in 80 B.C., this was the first *causa publica* in which Cicero was engaged. In his opening words, he apologizes, as it were, for his youth and lack of experience.

10. *Pro lege Manilia*: This title, derived from the proposer of the law, has no ancient authority. It was usually known as *De imperio Gn. Pompei*, a bill introduced to give Pompey extraordinary powers in conducting a war against Mithridates. This was the first speech that Cicero delivered before the people (*agere cum populo*), a privilege to which he was entitled by virtue of his election to the praetorship. Once again he speaks with feigned modesty, claiming that he is unfamiliar with the style of oratory befitting that platform.

Emperor Charles V (1500–1558)

Son of the duke of Burgundy and the heiress to Ferdinand and Isabella of Spain, Charles of Habsburg was born in 1500 and educated in the Netherlands. In 1506 he became duke of Burgundy and in 1517 King of Spain; two years later he was elected Holy Roman Emperor. His reign was characterized by his struggle with France which lasted over 30 years and by the Protestant Reformation which began in the German speaking lands of his Empire. It was also during his reign that Spain consolidated its New World empire and tried to contain the Turkish advance into Europe and the Mediterranean. In 1557 Charles abdicated and divided his immense dynastic inheritance between his brother, Ferdinand, who became Holy Roman Emperor and his son, Philip, who became King of Spain and ruler of the Habsburg territories in Italy, the Low Countries and the New World. Charles retired to a monastery where he died in 1558.

Philip II of Spain (1527–1598)

Charles V's son Philip II was born in 1527 and assumed rule of Spain, the Low Countries, Naples, Sicily, Milan and the Spanish Empire in the New World. He married Queen Mary I of England in 1554 and was given the title but not the authority of King. Philip extended his dominions through the conquest of Portugal and weakened Turkish power in the Mediterranean by defeating the Ottomans at Lepanto in 1571. However, during his reign the Low Countries revolted against Spanish rule, and the Armada sent to conquer England in 1588 was destroyed. Ruling his vast empire from his office in the enormous palace and monastery of the Escorial he had constructed near Madrid, Philip presided over the height of Spanish power and the beginnings of Spain's cultural Golden Age. Philip of Spain died in 1598.

———————

Chapter Thirty-Three

Advice to his son (Phillip II), 1555

I have resolved, my dear son, to remit to your hands the sovereignty of my dominions, having told you several times that I had formed this design .... Since the number of princes who have divested themselves of their supreme power in order to invest their successors with it is very small, you shall understand from this how great the love is that I bear to you, how thoroughly I am persuaded of your goodness, and how much I desire your increasing greatness, seeing that rather than remain in possession of the sovereignty over my realms to the end of my life (as do nearly all other princes) I prefer to follow such rare examples and reduce myself from sovereign to the status of a subject ....

I will not further stress this point, and I think I need not endeavor to exhort you to imitate the conduct which I have adhered to during the course of my life, nearly all of which I have passed in difficult enterprises and laborious employment, in the defence of the empire, in propagating the holy faith of Jesus Christ, and in preserving my peoples in peace and security. I will only say that at the beginning of your reign the two advantages you have—of being my son and of looking like me—will, if I am not mistaken, win for you the love of your subjects; in addition, you on your side must treat them so well that in due course you will have no need of memories of me to assist you in preserving their affection.

Do not imagine, my very dear son, that the pleasure of ruling so many peoples, and the freedom which flatters the feelings of sovereign princes, are not mixed with some bitterness and linked with some trouble. If one knew what goes on in the hearts of princes one would see that the suspicions and uncertainties which agitate those whose conduct is irregular torment them day and night, while those who govern their realms wisely and sensibly are overwhelmed by various worries which give them no rest. And truly, if you weigh in a fair balance, on the one hand, the prerogatives and preeminences of sovereignty, and on the other the work in which it involves you, you will find it a source of grief rather than of joy and delight. But this truth looks so much like a lie that only experience can make it believable.

You must know that the charge of ruling the realms which today I place upon your shoulders is more trying than the government of Spain which is a kingdom of ancient inheritance, firm and assured; whereas the acquisition of the states of Flanders, Italy, and the other provinces into whose possession you are to enter, is more recent, and they are exposed to more difficulties and upheavals, especially because they have for neighbors powerful and belligerent princes. Furthermore, the great number and vast extent of these states and kingdoms increases the cares and troubles of him who rules them; as the addition of a small piece to a reasonable burden will overwhelm him who carries it, or as superfluous food cannot but cause indigestion in a stomach which has taken sufficient nourishment ....

Remember, the prince is like a mirror exposed to the eyes of all his subjects who continually look to him as a pattern on which to model themselves, and who in consequence without much trouble discover his vices and virtues. No prince, however clever and skilful he may be, can hope to hide his actions and proceedings from them. If during his life he can shut their mouths and prevent them from making his irregularities and excesses public, they will after his death convey the memory of them to posterity. Therefore adhere to so just and orderly a conduct towards your peoples that, seeing the trouble you take to govern them well, they will come to rely entirely on your prudence and take comfort from your valor; and in this way there will grow between you and them a reciprocal love and affection ....

It is certain that people submit to the rule of their princes more readily of their own free will than when they are kept in strict bondage, and that one can retain their services better by love than by violence. I admit that the power which rests on a sovereign's gentle kindness is less absolute than that which rests only on fear; but one must also agree that it is more solid and enduring ....

A prince must preserve his credit with the merchants, which he will easily achieve if he takes precise care to pay them both their capital and the interest arising on it. You should especially act thus with the Genoese because, being involved in your kingdoms through the money they lend, they will be attached to you; without which you would have to garrison their city which they would not suffer without great difficulty. In this way you will make yourself master of Genoa, which is a most important place in Italy, just as the king of France has attached the Florentines to his interests through their trade with Lyons.

And since it is impossible for princes (especially those possessing several realms) to govern all alone, they must be assisted by ministers who will help them to carry so heavy a burden. From which it follows that it is extremely important to have honest and intelligent ones. I will therefore say a little more on this subject.

The three principal qualities called for in a minister are sound sense, love of his prince, and uprightness. Sound sense makes them capable of administration; love ensures that they have their master's interests at heart; and uprightness helps them to discharge their business efficiently .... But while it is difficult to find such men, you must do all you can, and spare no trouble, to acquire them when you meet them; for experience shows that all princes who have had this advantage have ruled their peoples with glory and success, although they themselves might be full of faults .... Certainly it is high wisdom in a prince, when by nature he is not sufficiently competent to govern his realms himself, to know how to choose those who are and to put trust in them. In this way he enjoys the abilities of several persons joined together, and he will gain much advantage, more than those who have only their own knowledge to fall back on. But that prince may be called very unfortunate who has neither the ability to rule by himself nor the good sense to follow wise counsels .... Do not think that any prince, however wise and able he may be, can do without good ministers ....

In criminal matters, where it is a question of life and other corporal pains, see to it that the judges modify severity with some mildness, and mildness with severity, and that they pay regard to the case, the persons, the circumstances of place and time, the manner in which the deed was done, and other like considerations. For those who govern states ought to accommodate themselves to the occasion and to the condition of affairs; otherwise they have reason to fear that they may be accused of having respect of persons. In effect, in order to follow the rules of sense and justice, one should consider the nature of cases, and when these are entirely alike one must proceed in the same manner; for injustice does not consist in judging now severely and now mildly, but in imposing different sentences in similar circumstances.

True, this would seem in part to contradict what I said before about laws being inflexible and immutable; but that referred to the dead law which should always be enforced according to its meaning and tenor. This is not so in the living law, which is the prince;[1] his ministers, in executing the dead law, must keep in mind the point of which we have just spoken, provided that in expounding the law they do not violate it. For the prince and the judges have a right to interpret law, and they should thoroughly examine all the circumstances of a case in order to arrive at an equitable decision .... Take care that your courts lean rather to mildness than to severity and cruelty, except that in particular cases, for the sake of example and to deter criminals, they should not fail to exact rigorous execution.

Lavish display on special occasions will give you great authority; ordinary dress, following common usage, will gain you popularity. Use the same with respect to your table and in other things, taking care that excess of show do not lead your subjects to dislike you, nor conformity with their habits and too much familiarity cause them to despise you. In peace time, you should engage in occupations worthy of a prince, such as doing things useful to your peoples, repairing bridges, improving roads, building houses, beautifying churches, palaces and squares, rebuilding town walls, reforming the religious orders, establishing schools, colleges, universities, law courts, and similar things .... But I ought to warn you that all this must be done without exacting new taxes from them, for their burdens are already grievous, no matter what purpose you have in mind when imposing them ....

Endnote

1. The contrast is between the enacted, positive law (dead, i.e., fixed) and the equitable discretion of the prince.